Student Cultural Diversity

Understanding and Meeting the Challenge

Third Edition

Eugene García

University of California, Berkeley

Houghton Mifflin Company

Boston • New York

Editor in Chief: Patricia A. Coryell
Senior Sponsoring Editor: Sue Pulvermacher-Alt
Senior Development Editor: Lisa Mafrici
Editorial Assistant: Sara Hauschildt
Associate Project Editor: Jane Lee
Editorial Assistant: Martha Rogers
Senior Manufacturing Coordinator: Priscilla Bailey
Marketing Manager: Jay Hu

Cover image: © Bildhuset AB/Photonica

Photo credits: page xviii, Bob Daemmrich/Stock Boston; page 35, Jean-Claude LeJeune/Stock Boston; page 118, Sven Marston/The Image Works; page 128, Susie Fitzhugh; page 135, Elizabeth Crews/The Image Works; page 155, Gale Zuker/Stock Boston; page 184, Susie Fitzhugh; page 282, Mary Kate Denny/Photo Edit; page 290, Michael Zide; page 346, Jean-Claude LeJeune/Stock Boston; page 366, Michael Zide.

Printed in the U.S.A.

Library of Congress Catalog Card Number: 2001131498

ISBN: 0-618-12208-7

56789-CRS-05 04

Brief Contents

Contents

Tables

Figures

Preface

My older sister had long looked forward to her first day of school. When the day arrived and she left for school with our mother, our older brothers and sisters reminded her of the importance of school and of receiving an education.

The schoolhouse was just a small, one-room building, yet it and the teacher were held in high esteem by the local community—a rural Colorado town of farm/ranch owners and laborers. During this time our siblings had picked up some English; however, the entire family spoke primarily Spanish. Our family's European and indigenous ancestors, who date back before the arrival of the Pilgrims on Plymouth Rock, had decided to stay in the territory ceded to the United States by Mexico in the Treaty of Guadalupe Hidalgo during the mid-1800s.

My sister will never forget her first day of school. She was asked by the teacher, "What is your name, little girl?" My sister responded, "Ciprianita." The teacher tried to pronounce the name and then respectfully requested, "Can I call you Elsie? It is my favorite name." In that one instant, my sister's linguistic and cultural heritage was politely and unintentionally challenged, and her "roots" metaphorically severed in my mother's presence. The teacher's intent was positive. She meant no harm. Scenes like these were common then and are still common today.

Elsie never performed well in school, yet my mother continued to send her to school along with her nine siblings. Elsie left high school before graduating, as she began to feel that other things in life, particularly family, religion, and work, were more important. These things made her feel wanted, respected, and successful; school did not.

This book is written in recognition of those children like Ciprianita, who are not understood by many educators because of the color of their skin, their language, or their culture. Some of these children are my own; others are children of my brothers and sisters; but most are just children marked by society because they are outside the "preferred" boundaries. Diversity is a wonderful gift to our society, but often it's an unrecognized gift—at times easily discarded or even scorned. Just as the motto of our nation is stated to be "e pluribus unum," meaning "out of many, one," the motto of this book is best articulated by its variation "e diversitate unum"—"out of many groups bonded by their humanity, yet distinct from one another, we form one nation."

It has always been the challenge of humankind to get along cooperatively and peacefully in the world. That challenge remains substantive and grows daily as our own existence becomes more and more dependent on our near and far neighbors' well-being. We know so much more today about meeting this challenge, especially in the domain of education. Educating all of our children to meet our highest expectations is possible. Like the fear of diversity, ignorance of how to meet the challenge is no excuse. This book's aim is to help eliminate both of these excuses.

Audience and Approach

Student Cultural Diversity: Understanding and Meeting the Challenge, third edition, is an introductory core text for courses on teaching culturally diverse students. The text is for one-semester, upper-level courses in *Multicultural Education, Teaching Culturally Diverse Students, Diversity in Families and Communities,* and *Language and Culture in Schools.* The text can also be a supplement in a variety of education courses. Teachers taking such courses increasingly ask, "How can I teach the entire range of students that I will find in classrooms today?" This volume responds to the new educational era of school reform by asking all educators to attend to the *five Rs:* In order to be effective for *all* students, reform must be Respectful, Responsive, Responsible, Resourceful, and Reasonable.

The Roots of Diversity

This book provides the basis for responsive teaching by exploring the roots of diversity. This basis consists of the social, cognitive, and communicative roots of diversity; how children of diverse backgrounds learn to think and communicate within their home, community, and school environments is the pivotal framework of this book. Language—from its early acquisition to its use to construct and communicate meaning—is treated fully as a key component of the roots of diversity.

The Responsive Teacher

An understanding of the roots of diversity in context helps teachers create classroom climates and instruction that are responsive to diverse students' needs. To connect concepts to active classroom practice, the theme of responsive teaching is integrated throughout the text narrative. Additionally, a feature called "Becoming a Responsive Teacher" presents practical classroom-oriented interludes in each chapter. Finally, helping teachers develop responsive pedagogy is the main topic of Part Three, "The Educational Response." Teachers who are truly effective learn to adjust their teaching strategies in response to the learning styles of individual students. The dual point consistently made by this book's approach is that (1) the roots of diversity provide understanding necessary for (2) meeting the challenge of responsive teaching.

Content and Revisions in the Third Edition

The third edition of the text consists of nine chapters divided into three parts. **Part One, "Student Diversity in Context,"** assesses the breadth and complexity of America's culturally diverse student population. Chapter 1, "Cultural Diversity in America's Schools," explores demographics and immigration trends, identifying more clearly the students we will be teaching today and tomorrow and the cultural and language backgrounds they bring with them. An expanded discussion of the increased "new immigration" and its educational consequences has been added. Moreover, the "Five Rs of Educational Reform" are introduced along with new marginal icons throughout the book to highlight examples of effective reform. Chapter 2, "Views of Culture and Education," provides a conceptual overview of culture: how the term is defined and what it means to be inside or outside of a particular culture. Chapter 3, "Educational Approaches to Students Cultural Diversity," examines past and present educational approaches to diversity. Where have we been successful, and where have we fallen short? How far have we come in providing equitable means and intellectual opportunities to a multicultural population? Coverage of "the constructivist perspective" is also included.

Part Two, "The Roots of Diversity," the core of the book, probes into the communication process itself and how teachers interact with their culturally diverse students and families. Chapter 4, "An Ecology of Family, Home, and School," describes methods of helping students build bridges between the sometimes incongruous worlds that they experience inside and outside the classroom.

Chapter 5, "Language and Communication," shows how language develops in early childhood and presents research on bilingualism and multilingualism; it also contains coverage of nonstandard dialects. A substantive discussion of standards-based reform along with issues related to authentic assessment have been added to this edition. Also new in this chapter is a concerned look at classroom instruction in "academic English." Chapter 6, "Language, Culture, and Cognition," examines the effects of social contexts—peers, the family, and the community—on the individual child's learning style and how well he or she performs in school. Instructional discourse for diverse students and the role of constructivism and cognition is also examined in this chapter.

Part Three, "The Educational Response," focuses on concrete ways in which educators can address the needs of culturally diverse students. Chapter 7, "The Effective Teacher: Preparation, Assessment, and Characteristics," looks at the preparation and characteristics the teacher of culturally diverse students must have, and what assessment methods may be used to determine his or her effectiveness in the classroom. Coverage of the school principal's role in effective schooling has been expanded. Chapter 8, "Effective Instruction of Linguistically and Culturally Diverse Children," examines the preparedness of the school itself, describing the qualities of some schools that have experienced success in educating multicultural populations. This chapter also makes recommendations on how other schools can share in this success. Chapter 9, "Educational Approaches at the Middle and Secondary School Level," addresses issues of diversity during the middle school and secondary school years. It is schooling during this critical adolescent period that sets the stage for high school completion and postsecondary education. This chapter provides real-life cases and examples to help meet the needs of readers who are going to be middle or high school teachers. An overview of educational "best practices" specific to the preparation of linguistically and culturally diverse students for postsecondary success has been added. Each chapter in this third edition has been completely updated with the latest statistics, research, and coverage of key topics.

Special Learning Features

Student Cultural Diversity: Understanding and Meeting the Challenge offers a number of valuable features designed to help students easily grasp and learn the material in the text.

- *Focus questions* at the opening of each chapter introduce the major topics to be explored.

- **New:** A *"five Rs" marginal icon* assists the reader in incorporating content into a model of effective school reform. This new feature places the text content in a reform context.

- *"Becoming a Responsive Teacher"*—a unique feature appearing at least once in each chapter—presents classroom situations drawn from the author's experience and from current studies and research. As a departure point, questions and activities in "Meeting the Challenge," a section within this feature, encourage students to reflect, then to respond thoughtfully and creatively to the diversity in real-world classrooms.

- *Marginal notations* draw attention to central points throughout the text and provide helpful landmarks for review.

- *Key terms* appear in boldfaced type so that their meanings are reinforced and can be more easily located.

- A *summary of major ideas* at the end of each chapter helps the student further understand and clarify what has been read.

- *"Extending Your Experience"* questions prompt students to apply their new understanding of diversity to their own lives and to the outside world. These questions will be especially helpful for students whose experience has primarily been among homogeneous populations.

- A list of *resources for further study* also appears at the end of each chapter, providing students with additional opportunities to read and learn. Expanded web resources can be found at the end of each chapter. These sites were live at the time of printing; however, we cannot guarantee that their URLs have not changed.

- A *glossary* at the end of the book defines important terms.

- A *references* section provides background for books and studies cited in the text, which students may wish to explore further.

- Houghton Mifflin's *Teacher Education Web Site* (found at *college.hmco.com,* then click on "Education") provides additional pedagogic support and resources for beginning and experienced professionals in education, including the unique "Project-Based Learning Site."

Acknowledgments

Grateful acknowledgment is given to an important set of colleagues and editors at Houghton Mifflin—Lisa Mafrici, Loretta Wolozin, and Sara Hauschildt—for their guidance, patience, and assistance throughout the book's development.

I would like to give special thanks to Julie Figueroa for her assistance. And a very special thank you to my wife, Erminda, who has always served as assistant, critic, and supporter.

Eugene García
Berkeley, California

Part One
Student Diversity in Context

In Part One we describe the scope and complexity of the population of culturally diverse students in the United States. In Chapter 1 we examine how the rapidly changing cultural and ethnic makeup of the nation as a whole affects our classrooms, particularly immigrant students in our schools. Who are the children we will be teaching, and what cultural and language backgrounds will they bring to the classroom?

Before turning to our discussion of cultural diversity in U.S. schools, we need to define what is meant by the term "culture." In Chapter 2 we provide such a conceptual overview. What does it mean to be a member of a particular culture, and how does cultural membership affect people's interactions both within and outside of that culture?

In Chapter 3 we supply a historical survey of American educational approaches to the teaching of culturally diverse students. What has been done? What remains to be done? Have we made significant strides in achieving educational equality?

Chapter 1
Cultural Diversity in America's Schools

Focus Questions

- What are some of the trends in immigration to the United States over the last two decades?

- What are the expected demographics of the U.S. student population in 2026?

- What changes in the economy can today's students expect?

- How do indicators of child and family well-being relate to educational achievement?

- What do the changing demographics of the U.S. student population imply for the training and assessment of teachers?

- How are language minority students defined, and what types of educational programs are designed to serve them?

- How do national and state policies affect language minority students?

> **"Not the best or worst of times, but times of challenge."**
> —*Tomás Arciniega*

An Introduction

This book is my attempt to write about our understanding of life in a diverse society, particularly as it relates to education in this country. There is no doubt that the historical pattern of education for culturally diverse populations in the United States is one of underachievement. This need not be the case in the future.

It has been useful for me to recognize that I am walking in varied and diverse cultures. But this is an experience everyone shares to some degree. Diversity within each individual is as great as diversity among individuals and their many cultures. We all live with diversity, some of us more than others, and no one escapes this challenge or its advantages and disadvantages.

Cultural and social diversity is not a new issue, of course; it has been a challenge through the ages. Early Hebrew scholars debated the issue of "us versus them," or the *hom* versus the *goy*. Plato and Aristotle differed vehemently over whether social diversity or social homogeneity was preferable among peoples in a nation-state. Plato concluded that homogeneity minimized political tensions and favoritism, whereas Aristotle, his student, concluded that diversity fostered inventiveness and creativity as well as the political compromises necessary for a democracy. Saint Thomas Aquinas argued that a similarity in people's approaches to God promoted their unity, while Martin Luther opted to cultivate religious diversity.

Today, in our "shrinking" world, as the United States and other nations are pulled together by communications and economics, our diversity becomes more visible and harder to hide. In addition, more and more people are worried about it. For example, the movement known as "English First" is passionately concerned that multilingualism will result in violent confrontations, whereas indigenous peoples just as passionately mourn the loss of their languages and cultures. Thus, although diversity has always existed, our social institutions need to address it today more directly than they have in the past, and it is crucial that our educational institutions help us address it successfully.

At the core of this volume are two beliefs:

To honor diversity is to honor the social complexity in which we live—to give the individual and the culture in which that person developed a sense of integrity.

To unify is absolutely necessary, but to insist on unity without embracing diversity is to destroy that which will allow us to unite—our individual and cultural dignity.

A Portrait of Change and Challenge

Mrs. Margaret Tanner's classroom in a sunny, southern California elementary school looks much like any other fifth-grade room. The walls are brightly adorned with the children's work, and an aura of busy concentration prevails. The playgrounds outside and the cafeteria down the hall complete a picture repeated countlessly in communities all over the United States. Mrs. Tanner's school was built in the 1950s, and the number of students it serves has remained around six hundred since its opening. This changed briefly for a five-year stretch during the enrollment boom of the late 1970s, when it served over nine hundred students and operated "split" morning and afternoon sessions. Mrs. Tanner has had as few as 19 students in her classroom and as many as 35, but on the average her daily attendance is between 26 and 28 students.

Mrs. Tanner has taught fifth grade in this very classroom, in this school, in a suburb of Los Angeles, for 21 years. She is a dedicated and committed teacher. When she accepted her initial teaching assignment, her students and most of the other people in her community shared many demographic characteristics: they were almost all middle class, white, and English speaking—the descendants of people who had emigrated to the United States from Europe during the nineteenth and early twentieth centuries. In short, they were all very much like Mrs. Tanner herself.

Demographic Shifts In that first decade of her professional career, however, demographic shifts began in her state. Los Angeles expanded and its suburbs multiplied, and her community became a haven for recently arrived Mexican immigrants and for other Spanish-speaking people coming to California from towns and cities in the southwestern United States. In that decade, the demographic makeup of Mrs. Tanner's fifth-grade class also began to change. Her white, middle-class students were joined by African American children whose parents had relocated from the southern United States, and by children who spoke Spanish in their working-class homes and commuted regularly between the United States and Mexico. The parents of these children, like the grandparents of her earlier students, had come to the United States to find employment and to achieve a higher standard of living for their families. Although these new students were not like her in some ways, Mrs. Tanner recognized their needs and abilities and felt just as committed to them as she had felt toward her first students.

Different Languages and Cultures

Since the second decade of Mrs. Tanner's tenure, further shifts in the population have continued to alter the demographics of her students dramatically. More and more, she is teaching children who speak a variety of languages in their homes and communities, including Spanish, Vietnamese, Russian, Hmong, Chinese, and Farsi. The communities in which these students live are made up of first- and second-generation Mexican immigrants, and first-generation Vietnamese, Hmong, Chinese, Iranian, Russian, and Central Americans. Many of these families have traveled to the United States to seek a better standard of living, but some were forced to escape politically unstable and other dangerous circumstances in their nations of origin.

Mrs. Tanner is quick to point out that her commitment and determination to serve these students is no less, and may be even greater, than it ever was. But she is also the first to admit that the diversification of her student body has challenged, to the very core, her own concept of her role as a teacher and her grasp of the skills necessary to teach effectively. As she sees it, the greatest challenge to her commitment as a teaching professional is the cultural diversity of her students, who come from different cultures, language backgrounds, and economic levels. Effectively teaching a classroom of over two dozen fifth-graders who come from radically different cultures and who speak different languages is not the job Mrs. Tanner was originally hired to do. Back in her first years as a teacher, she could fairly safely assume that all her students would respond similarly to a lesson and in ways that were familiar to her. Now, however, she can assume very little. In order to reach her diverse students while creating a cohesive learning environment, considerations of cultural and language differences must enter into her teaching strategies.

Teachers of the New Century

The changes and challenges Mrs. Tanner faces in her role as a teacher are being played out in classrooms all over the United States. Schools characterized by a culturally and linguistically diverse student population are soon to be the norm rather than the exception for new teachers of the twenty-first century. We need no crystal ball to see that the future for U.S. schools will mirror the changes that have occurred in Mrs. Tanner's classroom. The demographic shifts in our country's population are thoroughgoing and well documented. Groups of students once labeled minorities will become majorities, particularly in highly populated metropolitan areas where most of the student population is concentrated—areas where most of this country's students will either succeed or fail. Mrs. Tanner is a pioneer, a representative of things to come. And much like her own experience of self-examination regarding the practice of her profession, all of us will be required to take a fresh look at the assumptions underlying our current methods of teaching, learning, and schooling. Also, our commitment, like hers, to an increasingly diverse student population must never waver.

This book is dedicated to all the Mrs. Tanners of this country. Moreover, it is an attempt to address the many complex forces and issues that are likely to demand the attention of teachers for years to come. I hope the insights it offers and the discussions it engenders will be of service to the dedicated individuals who devote themselves to children within a variety of educational settings.

In this chapter, we focus on the demographic attributes of culturally diverse students in the United States. Clearly identifying and defining this population has not been an easy task for educators, and most of the categories of definition reveal more about the definer than the defined. The educational initiatives targeted at culturally diverse students have been variously synonymous with programs for "poor," "lower class," "immigrant," "at-risk," "underachieving," and "dropout" students. As Gonzalez (1990) has documented, the children thus categorized are usually perceived as "foreigners," "intruders," or "immigrants" who speak a different language or dialect or who hold values significantly different from those of the American mainstream. These perceptions have led policymakers (including the U.S. Supreme Court) to highlight the most obvious demographic characteristic—a racial or language difference—in their attempts to address widespread academic underachievement in a population.

In this chapter we will see that there are many other demographic characteristics that help us understand academic underachievement among culturally diverse students. Specifically, this chapter will provide:

1. An overall demographic assessment of factors related to the schooling of culturally diverse populations, including issues of poverty, family stability, and the "new immigrant."

2. An in-depth discussion of academic performance, including comparative data on high school dropouts, academic achievement, and funding for education.

3. A particular analysis of the challenges associated with the growing number of language minority students—that is, students who come to school with no or limited proficiency in English.

In all this discussion of demographic information, it is easy to lose sight of the actual significance of the numbers. Keep in mind that as cultural and linguistic diversity in our schools increases

*Perceptions
of Culturally
Diverse
Students*

arithmetically, the challenge to education increases geometrically and possibly exponentially. The schools of tomorrow will be transformed by our response today to a number of pressing variables and agendas. One of the most significant of these variables is the demographic reality of our school-age population.

The Extent of Cultural Diversity Among U.S. Students Today

Expecting a Different World

In contrast to the racial, ethnic, and linguistic diversity of U.S. students, the vast majority of teachers and administrators are white and speak English as their native—and only—language. Many are experiencing the daunting personal and professional challenge of adapting in adulthood to a degree of diversity that did not exist during their childhood.

A Changing Nation

The average teacher and administrator in his or her thirties or forties grew up in the 1950s, 1960s, or 1970s. Those who were raised in this period are likely to have attended schools dominated by others of their own ethnic group. It was not until their teens that most encountered the effects of the civil rights movement and other expressions of ethnic presence on a national level. Nor did they experience the swift increases in diversity that have occurred recently. Thus many of today's teachers and their parents grew up expecting a much different world than they now face.

This is not to say that diversity did not exist. To students of that era, however, diversity was probably not so evident because of segregated ethnic enclaves in housing and schooling and because of the less developed nature of mass communications. In addition, the prevailing "melting pot" ideology matched people's own observations: the children of immigrants should and did abandon their native language and culture in order to become "100 percent Americans."

But the 30-year period straddling the mid-century mark was an anomaly in our history. Until the 1930s, the story of the United States was the story of immigration. The grandparents of today's teachers, who grew up in the early 1900s and were often immigrants themselves, experienced increasing ethnic and linguistic diversity in the society of their youth.

Immigration: The Historical Basis of Diversity

The United States has always been a multicultural, multilingual society. To many Americans, the immigration movement that brought our ancestors to this country is a closed chapter, part of our national past. But from the perspective of the entire spectrum of American history, immigration has been the norm rather than the exception. In this century two generations of adults have grown up in a period of atypically low immigration, an experience that has shaped our perceptions of our country. The new reality is that, in terms of immigration, the United States of 2000 resembles the United States of 1900 more closely than the United States of 1950. Today's kindergartners will experience increasing population diversity over their lifetimes, just as their great-grandparents did.

A History of Immigration   From 1900 to 1910, nearly 9 million immigrants entered the United States, increasing the population by 10 percent. In the 1980s, about the same number of immigrants came to this country, but they accounted for only a 4 percent increase in a now much larger population. In the early decades of this century, and back as far as 1850, as many as 1 in 7 people in the United States was foreign-born. The current rate of 1 in 13 is high only in comparison to the low immigration rates of the 1950s and 1960s, when 1 in 20 Americans was foreign-born. By 2020, when today's kindergartners are in the workforce, the foreign-born population of the United States is again projected to be 1 in 7 people.

Because the United States is so closely identified with the English language, many people assume that Anglo-Americans have always formed the majority group in U.S. society. But the 1990 census reveals that only 13 percent of Americans claim English ancestry. They are outnumbered by the 15 percent whose families originated in Ireland—and many of these families did not speak English as a native language. An additional 5 percent identify their ancestry as "American"; many of these are Scottish Americans whose families have been in the United States for 9 or 10 generations. Thus, at most, about one-third of all Americans trace their ancestry to the various cultures and languages of Great Britain.

Today, nearly one-fifth of Americans live in a household in which a language other than English is spoken. In more than three-fourths of these households that language is Spanish; the next most common languages are Chinese, Russian, French, German, and Italian. Educating students from these immigrant families may seem like an entirely new challenge, but it is not; such students have always been in American schools in large numbers. Throughout most of our history, one in four or five white Americans grew up in an immigrant family.

From 1981 through 1990, more than 7.3 million people immigrated to the United States—a 63 percent increase over the previous decade. Table 1.1 shows a detailed breakdown of immi-

| Table 1.1 | Immigration to the United States by Region, 1820–1997, with Special Emphasis on 1971–1980, 1981–1990, and 1997 |

Region and Country of Origin	1820–1997	1971–1980	1981–1990	1997
All Countries	56,994,014	4,493,314	7,338,062	798,378
Europe	37,101,060	800,368	761,550	122,358
Austria-Hungary	4,342,782	16,028	24,885	1,964
Austria	1,828,946	9,478	18,340	1,044
Hungary	1,667,760	6,550	6,545	920
Belgium	210,556	5,329	7,066	633
Czechoslovakia	145,801	6,023	7,227	1,169
Denmark	370,412	4,439	5,370	507
France	787,587	25,069	32,353	3,007
Germany	7,083,465	74,414	91,961	6,941
Greece	703,904	92,369	38,377	1,483
Ireland	4,725,133	11,490	31,969	932
Italy	5,373,108	129,368	67,254	2,190
Netherlands	374,232	10,492	12,238	1,197
Norway and Sweden	2,145,954	10,472	15,182	1,517
Norway	801,224	3,941	4,164	391
Sweden	1,284,475	6,531	11,018	1,126
Poland	606,336	37,234	83,252	11,729
Portugal	501,261	101,710	40,431	1,690
Romania	204,841	12,393	30,857	5,276
Soviet Union	3,443,706	38,961	57,677	48,238
Spain	285,148	39,141	20,433	1,607
Switzerland	359,439	8,235	8,849	1,302
United Kingdom	5,119,150	137,374	159,173	11,950
Yugoslavia	136,271	30,540	18,762	9,913
Other Europe	181,974	9,287	8,234	9,113
Asia	5,019,180	1,588,178	2,738,157	258,561
China	914,376	124,326	346,747	44,356
Hong Kong	302,230	113,467	98,215	7,974
India	455,716	164,134	250,786	36,092
Iran	176,851	45,136	116,172	6,291
Israel	137,540	37,713	44,273	2,951
Japan	462,244	49,775	47,085	5,640
Korea	642,248	267,638	333,746	13,626
Philippines	1,026,653	354,987	548,764	47,842

Table 1.1	Immigration to the United States by Region, 1820–1997, with Special Emphasis on 1971–1980, 1981–1990, and 1997 (*cont.*)

Region and Country of Origin	1820–1997	1971–1980	1981–1990	1997
Asia (*cont.*)				
Turkey	412,327	13,399	23,233	4,596
Vietnam	458,277	172,820	280,782	37,121
Other Asia	1,030,718	244,783	648,354	52,072
North America	13,067,548	1,982,735	3,615,255	359,619
Canada and Newfoundland	4,295,585	169,939	156,938	15,788
Mexico	3,888,729	640,294	1,655,843	146,680
Caribbean	2,703,177	741,126	872,051	101,095
Cuba	748,710	264,863	144,578	29,913
Dominican Republic	510,136	148,135	252,035	24,966
Haiti	234,757	56,335	138,379	14,941
Jamaica	429,500	137,577	208,148	17,583
Other Caribbean	780,074	134,216	128,911	13,690
Central America	819,628	134,640	468,088	43,451
El Salvador	274,667	34,436	213,539	17,741
Other Central America	544,961	100,204	254,549	25,710
South America	1,250,303	295,741	461,847	52,600
Argentina	131,118	29,897	27,327	2,055
Colombia	295,353	77,347	122,849	12,795
Ecuador	155,767	50,077	56,315	7,763
Other South America	668,065	138,420	255,356	29,987
Other America	110,126	995	458	5
Africa	334,145	80,779	176,893	44,668
Oceania	204,622	41,242	45,205	4,855
Not specified	267,459	12	1,032	8,317

Source: U.S. Bureau of the Census, *Historical Statistics of the United States, Colonial Times to 1970,* 1975; U.S. Bureau of the Census, *Statistical Abstract of the United States, 1991,* 1990, Washington, DC: Author; U.S. Immigration and Naturalization Services, *Statistical Yearbook of Immigration and Naturalization Services,* 1999, Washington, DC: Government Printing Office.

gration to the United States by country of origin. Apart from the sheer magnitude of numbers, what are the characteristics of this immigrant population? In relative terms, which are the significant countries of origin? Perhaps more importantly, what are the greatest changes in immigration patterns and emerging immigration trends?

Significant Countries of Origin

For more than two decades, Mexico has remained the country of origin for the majority of U.S. immigrants. As Table 1.1 shows, an estimated 146,680 Mexican citizens emigrated here in 1997, exceeding the figure for any other nation. The Soviet Union ranked second with 48,238, and the Phillippines (47,842), China (44,356), Vietnam (37,121), and India (36,092) followed close behind. Table 1.2, showing the most recent data available, indicates that the rankings changed slightly by the mid-1990s, but Mexico continued to head the list. Among the changes since the 1980s, the decline in immigration from Cuba is especially notable.

Table 1.2	U.S. Immigrants' Country of Origin, 1997
Mexico	146,865
Philippines	49,117
Vietnam	38,579
Dominican Republic	27,053
China	41,147
India	38,071
Cuba	33,587
Ukraine	15,696
Jamaica	17,840
Korea	14,239
Russia	16,632
Haiti	15,057
Poland	12,038
Canada	11,609
United Kingdom	10,708
El Salvador	17,969
Colombia	13,004
Pakistan	12,967
Taiwan	10,853
Iran	9,642

Source: U.S. Immigration and Naturalization Services, *Statistical Yearbook of the Immigration and Naturalization Service,* 1999, Washington, DC: U.S. Government Printing Office.

During recent decades, which countries of origin exhibited the greatest rates of growth in immigration to the United States? Looking at the two tables, we can see that the number of Salvadoran immigrants increased dramatically in the 1980s, as many Salvadorans fled their war-torn country. Irish immigrants increased 178 percent from the 1970s to the 1980s but declined again by 1995. The average yearly numbers of Iranian and Haitian immigrants have more than doubled since the 1970s. For Poland, the yearly rate in 1995 was nearly four times the average in the 1970s, and figures for other Eastern European countries have risen as well. The Vietnamese immigrant community in this country grew at a rate of 62 percent between 1971 and 1990, and the number of Vietnamese who arrived in 1995 was even higher than the average for the 1980s. Mexican immigration, however, shows the most significant growth. Immigration from Mexico almost tripled from the 1970s to the 1980s and continued at a high level in the 1990s. This, combined with the fact that Mexico ranks first in actual numbers of immigrants, translates into perhaps the greatest impact on the U.S. population.

Growth Rates in Immigration

The New Immigration Phenomenon. As these statistics indicate, after a hiatus of half a century, a wave of immigration is once again transforming the United States. With more than a million immigrants, documented or undocumented, entering the United States each year, the foreign-born constitute the fastest-growing segment of our population, reaching 24.5 million in 1996, roughly 10 percent of the population, the highest proportion since World War II. Even more striking than the size of the immigrant population is its makeup. Since the passage of the Immigration Act of 1965, which eliminated national origin quotas, Asia and Latin America have replaced Europe as the main sources of newcomers to the United States. The largest groups come from Mexico (accounting for 27.2 percent of the 1999 foreign-born population), China, Cuba, India, and Vietnam. Today's immigrants also vary in their social and educational backgrounds and personal experiences. They come from the elite as well as from the most disadvantaged sectors of their societies. Some left to escape poverty, others were fleeing war or political persecution, and still others were attracted by better educational and economic opportunities. Some came directly to the United States; others arrived here after harrowing escapes followed by years in refugee camps.

The New Immigrant

Immigration today is part of an increasingly transnational phenomenon based on borderless economies, new communication technologies, and new systems of mass transportation. In recent years anthropologists, not always with robust data or analytical

Features of the New Immigration

rigor, have been arguing that the **"new immigrants"** are key actors in a new transnational stage (Suarez-Orozco, 1997; Portes, 1996). Today there is far more massive back-and-forth movement—not only of people but also of goods, information, and cultural symbols—than ever before. The European immigrants of the last century simply could not maintain the level and intensity of contact with the "old country" that is now possible. Furthermore, the continual nature of immigration to the United States constantly replenishes social practices and cultural models that would otherwise tend to ossify. In certain areas of the Southwest and Southeast, Hispanic immigration is generating a powerful infrastructure dominated by the growing Spanish-speaking mass media (radio, TV, and print), new market dynamics, and new cultural identities.

Culturally, immigrants significantly reshape the ethos of their new communities. This is perhaps the hardest aspect of immigration for native citizens to comprehend. For various psychosocial reasons, immigrants are, inevitably, active agents of change. We know much more—empirically and theoretically—about how the process of immigration changes immigrants than about how immigrants change their host communities. But there is little doubt in my own experience that they do so. In large cities like Los Angeles and small communities like Watsonville, California, a Sunday afternoon walk through a local park resembles the same walk (sights, sounds, food, play, etc.) one might take in Mexico City or Guadalajara.

Another feature of the new immigration to the United States is that immigrants today are entering a country that is economically, socially, and culturally unlike the country that absorbed—however ambivalently—previous waves of immigrants. Economically, the previous waves of immigrants arrived on the eve of the great industrial expansion in which immigrant workers and consumers played a key role. Immigrants today are part of a thoroughly globalized economy. Some theorists have argued that an important feature of the new economic landscape is its increasingly hourglass shape. Highly skilled immigrants are moving into well-remunerated, knowledge-intensive industries at a heretofore unprecedented rate (Waldinger and Bozorgmehr, 1996). However, at the other end of the hourglass, low-skilled immigrants may be locking themselves into the low-wage job sector in large numbers. A number of scholars have argued that unlike the low-skilled industry jobs of yesterday, the kind of jobs typically available to low-skilled new immigrants today do not offer prospects for upward mobility (Portes, 1996). This situation may have important implications for the long-term social mobility of large numbers of immigrants and their children.

Another current feature of immigration is the increasingly segregated concentration of large numbers of immigrants in a handful of regions. A number of sociologists have argued that as a result of an increasing segmentation of the economy and society, many low-skilled new immigrants "have become more, not less, likely to live and work in environments that have grown increasingly segregated from whites" (Waldinger and Bozorgmehr, 1996, p. 20).

Yet another way in which the new immigrant experience seems incommensurable with earlier patterns relates to the cultural ethos that today's immigrants encounter. New immigrants are entering American society at a time when what we might term a "culture of multiculturalism" permeates the public space. Certainly, a century ago there were no cultural models celebrating ethnic pride. Nathan Glazer's book *We Are All Multiculturalists Now* says it all. However, some observers fear that these new cultural models and social practices tend to undermine old-fashioned assimilation, American style (Chavez, 1995b).

It is, however, far from clear how, if at all, the new culture of multiculturalism will affect the long-term adaptations of immigrants, particularly of their children. If we examine the "holiest of the holy" issues of immigration and language, the data suggest that the new multiculturalism is indeed superficial. Today employers in Miami, the American city with the largest concentration of speakers of foreign languages, have trouble finding competent office workers who can function as professional Spanish speakers (Fradd, 1997b).

Immigrant Students in U.S. Schools

Although immigrants have affected all aspects of American life, nowhere is the changing demography of the United States more keenly felt than in education. First- and second-generation immigrant children are the fastest-growing segment of the U.S. population under age 15 (Fix and Passel, 1994). With more than 90 percent of recent immigrants coming from non-English-speaking countries, schools are increasingly receiving students who do not speak English at home and who have little or no proficiency in English. There has been an increase of almost 1 million immigrants in U.S. public schools (grades K–12) during the last 10 years, approximately 5.5 percent of the public school student population (Rumbaut and Cornelius, 1995). Keep in mind that it is difficult to determine the number of students who are classified as limited-English-proficient (LEP), the term used by the federal government and most states, because states determine the number of LEP students in different ways (Gandara,

Limited English
Proficient (LEP)
Students

1995). However, conservative estimates indicate that more than 2.1 million public school students in the United States are identified as LEP. They account for 5 percent of all public school students and 31 percent of all American Indian/Alaskan Native, Asian/Pacific Islander, and Hispanic students enrolled in public schools. The largest proportion of this population (more than 79 percent) are native Spanish speakers (Goldenberg, 1996). California has been particularly affected. The number of students classified as LEP in the state's public schools more than tripled from nearly 400,000 in 1981 to nearly 1.3 million in 1995 (García, 1999). Although these students were reported as speaking one or more of 54 different primary languages, some 80 percent speak Spanish as their native language.

Along with an increase in the sheer number of immigrant students who are at various stages of learning English, schools are also faced with a growing number of students who need extra academic instruction in addition to English as a Second Language (ESL) classes. Approximately 20 percent of LEP students at the high school level and 12 percent of those at the middle school level have missed two or more years of schooling since the age of six; 27 percent of those in high school and 19 percent of those in middle school are assigned to grades at least two years below their age/grade norms.

Immigrant
Population
Distribution

Because newcomers to this country tend to concentrate in certain areas, the responsibility for educating immigrant students is not evenly shared across the country. Accordingly, 82 percent of the immigrant students in K–12 public schools live in only five states—California, Texas, New York, Florida, and Illinois; more than 40 percent are in California. Dade County, Florida, is an example of an area with a school system struggling to serve a sudden, relatively recent influx of immigrants. Approximately one-quarter of the 330,000 students in Dade County during the fall of 1996 were born outside the United States, and the county continues to add an average of 1,322 foreign-born students each month to its rolls. At the same time, employment opportunities draw immigrants to smaller cities and even to rural areas, creating new challenges for schools in those areas (Lucas, 1997).

An increasingly diverse student population is hitting the schools at the same time that a record number of students in general (the "baby boom echo," a term used by demographers to refer to the children of the original baby boomers) are enrolling. In the fall of 1996, more than 51 million children entered school—a new national record. The Department of Education predicts that the number of students enrolled in school will not level off until 2006, when the student population reaches 54.6 million, almost 3 million more than in 1996. The greatest increase over the next decade will be in high school enrollments, which are projected to increase by 15 percent. Thus, schools already struggling with the influx of immigrant students will also be facing the strains of high total enrollments.

Understanding the Immigrant Student Population. Eddie Ruth Hutton, a high school teacher, describes what was the essence of the immigrant student experience for her first-generation Mexican immigrant students in 1942:

> Manuel Segovia, Esperanza Guadarrama, Cheepe Ochoa, Tibursio Torres, María Carríon. Strange names these and a hundred others representing the hundreds of strange boys and girls—first-generation Mexicans who each year enter the high schools of the Southwest.
>
> Most of these children come from the poorer homes in which diet and health are given little consideration. They are torn between the conflicting social customs instilled in them by their Mexican parents and those imposed upon them by a new society. They are apologetic for the peculiarities of their families, yet fearful of the alien social order in which they find themselves. (Hutton, 1942, p. 45)

This experience has changed very little for today's generation of Mexican immigrants and for many other immigrants. Lucas (1997) characterizes the experiences of these first-generation immigrants, particularly school-age children, as confronting a set of critical transitions. Most U.S. students undergo a set of important and critical transitions: from home to school and from childhood to adolescence. Immigrant children move through these same critical transitions as well as those associated with the transition to a new culture and language. How individuals confront and move through these transitions, individually and collectively, is the focus of the following discussion.

The term *immigrant* refers to those students (including refugees) born outside the United States but not those born and raised within the United States. Due to restrictive immigration laws, most new arrivals to the United States during the nineteenth century and the first half of the twentieth century were from Europe. Following the restructuring of America's immigration laws in the mid-1960s, however, this pattern was altered dramatically, and subsequently the changes have contributed to a new period of large-scale immigration to the United States that shows no signs of abating soon. Immigrants to America literally now come from all over the globe, with the nations of Asia and Latin America supplanting those of Europe as primary sources of new arrivals.

Immigrants'
Previous
Education

There are two very important educational dimensions to this new pattern of immigration. First, recent immigrants are simultaneously more educated and less educated than native-born Americans—a higher percentage of immigrants than native-born Americans have a bachelor's or graduate degree while a higher percentage of immigrants than the native-born also have not completed high school. Second, recent immigrants with high levels of education are disproportionately from several nations in east and south Asia while those with little schooling are largely from a number of Latin American countries. This situation is of great significance educationally. It is quite evident among immigrants that children from families in which the parents have had a great deal of education tend to achieve at much higher levels in school than children from families in which the parents have had little formal schooling (Rumbaut, 1997). Low levels of educational attainment are especially consequential for Mexican immigrants. They represent our largest immigrant group—and one of the least well-educated.

The large differences in education levels among immigrant groups are clearly illustrated in 1990 census data. Among 25- to 29-year-old adult immigrants (a segment containing many families with preschool or school-age children), 43 percent of the Asians had a bachelor's degree or higher while only 12 percent had less than a high school diploma. In contrast, just 4 percent of the young adult immigrants from Mexico had completed a college degree while 62 percent had not completed high school. These percentages were 12 percent and 33 percent, respectively, for other Hispanic young adult immigrants. These general patterns have continued among new immigrants in the 1990s.

Valdés (1996, 1998) has conducted studies of Hispanic immigrant families and the schooling of their children. The larger Valdés study (1996) focused on two males and two females. It took place during a two-year period and involved three middle schools, four new Latino focal students and their classmates, four different English-language teaching specialists (ESL teachers), and numerous subject matter teachers who had the focal children in class. It also involved interviews with school personnel, with students themselves, and with their parents. A subpart of the study's purpose was to examine how immigrant children who arrive in this country with "zero" English acquire English in schools. To address this issue, Valdés (1998) selected a middle school undergoing a rapid population shift and students aged 12, 13, and 14. In particular, two immigrant Hispanic students—one of Mexican origin and one of Honduran origin—were observed over a seven-year period.

The Immigrant
Educational
Experience Today

Lilian, the student of Mexican origin, was 12 years old when she first arrived at her California school. Previously, as a student in Mexico, she had developed a substantial reading ability in Spanish but had almost no English language or reading skills. Elisa, a 13-year-old Honduran immigrant, had completed sixth grade in her native country and also had substantial reading and writing skills in Spanish. Both Lilian and Elisa were eager to go to school and to learn English.

Mastery of English became the predominant focus of both of these students' schooling experience. Valdés (1998) concludes that both students had difficulty escaping "the ESL ghetto." This phenomenon is common for many Hispanic immigrant students: They are repeatedly placed in English-language-emphasis course work and instruction at the expense of access to grade-level-appropriate curriculum and instruction in subject-matter domains. The results for both Lilian and Elisa were predictable. Lilian dropped out of school at the age of 15. Elisa finished high school but has only recently begun to attend a community college, where her measured lack of English proficiency on a required placement test has forced her to enroll in more ESL courses. Valdés (1998) was led to conclude that "the students who had looked forward to schooling in the United States were disappointed" (p. 11).

Olsen (1997), in an effort similar to Valdés's (1996, 1998), followed a cohort of immigrant Hispanic and Asian students through their high school experiences at Madison High, a northern California urban school. This study attempted to address the issue of immigrant students becoming "American" and their experiences with instructors and curriculum. Olsen (1997) states that "the study illustrates [the] efforts and heartbreaks of those engaged in activity to provide more educational opportunity and equal access to schooling for immigrants, as well as the confusion, blindness, and concerns of those who resist changing their ways for them" (p. 239). Unfortunately, the study of the Madison High immigrant students offers a hard look at the ways in which schools still track students and determine very different futures for them based on race, class, and language. The immigrant students seemed to spend their educational time either being relegated to classes taught entirely in English, in which they were unlikely to thrive, or in separate "sheltered" English classes, where the emphasis was on English language development with little or no attention given to high school content-level curriculum. The immigrant students themselves reported that the key to becoming American was simply to learn English. At the same time, their teachers emphasized that the key to the students' educational success was mastery of basic skills and subject matter content. These teachers reported seeing students divided into academic levels as a result of their individual choices and efforts.

In essence, the teachers felt that any student could be success-ful—achieve at high levels and be meritorious—if he or she chose to do so and worked hard. The teachers' view of student achieve-ment contrasted dramatically with the immigrant students' views of their own experiences: "Pick your race and take your place" (Olsen, 1997, p. 241).

More specifically, Olsen concludes that the immigrant student experience is yet another important reflection of race and class negotiations and stratification in U.S. high schools that serve a diverse socioeconomic, racial, ethnic, and immigrant student body. Yet, particularly for immigrant students, taking one's place in the racial and socioeconomic hierarchy seemed to correspond with

1. The academic exclusion and separation of immigrants;

2. The extreme pressure placed on immigrants to give up their national identity and language.

Olsen (1997) is quick to point out that these phenomena are not uncontested. Students do try to rise to and overcome these chal-lenges. And as Rumbaut (1997) indicates, some do. Nevertheless, at Madison High, Hispanic immigrants were not likely to do so (Olsen, 1997).

The Challenge Will Continue. Immigration continues to make demands on our public schools at all levels. Most of the fiscal re-sponsibility for educating immigrant students is found at the state and local levels, where people have a vested interest in their schools. Although it is not unreasonable to expect the federal government, the unit of government that makes decisions about immigration policy, to bear the responsibility for funding some, if not all, of the costs of educating immigrant children, the imple-mentation of adequate programs will remain the responsibility of local school districts. Despite the immediate costs, the educa-tion of immigrant youth is an investment in the future of our communities.

California, Texas, and the rest of the United States are not alone in struggling with the predicament of how to deal with im-migrant youth. Most industrialized nations are also dealing with similar issues. What we are experiencing in the United States is part of a global phenomenon. The question of how to educate immigrant students is not one that can be addressed simply with reforms in immigration laws. The immigrant children who will be enrolling in our schools in most urban areas during the next five years are already residing in our communities. Programs for edu-cating them must already be in place when they arrive in our classrooms.

To make the transition from being an outsider to being an integral part of the U.S. workforce and society, immigrant youth must acquire cultural and technical skills through formal education. Portes and Rambaut (cited in Dugger, 1998), Cummins (1986), Heath (1989), and Ogbu (1987) have suggested that the schooling of immigrant children must be understood within the broader context of society's treatment of these students and their families both in and out of schools. No quick fix is likely under current social and educational conditions. There is no single attribute that is the only variable of importance in the education of immigrant youth. A more comprehensive view, one that includes an understanding of the relationship between home and school and one that integrates students' values, beliefs, histories, and experiences into educational strategies, is essential for the successful education of immigrant students.

When planning for the education of these students, we must remember that they are not a homogeneous group. Suarez-Orozco (1997) emphasizes the stresses and losses experienced by immigrant families that often affect their ability to help their children adjust to life in the United States. The acculturation process also tends to separate immigrant parents from their more acculturated children. When immigrant parents are preoccupied with the economic pressures of making a life for their families in the United States, immigrant youths often turn to peer groups for the support necessary for helping them adjust to their difficult surroundings. Issues in educating the second generation are very different from those involved in educating the first generation of immigrants. Many second- and third-generation youth become disenchanted with the school system, and when they experience difficulties in school environments, they turn to gangs or drop out of school altogether. Thus, for immigrant children and the children of immigrants, growing up American can either be a smooth transition or a traumatic confrontation. In some cases, even when they want very much to become indistinguishable from their American peers, they may still be viewed as outsiders. In other cases, they may be accepted as American but may also maintain a strong sense of ethnic identity (Zhou, 1997).

Measuring Racial and Ethnic Diversity

To document the racial and ethnic heterogeneity of our country's population, the U.S. Bureau of the Census uses a set of terms that place individuals in separate exclusionary categories: white, white non-Hispanic, black, and Hispanic (the latter with some five subcategories). Unfortunately, these terms are simplistic and ambiguous and do not accurately represent the true heterogeneity of the U.S. population. It is therefore important to note at the outset of this discussion that these categories are useful only as the most superficial reflection of our nation's true diversity. Given the forced-choice responses allowed them in census questionnaires, many U.S. citizens whose racial or ethnic identity crosses categories are compelled to answer inaccurately. Racially and culturally we are not "pure" stock, and any such measurement by the Census Bureau, by the Center for Educational Statistics, or by other social institutions that attempt to address the complexity of our diverse population is likely to result in only a vague sketch.

Vulnerability for Some Populations

However, once we grant the inherent restrictions on efforts to document population diversity in the United States, we must note that an examination of the available data does provide a suggestive portrait of our society. We can discern a sketchy outline of the specific circumstances of various groups within our nation's boundaries. That sketch depicts consummate social and economic vulnerability for nonwhite and Hispanic families, children, and students. On almost every indicator, nonwhites and Hispanics are "at-risk," meaning they are likely to fall into the lowest quartile on indicators of "well-being": family stability, family violence, family income, child health and development, and educational achievement. The census data also show that this specific population (usually referred to as the "minority" population) has grown significantly in the last two decades and will grow substantially in the decades to come. In the years ahead teachers in the U.S. schools will see increasing numbers of at-risk children in their classrooms.

Projected Trends for U.S. Schools

The most comprehensive report on the growing diversity of the student body in U.S. schools was published in 1991 by the College Board and the Western Interstate Commission for Higher Education. Entitled *The Road to College: Educational Progress by Race and Ethnicity,* this report indicated that the U.S. nonwhite and Hispanic student population would increase from 10.4 million in 1985–1986 to 13.7 million in 1994–1995. These pupils would constitute 34 percent of public elementary and secondary school enrollment in 1994–1995, up from 29 percent in 1985–1986. Enrollment of white students, meanwhile, would rise by only 5 percent, from 25.8 million to 27 million, and its share of the student population would drop from 71 percent to 66 percent in 1994–1995.

Projections for 2026

Figures 1.1 and 1.2 graphically display this astounding shift in student demographics. Figure 1.1 presents actual nonwhite and Hispanic K–12 public school enrollments from 1976 to 1986 and

Figure 1.1 **K-12 Public School Enrollment Projections, 1976–2026: Total Versus Nonwhite and Hispanic Enrollment**

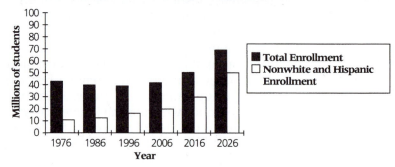

Source: U.S. Department of Education, Office for Civil Rights, *Directory of Elementary and Sec-ondary School Districts and Schools in Selected Districts:* 1976–1977; and 1984 and 1986 Elementary and Secondary School Civil Rights Survey. As cited in U.S. Department of Education, National Center for Education Statistics, *The Condition of Education,* 1991, vol. 1, *Elementary and Secondary Education* (Washington, DC: Author, 1991), p. 68.

projected enrollments based on changes in enrollment from 1976 to 1986 by decade through 2026. Figure 1.2 presents similar data but focuses on nonwhite and Hispanic student enrollments as a percentage of total enrollment. Each figure depicts a dramatic transformation projected for our nation's student body. Non-white and Hispanic student enrollment will grow from 10 million

Figure 1.2 **K-12 Public School Enrollment Projections, 1976–2026: Percentage of Nonwhite and Hispanic Enrollment**

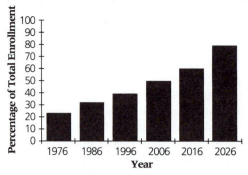

Source: U.S. Department of Education, Office for Civil Rights, *Directory of Elementary and Sec-ondary School Districts and Schools in Selected Districts:* 1976–77; and 1984 and 1986 Elementary and Secondary School Civil Rights Survey. As cited in U.S. Department of Education, National Center for Education Statistics, *The Condition of Education,* 1991, vol. 1, *Elementary and Secondary Education* (Washington, DC: Author, 1991), p. 68.

in 1976 to nearly 50 million in 2026. The percentage of those enrollments will rise from 23 percent to 70 percent of the total during this same time. Projections show that in 2026, student representation in our schools will be the exact inverse of what it was in 1990, when white students made up 70 percent of the enrolled K–12 student body.

It is of distinct educational significance that in 1986, 30 to 35 percent (3 million) of nonwhite and Hispanic students were identified as residing in homes in which English was not the primary language (August and García, 1988). Using these figures and extrapolating from the projections displayed in Figures 1.1 and 1.2, we found that by the year 2000 our schools were educating 6 million students who had limited proficiency in English. By the year 2026 that number will conservatively approximate 15 million students, or somewhere in the vicinity of 25 percent of total elementary and secondary school enrollments. In the next few decades, it will be virtually impossible for a professional educator to serve in a public school setting, or even in any private school context, in which the students are not racially, culturally, or linguistically diverse.

Indicators of Child and Family Well-Being

As many researchers have discovered, educational concerns cannot be appropriately addressed without attending to related indicators of child and family well-being. Children who are healthy and who live in safe and secure social and economic environments generally do very well in today's schools. Students from poor families, on the other hand, are three times more likely to become dropouts than are students from more economically advantaged homes (National Research Council, 1993). Students who reside in economically disadvantaged and socially dangerous environments are at risk for academic underachievement in today's and tomorrow's schools. Our earlier discussion of expected demographic shifts and projected trends in student enrollments is sharpened by a consideration of some economic and social realities. As noted previously, family income is correlated with academic performance. Family dislocations, uncertainty about one's future, and stress associated with poverty often undermine a child's ability to concentrate and to learn. Culturally and linguistically diverse students tend to live in situations that are not always compatible with a stable educational experience. Unfortunately, on a number of related measures of child and family well-being, the circumstances are bleak for this growing body of students.

Children Living in Poverty | According to the U.S. Bureau of the Census report *Poverty in the United States: 1995* (cited by National Center for Children in

Poverty, 1995), 5 million U.S. children under the age of 18 resided in circumstances of poverty. This represents approximately 20 percent of the total population in this age group and was an increase of some 2 million since 1970. Of the children counted, 6.5 million, or 45 percent, were nonwhite and Hispanic. Table 1.3 presents exact numbers and percentages of children in poverty for 1975 and 1986 and related projections through 2026. These projections indicate that unless poverty is checked in very direct ways, the number of children in poverty will more than double by the year 2026. More than half of them will be nonwhite and Hispanic.

The overall family circumstances expected for these children over the next decades are also alarming. Most children of elementary school age presently reside in families headed by persons under the age of 30. Figure 1.3 provides evidence that these families will be economically disadvantaged. The figure shows median income from 1973 to 1986 and projected income through 2026 for families headed by persons under the age of 30. All families in this category have experienced and are projected to experience a decrease in economic capability. Again, particularly vulnerable will be families headed by persons who are nonwhite and Hispanic. By 2026 the median annual family income for nonwhite and Hispanic families will drop to $10,000.

Table 1.3	Children 18-Years-Old and Younger in Poverty, Projected to 2026					
Race or Ethnicity	**1975**	**1986**	**1996**	**2006**	**2016**	**2026**
Total students (in millions)	12.3	14.2	16.4	19.4	23.1	27.9
White, non-Hispanic	6.7	7.8	8.8	10.1	11.6	13.2
Total minority	5.6	6.4	7.6	9.3	11.5	14.7
Black	3.8	4.0	4.2	4.4	4.5	4.7
Hispanic	1.7	2.4	3.4	4.9	7.0	10.0
Total percent of poor children	100	100	100	100	100	100
White, non-Hispanic	54.8	54.4	53.6	52.1	50.0	47.2
Total minority	45.2	45.6	46.4	47.9	50.0	52.8
Black	31.5	28.5	25.5	22.5	19.7	16.9
Hispanic	13.7	17.1	20.9	25.4	30.3	35.9

Source: U.S. Bureau of the Census, *Current Population Reports*, Series P-60, *Poverty in the United States*, various years. As cited in the U.S. Department of Education, National Center for Education Statistics, 1991, *The Condition of Education*, 1991, vol. 1, pp. 200–201, *Elementary and Secondary Education*, Washington, DC: Author.

Figure 1.3	Median Annual Income for Families Headed by Persons Under Age 30 (in 1986 Dollars), Projected to 2026

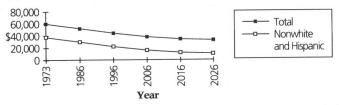

Source: C. M. Johnson, A. M. Sum, and J. D. Weill, (1988), Appendix: Table 3. As cited in National Center for Children in Poverty, School of Public Health, *Five Million Children: A Statistical Profile of Our Poorest Young Citizens* (New York: Columbia University, 1990), p. 47.

Implications of Poverty

What are the implications for education? Children in families with income below the poverty level are nearly twice as likely to be held back a grade level as their more advantaged classmates. Young people from low-income families also tend to leave school early and to enter the labor force to earn additional income for themselves or their families. While work experience during adolescence can have positive effects, recent research indicates that working more than half-time during the high school years can undermine academic performance (National Commission on Children, 1991). As for those students from homes in which English is not the primary language, over 90 percent in 1984 met poverty guidelines that allowed them to receive free or reduced-price lunches (Development Associates, 1984).

Much more eloquent than any quantitative analyses of this situation are the more intensive case studies that dramatically tell the disheartening educational stories of these underserved populations (August and Hakuta, 1997; Kozol, 1991; Rose, 1995; Valdés, 1997; Wong-Fillmore, 1991). Numerous expository in-depth studies have found that serious disruptions of individual, family, and community functioning occur when young children from nonmainstream backgrounds encounter the schooling process. There is much evidence, both in hard figures and in personal testimony, that members of culturally and linguistically diverse populations in the United States face social, economic, and educational problems.

Student Diversity and Educational Vulnerability

The inevitable conclusion to draw from patterns evident in the preceding indicators of child and family well-being is that school-age children and their families, particularly those who are nonwhite and Hispanic, will continue to be placed in economic and social situations that increase their social, economic, and educational vulnerability. Today's educators and educators of the future will be challenged by a student body of increasing cultural and linguistic diversity. Many of our students will come to school from situations that are already identified as educationally disadvantageous. Even though as educators we have little power to ameliorate those situations, we must heed their effects in the academic setting.

Three important and much-debated variables are key to understanding the real human consequences of educational vulnerability: dropout rate, measures of academic achievement, and educational funding policies:

Dropout Rate. A major indicator of academic success in the United States is completion of high school. One of the national educational goals adopted by the 1990 Educational Summit in Charlottesville, Virginia, and reinforced at a similar meeting in 1998, was to increase the U.S. high school completion rate to 90 percent by the year 2001. The dynamics of school completion are not well understood, however, and the cause-and-effect relationships involved are unclear (Fernandez and Shu, 1988). Much of the confusion stems from the variety of methods researchers have used to define what is meant by "completion." Fortunately, the National Center for Education Statistics (NCES) has begun to address this confusion. NCES issued two reports (Frase, 1989; Kaufman and Frase, 1990) that attempt to systematize our understanding of high school completion by defining the following set of dropout rates:

Types of
Dropout Rate
Reports

1. *Event rates report:* Compiled within a single year, an **event rates report** gives the percentage of students who left high school without receiving a diploma. This is a measure of the actual event of dropping out.

2. *Status rates report:* Compiled at any point in time, a **status rates report** gives the percentage of the population of a given age range who either (1) have not finished high school or (2) are not enrolled. This measure reflects the current status of a group in the whole population, including adults.

3. *Cohort rates report:* Compiled over a given time period, a **cohort rates report** describes what happens to a single group of students. This measure reflects changes in any given group over time.

Status and cohort reports provide a useful view of high school completion since they take into consideration what happens to students after they leave school. These reports indicate that high school completion rates for all persons aged 16 to 24 have generally declined in the last 20 years. In 1989, about 4 million persons in the United States aged 16 to 24 were high school dropouts. In 1994, by contrast, 32.6 million persons aged 16 to 24 were high school dropouts (NCES, 1996). Prior to 1994, an average of 87 percent of all U.S. students received their high school diploma or its equivalent by the age of 24; by 1994, that figure had fallen to 85.8 percent (NCES, 1996).

Comparative Dropout Rates | Moreover, both event and status reports show that nonwhite and Hispanic students drop out of high school at two to three times the rate of white students. Hispanic youth have the highest national dropout rate, African Americans the second highest, and whites the lowest. During the period 1987–1989 about 8 percent of Hispanic students dropped out of school each year, an event rate almost twice as high as that for white students; 7 percent of African American students dropped out during that same period. More revealing are the status report data. In 1989, among the population aged 16 to 24, only 67 percent of Hispanics had completed high school or its equivalency, versus 86 percent of African Americans and 88 percent of whites (Kaufman and Frase, 1990). Using the most recent data available, NCES (1996) reported that in 1994, of persons aged 18 to 24, 61.8 percent of Hispanics had completed high school or its equivalency, versus 83.3 percent of African Americans and 90.7 percent of whites. In other words, there was a decline in high school completion for Hispanics and African Americans and an increase for whites. These same data indicate that high school completion rates are lowest in metropolitan areas, which have the highest concentrations of nonwhite and Hispanic populations. Completion rates are highest in suburban areas.

Academic Achievement. We have determined that high school completion is problematic for nonwhite and Hispanic students. How do these students do while they are in school? The NCES (1996) also has generated a set of data that addresses this question. The most revealing data concern grade-level achievement as measured by standardized tests of academic achievement over the years 1989 to 1995. This measure attempts to assess the relative number of students who are not achieving at the academic level considered normal for their age, which is called the **modal grade level.** Table 1.4 summarizes these data by showing the percentage of 8-year-olds and 13-year-olds who are performing one or more years below the expected grade level. The data are presented by gender, race, and ethnicity.

Performance Below Modal Grade | This table indicates that the percentage of students performing one or more years below modal grade level has increased overall

Table 1.4 Academic Performance of U.S. Students According to Modal Grade Level

Percentage of 6- to 8-Year-Olds Enrolled Below Modal Grade, by Race and Ethnicity, 1989–1995

Year	All Students			White			Blacks			Hispanics		
	Male	Female	Average	Male	Female	Average	Male	Female	Average	Male	Female	Average
1989	21.4	25.1	18.1	22.4	26	18.6	19.6	21.7	17.5	21.9	23.7	20
1990	21.5	23.9	19.1	21.9	24.6	19	21.9	23.2	20.7	21.5	22.2	20.7
1991	21.2	24	18.2	21.3	24.4	18.1	21	22.9	19	21.8	22.7	20.8
1992	19.4	21.6	17.1	19.5	21.5	17.3	20.6	24.5	16.7	16.2	15.6	16.8
1993	18.7	21.2	16.3	18.8	21.4	15.9	20	21.8	18	18.9	19.1	18.9
1994	18.9	21.1	16.5	19.4	22	16.7	18.4	19.4	17.5	16.8	16.4	17.2
1995	17.5	20.2	14.6	17.7	20.5	14.7	16.8	18.8	14.8	14.4	11.4	17.5

Percentage of 12- to 14-Year-Olds Enrolled Below Modal Grade Level, by Race and Ethnicity, 1989–1995

Year	All Students			White			Blacks			Hispanics		
	Male	Female	Average	Male	Female	Average	Male	Female	Average	Male	Female	Average
1989	36.7	26.6	31.6	35	24.5	30	44.8	37.7	41.2	40	39.7	40
1990	36.2	25.7	31	33.3	23.2	28.2	52.7	39.3	46	40.2	34.9	37.5
1991	34.7	24.6	30	32.5	22.6	27.5	46.2	35	41	43.9	27.6	35.7
1992	37	24.6	31	35.8	23.2	29.5	44.5	31.2	38	42.5	25	33.7
1993	35.4	26.4	31	33.8	24.8	29.3	44.3	33.1	39	34.2	29	32
1994	35.6	26.7	31.1	34.4	25.7	30	39.9	32.3	36.1	36.3	28.5	32.4
1995	35.2	26	31	33.4	24.8	29.1	45	30.9	38	42.4	34.5	38.4

Source: National Center for Education Statistics, 1995, *The Condition of Education, 1995,* Washington, DC: U.S. Department of Education.

for boys and girls and for whites, blacks, and Hispanics at each age level over the period reported. For 8-year-olds, the percentage of students performing below modal grade level increased from 18.1 percent to 20.2 percent; for 13-year-olds, the percentage remained the same at 31 percent. It is important to note that the percentage almost doubled for all groups for ages 8–10 to 12–14 years of age. In addition, an interesting pattern emerges for black and Hispanic students. At the age of 8 in 1995, there is little difference in below-level performance for whites (14.6 percent), blacks (14.8 percent), and Hispanics (17.5 percent). But by the age of 13, the discrepancy is quite significant. Whereas 29.0 percent of white 13-year-olds performed below grade level in 1989, the figure was 38 percent for blacks and 38.4 percent for Hispanics. From roughly third grade to eighth grade, academic achievement drops off significantly for all students and even more so for blacks and Hispanics as compared with whites.

The unfortunate result is that by the eighth grade, 40 percent or more of black and Hispanic students are performing one grade level or more below expected and normal achievement levels. These findings, in concert with the previously discussed high school completion and dropout data, raise important educational concerns. Clearly, as the population of nonwhite and Hispanic students increases to an estimated 70 percent of the total U.S. student population in 2026, this underachievement will be an extreme waste of intellectual potential—a waste that we cannot afford in the least. Intervention of some sort will be necessary to avoid squandering our nation's valuable human resources.

Educational Funding Policies. Educational financing in the United States is not without its national, state, and local complications. On the average, 90 percent of any educational expenditure consists of tax dollars flowing directly from local or state sources. Less than 10 percent of these expenditures come from federal sources. Although funding for education increased substantially in the United States during the 1980s, education spending actually declined slightly as a proportion of the gross national product to just over 3.5 percent, which is the lowest for all "developed" countries. In real terms, overall state and local spending rose 26 percent between 1980 and 1988, but the federal share actually decreased by 2 percent (Committee for Economic Development, 1991b).

Keep in mind that non-Anglo-American and Hispanic children reside primarily in metropolitan areas in densely populated pockets of concentrated poverty and racial and ethnic segregation (Kozol, 1991). These children are likely to attend troubled schools with fewer resources and larger classes (*Beyond Rhetoric*, 1991). Moreover, these children have been more negatively affected than

Loss of Federal Support

others by recent changes in educational funding policies. The reduction of federal assistance to education, including funds for providing compensatory education and desegregating school districts, has reduced the fiscal resources directly available for the education of these children (Levin, 1986). Districts that cannot be integrated because they lack Anglo-American students are not eligible for enhanced funding available to establish science and math magnet schools, an emerging federal funding priority (Oakes, 1991). The educational personnel of such schools are not concerned with the educational buzzwords of recent years, such as "restructuring," "reform," "teacher empowerment," "site-based management," "teacher competencies," "outcome accountability," and "national goals." Instead, they are preoccupied with obtaining the bare necessities: windows, books, typewriters, classrooms with heat, working bathrooms, sufficient lighting, and long-overdue repairs and renovations (Kozol, 1991; Rose, 1989).

These schools have been transformed into institutions that must spend valuable time trying to secure the resources needed for basic survival. Much like developing countries, they seek alliances and petition for grants and loans from one source after another. These schools "beg" from city, state, federal, business, and charity sources. They do so only because the basic resources are not provided by present funding structures and formulas. In fact, those structures and formulas work to their disadvantage. These schools are in cities in which competition for tax dollars is great. These communities have high unemployment and underemployment and are pressed to provide a higher level of related social services. They are also competing to retain businesses. Such variables directly affect the resources that can be directed toward education.

Underfunding and "Fairness"

Most directly, students in these schools are underfunded, even in times that argue for "fairness" in school financing. As a society, we make it quite clear that we abhor the notion of social privilege. We strongly believe that an individual's financial background should not be a deterrent to educational success. Yet such a belief does not seem consistent with the ways in which we allocate educational resources. These fiscal disparities were identified over three decades ago. In 1968, in a now-famous legal case, Demetrio Rodriguez, a parent in the Edgewood School District in San Antonio, Texas, argued that his children were underfunded relative to children in an adjacent school district only a few miles away. In the Edgewood School District (which was 96 percent non-Anglo-American) residents paid a higher tax rate than did residents of the nearby district, which was predominantly Anglo-American. Edgewood was able to generate only $37 for each pupil, and with additional resources provided by the state, spent $231 yearly per student. The neighboring school district generated $412 per student on its own, and with state resources spent $543 yearly per student. This amounted to a differential of over 100 percent.

Coons, Clune, and Sugarman (1970) documented the distinct differential funding between "rich white" districts and "poor minority" districts identified in this legal action as a national phenomenon. They argued that in such funding there are discrepancies that are incongruous with the American ideology of fairness: "a differential of any magnitude the sole justification for which is an imaginary school district line" (p. 210). These boundaries and funding inequalities combined to make the public schools the institution that educated the rich and kept the poor uneducated (Coons et al., 1970).

Comparative
Per-Student
Spending

Preferential education for the rich and denial of education for the poor continues today. Table 1.5 provides an analysis of more recent educational funding differentials for school districts in New Jersey, New York, and Chicago. Arranged in order of per-pupil yearly expenditure, these data show that school districts with the greatest proportion of non-Anglo-American and Hispanic populations consistently spend the least amount per student.

Thirty years after research documented patterns in funding that were creating a "class" structure in education, with non-Anglo-American and Hispanic students at the lower end, we have achieved no substantive remedy. Court actions seeking such remedies are being revisited by the Edgewood School District as well as by school districts in California, Illinois, New Jersey, and New York. California's latest lawsuit (*Williams et al.* v. *State of California*, May 2000) targets both the district and the state because of unequal and detrimental funding of schools. Kozol (1991) sums up this situation best:

> These are Americans. Why do we reduce them to this beggary—and why, particularly, in public education? Why not spend on children here [in schools underfunded] at least what we would be investing in their education if they lived within a wealthy district like Winnetka, Illinois, or Cherry Hill, New Jersey, or Manhasset, Rye, or Great Neck in New York? Wouldn't this be a natural behavior in an affluent society that seems to value fairness in so many other areas of life? Is fairness less important to Americans today than in earlier times? Is it viewed as slightly tiresome and incompatible with hardnosed values? What do Americans believe about equality? (p. 41)

Table 1.5 Selected Per-Student Yearly Expenditures

School Funding in the Chicago Area (1988–89 School Year)		School Funding in New Jersey (1988–89 School Year)		School Funding in Six Districts in the New York City Area (Three-Year Period)		
School or District	Spending per Pupil	District	Spending per Pupil	District	1986-87	1989–90
Niles Township High School	$9,371	Princeton	$7,725	Manhasset	$11,372	$15,084
New Trier High School	$8,823	Summit	$7,275	Jericho	$11,325	$14,355
Glencoe (Elementary & Junior High School)	$7,363	West Orange	$6,505	Great Neck	$11,265	$15,594
Winnetka (Eementary & Junior High School)	$7,059	Cherry Hill	$5,981	Mount Vernon	$6,433	$9,112
Wilmette (Elementary & Junior High School)	$6,009	Jersey City	$4,566	Roosevelt	$6,339	$8,349
Chicago (average all grade levels)	$5,265	East Orange	$4,457	New York City	$5,585	$7,299
		Paterson	$4,422			
		Camden	$3,538			

Source: Chicago Panel on School Policy and Finance; Educational Law Center, Newark, New Jersey; Statistical Profiles of School Districts, New York State Board of Education; *New York Times.* As cited in J. Kozol (1991), *Savage Inequalities: Children in America's Schools,* New York: Crown, pp. 236–237.

A Wasted Resource

The most pressing argument for giving our attention to the previously mentioned signposts of educational vulnerability is the prospect of losing a significant body of our country's human resources at a time when we need all the resources we can muster. Added to this is the fact that young people lost from productive membership in our society often become a substantial resource liability. Estimates of fiscal resources diverted to high school dropouts throughout the United States in areas such as health services, unemployment, employment training, and social welfare reach billions of dollars yearly. Close to 85 percent of the people in the U.S. prison system are high school dropouts. Why can't our educational system invest in children so they become assets instead of liabilities? The irony of our predicament is most telling. The cost for a one-year stay in most state and federal prisons is nearly $30,000—the approximate cost, including tuition, fees, books, room and board, and miscellaneous, of sending a student to Harvard University for one year.

Costs of Low Educational Achievement

Recent efforts such as the Taylor Plan recognize the debilitating effect of educational vulnerability and work to find solutions. Patrick Taylor, a Louisiana state legislator and the author of the plan, has begun a campaign to revolutionize U.S. education. His program calls for guaranteed free college tuition and fees for any student who completes a high school education with a C-plus average and scores well on college entrance exams. In 1992 Taylor convinced the Louisiana state legislature to adopt the plan, which recognizes that keeping students in high school makes economic sense. In Louisiana, the long-term cost (loss in taxpayer revenue) associated with each individual who drops out of high school is estimated at $250,000. This estimate does not include the extra cost associated with dropouts who become involved in the criminal justice system, which is an additional $25,000 to $35,000 per person per year. In short, in terms of education, the old adage seems to apply: pay now or pay later. We will pay a lot more later.

Loss of Contribution to Society

Besides its monetary costs to our society, dropping out involves more intangible human costs. In my own family of ten siblings, the children of migrant farm workers, only four graduated from high school and only one—this one—had the opportunity to attend college. As in so many other families, the members of our household had the native intelligence, motivation, and work ethic to succeed in high school and beyond. Yet the circumstances of poverty, cultural and linguistic difference, and the absence of a responsive educational system led to the direct underdevelopment of the family's potential. This underdevelopment pertains not only to each family member's individual educational, economic, and personal growth, but also to his or her potential contribution to the family itself, to the community in which it is embedded, and to society at large. Considering the overall challenges faced by our country and our planet, continued neglect of this potential is a wastefulness we can no longer afford.

The Implications for Educators

The demographic and related information we have been discussing indicates that the diversity in our schools is a recent but an explosive and long-term phenomenon. Teachers, administrators, and other educational professionals who received their training over a decade or two ago were not encumbered by the challenges facing preservice teaching candidates today. A readiness to respond to the challenge presented by a highly diverse student body was not a recognized part of their training. Indeed, a decade or two ago relatively few individuals of minority status succeeded academically, with the result that even now the makeup of the teaching profession does not match the demographics of the students it serves. For the 1999–2000 school year, over 86 percent of the 2.7 million public and private school teachers and 103,000 school administrators were Anglo-American. Fewer than 12 percent were non-Anglo-American and Hispanic: 8 percent were African American, 3 percent were Hispanic, and fewer than 1 percent were American Indian, Alaskan Native, or Asian or Pacific Islander. In this same academic year, however, non-Anglo-American and Hispanic academic enrollment was at 30 percent (NCES, 2000).

Effective Teaching

It appears that in the near future the vast majority of schoolteachers and administrators will be Anglo-American, while the proportion of non-Anglo-American and Hispanic students will continue to increase rapidly (NCES, 1999). What significance does this hold for the training of teachers? Although it is difficult to pinpoint specific attributes of teachers that have served a diverse student body effectively, recent research efforts have attempted to identify some. Unlike earlier reports that identified and described effective programs only, recent reports have sought out effective programs and/or schools and then attempted to describe the specific instructional and attitudinal character of the teacher (Carter and Chatfield, 1986; Ladsen-Billings, 1994; McLeod, 1996; Pease-Alvarez, Espinoza, and García, 1991; Tikunoff, 1983; Villegas, 1991).

Skills of "Good" Teachers

Dwyer (1991) identifies four domains of instruction at which "good" teachers excel: (1) teaching for content knowledge, (2) teaching for student learning, (3) creating a classroom community conducive to student learning, and (4) displaying teacher professionalism. Villegas (1991) has extended these four domains for teachers who serve a student population that is culturally and linguistically diverse. She suggests that "good" teachers in these classroom contexts incorporate culturally responsive pedagogy, meaning that they adjust their teaching strategies in response to the learning styles of individual students.

Little Focus on Staff Quality

Concern for the effectiveness of teachers is not new. From the earliest days of education program evaluation, the quality of the instructional staff has been considered a significant feature (Heath, 1982; Ladsen-Billings, 1994). Unfortunately, for programs serving students of minority status, the evaluation of "effectiveness" has lately been consumed by an empirical concern for multicultural representation in the content of curriculum at the expense of an examination of teaching strategies themselves. For programs dealing with students with limited English proficiency, interest has centered only on the use or nonuse of the students' native language and the development of English-language skills (August and García, 1988). Very little consideration is given to the attributes desired in the professional and paraprofessional staff members who implement the myriad of program types that serve students in compensatory education. Typically, staff evaluation deals with the number of years of service and the extent of formal educational training (Olsen, 1988). Yet most

Educational Backgrounds of Today's Immigrant Students

Over the past two decades, U.S. classrooms have undergone a dramatic change. Anyone coming into contact with the school system—whether educator, student, parent, policymaker, or service provider—cannot help but notice the profound and continuous diversification of every facet of the student population: racial, ethnic, religious, and social. This trend is hardly new, but its accelerated pace is having a tremendous impact on our educational system.

Becoming a Responsive Teacher

Each year, thousands of school-age immigrant children arrive in the United States seeking a better life. Each enters school with his or her own unique educational history and life experiences. Consider the following examples:

Somxai and Souphanh. Somxai and Souphanh Noum, a teenage brother and sister, spent the last seven years in a refugee camp in Laos waiting for resettlement in another country. After six years with no schooling in the refugee camp, they were provided with a few months of "survival" English to prepare them for life in a new land and a new culture.

Swetlana. Swetlana Borishkevich, a teenage Ukrainian, attended regular classes in the Soviet Union through the eighth grade, but she was not able to fulfill her wish to enroll in vocational training in the Soviet Union because her family fled to Italy. From there, they came to the United States, where she is enrolled in a large secondary school in New York City.

José. José Cardenas, a Mexican immigrant who came to the United States with his uncle, attended school in Mexico only occasionally, since he had to spend most of his time helping on the family farm. Although José is a very mature 16-year-old, he has completed only

educational researchers will admit that the effect of any instructional intervention is directly related to the quality of implementation by the instructor. A recent report issued by the California Commission on Teacher Credentialing verified that because of high teacher turnover—and large numbers of misassigned teachers and classrooms staffed by teachers holding only emergency (that is, temporary and not state approved) credentials—a disproportionate number of poor and minority students are taught during their entire school career by the least-qualified personnel.

Continued   Educational Backgrounds of Today's Immigrant Students

the third grade. He now finds himself in an ESL program in Los Angeles with children who are much younger. He is embarrassed to be there and is quite bored with the endless drill. He can hardly wait to drop out of school and go to work in a fast-food restaurant.

Soo Jung Chu. Last year, Soo Jung Chu transferred from a prestigious Korean school to an American public school. Soo Jung Chu was at the top of his class in Korea. Now he feels intense frustration whenever he can't understand his schoolwork in English, but he is afraid to ask for help because it makes him feel dumb. He knows that the math class the school counselor placed him in is a "bonehead" class far below his mathematical abilities.

Meeting the Challenge

1. Imagine you are one of the students described previously. Write a journal entry expressing your thoughts and feelings about your first day of school in the United States. Which areas of the educational experience seem the most difficult? Which seem most exciting?

2. Select one of the young people described previously and suggest two alternative ways in which a classroom teacher might introduce the student to his or her new school peers. Remember the importance of first impressions.

3. If you were the classroom teacher for one or more of these students, what would you want to know about their family backgrounds? What would you want to know about their languages and the cultures of their countries of origin?

4. What are the implications for these students' lives if their educational needs are not met by our schools? List the job opportunities available to each one of them if they drop out of high school.

Problems in Training and Assessment

It is important to note that professional teaching organizations such as the National Education Association (NEA), the American Federation of Teachers (AFT), and the National Association for the Education of Young Children (NAEYC)—to name a few of the largest—have specifically addressed the need for teachers to receive special training in teaching a culturally diverse student body. Certification agencies, such as the National Council for

Special Training
Recommended

Accreditation of Teacher Educators (NCATE) and the California Commission on Teaching Credentialing, have included particular provisions related to "multicultural" education that institutions of higher education must implement in order to be accredited as teacher-training institutions and to ensure that their graduates will be considered viable candidates for state teacher credentialing.

Unfortunately, even though the need to train and assess teachers for competence in teaching culturally diverse students is a widely accepted idea, present modes of training and assessment remain highly problematic. The data quite clearly portray the problems in assessing individual professional competence. Present assessment practices can be criticized on several levels (McGahie, 1991; Shimberg, 1983; Sternberg and Wagner, 1986):

Criticisms of Current Assessment Practices

1. Although professional competence evaluations usually address only a narrow range of practice situations, teaching professionals engage in very complex planning, development, implementation, problem-solving, and crisis management. These endeavors usually require technical skills and knowledge that are not easily measured.

2. Professional competence evaluations are biased toward assessing formally acquired knowledge, likely because of the use of similar assessment for student academic achievement. We assess teachers the same way we assess students, even though we have differing expectations regarding these populations.

3. Despite the presumed importance of "practice" skills, professional competence assessments devote little attention to the assessment of enunciated practice skills. With regard to teachers of culturally diverse students, we do have some understanding of specific skills that might be necessary. Even so, because of the lack of specific research in this area, it remains difficult to articulate the exact skills to recommend for assessment.

4. Almost no attention is given to the assessment of what has earlier been identified as the "disposition" and "affective" domains of the teacher, discussed more specifically in Chapter 8. In recent analyses of "effective" teachers, these attributes were identified as being as significant for student learning as are content knowledge and practice skills (Ladsen-Billings, 1994; Pease-Alvarez, Espinoza, and García 1991; Villegas, 1991).

In addition to the preceding concerns, professional assessment instruments are subject to severe violations of reliability and validity. Feldt and Brennan (1989) have demonstrated that components of measurement error are highly inconsistent in professional teacher assessment. Test validity is also a fundamental problem.

Keep in mind that inferences about a teacher's professional competence or ability to practice are actually inferences about what the researcher has decided is important to measure. Test-makers construct an assessment, and soon are willing to say that whoever scores at a certain level on that assessment is competent. Underlying the assessment, however, is the often questionable legitimacy of the constructs the test-makers defined. What if their list of "most important teacher attributes" is not, in fact, particularly pertinent to classroom realities? We presently lack any definitive body of research and knowledge regarding the constructs that define good teachers in general and good teachers of culturally diverse students in particular. That knowledge base is developing, but it is presently inadequate (García, 1991a).

Questionable Basis for Assessment

The Language Minority Student

In our demographic discussion of student diversity, one distinctive subpopulation will receive selective attention because of its growing size, both relatively and absolutely, and its precarious situation within our educational institutions: **language minority students, who come to the schooling process without the language skills through which that process is communicated.** As the previous demographic data have indicated, in the next two decades in the United States, language minority students will comprise some 15 percent of K–12 enrollment. By 2026, these students are projected to make up nearly a quarter of our student body.

Language Diversity

Language minority students present a special challenge to our educational institutions because of their linguistic diversity. So much of what we do in the formal teaching and learning enterprise requires the effective communication of specific facts, concepts, ideas, and problem-solving strategies. Students with linguistic diversity encounter this teaching and learning enterprise not lacking in abilities but instead rich in communication skills that do not match those required in the classroom. If it is ineptly handled, this scenario is a formula for failure despite the intellectual gifts such students might possess.

The education of students who come to our schools speaking a language other than English has received considerable research, policy, and practice attention in the last two decades. The U.S. Department of Education and several private foundations have supported specific demographic studies and instructional research related to these students, from preschool through college. Congress has authorized legislation targeted directly at these students on six occasions (1968, 1974, 1984, 1987, 1994, and 2000), while numerous states have enacted laws and developed explicit program guidelines aimed at meeting their needs. Moreover, federal district courts and the U.S. Supreme Court have concluded adjudication proceedings that directly influence the education of language minority students. This significant attention has allowed answers to some important questions that were unanswerable less than a decade ago. The following discussion will highlight these questions and their respective treatment in light of emerging information regarding language minority students.

Who Are These Students?

I was one of these students when I entered elementary school in 1952. Spanish was my first language as well as my home language, although my older brothers and sisters and I had achieved significant English proficiency. In the present system of labels for such children, I would have been classified as *limited English proficient* (LEP) and would have been referred to as a "language minority student," "a linguistically and culturally diverse student," or an "English-language learner."

Attempts at Definition | As one searches today for a comprehensive definition of such a student, a continuum of attempts unfolds. At one end of the continuum are general definitions such as "students who come from homes in which a language other than English is spoken." At the other end are such highly operationalized definitions as "students who scored in the first quartile on a standardized test of English-language proficiency." Regardless of the definition adopted, it is apparent that this sort of student comes in a variety of linguistic shapes and forms. Over 189 distinct language groups have been identified in the language minority population in the United States. Even in the largest of these groups—the "Hispanic" population—some members are monolingual Spanish speakers while others are to some degree bilingual. Other non-English-speaking groups in the United States are similarly heterogeneous. And these subpopulations are culturally as well as linguistically distinct.

Thus it is highly problematic to describe the "typical" language minority student. However, put simply, we might agree that such a student is one who

- substantively participates in a non-English-speaking social environment,

- has acquired the normal communicative abilities of that social environment, and

- is exposed to a substantive English-speaking environment, more than likely for the first time, during the formal schooling process.

The various estimates of the number of language minority students compiled by the federal government (Development Associates, 1984, 1993; O'Malley, 1981; Waggoner, 1991) differ because of the particular definition adopted for identifying these students, the measure utilized to obtain the estimate, and the statistical treatment applied to generalize beyond the actual sample obtained. For example, O'Malley (1981) defined the language minority student population by establishing a specific cutoff score on an English-language proficiency test administered to a stratified sample of students. Development Associates (1984) estimated the population by using reports from a stratified sample of local school districts. Because of such differences in methodology, estimates of language minority students have ranged from 2,500,000 (Development Associates, 1993) to 4,600,000 (U.S. Bureau of the Census, 1991). Whatever its exact size, this population has the following attributes:

Statistics on Language Minority Students

1. Although these children reside throughout the United States, there is distinct geographical clustering. For example, about 75 percent of language minority children are found in Arizona, Colorado, California, Florida, New Jersey, New Mexico, New York, and Texas.

2. Of the language minority children in grades K–6 in 1993, 76 percent had a Spanish-language background; 8 percent were Southeast Asian (Vietnamese, Cambodian, Hmong, and so on); 5 percent were European; 5 percent were East Asian (such as Chinese and Korean); and 5 percent had language backgrounds designated as "other" (such as Arabic or Navaho).

3. In the 19 states most highly affected by the language minority issue in the national study done by Development Associates (1993), 17 percent of the total K–6 student population was estimated as language minority.

What Types of Educational Programs Serve These Students?

The staff of a school district with language minority students has many program options: "transitional bilingual education," "maintenance bilingual education," "English as a second language," "immersion," "sheltered English," "submersion," and so on (these are all the names of program types developed by the U.S. General

Accounting Office, 1987a). Ultimately, most staffs will reject such labels and instead decide to answer the following questions:

1. What are the native-language and English-language characteristics of the students, families, and communities we serve?

2. What model of instruction is desired?
   a. How do we use the native language(s) and English *as mediums of instruction?*
   b. How do we handle the instruction of the native language(s) and English?

3. What staff and resources are necessary to implement the desired instruction?

School district staff have been creative in developing a wide range of language minority student programs that attempt to respond to these questions by addressing the needs of (1) different language groups (Spanish, Vietnamese, Chinese, and so on); (2) different grade levels within a school; (3) different subgroups within a classroom; and (4) different levels of language proficiency. The result has been a broad and at times perplexing variety of program models.

These program initiatives can be differentiated by the way they utilize the native language and English during instruction. Development Associates (1993) surveyed 333 school districts in the 19 states that serve over 80 percent of the language minority students in the United States. For grades K–5, they report the following salient features of the instruction of language minority students:

Features of Current Programs

1. Ninety-three percent of the schools reported that the use of English predominated in their programs; conversely, 7 percent indicated that the use of the native language predominated.

2. Sixty percent of the schools reported that both the native language and English were utilized during instruction.

3. Thirty percent of the schools reported minimal or no use of the native language during instruction.

Two-thirds of these schools chose to utilize some form of bilingual curriculum to serve this population of students. However, one-third minimized or altogether ignored the native language in their instruction of language minority students. Recall that approximately three-fourths of language minority students in this country are of Spanish-speaking backgrounds. Programs that serve them have been characterized primarily as **transitional bilingual education,** which means that they offer a transition from early-grade

Spanish-emphasis instruction to later-grade English-emphasis instruction and eventually to English-only instruction.

For the one-third of the students receiving little or no instruction in their native language, two alternative types of instructional approaches likely predominate: **English as a second language (ESL)** and **immersion.** Each primarily uses English during instruction but does not ignore the fact that the students have limited English proficiency. However, the instructors in these programs do not need to be able to speak the native language of the students. Moreover, these programs are best suited to classrooms that have a heterogeneous non-English-speaking student population rather than those in which one non-English-speaking group predominates.

Federal and State Educational Policies

Now that we have identified the language minority student and examined how that student has been served, let us turn our focus to educational policy: first, federal legislative and legal initiatives, and second, state initiatives.

Federal Legislative Initiatives

The U.S. Congress set a minimum standard for the education of language minority students in public educational institutions in Title VI of the Civil Rights Act of 1964, which prohibits discrimination by educational institutions on the basis of race, color, sex, or national origin, and in the Equal Educational Opportunities and Transportation Act of 1974 (EEOA), which attempts to define a denial of constitutionally guaranteed equal educational opportunity. The EEOA provides in part that

> no state shall deny equal educational opportunities to an individual on account of his or her race, color, sex, or national origin, by the failure by an educational agency to take appropriate action to overcome language barriers that impede equal participation by students in its instructional programs.

The EEOA does not mandate specific education treatment, but it does require public educational agencies to sustain programs to meet the language needs of their students.

Bilingual Education Act | The Bilingual Education Act of 1967 (BEA) was designed to meet the educational needs of low-income students with limited English-speaking ability. This act was added to the larger and more comprehensive Elementary and Secondary Education Act of 1968 and became a continuing subcomponent of that act.

Grants were awarded to local educational agencies, institutions of higher education, or regional research facilities to (1) develop and operate programs for bilingual education, native history and culture, early childhood education, and adult education, as well as for programs to train bilingual aides; (2) make efforts to attract and retain teachers from non-English-speaking backgrounds; and (3) establish cooperation between the home and the school.

Five major reauthorizations of the BEA have occurred since its initial passage in 1968—in 1974, 1978, 1984, 1987, and 1994. As a consequence of the 1974 amendments (Public Law 93-380), a bilingual education program was defined for the first time as "instruction given in, and study of English and to the extent necessary to allow a child to progress effectively through the education system, the native language" (Schneider, 1976, p. 125). The goal of bilingual education continued to be a transition to English rather than maintenance of the native language. However, students no longer had to be from low-income backgrounds to participate. New programs were funded, including a graduate fellowship program for study in training teachers for bilingual education and another program for the development, assessment, and dissemination of classroom materials for bilingual education.

In the Bilingual Education Amendments of 1978 (Public Law 95-561), program eligibility was expanded to include students with limited English academic proficiency as well as students with limited English-speaking ability. Parents were given a greater role in program planning and operation. Teachers were required to be proficient in both English and the native language of the children in the program. Grant recipients were required to demonstrate how they would continue the program when federal funds were withdrawn.

The Bilingual Education Act of 1984 created new program options, including alternative instructional programs that did not require use of the child's native language. These options were expanded in 1987. State and local agency program staff were required to collect data, identify the population served, and describe program effectiveness.

The New National Educational Policies of 1994 and 2000

From this broader context, specific changes in policy with regard to language minority students developed in the reauthorization of the BEA in 1994. Typically, changes in national policy are related to crisis intervention: there is a problem, and it must be addressed quickly, usually with more political and philosophical rhetoric than action. In the past, national policy for serving linguistically and culturally diverse students and their families was driven to a large extent by this sort of "crisis" rationale. This meant that policies have been frequently short-sighted, inflexible, and minimally cohesive and integrated; they are not always informed by a strong knowledge base.

Titles I and VII of the Elementary and Secondary Education Act of 1965 (ESEA) are both prime examples of the disadvantages of a crisis-intervention approach to providing services to Hispanic language minority students. However, the 1994 reauthorization of the ESEA brought about the following concepts in developing new policy:

Policy Changes of 1994

1. The new knowledge base, both conceptual and empirical, must be central to any proposed changes.

2. Consultation with the professionals in the field is critical in order to profit from the wisdom of current policy, administration, curriculum, and instructional practice.

3. National, state, and local policies and programs must be cohesive in order to integrate services that are to be provided.

4. The demographic and budgetary realities of the present and of the coming decade must be acknowledged.

New policy directions, primarily those related to Titles I and VII of the ESEA, will be implemented according to these guidelines. (See Wiese and García, 1998, for a comprehensive description of the policy foundations of this reauthorization and García, 2000, for recent federal policy changes.)

We will now explore each of these guidelines in more detail to understand this new policy more fully.

Knowledge Base. Recent studies have documented the effectiveness of various educational practices related to linguistically and culturally diverse students in selected sites throughout the United States. The case-study approach of this research has included examinations of preschool, elementary, and high school classrooms. Teachers, principals, parents, and students were interviewed, and specific classroom observations were conducted to assess the dynamics of the instructional process. The results of these studies provide important insights into general instructional organization, literacy development, academic achievement in content areas (like math and science), and the views of the students, teachers, administrators, and parents.

Use of Research Findings

In brief, the studies have found that effective curriculum, instructional strategies, and teaching staffs are rooted in the sharing of expertise and experience through multiple avenues of communication. Effective curricula provide students with abundant and diverse opportunities for speaking, listening, reading, and writing, along with scaffolding to help guide them through the learning process. Further, effective schools for diverse students encourage them to take risks, construct meaning, and seek reinterpretation of knowledge within compatible social contexts. Within this knowledge-driven curriculum, skills become tools for acquiring knowledge, not ends in themselves (August and Hakuta, 1997).

An effective curriculum recognizes that any attempt to address the needs of linguistically and culturally diverse students in a deficit or "subtractive" mode is counterproductive. Instead, educators must be "additive" in their approach to such students; that is, the teachers must add to the rich intellectual, linguistic, academic, and cultural attributes and skills the students bring to the classroom. Moreover, programs for these students should be integrated and comprehensive. They should not be segregated, and the development of English and academic content mastery must be seen as equally important. The same educational goals are to be articulated for these students and *all other* students. In addition, federal efforts to assist local school districts, particularly in programs that may be perceived by parents as inappropriate for their children, should be clearly explained to the parents, and the parents should voluntarily agree to their children's participation.

Wisdom of Practice. Too often, in the heat of legislation and the political process, policy development is highly centralized under the control of various interest groups and professional policymakers. Therefore, with the 1994 and 2000 reauthorizations of the ESEA, new national policy initiatives were crafted in consultation with diverse constituencies. For linguistically and culturally diverse communities, the "usual players" in this process included the National Association for Bilingual Education; the Mexican American Legal Defense Fund, which has made specific legislative recommendations of major proportion; and other educational groups.

Using Reform
Expertise

This new legislation was also organized as a result of broader efforts at school reform. Of particular significance was the report by the Carnegie Foundation for the Advancement of Teaching, *The Basic School: A Community for Learning,* which acknowledged that there are key components of an effective school that need to be brought together in an integrated and cohesive manner. A good teacher in a good classroom is not enough to guarantee that effective learning will occur. Effective schools are those that reinforce the significance of the early school years and place a high priority on learning language and knowledge with cohesiveness. *The Basic School* is based on the concept of "best practice," a comprehensive plan for educational renewal that has as its goal the improvement of learning for every child. This same idea is at the core of new federal education policy.

The work of the Stanford Working Group was also significant in shaping the new policy. This group, funded by the Carnegie Corporation of New York, consulted widely with many individuals representing a broad spectrum of theoretical, practical, and policy expertise. In published reports and in various forums, it put forward a comprehensive analysis and articulated precise recommendations for policy and legislation related to linguistically and culturally diverse populations.

Thus, those who shaped the new policy proposals drew upon the shared wisdom from various established perspectives. Moreover, further changes, if they are to be effective, must be embraced by those individuals and organizations active in the field.

Cohesiveness. The new policy arising from the 1994 reauthorization of the ESEA also attempted to view provision of services to students in a comprehensive and integrated manner. Through the introduction of new legislation in Goals 2000, the U.S. Department of Education set the stage for the state-by-state development of standards. Then, with the 1994 reauthorization, an alignment of the goals initiative with specific goals and of the standards initiatives with specific resource allocation policies was accomplished. This alignment recognizes that federal, state, and local government efforts must be integrated if they are to be effective and efficient. Moreover, the federal role must allow for flexibility at the state and local levels while requiring that all children achieve at the highest levels.

Cohesiveness of Policy | The Title VII reauthorization of services to students with limited English proficiency is also highly congruent with the alignment principle. As such, Title VII is not seen as yet another intervention aimed at meeting an educational crisis in American education but rather as a key component of the integrated effort to address effectively the educational needs of students. Specifically, Title VII will continue to provide for leadership and increase national, state, and local educational services, professional development, and research related to linguistically and culturally diverse populations. Other programs, particularly Title I of the ESEA, will more directly increase the services needed by all students living in poverty, including those with limited English proficiency.

Demographic and Budgetary Realities. Over the last decade, large increases in the number of LEP students in our schools have occurred. In the last six years, that increase was nearly 70 percent, or approximately 1 million students. There is no reason to believe this trend will subside. Rather, it is important to recognize that the national presence of this population as well as its diversity are substantial. In the last decade 10 states have been added to the list of those with more than 2 percent of their student population designated as LEP. Today there are 20 such states, half of them with LEP student populations between 5 and 25 percent. Moreover, these LEP students are quite diverse, with over 180 language groups represented in programs funded under Title VII.

Pressures of Numbers and Money | Unfortunately, the fiscal resources needed to meet the growing and diverse demands of this population are not likely to be increased in any significant way. National, state, and local funding for this population has not grown in proportion to the increase in the number of students. Critics such as Linda Chavez (past presidential advisor to Ronald Reagan) and Congressman Bill Light of New York have indicated that bilingual education costs taxpayers between $5.5 and $15 billion yearly. How they arrive at those figures is a mystery, since federal funding for bilingual education in the last decade has ranged between $125 and $200 million yearly. A 4 percent increase in federal funds was requested by the Clinton administration in the past several years, but no major increases are likely to be requested in the near future. Although new legislation in the Improving American Schools Act (IASA) regarding the distribution of Title I funds to high-poverty areas should bring more resources to Hispanic language minority students, such funding will still be limited. This means that present resources must be utilized more efficiently.

Changing Title VII to Ensure Effective Schooling for Language Minority Students. The Title VII legislation of 1994 was part of a cohesive change in policy direction from the U.S. Department of Education. Title VII will continue to provide leadership and build the capacity of educational services, professional development, and research related to linguistically and culturally diverse populations. However, programs for language minority students are packaged in a comprehensive manner that recognizes the significance of Goals 2000, Title I and other ESEA programs, and state and local education efforts. This new federal legislation not only recognizes but also directly responds to the needs of linguistically and culturally diverse children. Title I legislation, for example, requires recipients to serve language minority students.

Improvements in Title VII | Within this framework, Title VII has undergone several changes. Direct assistance to local and state educational agencies has been the core federal service to LEP students. Under the new legislation, existing programs would be replaced by development and enhancement grants, comprehensive school grants, and comprehensive district grants. This new configuration recognizes the complexity of educational responses for language minority students as well as the necessity for locally designed and integrated programs. State review of proposals will reinforce the implementation of state plans for these students. In recent (2000) developments, funding for one thousand new two-way bilingual programs will be provided.

Other changes that relate to research, evaluation, and dissemination have been made in response to input from the field. Research activities will be developed by the U.S. Office of Bilingual Education and Minority Language Affairs, with required consultation from the field and enhanced coordination with other U.S. Department of Education research activities. Program evaluation requirements will be simplified to be more "user friendly" and directed at program improvement, assessment of student English proficiency, and academic outcomes and dissemination. To showcase the success of existing Title VII programs, there will be added emphasis on academic excellence programs that have effectively disseminated and demonstrated their expertise locally, regionally, and nationally. The work of Multifunctional Resource Centers and the Evaluation Assistance Centers will be merged with new comprehensive technical assistance and professional development efforts of the U.S. Department of Education.

After 25 years of efforts to develop a teaching force prepared to meet the needs of LEP students, this area remains a major challenge. Professional development programs will place renewed emphasis on such work, including a new career-ladder program. In addition to continuing attempts to prepare LEP teachers, opportunities for professional development through doctoral fellowships remain, and postdoctoral opportunities have been created to continue the development of a strong research and theoretical base.

These changes are framed by a commitment to the value of bilingualism and the belief that all children can meet high standards.

Over $1 billion in federal funding has been appropriated through Title VII legislation for educational activities (program development, program implementation, professional training, and research) for language minority students. In addition, other congressional appropriations (for vocational education, Chapter I, and so forth) explicitly target language minority students.

Federal Legal Initiatives

The 1974 U.S. Supreme Court decision in *Lau v. Nichols,* the landmark statement of the rights of language minority students, declares that LEP students must be provided with language support:

California: The "Minority Majority" State

Over the period 1987 to 1997, student diversity in California changed significantly. The number of students identified as LEP increased by a startling 20 percent (see Figures a–c). In fact, a major milestone was reached by 1988, when the majority of students in California's public schools were from ethnic and racial "minorities." Non-Hispanic Anglo-American students now constitute the minority of students in the schools and, based on demographic projections, will continue to do so.

Becoming a Responsive Teacher

The extent of the changes in the diversity of California's student population can be best appreciated by comparing the composition of the student population in 1987 with the "new" students who entered school between 1987 and 1990 (actually, new students who entered minus existing students who left). The accompanying graphs illustrate these differences. In 1987, 48 percent of all students were from ethnic and racial minority groups, and 13 percent were LEP. But of the new students who entered the schools in 1986–90, 92 percent were from ethnic and racial minority populations, and 65 percent were LEP. Clearly, the new students entering California's schools are much different from previous students.

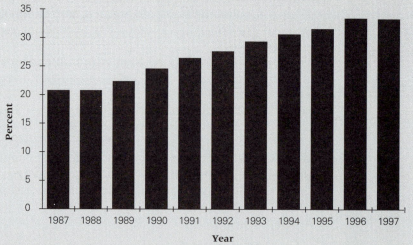

Figure a   **LEP Students in California Public Schools, Kindergarten through Third Grade, 1987–1997**

Source: California Department of Education, *Language Census Report for California Public Schools.* Sacramento: Author, 1997.

Continued   California: The "Minority Majority" State

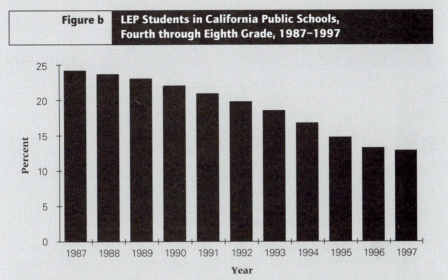

Figure b | **LEP Students in California Public Schools, Fourth through Eighth Grade, 1987–1997**

Source: California Department of Education, *Language Census Report for California Public Schools.* Sacramento: Author, 1997.

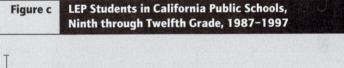

Figure c | **LEP Students in California Public Schools, Ninth through Twelfth Grade, 1987–1997**

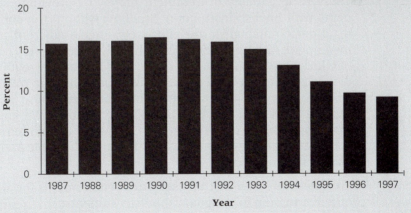

Source: California Department of Education, *Language Census Report for California Public Schools.* Sacramento: Author, 1997.

Continued   California: The "Minority Majority" State

Enrollment projections by the California Department of Finance suggest that these trends will continue throughout the 1990s. Total elementary and secondary enrollment is projected to increase by 47 percent during the next decade, or by 200,000 students per year, which is about three times the rate of growth in the 1980s. The proportion of students from minority populations is projected to increase from 54 percent to 63 percent during the same period.

Meeting the Challenge

1. Research the comparable elementary and secondary school enrollment data for your own state or city for 1986–2000. Are the trends similar to or different from those described for California? Construct a graph from the data if you can.

2. If you had been a teacher in the California schools during this dramatic shift in student demographics, what types of in-service training would have been helpful to you?

3. How might the social life of a school be affected by a significant increase in LEP students? As a teacher, what classroom methods would you use to encourage communication among students with different language backgrounds?

There is no equality of treatment merely by providing students with English instruction. Students without the ability to understand English are effectively foreclosed from any meaningful discourse. Basic English skills are at the very core of what these public schools teach. Imposition of a requirement that before a child can effectively participate in the education program he must already have acquired those basic skills is to make a mockery of public education. We know that those who do not understand English are certain to find their classroom experiences wholly incomprehensible and in no way meaningful.

Legal Rights of LEP Students   *Castaneda v. Pickard* (1981) set three requirements for an appropriate program for language minority students:

1. The program be based on a sound educational theory.

2. The program must be "reasonably calculated to implement effectively" the chosen theory.

3. The program must produce results in a reasonable amount of time.

The courts have also required appropriate action to overcome language barriers. "Measures which will actually overcome the problem" of limited English proficiency are called for by *U.S.* v. *Texas* (1981), and "results indicating that the language barriers confronting students are actually being overcome" are mandated by *Castaneda*. Therefore, local school districts and state education agencies have a responsibility to assess the effectiveness of special language programs on an ongoing basis. Other court decisions have delineated the requirements of professional training and the particular role of standardized tests.

State Initiatives

Twelve states have mandated special educational services for language minority students. Another twelve explicitly permit these services, and one state prohibits them. Twenty-six states have no legislation that directly addresses language minority students.

State policies for language minority students can be characterized as follows:

Variations by
State

1. Implementing programs that allow or require instruction in a language other than English (17 states).

2. Establishing special qualifications for the certification of professional LEP instructional staff (15 states).

3. Providing school districts with supplementary funds to support LEP educational programs (15 states).

4. Mandating a cultural component of LEP programs (15 states).

5. Requiring parental consent for enrollment of students in LEP programs (11 states).

Eight states (Arizona, California, Colorado, Illinois, Indiana, Massachusetts, Rhode Island, and Texas) impose all of these requirements concurrently. Such a pattern suggests continued state attention to issues related to language minority students (for details see Wiese and García, 1998).

Of particular interest is a subset of states that together are home to almost two-thirds of this nation's language minority students: California, Florida, Illinois, New York, New Jersey, and Texas. In these states, bilingual credentialing and ESL or some other related credentialing/endorsement is available. However, in only three of these six states is such credentialing mandated. Therefore, even in states with high numbers of language minority students, there is no direct concern for the establishment of specific professional standards. As Valencia (1997) suggests, because language minority students tend to be concentrated in a few districts within a state (as is particularly true of Chicanos in the Southwest), their presence does not exert a great deal of pressure statewide.

A new California state initiative is the most recent effort for state action to restrict the use of a language other than English in the delivery of educational services to non-English-speaking children. The new ballot measure identified as "English for All Children," or Proposition 227, passed by 61 percent of the vote on June 2, 1998, and proposes to

1. Require that all children be placed in English-language classrooms and that English-language learners be educated through a prescribed methodology identified as "Structured English Immersion."

2. Prescribe a methodology that would provide for a temporary transition period not normally to exceed one year.

3. Allow instruction in the child's native language only in situations in which a waiver is granted, is done so in writing, and is requested yearly by parents (also requiring a school visit by a parent), and

4. Prohibit native-language instruction only if the student already has mastered English and is more than 10 years old and if such instruction has been approved by the principal and the teacher.

Therefore, this "English Only" initiative allows bilingual education only through a waiver process for children less than 10 years old. Moreover, through another provision, teachers, administrators, and school board members would be held personally liable for fees and damages by the child's parents or guardians for not implementing any of the mandates of Proposition 227. Available data on the implementaion of Proposition 227 by local school districts indicate that little change in instructional practice has been realized (García and Stritikus, 2000). Districts and schools that already had bilingual education in place utilized the parent waiver to retain their programs.

The Five Rs of Educational Reform

These summonses to change educational practices in the face of continual increase in the number of culturally diverse students are not to be ignored. I have often been called upon to translate such calls in ways that might be helpful to the general public. In so doing, I have often called upon a set of recommendations that forms a particular mnemonic: "Remember the five Rs." Educational programs, initiatives, strategies, and policies that benefit these students are **respectful, responsive, responsible, resourceful,** and **reasonable.** Throughout this text you will find a special marginal icon next to discussions and examples of each of these criteria.

Respectful

Everyone wants respect. Parents want to be respected and want their children respected. Over and over again, it is common to hear language minority parents and their children say that they do not receive that respect in schools. The language minority child too often is seen as the student who is "different," a foreigner, the immigrant, the non-English speaker, the disadvantaged, someone who does not belong or who is "less" than others, and the school's mission becomes one of changing such students so they can belong. The most detrimental lack of respect for these students might be identified as the "*el pobrecito* syndrome*": "Oh, you poor thing—unwashed, of and in poverty, non-English-speaking immigrant; we sympathize with your circumstances and lower our expectations for what you might be able to learn." Sympathy is not what these students need. This is the point at which an educator or an educational system actually begins going down the slippery slope of lowering expectations and academic standards and begins to devise selection methods that separate the deserving from the nondeserving, the smart from the dumb, those with from those without a future. Consequently, culturally and linguistically diverse students find themselves at the bottom end of this continuum through no fault of their own. Educational programs, teachers, and administrators who serve these students well respect them for what they bring— their language, culture, and world view. Such providers do not see disadvantages that only place students at risk but instead see in these students resources that can be marshaled to meet learning goals, particularly high learning goals. There is acceptance and a respect that is to be honored and extended to all students and the families and communities from which they come. *Pobrecitos* they are not.

It was at the Pajaro Middle School that I first encountered the *el pobrecito* syndrome (García, 1989). The school was primarily serving Mexican American students, many of whom were first-generation immigrants. Some teachers actually felt that these students should not be in the country—or in their school. Several years later, the voters of California formally articulated this view

by passing Proposition 187, which eliminated educational services for noncitizens. Since these students did not speak English,
were poor, were members of gangs, and came from farm-worker
families, the majority of educators at the school felt that the most
they could do for them was to provide them with a basic, no-frills
education. These teachers thought that it was enough for an educational institution to take such students out of the fields. After
we analyzed the math and literacy curriculum for all seventh-
graders, we found that over an extended period of time, teachers
had been teaching fifth-grade skills to these seventh-graders.
This was not a teaching staff that had purposely set out to down-
grade instruction. They had not had sinister motives or goals.
When asked why they were teaching at these lower levels, their
response was, "We sympathize with [these students'] disadvantages and don't want them to fail." In other words, they considered these students *pobrecitos* (the disadvantaged ones).

That same staff, once it realized and began acting upon the
need to respect the language and culture of the students and to
raise its standards and academic expectations, developed and
implemented organizational and instructional changes that resulted in significant gains in the students' academic achievements in literacy, mathematics, and science. For culturally and
linguistically diverse students in particular, too much sympathy
for their circumstances can be highly detrimental; on the other
hand, too much respect is never handicapping. We too often
adopt the old adage, "You will need to earn my respect." Instead,
I am suggesting that we revise it: "I will begin by respecting who
you are, although you may lose that respect because of what you
actually do."

Responsive

It is not enough merely to have respect. Educational programs
and those individuals who teach in them must be directly responsive to the students and families whom they serve. Doing
this requires actively assessing the learning tools that the student
brings to the schooling process as well as encouraging the utilization of those tools to optimize student learning. It means shifting
the emphasis from needs assessments to "asset inventories."
However, it is not enough for a teacher just to know his or her
students well. He or she must also take that knowledge and make
it come alive when organizing and implementing teaching and
learning environments for those students. A former colleague of
mine once said, "The general can only be understood in [terms
of] its specifics." That is, we can come to know all of our students
in various intellectual ways, but until we can translate that

knowledge into the very specific ways in which we teach them, the maximum benefits of that intellectual knowledge will go unrealized.

My first encounter with the Puente Project resulted from a search of educational programs that supported Hispanic-language minority students in their efforts to attend four-year colleges (University of California, 1993). This program is an English-literature-based program for community college students preparing to transfer to a four-year college. The project adapted the community-college English literature course for Latino language minority students, most of whom were first-generation college attendees, in several important ways. First, it made sure to bring the instructors in the program together to learn about the students whom they would be serving. Many of these instructors were "standard" English professors, highly competent instructors yet personally unacquainted with the culture and the language of their students. Second, the curriculum of the course incorporated literature that utilized Spanish and Spanish and English code switching as well as standard English texts that reflected the students' personal or family experiences. Lastly, each student was paired with a mentor, usually a Latino college graduate working in the same community as the student and, if possible, one who had grown up in the same community as the student. The role of this mentor was not only to monitor and promote student progress but also to provide direct knowledge about how the educational system works while directly and indirectly providing a vision of what the future would hold for a college graduate. Students were expected to read, write, and otherwise meet the high and challenging standards of this course. I was amazed to find that students who participated in the Puente Project were accepted at four-year colleges at five times the rate that similar students who had not participated in the project were accepted. This phenomenon continues today, and the project has been extended to high school and middle school. It is a real and productive example of educational **responsiveness** to these diverse students. The Puente Project considered the experiences and skills of these students and adapted the curriculum and instruction to maximize their learning. It emphasized taking asset inventories in addition to doing needs assessments.

Responsible

In constructing new federal legislation in the Improving America's Schools Act, my U.S. Department of Education colleagues and I were continually confronted with the unequal achievements of selected students in U.S. schools (García and Gonzales,

1995). It became evident that nationally we did not have policy mechanisms in place for holding educational institutions accountable for these disparate educational results. Moreover, the general aggregate of achievement data did not reveal how subgroups of students were actually doing. For this reason, the Improving Americas Schools Act in Title I of that law now requires schools receiving federal Title I funds to report student achievement by race, ethnicity, gender, and socioeconomic status. Unfortunately, local schools and states do not always adopt disaggregation practices for achievement data on the basis of historically or currently relevant demographic categories.

Texas has taken an important lead in resolving this set of issues. A statewide accountability system administers achievement tests to each student in its schools on a yearly basis, publishes the disaggregated results of those tests by school, and provides school-based rewards in the form of new resources to those schools that make substantial progress. And, much like the legislation the U.S. Department of Education promoted and Congress passed in the Improving Americas Schools Act of 1994 and 2000, disaggregation of achievement data by ethnic, racial, gender, and economic status is required. In addition, students who are limited-English-proficient and have been receiving instruction in Spanish are administered academic achievement assessments in Spanish. Some have observed that the tests may still not meet high standards of content and may even be suspect due to their questionable reliability and validity. Yet, we now have a statewide system that seriously attempts to address the issues of educational accountability for culturally and linguistically diverse students. However, this type of **responsibility** is still the exception, not the rule. It must become standard practice so as to inform practices that can hold educators and educational agencies accountable for the educational progress of all students.

Resourceful

We often are told, particularly in education, that less is more and that throwing money at a problem is not the solution. Jaime Escalante, as portrayed in the popular movie *Stand and Deliver*, takes low-achieving students and by doing little more than engendering *ganas* (desires) in them, produces a cadre of mathematics success stories. For many students in similar circumstances, these adages sound hollow in the face of the challenges that they confront in everyday educational settings. *Ganas* are good, but a systematic effort to improve education on a variety of fronts is also needed.

The types of curricula and assessment and the expertise of instructors are critical resources in need of attention if language minority students are to do well. Teachers with the necessary instructional skills, classes of reduced size, and resources (time and money) for professional development can enhance educational **responsiveness** at all grades. At high schools, access to college preparatory, honors, and Advanced Placement courses requires redistribution of existing and addition of new resources in schools that have been historically organized to respond to *pobrecitos.*

After-school programs, specifically targeted in-school reading programs, and community-based support programs are not free. They require public and private resources that are not usually available. Yet such programs do not always require many resources. I was struck by the development and implementation of a high school completion program in Houston, Texas, that addressed the issue of **resourcefulness** very directly in response to a high dropout rate of poor African American and Latino students. Simply, the high school reorganized its physical space and instructional/support staff to keep the school open from 7:00 A.M. to 10:00 P.M. every day of the week. Doing this allowed many of these low-income students who needed to help their families by working during normal school hours to attend classes, complete assignments, and obtain counseling services at more convenient times. The high school completion rates and academic achievement of students tripled within one year. The program's additional costs were estimated at approximately $220 per year, but its benefits as attested to by parents, students, teachers, and administrators undeniably justified the expenditure.

Reasonable

We are right to pursue and insist on immediate solutions to the educational problems of language minority students. The U.S. Department of Education concluded that U.S. education needed "No More Excuses" (U.S. Department of Education, 1998). Yet the urgency of such conclusions must be tempered by and coupled with reasonable actions.

The anti–bilingual education movement exemplified by California's Proposition 227 but also evidenced in legislation in other states and in proposed federal initiatives aimed at immigrant students seeks to unreasonably restrict the flexibility of states and local school districts to respond to these students. These new policies mandate prescriptive instructional treatments, limit temporal access of programs to these students (from 1–3 years), and focus their efforts only on English-language development instead of on high academic achievement, all without concern for the accountability of the mandates they are imposing. Newly proposed grade-retention and "high stakes" testing practices may lead to large numbers of students dropping out of school or failing to graduate at a time when we as a country are promoting educational success for all students. Does this incongruity seem reasonable? Despite the situation's urgency and our best intentions, we need not act unreasonably.

Most often, as reasonable people address the five Rs, they are often seen nodding their heads. In almost all cases, these general guidelines are relevant to all students. I have tried, however, to make the strongest case possible that in order to ensure the present and future educational success of the increasing numbers of culturally and linguistically diverse students, applying these guidelines is absolutely critical. Educational policies and practices that respect who the students are, that respond directly to that knowledge base, that hold themselves responsible for academic outcomes, and that provide for and maximize new and existing resources organized in reasonable ways can make a huge difference.

In our University of California, Berkeley and San Francisco Unified School District school-reform efforts, we have found it reasonable to focus on one area of the academic spectrum—literacy—despite students' needs in the academic domains of math and science. This reasonable approach does not ignore the academic treatment of math and science. Instead, it acknowledges that we can only be effective in our efforts to reform instruction if we all are focused on the same goals and if these goals are realistic, given the available time and resources. Too often schools or teachers try to simultaneously reform, reinvent, and otherwise attempt to enhance every aspect of their instruction. Doing this is a laudable goal but too often an unreasonable one. It is also reasonable to understand that enhancing student achievement is not a short-term process. It will take years to reduce long-standing achievement gaps and to meet the high standards that we set for all students. Nationally, it has taken us more than two decades to erase the achievement gap between boys and girls in elementary-school math achievement. It seems reasonable to establish goals to reduce other achievement gaps, but we must also recognize that such reductions will take concerted efforts over reasonable periods of time.

Conclusion

Sometimes making sense of demographic data from the realm of education is like trying to make sense out of baseball by picking through the vast array of statistics printed in tiny type at the back of the sports pages. No one can develop a genuine feel for the game merely by examining the statistics, no matter how comprehensive, strategic, or ingenious those numbers may be. Numbers may never be able to fully convey the excitement experienced in the stands or on the field. Think for a moment about how you would describe your own formal schooling activities if you could answer only the statistical questions "How many?" "How much?" and "How long?" These questions allow you no room to tell the story of your educational experience.

We utilize demographic statistics in education, much as we use baseball statistics, to help us summarize the nature of the enterprise by describing the status of the groups and individuals involved. The demographic analysis in this chapter has presented specific status indicators with the warning that such description can add some depth to, but not total understanding of, the challenging issues that today's and tomorrow's educators face. To understand the quality of the educational experience of most culturally and linguistically diverse children, we will have to go beyond the numbers. For that we will need imagination—and a feel for the game.

Where do we start? What can these descriptive data tell us about the challenges facing us? It is undeniable that the students who will populate our schools, who will play the "game," will soon differ radically with regard to race, culture, and language. In less than two decades, one-half of the students in U.S. schools will be non-Anglo-American and Hispanic—and half of them will speak a language other than English on their first day of school. Teachers who receive their credentials today will likely be responsible for the education of a student body that is more diverse than at any other time in the history of U.S. formal education. This will be true at all levels of education.

The growing population of diverse students will begin their schooling with several strikes against them. They will be coming to the plate from social and economic circumstances that will leave them most vulnerable to the various pitches they will be asked to hit. Those pitches carry two powerful spins: a globally competitive climate in which educational success is an absolute must and a world in which our fundamental knowledge base is growing exponentially.

These students are likely to be equipped not with the best that money can buy but with the least that society is willing to allow them. They are likely to be "coached" by individuals who do not meet the highest standards or who themselves are learning to play the game as their own responsibilities and commitments change and increase. Many of these players will require coaching in a language not their own. They will need to acquire knowledge of the game along with facility in the language and culture in which the game is immersed.

Despite the immensity of their task and the difficulties stacked against these students, the data unequivocally indicate that the future of education rests with them. As they grow to represent the majority, their success will be our success, and their failure will be our failure. They—and we—must succeed. We have no other alternative short of calling off the game. But education, unlike baseball, is not an endeavor we can cancel or postpone when the weather looks bad. The U.S. educational system must rise to the challenge and accommodate students it has historically underserved.

Mrs. Tanner believes this is true. She is living this challenge and is not about to give up. There is no doubt that as a nation we have the resourcefulness we need to succeed, especially if we always remember the five Rs. The remainder of this book will address ways of identifying those resources and applying them to the task at hand.

Summary of Major Ideas

1. Educators in the U.S. schools face the challenge of teaching increasing numbers of children who are culturally and linguistically diverse. The education of these children must take into account demographic factors, issues of academic performance, language background, and child and family well-being.

2. The racial and ethnic makeup of the United States is more diverse than national census data indicate. The non-Anglo-American and Hispanic population, which is growing, is most at risk on indicators of child and family well-being: family stability, family violence, family income, child health and development, and educational achievement.

3. It is projected that non-Anglo-American and Hispanic enrollment will grow to approximately 70 percent of total school enrollment by 2026. And at this time nearly 25 percent of students will come from homes in which English is not the primary language spoken.

4. Today's students must be well prepared to meet the demands of a changing economy that requires workers to have more than the basic skills. In addition, the increasingly diverse U.S. and global marketplace will place a premium on those who can interact easily with others of various cultures and languages.

5. Students living in poverty are three times more likely to drop out of school than are students with economic advantages. It is projected that the number of children living in poverty will greatly increase by 2026.

6. The dropout rate is one indicator of educational vulnerability. The 1990 and 1998 Education Summits proposed the goal of increasing the U.S. high school completion rate to 90 percent by 2001.

7. Event and status rates reports show that non-Anglo-American and Hispanic students drop out of high school two to three times more often than Anglo-American students.

8. Most non-Anglo-American and Hispanic children are likely to attend schools with fewer financial resources and larger classes. Funding discrepancies between "rich" and "poor" school districts raise questions of fairness in education.

9. Effective teachers of students who are culturally and linguistically diverse excel in five domains: (a) mastering content knowledge, (b) teaching for student learning, (c) creating a classroom community for student learning, (d) teacher professionalism, and (5) incorporating culturally responsive pedagogy.

10. Professional teaching organizations, such as the National Education Association and the American Federation of Teachers, and some certification agencies have addressed the need to train educators to teach culturally diverse students. Nevertheless, the training and assessment of teachers of culturally diverse students remain problematic.

11. The language minority student is one who substantively participates in a non-English-speaking social environment, has acquired the normal communicative abilities of that social environment, and is regularly exposed to an English-speaking environment only during the formal school process. Roughly three-fourths of language minority children in the United States are from Spanish-speaking backgrounds.

12. Since the mid-1960s, a series of national policies have attempted to address the needs of language minority students. More recent changes in federal law have recognized the importance of developing programs that capitalize on the wisdom in the field, are cohesive and well integrated, and consider demographic and budgetary realities. The various state policies that focus on language minority students, even in states with high numbers of such students, are uneven in their approaches and their requirements.

Extending Your Experience

1. Describe the physical facilities, programs, and student demographics of your high school. What special materials were available for student use, such as computers, art and music supplies, and sports equipment? Research the school district expenditures for your state. How does your high school rank statewide in terms of per-student spending?

2. Design an elementary school whose sole purpose would be to respond to a student body of maximum cultural and linguistic diversity. As creator of this school, what are your requirements for staff credentials and experience, educational materials, and curriculum? Describe a typical classroom in your dream school.

3. Reflect on your regular personal interactions with people who are fluent in languages other than English. Is language diversity part of your daily experience? If not, how might you prepare yourself to teach in a linguistically diverse classroom?

4. Your best student has just informed you that she has to drop out of high school and get a job to help support her family. Part of her earnings will go to support her brother, who is in college. Her parents seem unconcerned and claim that since she will be getting married, it is not so important that she finish high school. What will you say to this student and her parents? What will you need to know about them before offering them helpful counsel?

5. You have 26 students in your fourth-grade language arts class, but only 20 textbooks are available, and your school has no budget for more. How will you make sure all of your students have the necessary materials for learning?

Resources for Further Study

Print Resources

August, D., and Hakuta, K. (1997). *Improving schooling for language-minority children: research agenda.* Washington, DC: National Research Council.

    This book is an essential tool that can be used by administrators, teachers, researchers, and policymakers who seek to understand and improve the current state of education for language minority students in the United States. Each chapter presents research literature, identifies remaining research needs, and discusses possible solutions regarding that chapter's particular topic. The book focuses on the relationships and outcomes that result when policy and practice intersect.

National Research Council (1998). *From generation to generation: The health and well-being of children in immigrant families.* Washington, DC: National Academy Press.

> This book documents the conditions of children according to their place of residence in the United States. To accomplish this goal, the book highlights existing literature as well as demographically profiling children. Similarly, careful attention is given to factors that aid or hinder the well-being of the children. Lastly, the authors campaign for adopting public policies and programs that recognize the needs of these immigrant children and use the information obtained to inform policy.

Portes, A. (1996). *The new second generation.* New York: Russell Sage Foundation.

> This edited volume focuses attention on providing as much information on recent immigrants as possible, especially on children who come from developing areas such as Asia and Latin America. This work compensates for the previous lack of information about these immigrants. Education, language, career expectations, and socioeconomic conditions are just a few of the important subjects that this work discusses to provide a better account of these immigrants' backgrounds.

Suarez-Orozco, M., and Suarez-Orozco, C. (1995). *Transformations: Immigration, family life, and achievement motivation among Latino adolescents.* Stanford, CA: Stanford University Press.

> This interdisciplinary (anthropology, psychology, and education) three-year case study thoroughly examines the experience of Latino (Mexican) adolescent immigrants. Immigration and family life are key factors that influence academic achievement among Latino students. This study deconstructs myths often used to malign these immigrant populations. Ensuring the academic success of these students can result in positive, long-term effects on the economic well-being of California and eventually on the national economy.

Waters, M. C. (1999). *Black identities: West Indian and American realities.* Cambridge, MA: Harvard University Press.

> The author discusses the experiences of immigrants from the West Indies, especially those of their children. Upon their initial arrival, she notices that their background knowledge of English, their skills and contacts, their self-respect, and their positive outlook toward American race relations brokers their interaction with the American economic structure. Unfortunately, the immigrants' positive outlooks on race relations quickly change when they experience blatant racial discrimination. Surprisingly, the author concludes that those students who resist Americanization, particularly the members of the second generation, are the most likely to prosper economically.

Wiese, A., and García, E. (1998). The Bilingual Education Act: Language minority students and equal educational opportunity. *Bilingual Research Journal, 22*(1), 1–18.

This article provides a thorough historical overview of the Bilingual Education Act. The authors focus on evaluating the objectives and results of this act from both current and historical perspectives in light of the debates on language diversity in schools presently occurring. This article strongly contributes to the discussions about the education of language minority students and also raises questions about the roles of administrators and teachers within this process.

Web Resources

Diversity Database: *http://www.inform.umd.edu/EdRes/Topic/Diversity*

This web site offers access to multicultural and diversity resources. This site accommodates the varied levels of knowledge that may exist among its potential users regarding multicultural and diversity issues. The mission of this site is to find ways to create a more responsive and respectful dialogue among family and schools.

The Education Alliance: *http://www.brown.edu/Research/The Education Alliance/*

This web site is geared toward creating a supportive learning community for educators, policymakers, researchers, and business and community agencies. It promotes such matters as advocacy at local and national levels, leadership training for districts and their employees, the design of curriculum responsive to languages and cultures, and networking among learning communities within local districts and at the national level.

ERIC Clearinghouse on Urban and Minority Education: *http://www.tc.columbia.edu/academic/iume/iume.htm*

The Institute for Urban and Minority Education (IUME) conducts research to better understand the experiences of diverse urban and minority group populations in the various institutions and situations that influence their educational development. IUME provides the knowledge necessary for establishing government policies and designing educational programs to support the educational advancement of ethnically and linguistically diverse groups.

National Clearinghouse for Bilingual Education (NCBE): *http://www.ncbe.gwu.edu/*

This web site collects, analyzes, and disseminates information relating to the effective education of linguistically and culturally diverse learners in the United States. Working in conjunction with other services, NCBE offers access to high-quality information to help states and local school districts develop programs and implement strategies to assist all students work toward high academic standards. This web site deals with such topics as the education of linguistically and culturally diverse (LCD) students in the United States. There is a strong focus on understanding how to implement and facilitate the relationship between practices and research as they relate to the education of LCD students.

Chapter 2
Views of Culture and Education

Focus Questions

- What are some of the social and economic changes that have resulted in new contexts for education in the United States?

- What are the group-oriented and the individual-oriented concepts of culture?

- How does the concept of culture prevalent in U.S. schools affect which practices are deemed appropriate for teaching culturally diverse children?

- What are some of the cultural demands of U.S. schools, and how might students respond if the demands of their home culture are different?

- What are the three ingredients for teaching effectively in a context of student cultural diversity?

- What is *cultural capital?* How do schools deter or enhance its development?

"A text without a context is a pretext."

The subject of this book is the increasing numbers of young people all over the United States whom I have referred to as culturally or linguistically diverse. In all our coming discussions of educational theories and practices, we must keep these children firmly in mind. They are our *students,* and, in a sense, they are our "text"—we will open the book of their educational experiences and read the signs of change that we as educators must follow. We will consider both the stories of individuals and the broader trends that generalize to groups of individuals. We will approach our "text" informed of a full range of social and educational issues that will help us be better readers of what is in store for schools in the United States.

This chapter lays out some of the contexts for education in the years to come. Social, economic, and cultural changes in the United States have raised questions about the proper role for our schools. The answers to these questions require a clearer understanding of our assumptions regarding culture and the individual and the part our schools are to play in transmitting culture to children. We will also look at the culture of school itself and examine the qualities that will be important for teachers of culturally diverse students.

New Contexts for Education

The accomplishments of all societies rest on the fundamental educational capabilities of their individual members. We must examine our past educational practices for successes and failures and use the present to rework and reenvision our goals for teaching and learning. We must look ahead and prepare our nation's children for the future. We will talk much in this book about change. Fortunately, continuing attention to educational reform in this country provides us with some solid information about changing social and economic circumstances that affect education. A variety of reports are produced yearly about our country's schools, ranging from preschool to higher education. The analyses and related reforms these reports suggest have focused our attention on many significant variables that influence our educational institutions today and others that will do so in the future. The following list highlights several of these new contexts for education:

- Economically, the United States finds itself at a significant competitive disadvantage relative to the growing emphasis on what **Global Marketplace** is termed the "global marketplace." International trade will be the arena for economic growth in the next century. At the present, only 10 percent of U.S. jobs are related directly to international trade. However, it is estimated that over the next two decades, this figure will increase to more than 50 percent. As activity in the global marketplace increases, the economic stability of our country will depend on how well we prepare the next generation for participation in this context.

- Education has become a major activity of institutions that are not primarily educational in nature. Only one-third of formal education occurs within primary, secondary, and postsecondary educational institutions. One example of this is the education the business sector provides to employees.

Career Flexibility |
- Today's sixth-graders will likely average 7 to 10 job changes in their lifetime and 2 to 3 changes in career. My father was an agricultural worker and died an agricultural worker. I have had four jobs but only one profession: teaching. My daughters may change jobs 10 times and experience 2 or 3 shifts in profession.

- Only 8 percent of tomorrow's jobs will require less than a high school education. Thirty-five percent will require at least a high school education, and a whopping 60 percent will require three or more years of postsecondary education.

- Eighty percent of new jobs will be in the information and service sector of the economy. This has been the fastest-growing part of our economy for the past two decades. Employees in this field must be flexible, computer literate, creative, and highly skilled at communication (preferably in more than one language), with good "people" skills.

- Major shifts in values over the past three decades have broadened the educational prospects for women in the United States. No longer limited to traditionally "female" professions such as teaching and nursing, young women are now training in large numbers for a broad spectrum of careers in business, law, and technical fields. The demise of gender-based barriers to economic participation has been accompanied by changes in a host of other issues, including sexual behavior, health and environmental concerns, and family priorities.

The Role of Schools

What is the role of the school in the midst of these new and developing circumstances? It seems evident that schools cannot provide adequate job-training skills. The job market described previously will be much too volatile, and employers themselves already find it necessary to provide their employees with job training tailored to specific tasks and functions. It thus appears that schools must take on several responsibilities, some similar to and others significantly different from the ones they have now:

1. Schools must serve children well with regard to the development of academic skills: "readin', writin', and 'rithmetic." Our society needs all its members to be able to communicate well and to be linguistically, mathematically, and technologically literate.

2. Schools must focus on the development of what I call "living" processes, involving students in curricula that enhance human relationships, critical thinking, and civic responsibility. An emphasis on process means attending to means as well as ends—that is, examining how individuals think through their ideas and actions and make decisions in addition to examining the ideas and decisions themselves.

3. Schooling for our increasing numbers of culturally and linguistically diverse students that will facilitate their present and future educational success must attend to the five Rs. Educational policies and practices that understand and **respect** who the students are should be directly **responsive** to that cultural and linguistic knowledge base, should be **responsible** for high academic outcomes, and should be **resourceful** in maximizing new and existing assets organized in ways that are **reasonable.**

Schooling for the Future: The Five Rs

In the new curriculum of the twenty-first century, schooling must become collaborative, highly social in nature, and process oriented. The lives of the young people now in school, even more than our own, will be characterized by continuous and dramatic social, economic, and technological change. As adults, these students must be able to react flexibly to these changing situations. They must be equipped with enough understanding, knowledge, and skill to act as well-informed members of society. They must be able to reflect on and analyze the perplexing array of social and individual problems that are part of modern life.

Cultural Change and Disruption

Change is never easy. The cultural shifts our nation is now undergoing take their toll on our individual and collective experience. Disruptions in the social fabric often lead to misunderstanding, miscommunication, and tension among people. In the most stressful situations, especially ones that involve economic hardships, people can feel pitted against one another, and old Growing Pains | hatreds and old ignorances may rise to block progress and growth. We will undergo more growing pains as the demographics of the U.S. population are transformed. In fewer than 20 years, 70 percent of California's students will be non-Anglo-American and Hispanic, and one-half will speak a language other than English on their first day of school. As we saw in Chapter 1, this same scenario is transforming schools in other states, including New York, New Jersey, Florida, Michigan, Illinois, and Texas. Such states will represent over 50 percent of the U.S. population in the near future.

We are a country of incredible cultural and linguistic diversity. We are singularly nationalistic—"American" to the core—but are still unaccepting of the diversity among us. Recent data on sociological perception suggest that over the past three decades, the Anglo-American majority of the U.S. population has not changed its stereotyped view of minority groups. The majority continues to perceive minorities as less intelligent, lazy, and of lower moral character. These findings are absolutely frustrating considering that within these same three decades, our country has witnessed a civil rights movement, a women's movement, and an equal educational opportunity initiative. Millions of dollars and, more significantly, millions of person-hours have been dedicated to addressing the inequalities and human injustices of our age.

Renewed Debate | The publication of *The Bell Curve* (Herrnstein and Murray, 1994) has reinvigorated a bitter public debate on significant scientific and societal issues, including a set of interrelated theories regarding the influences of genetic and environmental factors in the development of human intelligence; arguments over racial, ethnic, and group differences in intelligence; concerns about possible test biases; and questions concerning the implication of scientific research on these issues for education and public policy. Essentially the same argument—that race is related to innate intelligence—often coupled with the suggestion that African Americans and other selected people of color are genetically inferior, has continued for many years (Wigdor and Garner, 1982). Laosa (1995) suggests that, like a refractory strain of retrovirus, these issues tend to remain latent and from time to time resurge brusquely into the public consciousness.

At the political and policy levels, events in California and Texas are further examples of negative reactions to immigrant and minority students. In California, the passage of Proposition 187 in 1994, Proposition 209 in 1996, and Proposition 227 in 1998 set the stage for the development of a state policy that attempts to eliminate K–12 public education for undocumented immigrant students, that abolishes the use of affirmative action as a tool for providing equal educational opportunity in admission to public higher education, and that limits the use of bilingual education. These public policy intrusions, which rescinded the educational opportunities previously afforded immigrants and minority students (including women), have created a very different political climate for this population.

Language at Home and School

The context of "us versus them" is exemplified in the educational experience of many language minority children. In a nationwide survey of families, Wong-Fillmore (1991, 2000) found evidence of serious disruptions of family relations when young children learn English in school and lose the ability to use the language spoken at home. The study revealed that parents of language minority students fully recognize the importance of English and want their children to learn it at school, but they do not want this to happen at the expense of the home language. Many such parents expressed concern that their children would lose their native language and thus become estranged from their families and cultural heritage. Others reported that their children had already lost or were losing the home language.

Children's Loss of Home Language

An interviewer quoted in this study told the story of a Korean immigrant family whose children had all but lost the ability to speak their native language after just a few years in American schools. The parents could speak English only with difficulty, and the grandmother, who lived with the family, could not speak or understand English. She felt isolated and unappreciated by her grandchildren. The parents spoke to the children exclusively in Korean, refusing to believe that their children could not understand them. They interpreted the children's unresponsiveness as disrespect and rejection. Only when the interviewer, a bilingual Korean-English speaker, tried to question the children in both languages did the parents finally realize that the children no longer spoke or understood Korean. The father wept as he spoke of not being able to talk to his children. One of the children commented that she had never understood why her parents always seemed to be angry.

Systematic lack of support for students' home language has been pervasive in U.S. schools during most of the twentieth century. And difficulties caused by a family's inability to communicate are not manifested only in the home. On the contrary, family problems form the basis of children's problems, and those problems follow children into school, into the streets, and later into their work lives. When enough individuals have problems, our whole society has problems.

It may be years before the harm done to families by this situation is fully assessed. The experience of one family that had been in the United States for nearly 20 years displayed how breakdowns in communication can lead to the alienation of children from parents. As teenagers, the four children had completely lost their ability to speak or understand Spanish. They reportedly were ashamed of Spanish and did not acknowledge it when their parents spoke it, even though it was the only language their parents knew. The mother indicated that her 17-year-old son was having problems in school. He was often truant and was in danger of dropping out. She had tried to talk with him, but he didn't understand her. Their attempts at discussion ended in physical violence, with mother and son coming to blows when words failed them (Wong-Fillmore, 1991, 2000).

When we think about the numbers of families facing similar difficulties, the gravity of our national predicament becomes apparent. To prosper, we must find a way out of this situation and embrace the great and rich diversity of our culture. In the next section we shall discuss two different theories of culture and their implications for education in the United States.

What Is Culture?

When we speak of the **culture** that an individual belongs to, we are generally referring to the system of understanding characteristic of that individual's society or some subgroup within that society. This system of understanding includes values, beliefs, notions about acceptable and unacceptable behavior, and other socially constructed ideas that members of the culture are taught are "true." This is the common definition of culture employed by many anthropologists, who analyze the behavioral patterns and customs of groups of people. The word *culture,* however, can have a variety of connotations in general usage.

An Experiment in Definition | I recently asked a class of university juniors and seniors preparing for careers in education to break into small groups and identify very specifically attributes of their individual cultures. It was no surprise to me that one student responded, "I'm white. I have no culture." Such responses occur all too frequently. "Of course you have a culture," I answered as the other students scrutinized our interaction. "Everyone has a culture." They all went off, some a bit reluctantly, to complete the assignment.

At the end of the exercise, each group reported their findings and analysis. Yes, they all had a culture, but with a diverse set of students it was not easy to discuss individual cultural characteristics. These students, like most of us, usually do not sit down and expose their culture. They live it. They can recognize it when they see it. And they can determine when they are not in it, and that usually distresses them. These students also seemed distressed about speaking openly of their culture to one another, as if exposing it would leave them vulnerable to criticisms about who they were or what they might represent.

My students all survived their initial distress and discovered in a few minutes the basic tenets of the science of anthropology. To define a culture by its attributes might be a start, but this in itself is not particularly useful. The students did identify cultural attributes. They indicated that their cultures were made up of many distinguishable attributes: familial, linguistic, religious and spiritual, aesthetic, socioeconomic, educational, dietary, gender, **Problems of** and so on. The list was quite long. But what seemed quite evident **Definitions** was that they all came to the conclusion that this thing— culture— was not easy to define. To do so meant (1) defining these attributes in relation to specific individuals who live in distinct physical and social contexts and (2) taking into consideration the previous histories of those individuals and those social contexts. In short, they determined that culture is both complex and dynamic, yet for individuals living their cultures, it is quite recognizable.

We began this discussion with the ideas of novice educators and their conceptualizations of culture. Let us now turn to the "experts." Even professional anthropologists struggle with the same questions that bedeviled my students, but their thinking is more systematic, and that will help us.

The Group-Oriented Concept of Culture

The **culture concept,** with its technical anthropological meaning, was first defined by Edward Tylor in 1871 as "that complex whole which includes knowledge, belief, art, law, morals, custom, and other capabilities and habits acquired by man as a member of so-**Culture Is Learned** ciety" (Kroeber and Kluckhohn, 1963, p. 81). Since Tylor's time, anthropologists have advanced many other definitions of culture. These definitions, like Tylor's, commonly attempt to encompass the totality (or some subset of the totality) of humanity's achievements, dispositions, and capabilities. Virtually every anthropologist considers culture to be something that is learned and transmitted from generation to generation.

Culture Is Shared | Most definitions of *culture* include another dimension, the notion that culture is something that members of a group share. An anthropology textbook states, for example, that behaviors and ideas may be considered cultural only insofar as they are shared among members of a social group (Nanda, 1990). This formulation is useful for anthropological comparisons between societies or subgroups within societies. Its basic assumption, however, is that of uniformity among the cultural attributes of individual members of societies and subgroupings of societies. In this formulation, the primary focus of culture is some kind of group.

Anthropologists do acknowledge that members of all societies display individual differences in their behavior and thinking. That is to say, societies are characterized to some extent by intercultural heterogeneity. But these differences are not significant for anthropologists and usually are noted only insofar as they determine the "looseness" or "tightness" of a society's cultural system. When researchers in anthropology write their ethnographies, or their deep descriptions and analyses of any group, they tend to ignore individual variations and to abstract what they apparently consider "an essential homogeneity from the background noise of insignificant diversity" (Schwartz, 1978, p. 419).

Along these lines, anthropologist Ralph Linton defined *culture* as "the sum total of ideas, conditioned emotional responses and patterns of habitual behavior which the members of a society have acquired through instruction or imitation and which they share to a greater or less degree" (quoted in Kroeber and Kluckhohn, 1963, p. 82). Although ideas or learned behavioral habits need not be totally shared by everyone in a group, it is nevertheless this property of sharing, the commonality of attributes, that defines the domain of culture.

Educational Considerations. Some emphasis on shared traits is basic to any conceptual understanding of the role of culture in education. However, such an emphasis leaves little if any room for the recognition of each student's individuality within the framework of the culture concept. Individuality becomes the domain of psychology, relevant only to discussions of personality, while *culture* is used to refer to ideas and behaviors that prevail in the individual's group. Using the culture concept as a basis for theories of education might be appropriate if the goal is to educate (or reeducate) a group, as in modernization programs applied by developing countries to their peasant populations. But the focus of most education, as all who have taught for any time know, is the education of the individual student, not the education of his or her ethnic group.

Consequences for Teacher-Student Interaction

The relevance of this problem lies in the possible consequences of the **group-oriented concept of culture** for the perceptions and expectations of teachers in their interactions with culturally diverse children. A group-oriented concept may serve to distract the teacher's attention from the student's particular experience of culture-generating processes, in and outside of school. The culture concept adopted by the teacher greatly affects teacher-student interaction. The assumptions a teacher makes about the student's culture, whether right or wrong, may stereotype the student and thus preclude the flexible, realistic, and open-minded teacher-student interaction needed for effective instruction. The effect of this stereotyping on students is significant, since the educational process is fundamentally a process of social interaction, with socialization as a primary goal.

Stereotyping of Students

Let's consider an example of how the group culture concept might operate in a teacher-student interaction. Picture a situation in which the teacher is perplexed by some action or response by a student of minority status. A teacher who has studied some anthropological descriptions of the student's ethnic culture may leap to an interpretation of the student's behavior based on idealized characteristics anthropologists have attributed to that culture. The teacher may mean well, but to construe an individual's behavior solely on the basis of generalizations about group traits is to stereotype the individual, no matter how valid the generalizations or how well-meaning one's intentions.

It would be better for the teacher to encounter the student in the way anthropologists most often come to understand the people they study. Although they write about cultures in collective terms, anthropologists build their understandings through observations of individuals. The teacher's efforts to understand the individual student could (and should) be supplemented by knowledge of cultural attributes widely held in the student's ethnic community. But this fund of knowledge should be viewed only as background information. The question of its applicability to the particular student should be treated as inherently problematical. Many studies (for example, Cole, 1995; Rodriguez, 1989; Tharp and Gallimore, 1988) also caution educational personnel against hasty "ethnographic/cultural" generalizations on the grounds that all linguistic-cultural groups are continuously undergoing significant cultural changes.

Individual Differences

Even teachers who are of the same minority status as their students may be considered in some ways culturally different from those they are teaching. This observation is not recent. Guerra (1979) points to linguistic and other cultural variations both within (student-student) and between (student-teacher) generations of bilingual populations. Cuellar (1980) argues that one's understanding of the meaning and value of culture and language must take into account the fact that "a community's characteristics reflect the composition of the different generational cohorts in the different age strata" (p. 198). What this means is that the individual variation within cultures should be of particular importance to educators.

The Individual-Oriented Concept of Culture

The group culture concept is not the only instrument available for understanding individuals and groups. Fortunately, anthropological theory contains an **individual-oriented concept of culture** developed and used by a number of anthropologists with interests in psychology. As Schwartz (1978) notes, these theorists criticized the group culture concept for the way it can "lead one to imagine culture as floating somehow disembodied in the noösphere or, at best, carried by human beings as a conductor might carry an electric current containing information" (p. 434). Rather than work with an abstract idea of culture, these theorists were interested more in how culture was manifested in the lives of individual human beings.

An early expression of the individual-oriented concept of culture is seen in the work of anthropologist J. O. Dorsey. The American anthropologist Edward Sapir (quoted in Pelto and Pelto, 1975) wrote the following description of Dorsey's approach:

> Living as long as he did in close touch with the Omaha Indians, [Dorsey] knew that he was dealing, not with a society nor with a specimen of primitive man but with a finite, though indefinite, number of human beings who gave themselves the privilege of differing from each other not only in matters generally considered as "One's own business" but even on questions which clearly transcended the private individual's concerns. (p. 1)

Advocates of the individual-oriented concept of culture frequently describe a society's culture as a "pool" of constructs (rules, beliefs, values, etc.) by which its members conceptually

Culture as
Variable

order the objects and events of their lives. The participation of individuals in this pool is seen as variable. Spiro (1951), for example, distinguished between the cultural "heritage" of all members of a society (that which has been made available to them by their predecessors) and each individual's particular cultural "inheritance" (that portion of the group's heritage that the individual has effectively received, or "internalized," from the past). Schwartz adds that the individual also manipulates, recombines, and otherwise transforms these inherited constructs. This process of transformation, together with the outright creation of new constructs, is a major source of culture change (Schwartz, 1978). The individual's own portion of a society's culture is termed by Goodenough (1981) as a "propriocept," by Wallace (1970) as a "mazeway," and by Schwartz (1978) as an "idioverse." All of these specialized terms are variations on a core nature of culture: each individual assembles his or her own version of the larger culture.

For some of the anthropologists who employ an individual-oriented concept of culture, "the private system of ideas of individuals is culture" (Pelto and Pelto, 1975, pp. 12–13). Other anthropologists of like mind reject the implication in such a notion of individual cultures. As they see it, the contents of one subjective system alone cannot be considered a culture. Like Schwartz, these theorists consider a cultural system to consist of all the constructs available to a society's members. Nevertheless, the society is itself not the locus of culture; its individual members are. The culture thus is a distributive phenomenon in that its elements are widely distributed among the individual members of a society. A major implication of this **distributive model of culture** is a rejection of the traditional assumption of cultural homogeneity—that is, the idea that all members of a culture share all that culture's attributes. The distributive model instead implies that each individual's portion of the culture differs in some ways from that of any other.

| **Individual Is Locus of Culture**

According to Schwartz (1978), Wallace's antidote to the homogeneous view of culture is an overdose, leading to the opposite malady of ignoring the degree of cultural sharing that does occur between individuals. Schwartz's own model of culture takes into account both the sharing and nonsharing of cultural constructs between members of a society, and he argues that both are fundamentally essential to a society's viability. Diversity, he argues, increases a society's cultural inventory, whereas what any individual could contain within his or her head would make up a very small culture pool. Commonality then permits communication and coordination in social life. In Schwartz's (1978) own words:

> It makes as little sense to depict the distribution of a culture among the members of a society as totally heterogeneous and unique in each individual as it did to argue for complete homogeneity. We must dispense with the a priori assumption of homogeneity, but, similarly, we are not served by an a priori assumption of heterogeneity. (p. 438)

Educational Considerations. I view Schwartz's formulation of the distributive model of culture as the most appropriate for addressing issues of cultural diversity in the schools. This formulation permits, within the framework of culture, simultaneous recognition of a student's "ethnic" culture and of those characteristics that define the student as a unique individual. Students share with their ethnic peers constructs they do not share with others, but all individuals are in some ways different from their ethnic peers. The distributive model also permits recognition of traits that members of subgroups share with members of the larger culture, such as those acquired through acculturation.

Schooling is a major variable in **acculturation,** the process by which the members of a society are taught the elements of the society's culture. The acculturation process is a crucial consideration in the analysis of ethnic minorities in pluralistic societies.

Variety in Acculturation | Variety in acculturation also contributes significantly to the heterogeneity of ethnic cultures. Writing about the U.S. cultural subgroup labeled "Hispanic," Bell, Kasschau, and Zellman (1976) note that among Chicanos, "many have ancestors who came to North America several centuries ago, but others are themselves recent immigrants. Hence, a simple cultural characterization of [this] ethnic group should be avoided" (p. 7). These authors also caution against a simplistic view of the process of acculturation, noting that it "may not be linear, in the sense that one simply loses certain Mexican attributes and replaces them with Anglo attributes" (pp. 31–32). In other words, acculturation may be characterized by more complex combinations of attributes—and by ongoing recombination—rather than by simple substitution of Anglo attributes for the original ethnic ones.

Additive or Subtractive Acculturation | With regard to the effect of U.S. schooling, as Gibson and Obgu (1991) suggest, acculturation can be understood as either additive or subtractive. In her work with Punjabi Sikh immigrants, Gibson (1995) finds these immigrants to be quite eager to have their children succeed in U.S. schools. Yet she also reports that these same parents are just as anxious about their children's loss of important Punjabi cultural attributes. They would thus like to see an *additive* acculturation for their children—the acquisition of knowledge and skills of a new culture without rejection of the old. Yet in the schools these students attend, little or no attention is paid to the Punjabi culture. These schools practice a *subtractive* acculturation, often identified as assimilation, aimed at replacing the old culture with the new. Too often, U.S. schools adopt such subtractive acculturation practices, often without being cognizant of their effects.

Customs and Culture | The result of these various acculturation processes is wide differences among students within the same ethnic group. "But what about customs?" some people may ask. "If the family maintains certain ethnic customs, don't they help to minimize the effects of acculturation?" Chicanos, for example, might point out that nearly all members of their group recognize certain *costumbres*

Influential Teachers, Influential Students

These students will change American society.

    American society is not the same as it was a century ago, or even a decade ago, partly because of the different peoples who have come to our shores. Without the contributions of individual groups, we would not have such American icons as the Christmas tree, the log cabin, labor unions, and jazz. Jewish immigrants in the early part of this century made a key contribution—they demanded entry to college in such numbers that they transformed what had been a finishing school for the wealthy into an opportunity for individual advancement.

    Those college-bound students were fortunate to have teachers dedicated to their success, even if the teachers never anticipated that their efforts would have the far-reaching effect of helping to democratize higher education. Teachers of that era were selected not only for their formal credentials but also for their suitability as role models for the young. The impact of teachers on the life of young people can hardly be overestimated. Teachers represent a link to the adult world of educated, successful professionals. Especially for children from a different culture and language, teachers have a tremendous impact; they are their link to American society. Without the caring guidance of teachers, the immigrant and minority youth of today will readily learn how to eat at McDonald's, play video games, and watch MTV. But they will have great difficulty getting to college and becoming engineers, playwrights, or teachers themselves.

Meeting the Challenge

1. Write a letter to a young relative or friend. In this letter, describe some of the changes that have occurred in the world since you

Becoming a Responsive Teacher

(customs) that distinguish them from the larger society. Yet customs occupy a realm of culture that is more likely to belong to the public sphere than to form a specific part of an individual's subjective orientation. Referring to the "layered" nature of culture, anthropologist Benjamin Paul (1965) has observed that "what we call customs rest on top and are most apparent. Deepest and least apparent are the cultural values that give meaning and direction to life. Values influence people's perceptions of needs and their choice between perceived alternative courses of action" (p. 200).

    I purposely emphasize the problematic nature of cultural variability and sharing. The variable nature of acculturation and the

Continued Influential Teachers, Influential Students

were his or her age. You might mention specific political or social events or trends and your thoughts about them. Feel free to refer to any types of changes you have encountered that you feel have affected your life. Then, given your perspective as an older mentor for this young person, provide some suggestions about which aspects of schooling might help prepare him or her to confront change constructively. If you decide to send this letter, consider sharing any response from the addressee with your classmates.

2. Find out what student cultural centers are on your college or university campus and then visit each one. If possible, also visit cultural centers in the local community outside your campus. Gather leaflets and flyers and take some notes about the activities these cultural groups are planning. In class, compile a master list of events to attend over the semester and decide which ones interest you the most. Volunteer to attend an event and review it for your classmates.

3. You have been granted the opportunity to spend an entire day with an 8-year-old, a 12-year-old, or a 16-year-old student doing anything you want, wherever you want. This child is from an ethnic and linguistic background that is radically different from yours. In fact, you may not even have a shared language. What would you want this child to teach you about his or her world?

individual uniqueness that it engenders are, I believe, no less important for the education of culturally diverse students than are the "real" cultural differences between ethnic groups. Education must deal with both the individual and the culture.

I hasten to add that teachers who work with children from culturally diverse populations must be not only keenly aware of the instructional objectives of education but also knowledgeable about and sensitive to the impact that culture has on the student.

Culture as Central to Development and Education

Some scholars have made a persuasive case that typical definitions of culture do not appropriately address its significance in our understanding of human existence. Geertz (1973), for example, has suggested that culture is part of our continuous human endeavor to construct meaning out of life: "Humans are animals

Constructing
Culture

suspended in webs of significance that they spin. Culture is those webs, and the analysis of it is not an experiment in search of law but an interpretive one in search of meaning" (p. 83). According to this interpretation of culture, we are all similarly *constructing* culture in response to our own need to understand our circumstances and seek meaning for them. In this sense there will likely be many more similarities than differences in the ways in which individuals and groups construct culture. The specific context will vary, but not the basic goal.

Luria's (1928) and Vygotsky's (1929) notions of child development, cognition, and learning in relation to culture are also very instructive. They argue that cognition and learning emerge

Cultural Basis of Cognition through culturally mediated, historically developing, practical activity. In the most basic sense, human psychological processes arise simultaneously with forms of behavior and "tools" or artifacts that are utilized to modify material objects as a means of regulating human interactions with both the physical and the social world. These "tools" include tangible goods as well as communicative, cognitive, and other processes that allow knowledge of the use of tools to be transmitted to others (Luria, 1928). In this view, culture is the entire pool of tools accumulated by a social group in its historical existence. Individuals use these artifacts as they interact with their own world, and in doing so they continue to construct culture.

This view that human cognition and psychological processes have a social origin—artifact development in culture—has great implications for our construction of schooling. Vygotsky (1981) would go so far as to conclude that all forms of cognition and learning are social and therefore cultural in origin:

> Any function in children's cultural development appears twice, or on two planes. First it appears on the social plane and then on the psychological plane. First it appears between people as an inter psychological category and then within the individual child as an intra psychological category. . . . Social relations or relations among people genetically underlie all higher functions and their relationships. (p. 63)

In his research on child development, Cole (1995) follows this conceptual framework for understanding culture and human development. He concludes that teachers can be very important in organizing a child's environment so as to enhance the types of social experiences that lead to optimal development. He suggests that "it is the foundation upon which, in an ideal world, the education of children would be organized" (Cole, 1995, p. 111). We will explore this concept in Chapter 6 when we address specific roots of cognitive functioning and education.

It is important to note that as culture becomes more central to our analysis of development, learning, and schooling, all forms of cultural experience that generate diversity in our student populations need to be recognized. For example, children who are challenged by a physical and/or mental disability are exposed to cultural conditions different from those experienced by children who are not living with such challenges. Deaf populations have suggested that they develop in bilingual/bicultural social circumstances that are often not understood or addressed in our schools. The same can be said for children who are raised by caregivers whose sexual preference differs from that of the majority, or children who themselves express nonmajority sexual preferences. These examples suggest the importance of realizing that such students are immersed in a different cultural milieu and that issues of cultural diversity must be broadly defined. If culture in this sense comes to the center of our understanding of development and learning, it cannot be ignored in the classroom.

Culture and Disabilities

Race, Class, Gender, and Cultural Diversity

There are important issues in U.S. education concerning the relationships among race, class, gender, and cultural diversity. It is still quite apparent that the United States continues to struggle with the facts of racism (Weinberg, 1990), classism (Nieto, 1996), and sexism (Weis, 1988). In each of these cases, the basis for discrimination is the belief that those of one race, social class, or gender are either inherently superior or inferior.

The existence of such beliefs and the individual or institutional behavior that springs from them is not disputed here. Clearly, all educators must be vigilant with regard to these debilitating ideologies, especially within schooling practices. For example, the fact that students of one race, class, or gender are overrepresented in less challenging curricula (through the use of tracking or classroom grouping) and have consistently high dropout rates, poor attendance, and, of course, low achievement can be seen as potentially related to racism, classism, or sexism.

Culture and "isms"

What is different about my attention to culture as the central variable in schooling is a more comprehensive and useful understanding of these "isms." Racism serves as a good example. In the United States, most people are actually a mixture of races. Sometimes we even coin terms to indicate this mixture, such as *mulatto* (referring to someone of European and African background) and *mestizo* (referring to someone of European and indigenous American ancestry). Such individuals are not just examples of the racial mixture of this country. They also demonstrate the existence of new culture-creating groups whose characteristics may be either similar to or different from their ambiguous racial identities. Is it more useful, then, to focus on these individuals' "racial" character or on their cultural character? I suggest that an emphasis on their culture will be both more useful and more conceptually sound in education. This approach does not ignore the existence of racism or other "isms," of course; rather, it incorporates such factors into the cultural analysis.

The Role of Cultural Capital

A person's entire set of cultural relationships, not just in the family but across all the key social spheres, has been called his or her **cultural capital.** In effect, it is the cultural fund that the individual draws upon to support all the activities of life. Not only does it help protect and nurture the individual in family or family-like settings; it also plays a similar role in nonfamily-like institutions, especially the school. For healthy human development to occur, caretakers and other social agents (including teachers) must offer children systematic opportunities to construct the relationships that build cultural capital (Gordon, 1999; Valenzuela and Dornbusch, 1994).

But what of children who live in diverse cultural contexts? Is their cultural capital sufficient to protect and nurture their development, in school and elsewhere? Does school help them develop such capital, or does it in fact undercut the process?

Sociologists have not been particularly encouraging in their answers (Gordon, 1999; Mehan, Villanueva, Hubbard, and Lintz, 1996; Mirón, 1996; Romo and Falbo, 1996; Wilson, 1999). Stanton-Salazar (1997) summarizes a set of issues that all too often obstruct the development of the cultural capital of culturally diverse students:

Barriers to Developing Cultural Capital: Lack of Respect

1. Values based on social status, ethnicity, language, and gender may lead to such situations as the overrepresentation of Anglo-American males in gifted classes and of African American and Latino males in learning disability programs.

2. Barriers such as the inability of the school staff to communicate effectively in languages other than English may make school an uncomfortable experience for certain students.

3. Schools may use evaluation processes that hinge on the willingness of students, families, and the community to adopt the standards of the dominant group. For example, a state's new assessment activity for students of beginning reading may focus only on English and thereby ignore the fact that many children in the state are learning to read in a language other than English.

4. Distrust and detachment may be institutionalized. For example, a school may require teachers to report to the Immigration and Naturalization Service (INS) any students and families they suspect of being in the country illegally. The parents may respond by keeping their children away from school because of their fear of deportation (regardless of whether they are indeed legal residents).

5. Ideological mechanisms may limit the ability of people to seek and give help in the school, particularly in terms of the achievement of high academic standards. For example, the presence of the "*el pobrecito* syndrome" ("this poor kid syndrome") among instructional staff expresses the notion that children who are poor, immigrant, non-English-speaking, or from troubled families need the school as a protective and insulating environment. This frequently leads to lower academic expectations for the students. "What these kids need is a safe and loving place, not a challenging curriculum," teachers may think—when in fact the children need both.

Overcoming the Barriers: Being Responsive

This sociological analysis speaks volumes about how the school can impede the development of cultural capital among diverse student populations. But this need not always be the case. Various studies have documented how specific schools have attempted to overcome such barriers and promote cultural capital (August and Hakuta, 1997; García, 1997; Miramontes, Nadeau, and Commins, 1997; U.S. Department of Education, 1998). August and Hakuta (1997) comprehensively reviewed schools and classrooms in which linguistically and culturally diverse students have achieved high academic performance. Through their analysis of some 33 case studies, they identified the following factors as contributing to the students' success:

> a supportive school-wide climate, school leadership, a customized learning environment, articulation and coordination within and between schools, use of native language and culture in instruction, a balanced curriculum that includes both basic and higher-order skills, explicit skills instruction, opportunities for student-directed instruction, use of instructional strategies that enhance understanding, opportunities for practice, systematic student assessment, staff development, and home and parent involvement. (p. 171)

The Culture of the School

The school has many, if not all, of the characteristics that anthropologists and sociologists tell us belong to culture. It has tacit rules, patterns, formal structures of organization, and an ecological component. Most important are the tacit dimensions. We tend to think that school is all about learning "the three R's." Parents and children, and sometimes teachers themselves, do not recognize that the school makes cultural demands on students in addition to intellectual ones.

As in our earlier discussion of culture, a distinction must be made between competing concepts of the nature and purpose of **Competing** school. Recent research acknowledges that schools are social sit-**Concepts of** uations that are constructed through the interactions between **School** individuals (Feldman and Shen, 1971; Gardner, 1983). More traditional views represent schools as institutions with stable traits generally impervious to individual influence. It is important for educators to understand how our society views the concept of *school,* which underlies how we approach the teaching of students in schools. If we see teaching and learning as embedded within a cultural context, we are more likely to recognize that performance will vary as a function of that context.

Student Response to School Culture

Some examples from research into the cultural demands of school will demonstrate this point. Observing the classroom performance of Native American students, Phillips (1983, 1984) found that these students appeared to conform exactly to the **Observations** stereotype of "the silent Indian child." Phillips was puzzled, how-**of Students** ever, because her observations outside the classroom indicated that in this context these children were certainly not silent. She identified what is now considered an important aspect of school culture: **participant-structured demand,** or the demands of instruction that are imposed by the organization of the learning environment itself. She was able to make this discovery only because she observed the children across a number of situations—in community settings, in their homes, and in school.

Phillips found that classroom lessons imposed varying demands on the children. The classrooms were organized in an individualistic, competitive way. Children were expected to stand up alone in front of the classroom and to respond competitively to the **Contrasting** teacher's questions. The Native American children were not doing **Demands of** well in this arrangement. Phillips contrasted the demands of the **Home and** school with the demands of the home. There were definite de-**School** mands in each culture. In the homes of the Native American children, she found a culture in which children were working cooperatively in groups, not competitively. For an individual to stand out, to act on his or her own, independent of the group, was to violate the norm of the home. Conversely, it was to violate the norm of the classroom not to stand out. The children were thus caught in a bind between the competing demands of home and school.

Other studies have compared home and school cultures. Heath's (1982) work, conducted in a number of different areas, contributes a good deal to our knowledge base. In her study of low-income African American and Anglo-American Appalachian children, she found that their teachers, who came from different economic and cultural backgrounds, talked to children differ- | **Language Use** | ently than did the children's parents. Heath described a difference in language used between home and school. The school placed a great demand on children to display their knowledge. Children would often be asked a question for which the teacher already had the answer. If, for example, a child correctly answered the question "What time is it?" the teacher would respond not with "Thank you" but with "Very good," indicating that the child's knowledge had been tested. The teacher did not need the information. At home, however, when a child was asked, "What time is it?" the underlying assumption was that the child had information needed by another member of the family. Interestingly, middle-income parents often use a questioning strategy similar to the teacher's. They play games such as peek-a-boo that also have a dimension of information. But Heath found that in low-income families there was little imitation of the conversational demands of school. These children were not gaining practice at home with a linguistic device essential to their school performance.

The School's Response to Children

The school must allow cultural elements that are relevant to the children to enter the classroom freely. Some refer to this practice | **Importance of** | as **scaffolding.** With scaffolding, the school provides a set of sup- | **Scaffolding** | ports that utilize the child's home language, discourse style, participation orientation, and so on, thereby enabling the child to move through relevant experiences from the home toward the demands of the school as representative of the society. It is not a subtraction of culture, and it is not an attempt to reproduce home environments in the context of the school. Instead, the idea is to encourage the child to respect the demands of the school culture while preserving the integrity of the home culture.

We must first comprehend the fact that children—all children—come to school motivated to enlarge their culture. But we must start with *their* culture. We need not regard them, certainly not initially, as organisms to be molded and regulated. We look first to determine how they seek to know themselves and others and how their expertise and experience can be used as the fuel to fire their interests, knowledge, and skills. We look first not at their deficits—at what they do not know—but at what they need to know. Far from having deficits, they are rich in assets. As teachers, we enter their world in order to aid them and to build bridges between two cultures (Sarason, 1990).

Teaching in a Cultural Context

Respect Is
Not Enough

If educators better serve culturally diverse students by understanding cultural diversity and respecting individuality, have they fulfilled their obligations as teachers? I believe they have not. Our culturally diverse populations continue to be highly vulnerable in today's society and today's schools. We examined this social, economic, and educational vulnerability in the previous chapter. It is in all of our best interests for culturally diverse students to succeed. They will carry us all to either a bright or a beleaguered future.

Given the present circumstances and the magnitude of this challenge, what must we do? Sensitivity to "culture," while necessary, is not sufficient. Earlier we saw how even well-meaning teachers may stereotype students when trying to allow for cultural differences. There are three additional ingredients needed for effective teaching in a context of student cultural diversity:

- Personal commitment

- Knowledge of what makes a difference

- Educational leadership

Let's look more closely at these elements and take an inventory of them in our schools today.

Personal Commitment

We need not be fooled by liberal or conservative rhetoric. We have not achieved educational equality for our culturally diverse populations, and substantive progress in this area requires further resolve. It is often trumpeted that Head Start, school choice, restructuring, site-based management, cooperative learning, the whole-language approach, educational technology (computer-assisted instruction), and so forth have already or will soon reverse the pattern of underachievement among linguistically and culturally diverse populations. Clearly these contributions are important, but our own part in the U.S. educational system suggests that we as teachers should resist the notion of a miracle cure. No new methodologies, reorganizations, or curricula will

No Miracle Cures:
You need to be
Responsible

Responsible

satisfactorily address the problem of underachievement unless the individuals who implement these initiatives are deeply committed to the enterprise. Each of us must step up and be **responsible.** The change that is necessary must be fueled by the type of social energy that our nation has tapped in the past. As in the eras of President Kennedy's "New Frontier" or President Johnson's "War on Poverty," we must grasp the spiritual importance of this new educational challenge.

More than two decades after President Carter warned of a crisis of spirit in America—a warning that proved politically disastrous for him and a boon to rival Ronald Reagan—and with President Clinton having urged a national discourse on issues of diversity and unity, a broad spectrum of the nation's social and intellectual leadership is concluding that such concepts are as critically important now as they were in the 1960s. In fact, they say, the crisis has deepened. We are losing the faith that our children's days will be better than our own, and it is no longer possible to deny this fact—even to ourselves.

A consensus has emerged that a lack of confidence among Americans in the future and in one another lies at the heart of the nation's ills. A nation that passed much of the 1970s, in the aftermath of the Vietnam War, in search of its soul and self spent the 1980s and 1990s in what many see as a self-consuming materialism. We now enter the twenty-first century in a cynical, dispirited mood. "There is disturbing evidence to suggest that most forms of responsibility toward others have eroded in recent decades" (p. 101), asserts Derek Bok, former president of Harvard University, in his 1990 book *Universities and the Future of America.* The percentage of people who feel that most individuals in power try to take advantage of others has doubled over the past two decades and now exceeds 60 percent.

Importance of
Inspiration

It is difficult to believe that the picture is truly so bleak. Most of us know people who are generous and creative in their interactions with others—even heroic in small ways, considering the multiple stresses and strains of modern life. They work hard, tend to their families, and contribute to their communities. Many people care deeply about individual and collective welfare in the United States. It is possible that our current cynicism is simply a measure of disappointed idealism, of surprise and dismay that our work as a nation is not done and may never be done, and that we must continue to call upon the inspiration, resolve, commitment, and passion of everyone.

Some have argued that we have lost the ability to inspire our children. Others say we have lost the ability to inspire ourselves. But inspiration is the spark that leads to resolve and commitment, and we cannot afford to be without it. Borrowing from Jaime Escalante, the noted California educator depicted in the popular film *Stand and Deliver,* we will need *ganas*—the desire that fires the will to overcome great challenges.

Knowledge of What Makes a Difference

Individual Uniqueness

We will also need a new knowledge base. Recent research has pinpointed the problem of educational vulnerability. It has destroyed stereotypes and myths about the educational needs of culturally diverse students and laid a foundation upon which to reconceptualize present educational practices and to launch new initiatives. As we saw earlier in this chapter, the basis for change is a new understanding of individual uniqueness within a cultural context. No one set of descriptions or prescriptions will suffice for all students of a given cultural background.

Attributes of Successful Teachers

We should pay attention to what seems to work. As noted earlier, recent research summarized by the U.S. Department of Education (1998) and August and Hakuta (1997) has documented educationally effective practices with linguistically and culturally diverse students in selected preschool, elementary, and high school classrooms throughout the United States. The results show that the teachers of these classrooms were highly committed to the educational success of their students. They perceived themselves as instructional innovators utilizing "new" learning theories and instructional philosophies to guide their practice. Most of these teachers were involved in professional development activities such as small-group support networks with other educators. They had a strong, demonstrated belief in the importance of communication between the school and the home (several teachers were interacting weekly with parents) and felt they had the autonomy to create or change the instruction and curriculum in their classrooms, even if it did not exactly meet district guidelines. They had high academic expectations for all their students ("Everyone will learn to read in my classroom") and served as advocates for their students. They rejected any suggestion that their students were intellectually or academically disadvantaged.

This and other research shows that effective curriculum, instructional strategies, and teaching staffs are rooted in sharing expertise and experiences through multiple processes of communication. Abundant and diverse opportunities for speaking, listening, reading, and writing, along with home-to-school bridges that help guide students through the learning process, constitute an effective curriculum. Effective schools also encourage culturally diverse students to take risks, construct meaning, and reinterpret the knowledge they acquire as it applies to their lives. Within this curriculum, skills are taught as tools for acquiring further knowledge. Research into such effective programs should continue. The more we know about what makes them effective, the more equipped we will be to educate diverse student groups.

Educational Leadership

The leadership necessary to mobilize this growing commitment and knowledge will recognize four interlocking domains that pertain especially to teachers.

Knowledge Dissemination. We will need to disseminate knowledge about effective practices to those who can utilize it. This requires training, retraining, and more retraining of teachers. Individually and institutionally, new knowledge must be appropriated by people working in the field of education. It is of no use to students if researchers share their knowledge only among themselves. New avenues for knowledge dissemination and appropriation along with leadership in this domain are required.

Retraining Teachers

Professional Development. New knowledge alone does not automatically lead to a new set of pedagogical or curricular skills ready for use by practitioners. Knowledge must be transferred to teachers and adapted for use in specific instructional contexts. Time and energy must be devoted to the collaboration required between teachers and researchers to develop new skills. Moreover, these new pedagogical and curricular skills must be evaluated in the field—they must prove themselves effective for students. We will need to hold ourselves and others automatically accountable. Doing this requires leadership in both knowledge dissemination and professional skill development.

Disposition for Leadership. Many are called, but few will self-select. We need a generation of educational leaders who are willing to sacrifice, work very hard and very long, take risks, learn from failure, rise above frustration, rethink existing paradigms, and support and collaborate with their colleagues. Those who do not possess this set of dispositions must step aside, minimize obstruction, and otherwise admit that if they cannot be part of the solution, they will not be part of the problem.

Risk and Collaboration

Affective Engagement. We will need leadership that welcomes, adopts, nurtures, celebrates, and challenges our culturally diverse students. "They" must become "we." Anything short of raw advocacy every minute of every day will not suffice. Too many of these students have given up hope in themselves. We must not give up hope. Instead, we must instill hope.

Responsible

Mostly, educators need to act. Presidents, governors, and other politicians proclaim and set educational goals. Educators need to move beyond such proclamations. The task at hand is not only to see the future but also to enable it. With commitment, knowledge, and leadership, educators can enable the future for our culturally diverse society.

Conclusion

In this chapter, I have tried to establish a context for a more thorough discussion of the educational challenges facing this country's educators. The challenge stands for all students and specifically for those who are culturally diverse. This country's educational future will be much different from its educational past. We will have to be capable of responding to transformations in social structures and institutions, in global organization, and in values. Historically, our schools' efforts to merge diverse groups into a homogenized "American" culture have not resulted in academic success for culturally diverse students. However, new insights into educational concepts, research, and practices suggest that we can meet this challenge successfully.

In the chapters that follow, I will more clearly define the notions of culture outlined here and describe the interrelationships among social, cultural, and linguistic contexts for education. We must continue to build a knowledge base regarding children, families, communities, and schools. Research studies that add dimension to what we already know about culturally diverse students will be valuable pieces of the puzzle. However, as the preceding discussion has indicated, merely building this knowledge base is not enough.

I want to point out, before you turn another page, that the information in this book will not make a critical difference in the lives of many of our most educationally needy students. Even with all its theoretical underpinnings and its comments on research, pedagogy, curriculum, and educational philosophy, it is still only a book. It is a forum through which knowledge can be developed, examined, and transmitted. But this knowledge must be combined with action on the part of educators if the challenges I have articulated are to be met head-on and successfully overcome.

Summary of Major Ideas

1. Ongoing social and economic changes, in this country and worldwide, have produced new contexts for education in the United States. We need to prepare students for participation in

the global marketplace and for flexibility in their future careers. Projections show that in the near future 60 percent of all jobs will require some postsecondary education and 80 percent of new jobs will be in the information and service sector.

2. It is not the role of the schools to prepare students for specific jobs. Rather, schools must teach academic skills that develop students' intellectual abilities and that involve students in learning activities that enhance human relationships, critical thinking, and civic responsibility.

3. Despite its undeniable cultural and linguistic diversity, U.S. society still demonstrates an "us versus them" relationship between the Anglo-American majority and minority populations. This pattern of thinking is reflected in schooling practices, with negative results especially for language minority students. For example, recent state policy changes have eroded the educational opportunities offered to immigrant and minority students.

4. Culture is a system of values, beliefs, notions about acceptable and unacceptable behavior, and other socially constructed ideas characteristic of a society or of a subgroup within a society. The group-oriented concept of culture describes culture as a set of attributes that are shared by all the members of a group. The individual-oriented concept of culture describes culture as a set of attributes that are made available to members of a group but may not be shared by all members. The group concept of culture emphasizes cultural homogeneity, and the individual concept of culture emphasizes cultural heterogeneity.

5. Criticism of the group-oriented concept of culture as a basis for educational theory centers on the assumption of cultural homogeneity. It may lead to stereotyping children in terms of their cultural group identification rather than addressing children as unique individuals.

6. The distributive model of culture, which is based on the notion of cultural heterogeneity, implies that each individual's portion of a culture differs from that of any other individual. Because it recognizes the uniqueness of the individual, who is the focus of educational efforts, this concept may serve as a useful basis for educational theory.

7. Acculturation is the process by which the members of a society are taught the elements of the society's culture. There is much variety in the acculturation process within all societies. Variety in acculturation contributes to cultural heterogeneity.

8. As culture becomes a central variable in the concept of schooling, the definition of *cultural diversity* must be expanded in order to promote the development of students from all types of backgrounds. Issues of race, class, gender, and disability, which clearly form part of an individual's culture, can then be incorporated into the cultural analysis.

9. Schools must strive to promote the development of the cultural capital, or set of cultural relationships, of their diverse student populations.

10. An important aspect of school culture is *participant-structured demand*, a term that describes the demands of instruction that are imposed on children by the organization of the learning environment. Students for whom the cultural demands of home do not mesh with the cultural demands of school may not perform well academically. Different attitudes toward cooperation and competition and different uses of language at home and at school are two possible cultural variables.

11. Children enter school motivated to enlarge their culture. Building on what they already know instead of focusing on what they do not know is the goal of effective teaching.

12. Effective teaching in a context of student cultural diversity requires personal commitment, knowledge of what makes a difference, and educational leadership. Initiatives proposed by the educational leaders of tomorrow will focus on transmitting knowledge to teachers and developing new teaching skills. These leaders will be risk-takers who support one another's ideas and who celebrate student diversity in the schools.

Extending Your Experience

1. The text suggests that future job markets will require workers who are flexible and creative, skilled at communicating, and technologically literate. Outline some curricula that you think would develop these attributes in young people. As a further step, design a course for any grade level that focuses on developing children's awareness of three factors: human relationships, critical thinking, and civic responsibility.

2. Using your own words, and referring back to the chapter if necessary, explain the concepts of cultural homogeneity and cultural heterogeneity. Now list all your group memberships, both formal and informal: sets of friends and acquaintances, clubs, teams, and organizations in which you participate. Se-

lect one of these groups and describe what all its members have in common. Then describe how the members differ from one another. Write a few sentences introducing yourself to a new member of the group. Do you emphasize what you share with others, what makes you different, or both?

3. Using the categories listed in the text (familial, linguistic, religious and spiritual, aesthetic, socioeconomic, educational, dietary, and gender) and any others you can think of, characterize your cultural heritage—the systems of belief and thought in which you were raised. What portion of this heritage have you actually "inherited," or consciously incorporated into your own life? What portion, if any, have you rejected? Why?

4. Define *participant-structured demand* in your own words and describe how it operates in two of the courses you are taking. How do the cultural demands of these two class environments differ? Characterize your learning experience in each one. Write three serious recommendations to your instructor for altering the class culture to benefit your own particular style of learning.

5. Review the comments on cynicism by Derek Bok quoted in the chapter. Realize that if you are younger than 24, these comments refer to you. Do you feel that they accurately portray your vision of human nature? Interview five friends and describe their opinions on Bok's remarks. Using verbatim quotes from your friends, who may remain anonymous if they wish, present your findings to the class.

Resources for Further Study

Print Resources

Bigler, E. 1999. *American conversations: Puerto Ricans, White Ethnics, and multicultural education.* Philadelphia, PA: Temple University Press.

Bigler's ethnographic study examines the migration experience of working-class Puerto Ricans. The author explores the dominating theme of exclusion as it penetrates all aspects of their lives, especially school. This book explores the challenges and benefits presented when multiculturalism and bilingual education become the vehicles for inclusion.

Cole, M. (1996). *Cultural psychology: A once and future discipline.* Cambridge, MA: Belknap Press of Harvard University Press.

This volume touches very directly on the centrality of culture in the formation of the individual. The author traces the historical intellectual trail that has led to the prioritization of the ways in which culture serves the needs of individuality and thus argues that we cannot ignore the influence of culture on individual student development.

Kroeber, A. L., and Kluckhohn, C. (1963). *Culture: A critical review of concepts and definitions.* New York: Vintage Books.

The authors argue that culture is a general descriptive category of human nature. This definition allows cultures to have similar distinctive designs; however, the only changes culture can have are initiated by individuals because individuals create organisms that operate in groups. These groups or cultures are a direct result of individuals interacting at the concrete level. In short, cultures begin, continue, or change as the result of individual action.

Mahiri, J. (1998). *Shooting for excellence: African American youth and culture in New Century Schools.* New York: Teachers College Press.

Mahiri's book demonstrates how building on African American youth culture and experiences can foster student ownership and achievement in terms of literacy that takes place beyond the school. The author recognizes the power of responsive teaching and its transformative nature when there is space to value this kind of literacy. The end goal of this book is to demonstrate that making space, valuing, and integrating the literacy that takes place outside of the school is a means to enrich curricula that is purposeful and meaningful.

Moreno, J. (Ed.) (1999). *The elusive quest for equality: 150 years of Chicano/Chicana eduation.* Boston: Harvard Educational Review.

This edited volume offers a critical collection of readings that provide an overview of the educational conditions and experiences of Chicano/Chicana students. The book examines the experiences of these students through historical and contemporary perspectives. Within these two parts, the reader is given the opportunity to gain a greater understanding of the roles of policies and practice in the academic pipeline.

Nieto, S. (1999). *The light in their eyes: Creating multicultural learning communities.* New York: Teachers College Press.

Nieto masterfully presents a concise understanding of the various dimensions required to teach multiculturalism effectively, as well as exploring what it means to teach in multicultural contexts. This work documents the teaching experiences of teachers in multicultural contexts. His approach of working from a research and theory base only enhances the narrative provided by the teachers. Beyond identifying challenges, this book makes an important contribution toward empowering teachers.

Rose, M. (1995). *Possible lives: The promise of public education in America.* Boston: Houghton Mifflin.

This author accurately describes the lives of students and educators who are confronting the challenges of cultural diversity and rising above expectations of failure. A touching, thoughtful, and highly articulate account of real people in real schools who are beating the odds against them, it is a must read for any future teacher.

Schwartz, T. (1978). Where is the culture? Personality as the distributive locus of culture. In G. Spinder (Ed.), *The making of psychological anthropology* (pp. 197–218). Berkeley: University of California Press.

The author presents a model of culture that is neither homogeneous nor heterogeneous but instead a conglomeration of similarities and differences. Both culture and individual are constantly changing, but it is essential to recognize that even while changing, both are still stable and inherent. The author argues that individuals are the driving force behind cultural change, yet maintains that such change affects other individuals and creates and re-creates culture.

Valdés, G. (1996). *Con respeto: Bridging the distances between culturally diverse families and schools: An ethnographic portrait.* New York: Teachers College Press.

This volume traces the development of Mexican American migrant children and their families as they confront the world both inside and outside the family, with a particular emphasis on how schooling intersects with this process. Through in-depth case studies, the reader comes to know each family and the intricate ways in which they address their own cultural practices and those they are facing through contact with the schools.

Web Resources

Cultural Diversity and Early Education: What children bring to school: *http://www.nap.edu/readingroom/books/earlyed/chapter3.html*

This web site identifies the impact of student culture, social organization, and home language on children's learning styles.

The Social Context of Education: *http://nces.ed.gov/pubs*

This web site draws attention to ways in which schools can meet the academic, social, and emotional needs of a demographically diverse student body.

Chapter 3
Educational Approaches
to Student Cultural Diversity

Focus Questions

- What is *Americanization*, and what concept of culture underlies it?

- How have legal reforms in educational equity and the movement toward multicultural education in U.S. schools affected the education of culturally and linguistically diverse children?

- What are the shortcomings of educational equity and multicultural education as approaches to understanding the educational needs of diverse populations?

- What are two new theoretical perspectives that attempt to explain why culturally diverse children often fail academically?

- How does the constructivist approach to knowledge provide the basis for a new pedagogy?

> "Equity and pluralism in schools do not address diversity."

In our efforts to understand the effects of cultural diversity in the schools, we use theories of language, learning, thinking, teaching, socialization, and culture (García, 2001). Research pertinent to education has expanded its scope in recent decades. What was once considered the study of values and behavior (Mead, 1939a; Skinner, 1957) has become today an interlocking study of elements from linguistics, psychology, and sociology. Findings in each of these areas are independently significant, but together they help us understand the nature of the cultural experience at both micro and macro levels. Educators, for example, can focus on smaller units of social analysis, such as a speech event, for insight into a student's experience. We can also broaden the view to a larger unit of social analysis, such as social class, for vital contextual information. For teachers of culturally and linguistically diverse students, the issue of culture—what it is and how it directly and indirectly influences academic learning—is the nexus of the issue.

This chapter concentrates on the schooling initiatives that have been targeted at culturally diverse students in the United States. In so doing, it discusses the way in which educational research, theory, policy, and practice of significance to these students converge. We will look beneath the variety of action plans and programs that have been devised for culturally diverse students and reveal the educational concepts and theories used as a foundation. We will find that definitions of culture and assumptions about cultural differences largely have determined past and determine present educational practices.

A Historical Survey

Within the past few years, educational approaches related to culture and education have shifted from an early focus on "Americanization" (Dewey, 1921) to concerns about educational equity (Ramirez and Castaneda, 1974) and then to multicultural education (Banks, 1981; Banks, J., and Banks, C. A., 1995; Gay, 1997; Sleeter and Grant, 1999). More recent approaches center on the "effective" instruction of children from culturally and linguistically diverse groups (August and Hakuta, 1997; Gandara, 2000; García, 1991c, 1995; Purkey and Smith, 1983; Rose, 1995). This section introduces these earlier educational approaches and explains how they developed from past theory and data on culture and education. Later sections will discuss newer approaches based on a broader understanding of cultural diversity as it relates to schooling. You will see that the linguistic, cognitive, social, and educational research and theory developed over the past two decades have dramatically reshaped our view of cultural "difference" in education.

Americanization

As I described in Chapter 1, at various times in its history—including its recent past—the United States has been a major destination for immigrants. The 1990 U.S. Census, for example, identified some 20 million immigrants, with nearly 6 million children living with immigrant parents and another 2 million foreign-born children (Smith and Edmonston, 1997). By 1996, the immigrant population had grown to 25 million, with an even greater increase in the number of children (Rambaut, 1997). According to Rambaut (1997):

1. Mexicans are by far the largest legal and undocumented immigrant population in the United States. They also have the lowest educational levels of any major ethnic group, native- or foreign-born.

2. Since the 1960s, Filipinos have formed the second largest immigrant population. They have the lowest poverty rate of any sizable ethnic group in the country.

3. Since 1975, immigrants from Vietnam, Cambodia, and Laos have formed the largest refugee population. Compared with refugees from Central America, the Balkans, or the former Soviet Union, they have the highest rates of poverty and welfare dependency in the country.

In short, the student diversity in the United States has been and continues to be driven by these dramatic increases in immigration, which in turn have driven the educational responses to this diversity.

Historically, **Americanization** has been a prime institutional education objective for immigrant and culturally diverse children (Elam, 1972; Gonzalez, 1990). Based on the sociological theory of **assimilation,** Americanization is an approach to acculturation that seeks to merge small ethnic and linguistically diverse communities into a single dominant national institutional structure and culture. Traditionally recognized as a solution to the problem of immigrants and ethnicity in the modern industrialized United States, Americanization is the "melting pot" solution.

Americanization schooling practices were adopted whenever the population of culturally and linguistically diverse students rose to significant numbers in a community. The government established special programs and applied them to both children and adults in urban and rural settings. The desired goal of Americanizing students was to socialize and acculturate the diverse community. In essence, the reasoning went, if schools could teach these students to speak standard English and to accept "American" values, then educational failure could be averted. Ironically, social economists have argued that such efforts to assimilate immigrant populations were coupled with systematic attempts to maintain disparate social and economic conditions between them and majority populations. Indeed, more than anything else, past approaches to addressing the educational problems of minority populations have actually preserved the political and economic subordination of these communities (Spencer, D., 1988).

Many immigrant populations have come to the United States in the last century. In 1921, Thomas and Park (1921b) argued that the "Old World" consciousness of immigrants would eventually be overcome by modern American values. Recent analysis by Gonzalez (1990, 1999) and D. Spencer (1988) shows, however, that Americanization did not evenly affect all immigrant groups. There are a number of reasons for this. According to Gonzalez (1990, 1994, 1999), there are important distinctions between the experience of European immigrants and that of other immigrant groups:

Different Immigrant Experiences

1. The Americanization of the non-European community has been attempted in a social context that continues to be highly segregated. African American, Hispanic, and other non-Anglo-American students are more segregated today than they were three decades ago.

2. The assimilation of these non-Anglo-American groups had both rural and urban aspects, whereas the European immigrant experience was overwhelmingly urban.

3. Assimilation was heavily influenced by the regional agricultural economy, which retarded a "natural" assimilation process.

4. Slaves and immigrants from Africa, Mexico, Puerto Rico, and other Latin and Asian countries could not escape the economic and political stigma assigned by the United States, an advanced industrialized nation, to their semi-industrialized, semifeudal lands of origin. Many such immigrants came from

regions under U.S. domination. This relationship led to a very constrained immigration pool, with only farm and low-skilled labor immigrating continuously to this country. None of the European nations had such a relationship with the United States, and thus their national cultures tended to be perceived as being relatively equal to that of the United States. This factor alone would have significantly affected the manner in which Americanization was applied to immigrants of non-European background.

American Indians: An Example

Although many immigrant groups have been subjected to the Americanization phenomenon, the effects of this process can be seen most dramatically on the indigenous population of the United States during the late nineteenth and early twentieth centuries. After the American Indians had been segregated on federal reservations, boarding schools were established for their children. At an early age, sometimes as young as four or five, Indian children were removed from their families and placed in schools hundreds or thousands of miles away. The clear goal of such removal was to wash these children clean of the native and tribal influences regarded as negative by the majority of U.S. society.

As students in these boarding schools, Indian children were forbidden to speak their native languages, to practice their native religions or traditions, or to wear their usual dress. They were often forbidden to return to the reservation for visits. At the same time, they were taught English, "proper" manners of behavior, and other standard school content, and were subjected to Christian missionary efforts. In short, this major national effort at education, requiring significant economic and social resources, was built on a policy designed to rid these children of "negative" cultural attributes while instilling new "positive"—that is, "American"—cultural attributes. The goal was to rehabilitate a problematic cultural group over time through the use of U.S. schools. The focus was on the young. The actual result, many American Indians have argued, was the anguish of young children and their families at separation, the loss of tribal responsibility and authority over the young, and the accelerated loss of the culture and language of indigenous peoples (Banks, C. A., and Banks, J., 1995).

It can be argued that Americanization still underlies many programs aimed at culturally diverse students (Nieto, 1994; Olsen, 1997; Portes and Rumbaut, 1996). For these students American**Elimination of Differences** ization unfortunately still means the elimination not only of linguistic and cultural differences but also of an "undesirable" culture. Americanization programs seem to be based on the incorrect assumption that in the United States a single homogeneous ethnic culture is in contact with a single homogeneous nonethnic one, and that the relationship between the two is not one of equals. The dominant community, enjoying greater wealth and privileges, claims its position by virtue of cultural superiority (Ogbu, 1987a). In one way or another, nearly every culturally diverse child, whether born in the United States or elsewhere, is likely to be treated as a foreigner, an alien, or an intruder.

In 1923, the superintendent of the Los Angeles schools voiced an eerily familiar complaint in an address to district principals: "We have the [Mexican] immigrants to live with, and if we Americanize them, we can live with them." Unfortunately, even today the objective is to transform the diversity in our communities into a monolithic, English-speaking, American-thinking-and-acting community. As many have done throughout the century, this attitude was echoed in 1990 by Ken Hill, a superintendent in the California schools who has received national and state distinction for his efforts to serve a large number of African American, Mexican American, and Asian American students: "We've got to attend to the idea of assimilation and to make sure that we teach English and our values as quickly as we can so these kids can get in the mainstream of American life" (quoted in Walsh, 1990, p. B14). (It is important to note that at the time Hill made his statement, the dropout rate for non-Anglo-American students in his district was over 40 percent [Matute-Bianchi, 1990].)

The Americanization solution has not worked. Moreover, it depends on the group-oriented concept of culture, which, as we saw in Chapter 2, leads to mistaken notions about cultural difference. The Americanization philosophy presumes that culturally

Children as Culturally Flawed

different children are as a group culturally flawed. To "fix" them individually, we must act on the individual as a member of a cultural group. By changing the values and language of the group, we will have the solution to the educational underachievement of students who represent these groups. In essence, the groups should "melt" into one large and more beneficial so-called American culture. Research has shown, however, that this "melting" does not in fact occur.

Our educational efforts have been responding quite ignorantly with regard to the processes by which individuals and groups actually come together to form culture. The challenge facing educators with regard to culturally diverse students is not to "Americanize" them but rather to understand them and to act responsively to their specific diversity in order to achieve academic success for *all* students. In recent decades, this realization has led directly to issues of educational equity.

Educational Equity

No one argues about the significance of education in this country. We are all quite convinced that an educated society is beneficial for enhancing individual well-being, improving our standard of living, and maintaining a democratic society (Dewey, 1921). Moreover, education is perceived as a vehicle for achieving the "American Dream." It is not surprising that many organizations in the United States, from large businesses to small community groups, have attempted to initiate and maintain educational endeavors in conjunction with efforts in the public schools. In fact, what with the many courses, workshops, seminars, conferences, and other structured learning opportunities available today, people are exposed to more formal educational experiences outside of the typical K–12 system than within it. Clearly in our society, education, from cradle to grave, is important to our citizens.

If this is so, then equal access to educational opportunities must be a corollary to this basic value. This was clearly brought home by the U.S. Supreme Court decision of 1954 in *Brown v. Board of Education*. This landmark case concluded that the separate, segregated education provided for African Americans was unequal to the education provided for Anglo-Americans. The Court argued that every effort must be made to address equal access to education regardless of race. Significant congressional actions during the 1960s and 1970 reinforced this decision for Hispanic Americans, Asian Americans, Native Americans, and women. The major legislative piece was the 1964 Civil Rights Act. Title IV of that act banned discrimination on the grounds of race, color, or national origin in any program receiving federal financial assistance (Title VII addressed educational equity across gender). Not coincidentally, the Elementary and Secondary Education Act (ESEA) of 1965 began to provide millions of federal dollars in assistance to state and local school systems. If these schools were to use these federal funds, they were to be held accountable to the standard of nondiscrimination.

This legislation directly banned recipients of federal resources from "restricting an individual in any way in the enjoyment of any advantage or privilege enjoyed by others receiving any service, financial aid or benefit under the [federally] funded program." Importantly, the recipient of federal funds was also prohibited from using criteria or methods that would have the effect of undermining the objectives of the federally funded program for individuals of a particular race, color, or national origin. Other provisions of this legislation provided the possibility of a private cause of action (a lawsuit) against a federally funded institution to rectify issues of discrimination. This meant that students and

Legal Redress Allowed

their parents were not required to wait until the federal government noticed that a funded program was out of compliance. Instead, they could independently move the courts to seek relief. And they did. A barrage of legal action aimed at correcting educational inequities soon followed.

The 1994 overhaul of the ESEA (which is now known as the Improving America's Schools Act, or IASA) redirected some $11 billion in federal yearly appropriations to educational institutions, mostly K–12, throughout the country. The terms of the reauthorization, while acknowledging the acute need to serve the diverse student population, also recognized the following:

Central Points of IASA

1. The new knowledge about which programs are effective and why must be central to any proposed changes.

2. New policy must capitalize on the wisdom of current policy, administration, curriculum, and instructional practice.

3. Policies and programs must be cohesive in order to integrate the services that are to be provided. This cohesiveness should reflect the partnership among national, state, and local educational policies and programs.

4. The very limited amount of money for new programs that is available today and for the near to distant future must be acknowledged. Therefore, federal resources must be utilized in systemic reform efforts that minimize the notion of "compensatory" education and instead help educators to formulate and implement programs that allow *all* children to achieve to high academic standards.

(For a broader discussion of the policies, see Chapter 1; for a comprehensive description of the policy foundations of the 1994 reauthorization, see García and Gonzalez, 1995; Wiese and García, 1998.)

In these 1994 legislative initiatives, the emphasis on *all* children is particularly relevant to the country's diverse student population, and it reflects an awareness that some children were systematically not benefiting from their educational experiences. Through the introduction of new legislation in Goals 2000, the U.S. Department of Education had already set the stage for the state-by-state development of educational standards. Then, with the passage of the IASA, the goals-and-standards initiative was aligned with the allocation of resources for specific policies. This alignment recognized that federal, state, and local government efforts must be coordinated to enhance effectiveness and efficiency. Moreover, the federal role must allow flexibility at the state and local levels while requiring that all children achieve at the highest levels.

This new policy is a first attempt to use federal support to unite equity and excellence in state and local educational endeavors. It is also one of the first instances in which federal policy has attempted not only to emphasize equal educational opportunity but also to focus on educational achievement outcomes that are based on high academic standards for all students. The results of this new policy are yet to be assessed.

Language Barriers Must Be Overcome

Other administrative and legislative actions have addressed further aspects of equal educational opportunity. For example, in 1970 the U.S. Department of Health, Education and Welfare issued a memorandum, later referred to as the **May 25 memorandum,** that clarified the mandate of the 1964 Civil Rights Act with respect to non-English-speaking students: "Where a liability to speak and understand the English language excludes national origin minority group children from effective participation in the educational program offered by a school district, the district must take affirmative steps to rectify the language deficiency in order to open instructional programs to these students." The Equal Educational Opportunities and Transportation Act of 1974 converted this administrative protection for language minority students into formal law. The act makes "the failure by an educational agency to take appropriate action to overcome language barriers that impede equal participation by its students in its educational programs" an unlawful denial of equal educational opportunities.

Taken together, these legal and legislative initiatives directly related the value placed on education in U.S. society to the educational needs of culturally diverse populations. Every child, regardless of race, color, national origin, or language, is legally entitled to the benefits of equal educational opportunity. This movement toward equal educational opportunity pervaded our schools for over a decade and still drives many initiatives designed for culturally diverse students. But equal access to education has not been the only stimulus behind our attention to culturally diverse students.

Multicultural Education

During the late 1970s and early 1980s and into the 1990s, the educational establishment and representatives of minority groups themselves began to confront another important educational issue of particular consequence to culturally diverse students. Mostly aimed at curriculum reform, this debate suggested that the content of curriculum taught in U.S. classrooms should reflect the diverse character of the nation's population. A **multicultural education** was recommended for several reasons. First, advocates argued that the curriculum should better represent the actual contributions made by various cultural groups to this country's society. They criticized prevailing curriculum for its unbalanced perspectives emphasizing only Western European values, history, literature, and general world view (Banks, 1982). The United States is not one monolithic culture, these critics claimed, and the curriculum should reflect its true cultural diversity. Second, a multicultural curriculum would educate children of majority status as to the many accomplishments and contributions to U.S. society by individuals of minority status. This would at the same time reaffirm the significance of the minority group to the larger society and help develop positive self-esteem in children of minority status (García, 1983b). Third, multicultural education was perceived as a school reform movement aimed at changing the content and process of education within schools. Its goal was not to stop at merely providing equal educational opportunity but to go further and enhance the schooling experience for all students (Grant and Sleeter, 1987; Sleeter and Grant, 1999).

Goals of
Multicultural
Education

The concept of multicultural education gave rise to several distinct approaches to the instruction of students in general and of culturally diverse students in particular. However, the major impact of this reform movement has been in the area of **curriculum**—that is, the area of schooling that addresses the content of instruction. In essence, this major reform attempted to address what students should be learning. The movement made it quite clear that we needed to know more about this country's diverse cultural groups and that after we had uncovered such knowledge, we needed to dispense it in our everyday schooling endeavors.

Focus on
Curriculum

Disparate Goals of Multicultural Education. The overall agreement about the importance of including curriculum that addressed diversity was quite significant, since there was some disagreement about the goals of curriculum reform. Sleeter and Grant (1987, 1999) and Gay (1997) have provided an excellent review of the varied goals and the overall limited consequences of the multicultural education reform movement on American education.

Within a model described as "Teaching the Multiculturally Different," one goal was to assist educators charged with helping culturally different students succeed in mainstream schooling. Although this model did not directly cite the need to assimilate children of different backgrounds into the mainstream, this seemed to serve as its major goal. The prescription for success was usually subtractive in nature. That is, children with different cultures and languages were asked to leave behind these attributes through the assistance of bridgelike educational programs that promised access and success in academics and later in other

A Bridge
to Success

Assimilation Doesn't Equal Success

Becoming a Responsive Teacher

How can schools cope with the diversity presented by their students? Should they harken back to the model of education developed in the early decades of this century to deal with the huge numbers of immigrants, when educators responded to increasing cultural and linguistic diversity among their students by attempting to accelerate their assimilation into the American mainstream? Their mission was to Americanize immigrants by replacing their native language and culture with those of the United States. Educators confidently sought to fit newcomers into the American mold by teaching them the English language and literature, a sugarcoated version of American history, and a respect for the U.S. political system and civic life.

Although some recommend a similar approach today, it is no longer possible even to describe American culture with confidence; into what mold should educators seek to place all children? There is no single definition of American culture; multiple definitions have been informed by ethnic minority voices.

We also have never counted the cost of the Americanization philosophy. How many children were estranged from their family and culture; how many grandparents of today's teachers lost their native language; how many worked a lifetime on the assembly line when they should have gone to college; how many became ashamed of who they were?

When immigrant students become shining academic stars, their success is often attributed to the values and habits of their native culture rather than their Americanization. There is some evidence that assimilation may actually inhibit academic success. Studies of Mexican, Indian, and Vietnamese immigrants all suggest that those who maintain a strong identification with their native language and culture are more likely to succeed in school than those who readily adopt American ways (Rambaut, 1997).

societal domains. This type of multicultural education was regarded as a temporary, highly directed educational endeavor that would lead to a melting pot of a successful and more homogeneous student population.

Early versions of the federal program known as Head Start reflected this multicultural approach. For preschool children aged three and four, Head Start, and its extension for the early elementary student, Follow Through, were perceived as bridges to the mainstream academic environment. Other compensatory educa-

Continued   Assimilation Doesn't Equal Success

Meeting the Challenge

1. Research seems to indicate that assimilation does not serve culturally diverse students. Since it nevertheless persists as a response to cultural difference, who or what might it serve?

2. How would you define the culture in which you live? Develop a list of at least 10 highlights of this culture that most accurately characterize it. Your list may include values, events, people, places, or things both past and present that you consider culturally significant. Compare your list with those of your classmates. Make a separate list of all the items others selected that are surprising or unfamiliar to you. Why were these items not on your list?

3. Consider these three Filipino children:
   (a) Renaldo has recently arrived in the United States from the Philippines with his parents and three brothers.
   (b) Carlo and his three brothers were born in the United States, as were both of their parents. Carlo's grandparents emigrated from the Philippines when they were in their twenties.
   (c) Joshua was born in the Philippines but was adopted at birth by Anglo-American parents. His three adoptive brothers are also Anglo-American.

   Explain the variety in acculturation these three children have experienced. Describe how an approach to education based on assimilation might affect each child. Alternatively, if you had all three of these children in class, how would you build on each one's specific relationship to language and culture?

tion programs, such as Title I programs that address underachievement directly, were also meant to provide underachieving students with bridges to achievement. They are, however, still too often perceived as temporary and compensatory means of helping unsuccessful students make the transition to success through a process likened to natural cultural assimilation. In such assimilation, immigrants with very diverse cultures and languages come to embrace mainstream American values and to acquire English as their main mode of communication. Schools were asked to serve, positively, as an organized vehicle to hasten this natural process.

It must be noted that this perspective on multicultural education did stress the importance of cultural diversity among the students, families, and communities served. In this way, it was definitely distinct from earlier educational strategies of Americanization. The practice of taking American Indian youngsters from their families and placing them in boarding schools far from their homes was not meant primarily to serve as a bridge to American society. It was devised instead to be a direct break with a child's original but negatively perceived language and culture (Crawford, 1995; Phillips, 1983).

Enhancing Human Relations The bridging goal of some multicultural education efforts was at times combined with the goal of enhancing human relations (Banks, C. A., and Banks, J., 1995; Colangelo, Foxley, and Dustin, 1982). Such a result was seen as best achieved by learning about and with each other. In so doing, the members of diverse populations would be able to understand one another, and as a corollary, improved communication and social relations would develop. Distinct from programs of assimilation and bridging, educational programs reflecting this approach to multicultural education asked students to learn about other groups not like their own and to utilize this new knowledge to enhance social accommodation of diversity—"Let's learn to get along better."

The most dramatic example of a large-scale program of this type comes from Canada. In the province of Quebec, French-speaking populations (Francophones) were in constant social and economic dispute with English-speaking populations (Anglophones). The solution to this problem in social relations was Bilingual-Bicultural Immersion Education. Anglophone children were placed in French-only schooling programs for the first three years of their educational experience. The goal of the program was for children to acquire knowledge of both the language and the culture of Francophones, with the expected product of better human relations. Evaluation of these programs indicates that these expectations were achieved without any loss in academic achievement resulting from children learning in a language other than their own home language (Swain and Lapkin, 1991). Swain and Lapkin (1991) point out that in Canada, French speakers and English speakers are socially equal. This is not true of language-diverse groups in the United States.

Respecting Diversity Yet another approach to multicultural education has been much more activist in nature. Its goals serve to promote respect for diversity. In addition to acquiring and disseminating information about the cultural diversity of the U.S. population, this approach is aimed at developing intellectual and societal acceptance of cultural diversity as a goal in and of itself (Fishman, 1990; García, 1997; Garcia, R., 1979; Gay, 1975, 1997; Gollnick and Chinn, 1986; Grant, 1998; Ovando and McLaren, 1997).

Most popular and influential in the past decade, work in this area has attempted to bring together issues of race, ethnicity, gender, and social class. The thrust of such initiatives has been to permeate the curriculum with issues of diversity—in literature, social thought, scientific approaches, historical construction, and so on—while at the same time serving up criticism of "standardized" curricula, particularly those that reflect Western European contributions as the norm. A corollary of this approach is the overall multicultural and social reconstructionist perspective (Appleton, 1983; Suzuki, 1984). In this view, students are asked to become social critics, particularly in terms of issues of social injustice. Proponents argue that adoption of this multicultural educational approach would rid society of pervasive social injustices inflicted on the basis of race, ethnicity, and gender.

A Focus on Social Injustice

Such a proactive stance toward multicultural education is exemplified by programs in U.S. bilingual education. In the past decade, **double immersion** programs have been introduced into large Latino school districts in California, New York, Texas, Illinois, and Florida. The goal of a double immersion program is to produce a student population that is bilingual and bicultural. For non-Latino, English-speaking students, the goal is English and Spanish language and literacy. Beginning in kindergarten, these students are exposed to Spanish-language instruction in classrooms with Spanish-speaking students and to a curriculum that addresses bicultural concerns. For Latino students in the programs, the goals are the same. These aims are in concert with the notion of actively promoting cultural diversity, with a healthy academic respect for the linguistic and cultural attributes of the diverse students involved (Lindholm and Christiansen, 1990, 1997).

Similar programs in the public schools of San Francisco, San Diego, Detroit, New York, and Chicago are housed in **magnet schools.** The purpose of a magnet school is to attract a highly diverse set of students around a thematically designated curriculum that is multilingual and multicultural. Such programs attempt to integrate African American, Latino, Asian, and other culturally diverse student populations by recognizing diversity as a positive ingredient in addressing the agendas of equal educational opportunity and multicultural education (Grant, 1991, 1998).

An Appraisal of Progress. Attention to multicultural education in this country over the past two decades has fired numerous debates and resulted in substantive accomplishments. Publishing companies have launched new curriculum efforts to address claims by proponents of multicultural education of bias in publishing (Gollnick and Chinn, 1994). Teacher-training programs have been required to provide specific training in student cultural diversity at the preservice level (California Commission on Teacher Credentialing, 1991). School-based programs such as the magnet and double immersion bilingual education programs described earlier find their roots, at least partially, in the values and goals of multicultural education.

The previous discussion has attempted to locate multicultural education in three broad categories based on distinct but not necessarily exclusive goal agendas. We have seen that these goals range from bridging and assimilation for culturally diverse students to enhancement of human relations, to active promotion of cultural diversity as a societywide goal. Keep in mind that all the goals of multicultural education build upon previous and ongoing initiatives that address the basic issue of equal educational opportunity: no child should be denied the benefits of education. These two educational approaches have provided an alternative to the traditional response of Americanization to the growing presence of cultural diversity in our schools.

Beyond Multicultural Education

Since the time of Socrates, educators and philosophers have argued for a kind of teaching that does more than impart knowledge and teach skills. Knowledge and skills are important enough, the argument goes, but true education and real teaching involve far more: helping students understand, appreciate, and grapple with important ideas while developing a depth of comprehension of a wide range of issues.

Yet teaching aimed at these important goals is presently most notable for its absence from U.S. classrooms. Goodlad (1984), for example, reports that:

> A great deal of what goes on in the classroom is like painting-by-numbers—filling in the colors called for by numbers on the page. . . . [Teachers] ask specific questions calling essentially for students to fill in the blanks: "What is the capital city of Canada?" "What are the principal exports of Japan?" Students rarely turn things around by asking questions. Nor do teachers often give students a chance to romp with an open-ended question such as "What are your views on the quality of television?" (p. 108)

If this portrait is true in mainstream American classrooms, it is even more true in classrooms with low-income, linguistically and Low-Level Skills | culturally diverse children. Because of the perception that these students fundamentally require drill, review, and redundancy in

CURRY COLLEGE

1071 Blue Hill Avenue
Milton, Massachusetts 02186-2395

617-333-
2243

Tel: (617) 333-2255
Fax: (617) 333-2045
jbresnah0104@curry.edu
www.curry.edu

Gail Koonie

John A. Bresnahan
Director of Graduate
Enrollment & Student Services

order to progress academically (Brophy and Good, 1986), their learning opportunities are likely to be excessively weighted toward low-level skills and factually oriented instruction. As important as skills and facts undoubtedly are, no less important are more cognitively demanding learning opportunities that promote, as the philosopher Mortimer Alder (1982) has written, the "enlarged understanding of ideas and values" (p. 23).

The lack of attention to higher-level cognition is only one of the systemic problems that continue to exist despite decades of efforts for equal educational opportunity and multicultural education. As much as they have contributed to changing demands in U.S. schools, these efforts have failed to address a number of important educational concerns. For the most part they have lacked a strong theoretical foundation. They have addressed curriculum only—not instructional methods or pedagogy. They have produced many single case studies of ethnic groups but little empirical data to substantiate the positive effects of implementation.

As described in Chapter 1, academic achievement in many culturally diverse populations has not been enhanced significantly over the past decades. Action for equal educational opportunity has generated legislative and legal policy along with concomitant resources to address this core societal value. But such action has not considered, in any comprehensive manner, how educational equity should be achieved. Educational attention in and around multicultural education has espoused important societal values and has led to advances in a number of educational fronts. But still it has not produced a set of comprehensive strategies that address the educational concerns it has raised (Sleeter and Grant, 1987). Essentially, the result of these initiatives in educational equity and multicultural reform has been to raise even more issues. This is no small feat, considering the many-headed character of U.S. schools.

The era of equal educational opportunity and multicultural education has left us a clearly identifiable legacy: educational endeavors related to culturally diverse students have been prag-

Lack of Theory | matically oriented. That is, they have focused on a set of problems—discrimination, segregation, underachievement, low self-esteem, and non-English proficiency, to name a few—and have forwarded programs to address them. These pragmatic efforts tended to lack any substantive theoretical underpinnings. The proposed solutions were driven by somewhat ambiguous social values associated with educational equity and pluralism. Conversely, a more theoretical approach would still consider the problems of discrimination, underachievement, and segregation but would first attempt to understand why such problems exist. We could then develop solutions from a storehouse of understanding (Cole, 1996; García, 1991c; Tharp, 1991).

Another legacy of the past three decades of educational activity, particularly in the area of multicultural education, is the extended case study approach to cultural diversity (Nieto, 1992). The educational community has produced an extensive research literature on the characteristics of different racial, ethnic, and ethnolinguistic groups. The goal of this work was to document the cultural and linguistic attributes of various groups in the United States so that these attributes could be better understood and utilized to serve students. It was not uncommon to learn from these research studies, for example, that American Indian children were nonverbal (Appleton, 1983), that Asian American children were shy (Sue and Okazaki, 1990), that Mexican American children were cooperative (García, 1983b, 1995, 2001), that African American children were aggressive (Boykin, 1983), and that Anglo-American children were competitive (Kagan, 1983b).

Stereotypes Promoted

Although this case study work was meant to advance our understanding of culturally diverse students, it often had the effect of promoting stereotypes. Moreover, it did not recognize the axiom implicitly understood by social scientists who study culture: there is as much heterogeneity within any cultural group as there is among cultural groups. (See Chapter 2 for an extended discussion of this issue.) Unfortunately, descriptively useful indicators began to take on explanatory values: if that student is Mexican American, she must be cooperative and speak Spanish. The problem arose when educators tried to apply case study information in the classroom. They developed educational programs to address the cultural attributes identified only to discover, for example, that many Mexican American children were not cooperative and did not speak Spanish. If all Mexican Americans are not alike, if all African Americans are not alike, if all American Indians are not alike, then what set of knowledge about those groups is important educationally? What overarching conceptualization of culture is truly useful for understanding the educational framework of culturally diverse groups?

New Theoretical Perspectives

Before we address the preceding questions directly, it seems appropriate to frame this discussion in terms of a continuum of educationally relevant theory. At one end of this continuum, theorists argue that serving culturally diverse populations calls for a deeper understanding of the interaction of a student's culture and the prevailing school culture (Nieto, 1999; Tharp, 1989). At the other end, theorists claim that any population of students, no matter what their cultural background, will achieve academically if the appropriate teaching methods are implemented. Next, we shall examine these two perspectives and other ideas that fall in between them.

A Continuum of Theories

The claim that culture plays a role in educational underachievement is supported by a wealth of research suggesting that the educational failure of diverse student populations is related to a "culture clash" between home and school. Evidence for this claim comes from Boykin (1986) for African American students; from Heath (1983) for poor Anglo-American students; from Wiesner, Gallimore, and Jordan (1988) for Hawaiian students; from Vogt, Jordan, and Tharp (1987) for Navaho students; from García (1988) for Mexican American students; and from Rodriguez (1989) and Bigler (1999) for Puerto Rican students. In essence, these researchers have suggested that educational endeavors that do not

Cultural Dissonance

attend to the distinctiveness of culture are likely to result in failure for certain students. Theoretically, these students do not succeed because the difference between their school culture and their home culture creates an educationally harmful dissonance—a home-to-school "mismatch." Sue and Padilla (1986) directly enunciate this position by asserting that "the challenge for educators is to identify critical differences between and within ethnic minority groups and to incorporate this information into classroom practice" (p. 62).

Using What "Works"

At the same time, however, other research supports the theoretical position that the academic failure of any student rests on the failure of instructional personnel to implement what is known to "work." In other words, it is not a mismatch of cultures that is to blame so much as the failure of instructional programs to utilize appropriate general principles of teaching and learning. Using the now-common research tool of **meta analysis,** which is a method of analyzing and summarizing large numbers of research studies, Walberg (1986b) suggests that a synthesis of educational research identifies robust indicators of instructional conditions with academically significant effects across various conditions and for various student groups. Other meta analytic reviews (Baden and Maehr, 1986; Bloom, 1984; Slavin, 1989) agree. Among the specific instructional strategies proposed as candidates for "what works with everyone" are direct instruction (Rosenshine, 1986), tutoring (Bloom, 1984), frequent evaluation of academic progress (Slavin, Karweit, and Madden, 1989), and cooperative learning (Slavin, 1989).

This research also identifies expectations as significant factors in underachievement. Levin (1988) and Snow (1990) have suggested

Motivations and Expectations

that students, teachers, and school professionals in general have low academic expectations for culturally and linguistically diverse students. Again, as popularized in the film *Stand and Deliver,* raising student motivation in conjunction with enhanced academic expectations and challenging curriculum is a prescribed solution. The assumption of theorists at this end of the continuum is that the educational failure of culturally diverse populations can be reversed by the systemic and effective implementation of general principles of instruction understood to work with "all" students.

Explanations for Lower Achievement

Interspersed within this continuum are other theoretical approaches that attempt to explain the academic underachievement of culturally and linguistically diverse students. Friere (1970) has argued that educational initiatives cannot expect to lead to academic or intellectual success under social circumstances that are oppressive. He and others (Cummins, 1986; Pearl, 1991) suggest that social oppression experienced by students taints any curriculum or pedagogy, however "successful" it is in general, and that only a pedagogy of empowerment can fulfill the lofty goals of educational equity and achievement.

Similarly, Bernstein (1971), Laosa (1982), Wilson (1987, 1999), and Anyon (1997) address underachievement by pointing to socioeconomic factors that influence the way schools and instruction are organized. When a group of people is exposed, over generations, to poverty and debilitating socioeconomic conditions, the teaching and learning process for children at home, in the community, and in the schools will suffer. The result is disastrous, long-term educational failure and social disruption of family and community. Ogbu and Matute-Bianchi (1986) and Ogbu (1999) offer a broader sociological perspective. They describe this country's present social approach to several immigrant and minority populations as "caste-like." In this attempt to explain underachievement, these theorists claim that certain populations are perceived as forming a layer of U.S. society that is not expected to excel academically or economically. These social expectations are reinforced until they become self-perceptions adopted by the members of "caste-like" populations, with academic underachievement and social withdrawal as the inevitable result.

So far we have discussed some of these new theoretical perspectives in only a general way. Throughout the rest of this book, we will examine them more comprehensively. You should realize, however, that the continuum of theories I have represented as ranging from "cultural mismatch" to "general principles" is not a set of incompatible approaches. Instead, as this brief introduction has indicated, a wide variety of scholars have seriously attempted to understand why so many culturally and linguistically diverse students are not well served by educational institutions in the United States today. These conceptual contributions are not limited to espousing the principles of multicultural education or recommending policies of educational equity. They go farther, and they dig deeper. The theoretical approaches useful to us address the issues of educating a culturally diverse population by searching out explanations for the present unsatisfactory situation.

These contributions take into consideration the work of Friere (1970), Cummins (1979, 1986), Ogbu (1987a), Rose (1996), and Tharp and Gallimore (1988). This research suggests that the educational vulnerability of culturally diverse students must be understood within the broader context of the circumstances for children in U.S. society. No quick fix is likely under social and schooling conditions that mark students for special treatment according to a category of cultural difference without consideration for the psychological and social circumstances in which each student—as an individual—resides. These theorists warn us against isolating any single attribute (poverty, language difference, learning potential, etc.) as the only variable of importance. More comprehensive views of the schooling process urge an understanding not only of the relationship between home and school but also of the psychological, sociological, and cultural incongruities between the two, and the resulting effects on learning and achievement (Cole, 1996; García, 2001; Valdes, 1997).

Broader Approaches

The Constructivist Perspective

How do we as educators begin to understand such a complex set of interactions? One framework for understanding is founded on the concept of **act psychology.** First formulated at the end of the nineteenth century, this concept proposes a model for human cognitive processes, or how we come to know. It focuses on the assertion that the mental functions of perceiving, remembering, and organizing—ultimately, knowing—are all acts of construction (Barlett, as cited by Cole, 1996). It also asserts that what we know is closely related to the circumstances in which we come to know it.

The term *construction* is particularly apt. Have you ever watched a large building evolve under construction? Scores of people and tons of material are marshaled and organized, and a structure rises seemingly out of chaos. Remember, though, that the process is not without its glitches. Days of rain may halt or alter construction, and the entire project is subject to the availability of supplies, not to mention the willingness of people to work together. The architects must consider features of the surrounding terrain and adjust their designs accordingly. In short, construction has a context, a

set of local circumstances in which it happens. These circumstances greatly affect the final form of the building.

Construction of Knowledge

The **constructivist perspective** is rooted in the notion that human knowledge is the result of continual building and rebuilding. Our "construction materials" consist of the give-and-take between the organization and content of old information and new information, processes of organizing that information, and the specific physical and social circumstances in which this all occurs. We come to understand a new concept by applying our knowledge of previous concepts to the new information we are given. For example, in order to teach negative numbers, a math teacher can use the analogy of digging a hole: the more dirt you take out of the hole, the greater the hole becomes; the more one subtracts from a negative number, the greater the negative number becomes. But a math teacher cannot use this example with children who have no experience digging holes. It won't work. As you can see, this theory of how the mind works implies that continual revisions (or "renovations," as an architect might say) are to be expected. Therefore, when we organize teaching and learning environments, we must recognize the constructivist nature of those environments. As educators, we "build" teaching and learning environments out of what we know and how we come to know it. And we must continue to build. To ignore that is to discount the relevance of previous educational environments to the ones we are considering now. They got us to today, but that does not mean they will get us to tomorrow.

A New Pedagogy

Embedded in the constructivist approach to education is the understanding that language and culture, and the values that accompany them, are constructed in both home and community environments (Cummins, 1986; García, 2001; Goldman and Trueba, 1987; Nieto, 1999). This approach acknowledges that children come to school with some constructed knowledge about many things (Moll, 1996) and points out that children's development and learning are best understood as the interaction of past and present linguistic, sociocultural, and cognitive constructions (Trueba, 1988b, 1999). A more appropriate perspective on learning, then, is one that recognizes that learning is enhanced when it occurs in contexts that are socioculturally, linguistically, and cognitively meaningful for the learner. These meaningful contexts bridge previous "constructions" and present "constructions" (Diaz, Moll, and Mehan, 1986; Heath, 1986; Moll, 1998; Wertsch, 1985).

Meaningful Contexts

Such meaningful contexts have been notoriously inaccessible to culturally diverse children. On the contrary, schooling practices often contribute to their educational vulnerability. The monolithic culture transmitted by U.S. schools in the form of pedagogy, curricula, instruction, classroom configuration, and language (Walker, 1987) dramatizes the lack of fit between the culturally diverse student and the school experience. The culture of U.S. schools is reflected in such practices as:

1. The systematic exclusion of the histories, languages, experiences, and values of these students from classroom curricula and activities.

2. "Tracking," which limits access to academic courses and justifies learning environments that do not foster academic development and socialization or perception of oneself as a competent learner and language-user.

3. A lack of opportunities to engage in developmentally and culturally appropriate learning in ways other than by teacher-led instruction.

This rethinking of the pedagogy of U.S. schools has profound implications for the teaching and learning enterprise, especially as it relates to culturally diverse students. The new pedagogy is one that envisions the classroom as a community of learners in which speakers, readers, and writers come together to define and redefine the meaning of the academic experience. Researchers variously describe it as a pedagogy of empowerment,

Community of Learners

cultural learning, or a cultural view of providing instructional assistance and guidance. Whatever its designation, it allows for respect and integration of the students' values, beliefs, histories, and experiences and recognizes the active role that students must play in their own learning. This responsive pedagogy utilizes students' present knowledge and experiences as a foundation for appropriating new knowledge. For language minority students, this means using instructional strategies that incorporate the student's native language or bilingual abilities. Language is a substantial part of the social network within which children construct knowledge.

Redefining the Teacher's Role | A responsive pedagogy for academic learning also requires a redefinition of the instructor's role. Instructors must become familiar with the cognitive, social, and cultural dimensions of learning. We need to recognize the ways in which instructional, assessment, and evaluation practices affect learning. We should become more aware of the purpose and degree of implementation of the classroom curriculum and understand its full impact on students. Specifically, we need to be alert to the configuration of the classroom environment and the ways in which students interact with one another and with teachers. Instructors must also recognize that helping students learn often requires allowing them to display their knowledge in ways that suggest their competence as learners and language-users. Once we begin to rethink all these dimensions of our role as educators, classrooms in U.S. schools will be equipped for the task of ensuring academic success for culturally diverse students.

Finally, teachers must question myths about learning processes and about the potentially underprepared student. In particular, we must debunk myths about students who come from households of lower socioeconomic status or ones where English is not the primary language. For educators who embrace the concept of a responsive pedagogy, new educational horizons for themselves and their students are not only possible but inevitable.

Responsive Learning Communities

The learning environments that we consider essential to the development of a responsive pedagogy have been referred to as "effective schooling" (García, 1997) and "high-performance learning communities" (Berman, 1996). Regardless of the specific term used, these environments must address issues of student diversity in order to maximize their potential and to sustain educational improvement over time. To examine the challenge presented to today's schools by the social, cultural, and linguistic diversity of their students, Table 3.1

The Learning Environment |

Table 3.1	**Conceptual Dimensions of a Responsive Pedagogy: Addressing Cultural and Linguistic Diversity in High-Performance Learning Communities**

Schoolwide Practices

- A vision defined by the acceptance and valuing of diversity—Americanization is *not* the goal
- Treatment of classroom practitioners as fellow professionals and colleagues in school development decisions
- An atmosphere of collaboration, flexibility, and enhanced professional development
- Elimination (gradual or immediate) of policies that apply categories to diverse students that render their educational experiences inferior or limiting for further academic learning
- Reflection of and connection to the surrounding community, particularly the families of the students

Teacher Practices

- Bilingual/bicultural skills and awareness
- High expectations of diverse students
- Treatment of diversity as an asset to the classroom
- Ongoing professional development on issues of cultural and linguistic diversity and practices that are most effective
- Curriculum development that addresses cultural and linguistic diversity through the following means:
  1. Attention to and integration of home culture and practices
  2. Emphasis on maximizing student interactions across categories of English proficiency, academic performance, length of time in the United States, etc.
  3. Regular and consistent attempts to elicit ideas from students for planning units, themes, and activities
  4. Thematic approach to learning activities that integrates various skills, events, and learning opportunities
  5. Focus on language development through meaningful interactions and communications rather than on grammatical skill-building that is removed from its appropriate context

summarizes the conceptual dimensions that must be reflected in high-performing, responsive learning communities.

Conclusion

A focus on the content of specific cultures, such as that advocated in the multicultural education reform movement, is useful but will not be enough to attain educational equity for culturally diverse students. Similarly, the search currently under way for general principles of learning that work for all students must be redirected. Educational researchers and teachers themselves need a broader view that provides some explanation for pervasive underachievement among culturally diverse student populations. How do individuals with diverse social, cultural, and linguistic experiences construct knowledge—or "make meaning"? How do they communicate and extend that meaning, particularly in the social contexts we call *schools?* These are the vital questions for today's and tomorrow's educators, and finding answers will require a solid theoretical framework.

We must develop an in-depth understanding of the "meaning-making" process. We need to couple a grasp of socialization processes in and out of schools with a clear-eyed examination of our present pedagogy. Our mission is first to understand the relationships among language, culture, and the learning process. Only then will we be ready to transform our understanding into recommendations for a responsive pedagogy and curriculum. The rest of this book pursues these two goals.

Summary of Major Ideas

1. Approaches to the education of diverse student groups in the United States have shifted from Americanization to a focus on educational equity and multicultural education. More recent approaches are based on broader theoretical frameworks that consider the roles of language and culture in education.

2. Americanization, or the "melting pot" solution to cultural diversity, seeks to assimilate, or merge, small ethnic and linguistically diverse communities into a single dominant national culture. It is an approach to acculturation that is based on a group-oriented concept of culture and the notion of cultural homogeneity as a desirable goal.

3. Members of non-European immigrant groups experience the process of Americanization differently than do members of European immigrant groups. This is because, comparatively, non-European immigrant groups are (a) subject to more ongoing segregation in the United States; (b) concentrated in both urban and rural areas; (c) more dependent on the U.S. regional agricultural economy; and (d) stigmatized by the low economic and political status of their countries of origin.

4. Native American children were subjected to Americanization on a large scale early in this century. Americanization underlies any educational approach that assumes that some children are culturally flawed and have undesirable cultural attributes that should be eliminated or "fixed."

5. The U.S. Supreme Court decided in 1954 in *Brown v. Board of Education* that separate educational facilities for African American students were not equal to educational facilities for Anglo-American students and that U.S. schools must provide equal access to education regardless of race. The 1964 Civil Rights Act, the Elementary and Secondary Education Act of 1965, the May 25 memorandum of 1970, and the 1974 Equal Educational Opportunities and Transportation Act together legally require equal educational opportunity for every child in the United States regardless of race, color, national origin, or language.

6. New policies emerging from the 1994 reauthorization of the Elementary and Secondary Education Act have recognized the acute need to serve the culturally diverse student population in a comprehensive and integrated manner.

7. The concept of multicultural education began as a criticism of school curricula that focused only on Western European values, history, literature, and general world-view. The movement toward multicultural education advocated reform of curricula to reflect more accurately the truly diverse nature of the nation's population. Multicultural education was expected to highlight contributions to U.S. culture by individuals of minority status in order to offer children of majority status alternative perspectives and improved self-esteem.

8. As a reform movement, multicultural education had three main emphases, which sometimes were contradictory: (a) to provide a bridge to success for culturally diverse children through programs such as Head Start, by which they would be assimilated into the mainstream academic environment; (b) to enhance human relationships by teaching students from different cultures how to understand one another; and (c) to promote respect for diversity by portraying cultural diversity as a desirable social goal.

9. Two multicultural educational approaches that promote diversity and oppose the notion of assimilation are double immersion programs in bilingual education and magnet schools. Double immersion programs produce students who are bilingual and bicultural. Magnet schools offer a thematically designated curriculum that is multilingual and multicultural.

10. Because they lack a strong theoretical foundation, initiatives in educational equity and multicultural education have only partially addressed educational issues of concern to culturally diverse students. They have focused on developing programs to address educational problems at the expense of fully understanding why the problems exist. The extended case study approach, favored by researchers who sought to document the attributes of different cultural groups, often had the unintended effect of promoting stereotypes.

11. New theoretical perspectives on the educational needs of culturally diverse populations span a broad continuum. Some researchers claim that educational failure is related to a mismatch between home and school cultures. Others claim that students fail academically because schools do not utilize principles of effective teaching and learning. Still other theorists point to social oppression, socioeconomic status, and social expectations for certain groups as keys to understanding educational underachievement.

12. More comprehensive perspectives on education focus on both the psychology of the individual student and the sociocultural context in which the student lives. These theories attempt not only to explain the relationship between home and school but also to reveal how learning and achievement are influenced by psychological, sociological, and cultural variables.

13. The constructivist approach to education is based on a specific model of how humans come to know and to understand. It proposes that humans gain knowledge by constructing it— by comparing and organizing old and new information within a surrounding local context or environment that greatly affects the final form the knowledge will take. This approach acknowledges that children come to school with constructed knowledge about many things.

14. In U.S. schools, culturally diverse children often are confronted with contexts for education that do not allow them to apply and extend their constructed knowledge. Such students are vulnerable to failure when faced with schooling practices that exclude their histories, languages, experiences, and values; that feature tracking; and that limit opportunity to learn in ways other than by teacher-led instruction.

15. A pedagogy that is responsive to culturally diverse students utilizes their constructed knowledge as a foundation for appropriating new knowledge. It also incorporates the students' native languages or bilingual abilities. In order to respond effectively to

these students, teachers must become more familiar with the cognitive, social, and cultural dimensions of learning.

Extending Your Experience

1. Research the history of school desegregation efforts in your state during the 1960s and 1970s. Outline the results of any major state court cases you uncover. Look back through the magazine and newspaper coverage of the time, and characterize the nature of the national public debate over educational equity. Prepare a list of three comments to report to the class about your findings.

2. Interview an older friend or relative who immigrated to the United States as a young person. Keeping in mind what you learned in this chapter about Americanization and assimilation, create a list of questions to ask this person about his or her experience in a new culture. What aspects of the original culture did he or she have to give up or change?

3. What role do you think teacher expectations play in students' accomplishments? How have high or low expectations from teachers influenced you? Create a written portrait of a particularly inspiring teacher you have had, exploring the possible sources for the inspiration you felt. Share your portrait with your classmates.

4. Reflect on a time in your own experience—whether in school or in a particular social situation—when you felt most like a foreigner or an outsider. Describe your feelings. What about the situation made you feel this way? Was it the way other people treated you? Was it something you were expected to do that you did not know how to do? What might have made you feel less excluded? As a teacher in a classroom of culturally diverse students, how can you be sensitive to a child's experience of outsiderness? What about tracking?

5. Is school the proper forum in which to discuss social issues centered on race, ethnicity, gender, and social class? Should students be encouraged to develop a critical, analytical perspective on social injustice? What types of questions do you yourself have about the unfairness and inequities you perceive in our society? List as many of your questions as you can, and then be prepared to share them in class.

6. Imagine that you are suddenly immersed in a culture completely different from the one in which you grew up. What

aspects of your constructed knowledge about your own culture will be helpful to you as you join this new culture?

Resources for Further Study

Print Resources

Banks, J., and Banks, C. A. (1995). *Handbook of research on multicultural education*. New York: Macmillan.

> This volume offers a wealth of information related to multicultural
> education. An excellent resource tool, it addresses theoretical as well
> as practical issues along with an extremely comprehensive set of arti-
> cles by leading authors in this field.

Cummins, J. (1986). Empowering minority students: A framework for intervention. *Harvard Educational Review, 56*(1), 18–35.

> The author offers a theoretical framework for analyzing the school
> failure of minority students and the relative lack of success of com-
> pensatory education, bilingual education, and LEP programs, arguing
> that these attempts were unsuccessful because of the inflexibility of
> teachers, students, schools, and minority communities.

Oakes, J. (1990). *Multiplying inequalities: The effects of race, social class, and tracking on opportunities to learn mathematics
and science*. Santa Monica, CA: Rand Corp.

> This publication assesses the opportunities given to underrepre-
> sented and low-achieving groups of students to succeed in scientific
> and technological domains. Statistical reports and economic trends
> paint a dismal picture for the future. This deficiency can affect the
> economic well-being of the nation, as our educational system loses
> important human capital.

Ovando, C. J., and McLaren, P. (Eds.). (2000). *The politics of multiculturalism and bilingual education: Students and teachers
caught in the crossfire*. Boston: McGraw-Hill.

> This is a collection of essays that critically explore the dimensions of
> multiculturalism in terms of politics and morality. They also examine
> the roles of teachers and students and the issues that they confront
> within the teaching and practice of multicultural education.

Romo, H. (1999). *Reaching out: Best practices for educating
Mexican-origin children and youth*. Charlston, WV: Clearinghouse on Rural Education and Small Schools.

> Romo examines the educational experiences of Mexican Americans
> through a multi-lens analysis. The author comprehensively profiles
> the current state of education for Mexican Americans by focusing on
> family-school partnerships, gender issues, language and literacy, and
> the dimensions of teaching and learning.

Sleeter, C. E., and Grant, C. A. (1999). *Making choices for multicultural education: Five approaches to race, class, and gender* (3rd ed.). Upper Saddle River, NJ: Merrill.

> The authors provide a framework for educators who are interested in dealing with misunderstandings about multicultural education. The term *multiculturalism* is examined and described, and various other definitions for it are criticized. Specific educational strategies are also discussed.

Web Resources

The Center for Research on Education, Diversity, and Excellence (CREDE): *http://www.cal.org/crede*

> This is a research-based web site that offers information that identifies and develops effective educational experiences for diverse learners.

Multicultural education: Strategies for linguistically diverse schools and classrooms:
http://www.ncbe.gwu.edu/ncbepubs/pigs/pig16.html

> This site addresses the practical side of multicultural education by discussing sample lessons as well as curriculum, and also provides additional resources. The overall goal is to provide insight into how to create a classroom that is responsive to the diversity of the student body.

Part Two
The Roots of Diversity

How much do we know about the development process as it relates to the culturally diverse student? Part Two addresses teaching and learning as they relate to research into children's social, linguistic, and cognitive development.

What do current research findings indicate about the relationship between linguistic and cognitive development? Chapter 4 describes the relationships among students' family, school, and peer cultures and suggests how they combine to affect students' engagement with learning. Which aspects of the school environment help (and which hinder) students bridge the gap between home and school? Chapter 5 traces the steps in language development and discusses research into multilingualism and use of dialect.

Finally, what role does culture play? Chapter 6 examines the social context of learning and the roles of the family, the peer group, and the community in the school achievement of individual learners. It also describes instructional strategies that can help all students become more effective communicators.

Chapter 4
An Ecology of Family, Home, and School

Focus Questions

- What might prevent children from making successful transitions between their multiple cultures?

- What is the role of the family in the socialization of culturally diverse children?

- What are ethnic images, and how might they influence a child's concept of self?

- How does the cultural systems approach account for persistent educational underachievement among culturally diverse populations in the United States?

- What is the difference between voluntary and involuntary minority population?

- How can schools develop and sustain their partnerships with students' families and communities?

- What are the advantages of scaffolding and the disadvantages of tracking and ability grouping?

> "In the seed lies critical ingredients for future growth, but the initial nurturance of that seed also determines the same growth."
>
> —CONRAD LORENZ

In any culture, important socialization practices formed within the context of family and home circumstances set the stage for a child's development for years to come. This chapter focuses on understanding students' multiple cultures and the transitions among them. It is my hope it will also provide information that will assist educators and others who work with students to build bridges across these cultures. We will look at family, school, and peer cultures, at the interrelationships among them, and in particular at how these cultures combine to affect children's engagement with learning. Of particular interest to us are the features in school environments that either aid or impede students' transitions between home and school.

The Meeting of Cultures

Before we can discuss the bridges we want to build across students' multiple cultures, we must identify the nature of the lines that separate these cultures. Some such boundaries are neutral in that sociocultural components experienced by the people on each side of the boundary are perceived as equal. When boundary lines are neutral, movement between cultures occurs with relative ease because the social and psychological costs to the individual are minimal. Alternately, when cultural borders are not neutral and when separate cultures are not perceived as equal, then movement and adaptation across borders are frequently difficult because the knowledge and skills in one culture are more highly valued and esteemed than those in the other. Although it is possible for students to navigate nonneutral borders with apparent success, these transitions can produce psychological effects that are invisible to teachers and others. Moreover, when the psychosocial consequences of adaptation across borders become too great for individuals to face, cultural boundaries become impenetrable barriers.

Cultural Boundary Lines

Earlier research generally has focused on families, peers, and schools as distinct cultural entities. We know that any one of these components can powerfully affect the direction in which students are pulled. For example, dynamic teachers, vigorous schools, and educational programs targeted to override the negative effects associated with low socioeconomic status, limited motivation, and language and cultural barriers can produce committed, interested, and academically engaged individuals (Abi-Nader, 1990a; Edmonds, 1979a; García, 1997; Heath, 1982; Joyce, Murphy, Showers, and Murphy, 1989; Slavin, 1989; Vogt, Jordan, and Tharp, 1987; Walberg, 1986a). Likewise, research on peer groups has described the potency and force with which members pull young people toward the norms of groups (Coleman, 1963; Eckert, 1989; Romo and Falbo, 1996; Ueda, 1987). We know too that family indices, such as socioeconomic status and parents' educational levels, are important predictors of students' engagement within educational settings (Jencks et al., 1972), as are cultural expectations and beliefs (Banks, C. A., and Banks, J., 1995; California Tomorrow, 1997; Clark, 1983; Erickson, 1987; Fordham, 1988; Gibson, 1987; Hoffman, 1988; McDermott, 1987; Ogbu, 1983, 1987a; Spindler, 1987; Spindler and Spindler, 1989; Suarez-Orozco, 1985, 1987; Trueba, 1982, 1999; Trueba, Moll, Diaz, and Diaz, 1982; Valdés, 1996). In other words, we know a great deal about how aspects of families, schools, teachers, and peer groups independently affect educational outcomes. But we need to know how these worlds combine in the day-to-day lives of students to influence their engagement within school and classroom contexts.

Influence on Students

As we attempt to create optimal school environments for increasingly diverse populations, educators need to know how students negotiate borders successfully—or, alternatively, how they are impeded by barriers that prevent their successful negotiation not only within an institutional context but also with peers who are different from themselves. Figure 4.1 attempts to portray graphically the interaction of cultures that students must learn to negotiate.

Although we still have much to learn about the complex interactions of culture, socialization, and education, at least now we are asking the right questions. That is, recent research focuses on understanding and facilitating successful interaction among cultures rather than on discounting the attributes of minority cultures to accommodate those of majority cultures. Sadly, this has not always been the case. In Chapter 3 we saw that for a long time U.S. schools have considered the unique language development of culturally diverse children as a limitation. The social attributes

Difference Seen as Negative

Figure 4.1   A Model of Children's Multiple Cultures

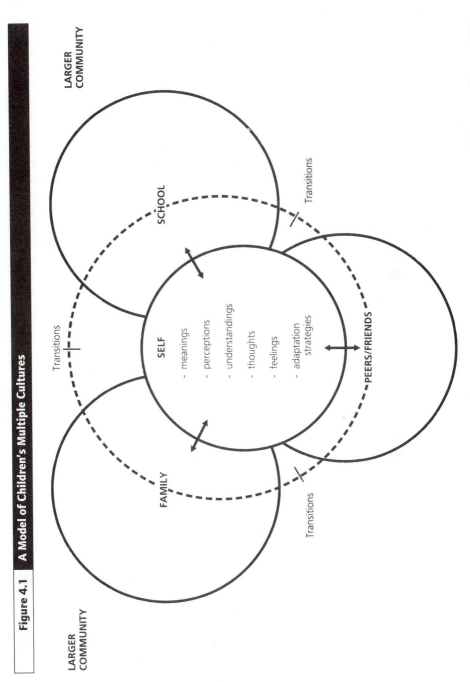

Source: Adapted from *Students' Multiple Worlds: Negotiating the Boundaries of Family, Peer, and School Cultures* (p. 56), by P. Phelan, A. L. Davidson, and H. T. Cao, 1991, Stanford, CA: Center for Research on the Context of Secondary Teaching.

133

of these children's family and home environments likewise have been viewed as detrimental to the students' social, economic, and educational success.

The desired effect of "Americanizing" students and adults was to socialize the culturally different community into the dominant culture. The early response was an attempt not only to change but also to segregate culturally diverse student populations to better serve these children while not contaminating the others.

Socializing Difference | Legally segregated schools thus arose for African Americans, Mexicans, Chinese, Jews, Germans, Poles, and others. Chapter 3 also described how American Indian students were segregated into government schools many thousands of miles away from their families and communities. The belief was that if schools could serve as the social institution that taught students English and instilled "American" values, then the negative social and economic conditions of these populations could be eradicated.

Americanization continues to be the goal of many programs aimed at culturally diverse populations in the United States. For students, Americanization means the elimination not only of linguistic and cultural differences but also of an undesirable culture. This schooling approach does not recognize the significant boundaries that exist between a student's family, community, and school and the necessity of providing students with transitions and bridges across these borders. Instead, it considers only the most negative perceptions of these differences while ignoring the positive effects of the interaction that always have and always will occur when cultures meet.

The Role of the Family in the Socialization of Children

Although the concept of Americanization has predominated in U.S. society, educational research during the last two decades has begun to regard ethnic culture as more than a target for elimination. Building on a foundation established by the noted anthropologist Margaret Mead (1937), more recent researchers have begun to explore socialization as a means by which cultural differences can be understood as opposed to eliminated (notably Gallimore and Tharp, 1989; Kagan, 1983b; Lave, 1988; McClintock, 1974; Nieto, 1979, 1992; Soto, 1997; Valdés, 1996; Valsiner, 1989).

One of the most significant functions of **socialization** is the transmission of values. By socialization, Mead (1937) and McClintock (1972) refer to the process through which prescriptions (ideas about what one should do) and prohibitions (ideas about what one should not do) are transmitted to members of the social

Agents of Socialization | group. The traditional view of socialization generally presented in the literature has emphasized the family, including siblings and members of the extended family, as important agents of socialization. More recent conceptualizations (e.g., Hetherington and Parke, 1988) have considered socialization agents outside the family, such as teachers, peers, the media (especially television), and other persons with whom the child regularly comes into contact.

Several authors have discussed the variables associated with family background, family structure, and the broader social ecology that influences the socialization experiences of culturally diverse children (Comer, 1997; Keefe and Padilla, 1987; Knight, Bernal, and Carlos, 1988; McClintock, Bayard, and McClintock, 1983; Whiting and Edwards, 1988). The variables of family structure shown to be related to the parents' socialization goals include (1) the strength of familial interdependence, (2) the pattern of status in relationships within the family, and (3) family size (see McClintock et al., 1983, for more details). Strength of familial interdependence consists of feelings of family solidarity as well as attachment and commitment to the family.

Family Variables |

How Home Life Shapes Classroom Behavior

Maria was identified by her first-grade teacher as very quiet. She hardly ever participated in classroom discussions. Even when the teacher specifically invited her to participate, she was very reticent. She did very well on individual activities, but the teacher worried about her shyness.

Becoming a Responsive Teacher

A videotaping project was scheduled for her classroom as part of a larger research project exploring the language development of the children. The teacher made a request to make a special effort to videotape Maria's interactions during specific whole-group lessons. These videotapes indicated that Maria was paying close attention to the teacher but never volunteered to participate and at times avoided eye contact with the teacher when the teacher attempted to make eye contact with her.

Another aspect of the videotaping captured students working together in small groups at "learning stations" that the teacher had throughout the room. During one of those tapings, Maria was observed leading a group of five students through the exercises at the station. She was quite verbal, asking the other students questions and directing their activity. In addition, the students in the group looked to her for guidance, overtly requesting her assistance. Subsequent videotape recordings of similar small-group interactions in which Maria participated always showed Maria playing an active or even a leading role. Yet, on the very same days, Maria continued to be nonparticipatory within any lesson activity led by the teacher.

The teacher was very interested in these contrasting behavior patterns. She watched the videotapes herself and was deeply puzzled by the distinct ways in which she saw Maria behave. Here was her shy Maria acting not shy at all—in many cases actually looked upon as a leader by her peers.

The teacher decided to ask Maria about her family circumstances and was not surprised by the answers. Maria was one of eight children—five older than she and two younger. Her parents and older brothers worked in the local fields, and Maria took major responsibilities for caring for her younger brother and sister whenever her mother was unavailable. Her family lived in a two-bedroom house that required sharing of space and related resources. "Mom and Dad made the rules and enforced them," Maria said—you respected their wishes;

Continued   How Home Life Shapes Classroom Behavior

you knew they knew best. When Maria was asked if she was ever consulted regarding her opinions, impressions, or suggestions, she politely indicated that Mom and Dad knew best: it would be disrespectful to offer any opinions.

The teacher now understood Maria's hesitancy in responding to her during group lessons. The teacher as adult was a person to be respected—she knew best. Maria would likely never volunteer opinions or in any way challenge the authority of the teacher. However, in small-peer-group circumstances, she seemed to be making use of her caretaking skills—those practiced and appropriately regarded in her family. Without the necessary attention of the teacher, this culture clash could have had negative educational consequences for Maria. The teacher's perceptions of Maria's choice not to respond during formal instruction could have led to an impression that Maria could not participate—that she was uninterested, unmotivated, or lacked the ability to handle the academic content in the lessons.

Needless to say, the teacher appreciated the new-found information. She understood that Maria worked best in small groups and that she needed to develop the ability to participate in larger groups led by adults.

Meeting the Challenge

1. Share the previous story about Maria with a few of your friends outside of this class. Describe the teacher's observations about Maria's two different behaviors and ask your friends why they think she would act so differently. After they offer some ideas, explain to them the concept of home-school culture clash and how it may influence children's learning experience. Report the results of your discussion to your classmates.

2. If the previously described small "learning stations" had not been an established part of Maria's classroom, what impression would her teacher have continued to have about her?

3. What is shyness? Compare your definition with those of your classmates. Describe learning environments that have made you feel reticent about participating and why.

There is some empirical evidence of particularly close family ties among Mexican American families (Keefe, 1979; Keefe, Padilla, and Carlos, 1979b). For example, research comparing Hispanic families with Anglo-American families suggests that Hispanic families demonstrate closer relations and greater loyalty among members, more frequent visits among relatives, parental encouragement of family-centered interactions, fewer opportunities for children to invite friends into the home, less freedom for children to play away from home, greater disapproval of children who contradict authority, and fewer decision-making opportunities for children. Similarly, Johnson, Teigen, and Davila (1983) found parents of Mexican backgrounds to be relatively demanding and restrictive of children compared with Anglo-American parents. Although we must be cautious of stereotyping all Hispanic families as showing strong interdependence among family members, McClintock et al. (1983) have speculated about the implications of this characteristic for a child's exposure to nonfamilial peers. Because of the greater emphasis on family-oriented interactions and within-family competition, it may be less relevant for a Hispanic child to compete with Anglo-American peers for recognition and rewards.

A related study of individual and cooperative socialization values explored the links between individuality and family connectedness in European American, Chinese American, Filipino American, Vietnamese American, and Hispanic American adolescents (Cooper, Baker, Polichar, and Welsh, 1991). Members of the three Asian American groups and the Hispanic American group reported much more concern for familial values than for the individual. In addition, members of these groups were much more likely to consider their siblings and peers, rather than their parents, as major sources of assistance and advice. By contrast, Anglo-American adolescents were much more individualistic in their perception of themselves in the family and more likely to seek out parents and adults for critical advice or support. Similarly, Seginer's (1989) study of the socialization of Arab adolescents found that older sisters play a key role in this process. These adolescents see their sisters as important consultants regarding the outside world, future plans, social relations, and education. Mothers are consulted only about pubertal changes, and fathers are consulted about permission, money, and political issues.

Still further evidence of cultural diversity in socialization practices comes from research on Native Alaskan families (Henze, Regan, Vanett, and Power, 1990). Interviews with Yup'ik families yielded a pattern of socialization that was centered not on the family but instead around those activities that are required for survival: the "men's house" provides instruction for boys in all

Diversity in
Socialization aspects of community life, and the home is where women transmit information to girls. This gender-separate social structure evolved over many years as the functions of each gender were organized to meet the harsh survival challenges of the group's environment. The concept or structure of a core nuclear or extended family is nonexistent in this culture. Moreover, as other studies of American Indian cultures have revealed (Tharp, 1989), Yup'ik children are expected to learn by carefully observing adults or older peers and siblings, without asking questions or interrupting activities. Such diverse socialization practices have too often been interpreted as deviant instead of merely different. We review these examples here to reinforce the overall thesis that the environment of children outside of school sets the stage for their lifelong patterns of social relations, including those that are important in the schooling process.

The Concept of Ecology

In this chapter, we shall use the concept of *ecology* to gain an understanding of the family, community, and school environments of children. **Ecology** is the study of the relationships between an organism and its environment.

Ecology of the Family. Valdés (1996), Delpit (1995), García and McLaughlin (1995), and Soto (1997) have documented in great detail the ecology of minority families as it relates to the schooling of their children. The findings can best be summarized by the conclusion that these families are under siege (Soto, 1997). Interviews with parents, children, and teachers revealed that, in general, these families seem to be immersed in hostile educational and community settings. Even in communities that have rich ethnic traditions of language and culture, poor families from diverse linguistic and cultural backgrounds, as well as some immigrants and certain other minorities who are socially well established, report feeling that they are perceived as a threat to the status quo (Nieto, 1992; Soto, 1997; Valdés, 1996). As Soto (1997) reports of Puerto Rican families in Pennsylvania, many parents have adopted a "swallowing hard" approach to these circumstances. Particularly harmful is the educational system's preference for advocacy by parents combined with the Puerto Rican parents' adaptive stance of passivity. In general, the parents know very well that their children are not doing well at school and that they are not welcomed there as other children are welcomed. Yet the parents believe that by not advocating (some would say, not complaining) and by "swallowing hard," they are actually improving their children's situation in school.

Attributes of
Successful
Families

There are, however, certain attributes of linguistically and culturally diverse families that can help promote children's success in school (Soto, 1997; Valdés, 1996). In a "successful" family, for example, the children are often raised bilingually with a clear appreciation for being bilingual and bicultural. Such families devise strategies to ensure that the children can use *both* languages in the home and community, and great importance is attached to such ability. These families also foster the children's pride in their culture's traditions through a variety of means, including intergenerational contacts, extended family interactions, and observance of special traditions (such as making *pasteles* and *tamales* at Christmas)—all of which require regular commitments of time and space.

Moreover, "successful" families support and nurture an appreciation of education for all family members. A micro learning community flourishes in the home, with parents teaching children, children sometimes teaching parents, and siblings and extended family members teaching one another. There is an overarching respect for each person's potential and actual contribution to the family. As Valdés (1996) indicates, these families are built on the notion that members act *con respeto* (with respect) toward one another.

Social Ecology

Factors in
Social Ecology

Besides the ecology of the family and the community, the broader social ecology has also been suggested as an important determinant in the socialization of children (Kagan, 1984; Keefe and Padilla, 1987). The social ecology includes such factors as the urbanization level of the community in which the child lives, the socioeconomic status of the family and the community, the nature of the minority status of other cultural groups in the community, and prevailing views about these cultural groups in the larger society.

In many ways, a more rural environment and/or an environment of relatively low socioeconomic status may lead to socialization experiences that foster interdependency, respect for others, and more sharing of resources. In contrast, a more urban environment may lead to socialization experiences that cultivate independence, competitiveness, and more reliance upon social supports that are external to the family. There has been some empirical demonstration of a relationship between the social behaviors of children and urbanization level (e.g., Kagan, Knight, Martinez, and Espinosa-Santana, 1981) and socioeconomic status (Knight and Kagan, 1977). Minority status may lead to considerable variability in socialization experiences simply because children from a minority population generally have direct contacts with members of the minority group as well as with members of the Anglo-American majority (Ogbu, 1982a, 1987a).

An Ecological System

The model of socialization briefly presented here suggests that characteristics of family background and structure and the broader social ecology are important determinants of the socialization practices to which children are exposed. We have barely scratched the surface of the many cultural differences that exist in socialization practices. Nonetheless, such conceptual rethinking of the child, the family, and the broader society as an ecological system is a far cry from the traditional tendency to regard cultural difference as a negative social attribute to be eliminated. Enlightened understanding of diverse student cultures cannot be founded on the Americanization strategy of taking all who are not "American" and making them "American." We will gain a clearer picture of the future for culturally diverse students in this country if we set aside issues of Americanization and instead concentrate on examining the nature of social variables and their relationship both to "cultural differences" and to educational practices and outcomes.

Ethnic Image and Its Effects

In recent decades, American society has made considerable progress in the area of race relations. Today many Anglo-Americans are more supportive of integration and racial equity than in the past (Oakes and Lipton, 1999). Federal and state governments have instituted numerous programs to promote integration and to assist members of minority groups in their efforts to attain educational and economic equality of opportunity (e.g., through busing, affirmative action, and minority contracting). In the next section we will discuss the findings of research studies that explore the ethnic images that continue to prevail in our society despite this progress toward equity.

Ethnic Images in Society

Two Questions

Recent research has explored shifts in racial tolerance and in people's images of different ethnic groups. This work has addressed two questions: (1) What are people's images of several major ethnic groups along various dimensions? (2) Do these images influence attitudes and behaviors toward those groups?

In this discussion, **ethnic** is used as a general term to refer to seven groups of people (whites, Jews, African Americans, Asian Americans, Hispanic Americans, Native Americans, and white

Southerners) who are differentiated partly by race, religion, nationality, and region of origin. **Ethnic images** describes people's general beliefs about cultural groups, in particular beliefs about group characteristics and attributes. We use the term *images* rather than words such as *stereotypes* or *prejudices* to avoid some of the baggage that is frequently associated with these words. For example, stereotypes and prejudice are often considered to contain a component of irrationality and to involve such fallacious thinking as improper generalization, excessive categorization, and rejection of counterevidence (Allport, 1954; Jackman, 1973; Schuman and Harding, 1964).

Contemporary relations between cultural groups in the United States cannot be understood without an examination of the images members of these groups have of themselves and of other groups. The notion that Americans are creating a color-and-creed-blind society is easily disabused by the data on ethnic images collected in the 1990 General Social Survey (Smith, 1990). First, these data indicate that people are willing and able to rate

Rating of Ethnicities others on the basis of their ethnicity. Second, with one exception, minority groups were evaluated more negatively than whites in general. The one exception among minority groups was Jews, who were rated more favorably than whites on each characteristic except patriotism. No other group scored above whites on any characteristic. In this study, Jews were rated most positively overall (first on wealth, industry, nonviolence, intelligence, and self-support, and third on patriotism). Asian Americans and white Southerners were ranked next (second or third) on almost every dimension. Finally, African Americans and Hispanic Americans were ranked last or next to last on almost every characteristic.

Ethnic images also are associated with the social distance that people wish to maintain between themselves and the members

Desired Social Distance of other groups. As the rating scale for each group moves from positive to negative, people are less favorable toward living in a neighborhood where half of their neighbors are from particular groups and toward having a close relative marry a member of one of those groups. All the groups showed a significant relationship between ethnic images and desired social distance, but the relationship between these factors for Jews and white Southerners was modest, whereas the relationship for African Americans, Asian Americans, and Hispanic Americans was strong.

This research shows that images about ethnic groups are significant predictors of support for racial integration and desired social distance. Despite the demonstrable progress in tolerance of cultural difference over the last several decades, ethnic images are still commonplace in contemporary U.S. society. On the whole, these images are neither benign nor trivial. Most members of the majority population in the United States see most minority groups in a decidedly negative light on a number of important characteristics. African Americans and Hispanic Americans in particular receive very low ratings. These negative ethnic images in turn help shape people's attitudes toward civil rights and racial integration. Ethnic images remain important determinants of public opinion on affirmative action, school desegregation, and many other group-related issues.

In considering explicit theories of the importance of race, Delgado (1995) describes features of a **Critical Race Theory (CRT).** Critical Race Theory begins with one basic insight: Racism is normal, not aberrant, in American society. Formal equality can do little about the business-as-usual forms of racism that people of color confront every day and that account for much misery, alienation, and despair. CRT's challenge to racial oppression and the status quo sometimes takes the form of storytelling, in which writers analyze the myths, presuppositions, and received wisdom that make up the common culture about race and that invariably render Hispanics, African Americans, American Indians, and other minorities "one-down" (Delpit, 1988; Ladson-Billings and Tate, 1995, Renato, 1993; Vizenor, 1998).

Moreover, CRT proposes an analysis of "interest-convergence." Developed by Derrick Bell (1980a), this idea holds that Anglo-American elites will tolerate or encourage racial and ethnic advances only when they also promote Anglo-American self-interest. President Clinton had hopes that as the nation entered the twenty-first century, the attention directed toward African Americans and other minorities in America would differ from that given them at the beginning of the twentieth century. Unfortunately, as Cornell West (1999) argues, for nearly a century, since the writings of W. E. B. Du Bois, the nation has confined discussion about race in America to "problems" that people of color pose for society—meaning the Anglo-American majority—rather than consider what this way of viewing people of color reveals about us as a nation. National discussions, with different spins and various twists, have recently begun to feature a particularly negative tone when focusing on African American, Hispanic, Asian, and Anglo-American relations. Race and ethnicity seem to continue to drive us apart, but, as race theorists have concluded, they do so to the disadvantage of minorities and to the advantage of Anglo-Americans.

CRT, which indicates the existence of socially constructed disadvantages, takes on special significance for schooling in the United States. At one level, it means that the society as a whole must come to understand that these social constructions may lead to academic underachievement for culturally, linguistically, and racially diverse students. The curriculum therefore must take on a special mission to engage all students in learning about these so-cial contructions. In essence, we are all responsible for the social construction of these inequities; therefore, we are all similarly re-sponsible for their deconstruction. But of special significance is the need to engage the "disadvantaged" directly in understanding their own circumstances and the reasons for those circumstances and in the critical analysis of how they might overcome such cir-cumstances (Aronowitz and Giroux, 1991). It becomes incumbent upon educational institutions to embrace a "critical pedagogy" (Giroux, 1992) that seeks to equip those disadvantaged by existing social structures and organizations with the intellectual means to remove those encumbrances.

Effects of Ethnic Images on Children

How do ethnic images shape a child's personality? Following from the work of Smith (1990), personality may be understood as a structure that reconciles children's interpreted experiences and emotional states. Those experiences and emotions, in turn, are shaped by the social attributes ascribed to an individual by oth-ers. A sense of ethnic identity is part of that synthesis. In a world populated by people of many different ethnic backgrounds who often interact and conflict with each other, a child's developing sense of ethnic group identity is an important social issue. Sev-eral studies of the development of ethnic identity have focused both on children's ability to identify their own ethnic group and on their attitudes toward their own and other groups (McAdoo and McAdoo, 1985).

Research performed by Clark and Clark (1939) was perhaps the most famous inquiry into the development of ethnic identity, be-cause the results became evidence that led the U.S. Supreme Court to declare racially segregated education illegal. In the Clarks' work, African American and Anglo-American children aged three years and older were presented with pairs of dolls rep-resenting each ethnic group. On successive trials the children were asked to choose "which boy [doll] you would like to play with" or "which girl [doll] you don't like." The Clarks reported that most of the youngest children distinguished between the gender categories of the dolls and that both the African American children displayed a preference for the Anglo-American dolls. These results were interpreted by the justices of the Supreme Court as evidence that segregation resulted in the development of a negative sense of self among African American children. Studies conducted since the 1950s both confirm the Clarks' origi-nal findings (McAdoo and McAdoo, 1985; Spencer, M. B., 1988) and extend them to other minority ethnic groups, including Na-

Negative Self-Concept

tive Americans (Beauf, 1977). In all of these studies, children of minority groups were more likely to prefer Anglo-American dolls.

Importantly, these same studies have cast doubt on the notion that children from minority ethnic groups acquire a generalized negative self-concept. Beauf (1977), for example, reports incident after incident in which Native American children who display a preference for Anglo-American dolls also demonstrate with devastating accuracy an understanding of the economic and social circumstances that make their lives difficult in contrast with the lives of Anglo-Americans. Five-year-old Dom was given several dolls representing Anglo-Americans and Native Americans (whose skins were represented as brown) to put into a toy classroom.

Recognition of Inequalities

Dom: (holding up a white doll) The children's all here and now the teacher's coming in.

Interviewer: Is that the teacher?

Dom: Yeah.

Interviewer: (holding up a brown doll) Can she be the teacher?

Dom: No way! Her's just an aide. (Beauf, 1977, p. 207)

In Beauf's view, the choices children make when presented with pairs of dolls that represent different ethnic groups are less an expression of their self-concept than of their desire for the power and wealth of the Anglo-Americans with whom they have come into contact.

Other recent research has shown that when psychologists attempt to test the social concepts and self-concepts of young children, their expressed ethnic preferences change according to the circumstances. McAdoo and McAdoo (1985) report that the degree to which African American preschoolers show a preference for Anglo-American dolls has decreased relative to the results obtained in studies performed prior to the 1960s. She does not speculate on the reasons for these trends, but the end of racial segregation and several decades of political and cultural activism in the African American community are likely candidates. This conclusion is reinforced by Beauf's (1977) finding that young Native American children whose parents were active in promoting Native American cultural awareness and social rights chose dolls representing Native Americans more often than children whose parents took little interest in Native American affairs.

Environment and Self-Concept

Additional evidence of the power of the environment to shape children's ethnic preferences comes from an experimental study that rewarded children aged three to five for choosing black versus white pictures of animals and people (Spencer and Horowitz,

1973). Initially all the children showed a preference for white stimuli (both animals and people), but after training sessions in which they received symbolic rewards (marbles that could be traded for cookies) for either choice, all children displayed a marked preference for black stimuli, and that preference remained intact over a period of several weeks.

In sum, the results of studies on ethnic identity indicate that children are aware of differences by the time they are four years old. At the same age, or not long after, they also become aware of and form judgments about their own ethnicity. These views, as well as their attitudes toward other people's ethnicity, seem to depend on both the beliefs of their adult caregivers and the perceived power and wealth of their own ethnic group.

A Cultural Systems Account of Underachievement

So far in this chapter we have discussed the relationship between culture and education by concentrating on issues of family, home, and socialization practices experienced by individual students. By its very nature, such a "micro" approach focuses on an individual student's social contact with parents, siblings, peers, and other representatives of social institutions. These interactions are seen as forming and guiding the student's communicative, cognitive, social, and educational development. In short, these interactions prepare the way for either educational success or educational failure.

An alternative to this intense focus on the individual student is the "macro" approach proposed by a number of anthropologists and sociologists. This approach broadens the examination to the cultural system. A system is a network of interrelating elements that form a complex whole. A cultural system, then, is a group of interacting cultural elements. The **cultural systems approach** to education considers the organization of a society, specifically the roles and status assigned to cultural groups within a society, to be a major determinant of educational underachievement (Gibson and Ogbu, 1991; Ogbu, 1982a, 1987b, 1992b; Ogbu and Matute-Bianchi, 1986; Solorzano, 1997b; Stanton-Salazar, 1997). Known by such names as the *structural inequality theory* (Gollnick and Chinn, 1990), *institutional racism* (Ovando and Collier, 1985), the *perceived labor market explanation* (Erickson, 1987), and most notably, the *secondary cultural systems theory* (Ogbu, 1992a, 1999), this approach suggests that the specific social placement of a cultural group within the broader social fabric will directly affect the values, perceptions, and social behavior of members of that group.

Broader Approach |

As it pertains to the education of culturally diverse groups in the United States, the cultural systems approach suggests that members of minority groups become convinced by the overall social order that their "place" in society is distinctively disadvantaged. In essence, students from minority backgrounds recognize that they are generally perceived as less intelligent, lazy, and dependent, and begin to take on these attributes themselves, particularly in response to perceptions held by social groups that wield political and economic power. As we saw in the previous section, the ethnic images that label some cultural groups as "lesser" have long persevered in our society despite outward signs of progress.

Ogbu (1999) has been an important spokesperson for the cultural systems approach to understanding the disproportionate school failure of some minority populations in the United States and throughout the world. His analysis carefully distinguishes **Types of Minority Groups** between immigrant or voluntary minorities and nonimmigrant or nonvoluntary minorities (also called "castelike," "outcast," or "pariah" minorities). The term *minority* suggests a group that is smaller numerically. When considered in a social context, however, minority usually refers to a group that is subordinate to a dominant group by a negative power relationship. Numerical majority does not guarantee a group dominant status. In Latin America, India, and Africa, for example, millions of native peoples historically were in a subordinate position to a minority of colonial powers (Oakes and Lipton, 1999).

Ogbu's (1999) analysis suggests that members of voluntary and involuntary minority groups may live in the same society and experience the same circumstances: prejudice, discrimination, residential segregation, inferior education for their children, and exclusion from desirable jobs. However, voluntary minorities often do well in school and sometimes are more successful academically than students in the dominant group. In the United States, for example, East Asian students often test higher on standardized testing than Anglo-American students. By contrast, involuntary minorities such as African Americans, Hispanics, and American Indians consistently have problems in school, perform below grade level, and have high dropout rates.

Ogbu and Matute-Bianchi (1986) elaborate on a conceptual framework regarding the distinction between voluntary and involuntary minority groups. Table 4.1 defines these two types of minority status. Tables 4.2 through 4.5 further describe these groups and chart their responses to and interpretations of prejudice and discrimination, based on a synthesis of Ogbu and Matute-Bianchi (1986) and Ogbu (1992a).

Table 4.1	Terms of Minority Status

Voluntary Minority

1. Moved voluntarily to host society
2. Chose to emigrate for
    a. greater political freedom (including escaping death, imprisonment, or torture in homeland)
    b. economic well-being
    c. better overall opportunities
3. Experience in host society may include prejudice, exploitation, and discrimination in the form of
    a. residential segregation
    b. inferior education for their children
    c. job ceiling: exclusion from jobs even when qualified (particularly desirable jobs)
    d. low wages
    e. cultural and intellectual derogation
4. Primary cultural discontinuities (cultural and language barriers)
    a. existed before minority group came into contact with dominant group
    b. are perceived as barriers to be overcome to achieve goals of immigration
    c. are specific; have to do with "content"
    d. cause initial problems for teachers, peers, and learning but diminish over time; are attributed to deficiencies in cultural assumptions

Involuntary Minority

1. Involuntarily incorporated through slavery, conquest, colonization, birth, and relegated to menial status
2. Did not choose to emigrate
3. Experience in "host" society is one of prejudice, discrimination, and exploitation in the form of
    a. residential segregation
    b. inferior education for their children
    c. job ceiling: exclusion from jobs even when qualified (particularly desirable jobs)
    d. low wages
    e. cultural and intellectual derogation
4. Secondary cultural discontinuities (cultural and language barriers)
    a. arose as coping mechanisms after minority group was subjected to the power of dominant group
    b. are perceived as markers of social identity to be maintained
    c. are general; have to do with "style" (interaction, communication, cognition, learning)
    d. cause problems that do not tend to diminish over time; are attributed to social opposition and negative personal characteristics

Ogbu (1992a) proposes that the cultural models for voluntary and involuntary minorities differ in five key elements:

1. A frame of reference for comparing present status and future possibilities (see Table 4.2)

2. A folk theory of how to succeed, especially through education (see Table 4.3)

3. A sense of collective identity (see Table 4.4)

4. A cultural frame of reference for judging appropriate behavior and affirming group membership and solidarity (see Table 4.5)

5. An assessment of the extent to which one may trust members of the dominant group and the institutions they control

Table 4.2	Frame of Reference for Comparing Present Status and Future Possibilities

Voluntary Minority

1. **Positive dual frame of reference:**
   a. compare life in host society to that in homeland ("there")
   b. perceive position "here" to be much better
   c. perceive themselves as foreigners, outsiders, guests
2. Believe that "foreigners" must tolerate prejudice and discrimination of dominant group to achieve emigration goals; not highly influenced by such negative factors.
3. View situation as temporary because
   a. they can return home
   b. they can emigrate elsewhere with wealth and credentials
   c. it will improve through education and hard work
4. **Perception of job ceiling:**
   a. menial position "here" compared with worse position at home
   b. exclusion from better jobs is caused by "foreigner" status, inability to speak the language, education elsewhere

Involuntary Minority

1. **Negative dual frame of reference:**
   a. compare life to that of members of dominant group
   b. perceive position to be much worse
   c. perceive themselves as denigrated and subordinated members of dominant society
2. See no justification for dominant group's belief that minorities are biologically, religiously, socially, and culturally inferior; highly influenced by such a negative attitude
3. View situation as permanent and institutionalized because
   a. they have no other home
   b. they cannot leave present circumstances
   c. it will not improve through education and hard work
4. **Perception of job ceiling:**
   a. menial position compared with jobs held by dominant group members
   b. exclusion from better jobs is caused by the fact that they are a disparaged group relegated to menial position

According to Ogbu (1992b), "the different cultural models resulting from these differing theories and frameworks are learned by the children and shape the attitudes, knowledge and competencies they bring to the school" (p. 141).

As a theoretical framework, this conceptualization of educational underachievement allows us to begin to understand the

Table 4.3	Folk Theory of How to Succeed

Voluntary Minority

Value education, hard work, and individual effort as a means of "making it" and diminishing discrimination. As a result,

1. accept parts of the mainstream dominant culture
2. adopt the challenge of assimilating into the dominant culture

Involuntary Minority

Do not perceive education, hard work, and individual effort as a means of "making it"; believe discrimination is permanent. As a result,

1. reject the value system of the mainstream dominant culture
2. develop a folk theory in opposition to the values of the dominant group

Table 4.4	**Sense of Collective Identity**

Voluntary Minority	Involuntary Minority
Maintain a sense of the social identity they had before emigration, at least through the first generation. Thus,	Form a new sense of peoplehood or social identity in opposition to the "oppressor." Thus,
1. may not approve of certain aspects of dominant culture or want to be like dominant group members, but do not develop oppositional identity	1. identity is forged from group's ancestral heritage and present interpretations of discrimination and denial of equal treatment

reasons for different educational outcomes for different populations of students. For example, Suarez-Orozco (1987) proposes that the different Hispanic American groups—Mexican Americans, Puerto Rican Americans, and Americans of Cuban, Central American, and South American descent, as well as recent refugees from Central America—are distinct populations and should be understood as such. They face different issues and have different patterns of educational adaptation. Suarez-Orozco (1985) reports that whereas nationwide one-fourth of Mexican Americans aged 25 or older had less than five years of schooling, the same was true for only 6 percent of other Hispanics. In the southwestern states, only 60 percent of Mexican Americans were reported to have graduated from high school compared with 86 percent of Anglo-Americans. Many Central American refugees, however, are experiencing school success.

Different Educational Outcomes

Table 4.5	**Cultural Frame of Reference for Judging Appropriate Behavior and Affirming Group Membership and Solidarity**

Voluntary Minority	Involuntary Minority
1. Alternation model: group members	1. Cultural inversion model: group members
a. believe it is possible and acceptable to participate in two different cultures or two different languages for different purposes, alternating one's behavior to the situation	a. assume it is not possible or appropriate for the same individual to participate in cultures of the dominant group and of the minority group
b. become acculturated without assimilating; dominant culture is not seen as threatening; believe it is necessary to cross cultural boundaries to achieve emigration goal	b. experience linear acculturation; crossing cultural boundaries is seen as threat to minority identity, culture, and language
	c. communicate disapproval for "acting white"
2. Stress cultural values of the homeland in family and community but believe that members	2. Stress collective efforts and struggle, so members
a. must accept the rules of the host society	a. legitimate civil rights activities as well as rioting to change rules because the rules don't work for them

An ethnographic study of two hundred Central American refugees at two schools in San Francisco found that the ideas these new immigrants had developed about the nature of opportunity in this country allowed them to succeed academically. This success was surprising. These students "were routinely routed to overcrowded, understaffed, poor inner city schools, into a poisonous atmosphere of drugs and violence," where teachers were afraid of their students (Suarez-Orozco, 1985, p. 125). They learned English quickly but were tracked into low-level classes they had already completed in their own countries. Yet many were highly motivated to persevere and to succeed in school. The Central American immigrants were perceived by their teachers as desirable students—eager to learn, appreciative, polite, respectful, and hard-working.

According to Suarez-Orozco (1987), these recent Central American immigrants developed a dual frame of reference in which they compared their situation in the United States with that in their homeland. Most perceived that they had more and better opportunities here. The students believed it was self-evident that the future was open to them. Their parents overlooked the difficulties and emphasized the positive: the United States was fairer; schools, hot lunches, and libraries were free; and teachers seemed sincerely interested in their students. These immigrants developed a folk theory of "making it" in which education became the single most significant factor in getting ahead. This was in contrast to the method of getting ahead at home, which was based on connections: "who you know." In the United States, they felt, getting ahead was based on "what you know." The students believed their parents were doing everything they could for them and in turn felt a duty to succeed and to remove other loved ones from dangerous situations in the homeland. No matter how bad things were here, they were not as bad as at "home."

How to Get Ahead

With a similar interest in distinctions between minority groups, Matute-Bianchi (1990) focused on diversity within a population of students of Mexican descent at Field High School on the central coast of California. Conducted between 1983 and 1985, her ethnographic research included interviews with teachers, counselors, aides, administrators, students of Mexican descent, and her own observations. From this research she distinguished among five major categories or "cultural" groups of students of Mexican descent:

1. *Recent Mexican immigrants:* Self-identify as "Mexicanos"; have arrived in the last three to five years; refer to Mexico as home; came to the United States for economic opportunity; considered "unstylish" by other students; proficiency in

Spanish (oral and written) tends to be an indicator of school success.

2. *Mexican-oriented:* Maintain a strong identity as Mexicano; frequently Mexican-born but have lived in the United States most of their lives; parents are immigrants; tend to be bilingual; adept at academic work in English, having received most schooling here; speak English with school personnel, Spanish and English with peers, Spanish at home; active in Sociedad Bilingüe (Bilingual Society); proud of Mexican heritage; many students with Spanish surnames who are in college prep from this group.

3. *Mexican Americans:* U.S.-born English speakers who are much more U.S.-oriented than previous groups; may not speak Spanish at home unless necessary; participate in mainstream activities; tend not to call attention to their ethnicity; include some of the most esteemed students of Mexican descent in the school; described by staff as "totally acculturated."

4. *Chicanos:* At least second generation of their family in the United States of Mexican descent; loyal to their own group and avoid school activities; call themselves "homeboys" and "homegirls," call academically successful students "schoolboys" or "wannabes" ("want to be white"); among the most alienated students in the school.

5. *Cholos:* Smallest group in the school; noted for culturally distinct style of dressing that represents an identity that is neither Mexican nor American; "gang-oriented" or "gang sympathizers"; "low riders" (drive vintage and modern automobiles that are altered to sit low on the ground and decoratively painted to reflect cultural ideologies); perceived to be gang members; feared and held in contempt by other students of Mexican descent and mainstream Anglo-American students.

Patterns in School Performance | Matute-Bianchi emphasized the different forms and functions of ethnic labels and self-identity in immigrant and nonimmigrant Mexican groups in the United States. She traced the relationships among these factors to variations in school performance and discovered a pattern of school success among immigrant Mexican-oriented students and of school failure among nonimmigrant Chicanos. The two groups were perceived differently by teachers and students, and members of the groups themselves had different perceptions of what their futures held in terms of employment.

According to Matute-Bianchi, the successful students of Mexican descent were achievement- and goal-oriented. They saw a connection between high school success and adult success. They defined success as having a nice car, a nice house, a good job, and no money worries. They wanted to go to college, although they were not sure of a career choice. They had both Anglo-American and Mexican role models in school. Most stated that interest and support from their parents were essential to their school success, which they defined as the result of attending school regularly, doing homework, asking for help, getting along with teachers, and working "as hard as you can." Some had received support from teachers and counselors.

The Chicanos and Cholos expressed the desire to get good jobs but did not have an idea of how that was accomplished. They did not feel a connection to the future in a positive way and lived for the moment or the weekend. They doubted that they would graduate, even though they wanted to. They had little exposure to occupations other than the menial and physically difficult jobs of low status at which their parents worked. They could not think of one successful adult of Mexican descent whom they knew well. Although they expressed desire to do well, they exhibited behaviors that resulted in school failure: truancy, disruptive behavior, failure to bring books and homework, poor performance in class, and failure to pass enough classes to maintain academic standing. They were apathetic and defiant of school culture.

In Gibson and Ogbu (1991) similar findings in fieldwork carried out in Saint Croix (U.S. Virgin Isands) during the 1970s to study the relationship among ethnic identity, immigrant status, and school performance are described. Their results were similar to those of Matute-Bianchi (1990). In the Saint Croix public schools, immigrants were more successful than natives, even though they were similar in class status, color, and cultural background. This

pattern shows up in other settings. In the United States, for example, "Asian Americans (Koreans, Japanese, and Chinese) are the only minority group whose academic achievement surpasses that of whites" (Lee, 1991, p. 3). They exhibit higher college attendance rates and higher achievement scores than the Anglo-American majority. But Korean students, who in the United States achieve as well as Japanese students, do not fare as well in Japan, where they have much lower achievement rates than Japanese students. In Japan the college attendance rate of Korean high school graduates was less than 60 percent of the rate of Japanese high school grads. Lee (1991) suggests that the historical experience of Koreans in these two host societies provides valuable insight into the effect of cultural systems on academic achievement.

Specifically, Lee argues, Koreans have had an increasingly positive image in the United States for two reasons: (1) Korea has become of strategic and economic importance to the United States, and (2) most Koreans in the United States are educated people with middle-class backgrounds. With the exception of physicians, however, Koreans have found it difficult to enter the U.S. middle-class mainstream because of the language barrier, their inability to transfer skills acquired in Korea, and discrimination against them in large businesses.

Although some claim (Erickson, 1987) that Ogbu (1986) sees "a social revolution" as the only way out of the situation involuntary minorities find themselves in, Ogbu (1999) does not in fact reach that conclusion. What he does stress is that educational practices and programs must be based on appropriate research. He points out that many intervention programs are based on the idea that ethnic minorities are "culturally deprived," "culturally deficient," or "socially disadvantaged" and that the school's role is to "redeem" them. He differentiates between "improvement research" and "explanatory research." He is interested in providing explanatory research, in particular comparative ethnographic research, "the long range goal of which is to provide knowledge for better and more effective educational policy as well as for preventative and remedial efforts" (Ogbu, 1987a). He cautions against instigating educational change without first understanding both the "micro" and the "macro"—the individual and the societal—aspects of underachievement in ethnic minority populations.

Research That Explains

Responsible

Educational Implications

A distinction can be made between ethnic studies (the study of ethnic groups) and a sociocultural approach to language, culture, and education. This distinction does not diminish the significance of ethnic studies. From the point of view of schooling practices, however, approaching contexts of learning for culturally diverse youth with a focus on ethnic studies poses difficulties—and, in fact, can be dangerous. Because it is impossible for educators to acquire complete ethnological knowledge of the student groups they will encounter, the knowledge they do acquire tends to be laden with stereotypes. These stereotypes in turn often lead to the assumption of cultural deprivation: Because a culture is different, it is deficient. Educators should focus on understanding the intersection of the school context with the student's family, home, and community contexts, not only on understanding the differences among ethnic cultures.

Ethnic Studies Alone Are Insufficient

Educational Implications of Family Diversity

Soto (1997) has offered advice that can help schools serve the families of culturally diverse students. In Soto's study, the families themselves articulated the need for schools to move away from paradigms of shame to paradigms of compassion—that is, the need for schools to overcome an oppressive climate that devalues the language and culture of the home. When culturally diverse families were asked, "What advice do you have for schools?" the following themes emerged:

Families' Advice for Schools

1. *Provide culturally diverse students with access to quality programs.* Families envisioned "quality programs" as those in which the following conditions prevail: children's linguistic and cultural gifts are valued; expectations are high; academic learning is the norm; humanistic and democratic approaches are implemented; culturally diverse children are well represented in gifted programs; leaders are created; teachers care about the children; the classrooms are clean and brimming with colorful materials; children learn about technology; creativity is appreciated; communication between school and family takes place; problem-solving is evident; all children experience a world of equity and justice.

2. *Implement programs that preserve home languages and cultures.* Parents valued highly those instances of schooling that

acknowledged parental language and culture. Parents were most appreciative when the teachers communicated with them in Spanish and regarded the use of Spanish in the classroom as a positive educational attribute.

3. *Integrate caring and humanistic approaches to learning.* Early, painful educational experiences of culturally diverse students who had nevertheless done well in school led parents of these "success stories" to conclude that children find it difficult to overcome oppressive educational climates. Parents reported that their children had done well academically despite the system, not because of it.

4. *Accept the fact that institutions of learning are not the only knowledge brokers in society.* Schools must become respectful of the knowledge and wisdom families can impart.

5. *Model ways of encouraging linguistic and cultural integrity at school.* Celebrating culturally relevant holidays and customs was particularly appreciated. Similarly, the school's understanding of extended family responsibilities, such as grandparents' or siblings' role in caretaking, was valued by the families in the study.

6. *Initiate mentoring relationships for minority students.* The mentoring roles described by the families were often quite simple and mechanical in nature. Helping students with college applications was one suggestion. In addition, establishing "ways of relating" to children that reflect high expectations and value persistence was important for parents.

7. *Interact and communicate in ways that value the linguistic and cultural background of families.* If children see that the adults in their learning environment value the language and culture of their homes, it stands to reason that they will gain pride in their families. The human relations and communicative patterns children observe in the "worlds of childhood" can have a long-lasting impact on how they regard themselves, their family, and their nation.

8. *Provide ethical and knowledgeable advice.* The parents raised such issues as the following: Is it ethical for schools to encourage families to speak only English at home? Is it ethical for schools to devalue children's home language and culture? Are schools offering knowledgeable advice about the optimal education practices for diverse learners? The families interviewed perceived schools as being neither knowledgeable nor ethical on matters affecting the daily educational realities of their children.

Power and Privilege in Parent Involvement

Too often, involvement models are derived from a tradition of democratic educational philosophy in which education and schooling are viewed as politically neutral forces that serve as a form of social amelioration. From this perspective, the various models for parent involvement are conceived as programs to strengthen the school's role as a meritocratic ladder for individual social mobility. Although schools do provide a means of social mobility, it is, in fact, severely constrained for marginalized culturally and linguistically diverse groups. Yet the democratic perspective gives little attention to the legacy and extant conditions of injustice that are fundamentally and systematically structured into schooling. This lack of attention diminishes the reality of the political, economic, and racial conflicts that are deeply embedded in the educational system.

What is missing, then, is a recognition of the dynamics of power, authority, and control that underlie the experiences of all parents on the political terrain of public education (Fine, 1993). Family-school policies informed by the democratic perspective—and its attendant aversion to issues of power—are characterized by the promotion of a model of consensus (reflected in the common usage of the term *partnership*) and an emphasis on increasing an individual parent's participation in education (Lareau and Shumar, 1996).

Unfortunately, refusing to acknowledge the presence of that which we do not wish to see will not cause the problem to disappear, and, as in this case, can instead serve to maintain privilege. According to Ruth Frankenburg (1993), this approach is indicative of a particular "discursive moment" that she labels "power evasiveness," which is currently widely represented in the public's thinking. Power evasiveness selectively acknowledges difference but succumbs to "power-blindness" when considering the power imbalances underlying the link between differences and inequality.

Researchers who contextualize family-school connections within deeper patterns of social inequality address power head-on:

> I suggest that "power" undergirds the knowledge required on the part of parents to deal with school. . . . Power is the capacity to produce intended, foreseen, and unforeseen effects on others to accomplish results on behalf of oneself. How one utilizes power determines the extent to which individuals or organizations access valued resources. (Delgado-Gaitan, 1991, p. 22)

Parental involvement is an issue of power, and power is not equally distributed across social groups. But because power relations are rooted in the larger inequalities of American society, they are sometimes not noticed. (Lareau and Shumar, 1996, p. 30)

Put simply, these researchers suggest that the ways in which schools care about their students are reflected in the ways in which they care about the students' families. Proactive efforts to involve parents always seem to be on the agenda of elementary schools, but the effort tends to waver in later years of schooling. In addition, parent involvement is unfortunately often more rhetoric than reality in schools that serve a highly diverse population. But as Edwards (1995) and Epstein (1995) point out, this need not be the case, and they have identified several important components related to developing a strong and functional partnership between home and school:

1. *Development of parenting:* Educational and related agencies can organize ways in which basic information on parenting and child and family development can be conveyed to families. Since all parents are learning while doing, support for that learning process can be useful for the parents, the children, the family, and the educational staff.

2. *Family-school communication:* Systematic and ongoing communication between the family and school is critical. This can be accomplished both formally and informally, utilizing school events, teacher-parent conferences, home visits, parent journals, and student portfolios. Communication from the school in the language of the family lays the groundwork for developing a trusting relationship, which in turn will allow parents to become more aware of and involved in their important role in the education of their children.

3. *Parental participation in school governance:* Most local, state, and federal education policies require some sort of parental involvement in the governance and/or decision-making activities of the school. Yet such participation is too often peripheral (Edwards, 1995), selective, and constrained. Although parental participation does not mean that parents should "control" the school, it ought to be more than window dressing.

4. *Families and cultural groups in the school:* Many schools actively recruit volunteers or instructional assistants from their students' families or from representatives of linguistic and/or cultural groups that reside in the community. Such efforts do much to enhance the partnership opportunities and involve families directly in the educational process. This is particularly useful for immigrant families and communities, who can

begin to learn about the educational process first-hand through such participation in the schools.

5. *Home support for teaching and learning:* Too often, poor and non-English-speaking parents come to the conclusion that they cannot help their children with homework or related academic assignments. They themselves have likely not had the same educational experiences as their children or have had a history of educational failure. Yet even if this is the case, they can be a critical motivational and structural support for their children's academic success. As indicated earlier in this volume, parents of successful students and parents of those who are less successful display little difference in their aspirations for their children's school achievement. Often the difference lies in the parents' instrumental knowledge, not in their academic knowledge, as it relates to helping their children become academically successful. *Instrumental knowledge* refers to those understandings about what is expected, required, and acceptable at school. All parents, once armed with this type of knowledge, can play a key role in their children's school success, even if they cannot directly assist them with academic subject matter. More direct efforts at enhancing family participation in teaching and learning, such as family math and family literacy programs, have quite effectively involved parents in content-area instructional support for their children.

Epstein (1995) has elaborated on many of these areas of parental and family involvement. Table 4.6 provides an excellent summary of the types of involvement and related practices that she has identified in her national studies of school/ family/community partnerships; Table 4.7 offers challenges and redefinitions of these sorts of partnerships, including issues of "power" sharing.

Building Bridges Between Diverse Cultures

In Chapter 2 we saw how school and the classroom arrangements within it can be seen as analogous to a culture. The classroom has many explicit cultural elements, but it also has hidden cultural dimensions that Phillips (1984) and others have described. Children themselves often feel deeply the numerous cultural demands of the school.

Some of the classic work on this issue has been done by Labov (1972b), who studied the same group of children across different social domains of the school culture. Specifically, he observed educational testing encounters arranged in a number of ways.

Table 4.6   School/Family/Community Partnerships: Types and Sample Practices

Type 1 Parenting	Type 2 Communicating	Type 3 Volunteering	Type 4 Learning at Home	Type 5 Decision-Making	Type 6 Collaborating with Community
Help all families establish home environments to support children as students.	Design effective forms of school-to-home and home-to-school communications about school programs and children's progress.	Recruit and organize parent help and support.	Provide information and ideas to families about how to help students at home with homework and other curricumum-related activities, decisions, and planning.	Include parents in school decisions, developing parent leaders and representatives.	Identify and integrate resources and services from the community to strengthen school programs, family practices, and student learning and development.
Sample Practices	**Sample Practices**	**Sample Practices**	**Sample Practices**	**Sample Practices**	**Sample Practices**
Suggestions for home conditions that support learning at each grade level. Workshops, videotapes, and computerized phone messages on parenting and child-rearing at each age and grade level.	Conferences with every parent at least once a year, with follow-ups as needed. Language translators to assist families as needed. Weekly or monthly folders of student work sent home for review and comments.	School and classroom volunteer program to help teachers, administrators, students, and other parents. Parent room or family center for volunteer work, meetings, and resources for families.	Information for families on skills required for students in all subjects at each grade. Information on homework policies and how to monitor and discuss schoolwork at home.	Active PTA/PTO or other parent organizations, advisory councils, or committees (e.g., curriculum, safety, personnel) for parent leadership and participation. Independent advocacy groups to lobby and work for school reform and improvements.	Information for students and families on community health, cultural, recreational, and social support, and other programs or services. Information on community activities that link to learning skills and talents, including summer programs for students.

Parent education and other courses or training for parents (e.g., GED, college credit, family literacy).

Family support programs to assist families with health, nutrition, and other services.

Home visits at transition points to preschool, elementary, middle, and high school. Neighborhood meetings to help families understand schools and to help schools understand families.

Parent/student pickup of report card, with conferences on improving grades.

Regular schedule of useful notices, memos, phone calls, newsletters, and other communications.

Clear information on choosing schools or courses, programs, and activities within schools.

Clear information on all school policies, programs, reforms, and transitions.

Annual postcard survey to identify all available talents, times, and locations of volunteers.

Class parent, telephone tree, or other structures to provide all families with needed information.

Parent patrols or other activities to aid safety and operation of school programs.

Information on how to assist students to improve skills on various class and school assessments.

Regular schedule of homework that requires students to discuss and interact with families on what they are learning in class.

Calendars with activities for parents and students at home.

Family math, science, and reading activities at school.

Summer learning packets or activities.

Family participation in setting student goals each year and in planning for college or work.

District-level councils and committees for family and community involvement.

Information on school or local elections for school representatives.

Networks to link all families with parent representatives.

Service integration through partnerships involving school; civic, counseling, cultural, health, recreation, and other agencies and organizations; and businesses.

Service to the community by students, families, and schools (e.g., recycling, art, music, drama, and other activities for seniors or others).

Participation of alumni in school programs for students.

Source: Joyce Epstein, May 1995, "Epstein's Framework of Six Types of Involvement and Sample Practices" from *Phi Delta Kappan*, p. 704. Reprinted by permission of Joyce Epstein.

Table 4.7   Challenges and Redefinitions of the Types of School/Family/Community Partnerships

Type 1 Parenting	Type 2 Communicating	Type 3 Volunteering	Type 4 Learning at Home	Type 5 Decision-Making	Type 6 Collaborating with Community
Challenges	Challenges	Challenges	Challenges	Challenges	Challenges
Provide information to *all* families who want it or who need it, not just to the few who can attend workshops or meetings at the school building.	Review the readability, clarity, form, and frequency of all memos, notices, and other print and nonprint communications.	Recruit volunteers widely so that *all* families know that their time and talents are welcome.	Design and orgnaize a regular schedule of interactive homework (e.g., weekly or bimonthly) that gives *students* responsibility for discussing important things they are learning and helps families stay aware of the content of their children's classwork.	Include parent leaders from all racial, ethnic, socioeconomic, and other groups in the school.	Solve turf problems of responsibilities, funds, staff, and locations for collaborative activities.
Enable families to share information with schools about culture, background, and children's talents and needs.	Consider parents who do not speak English well, do not read well, or need large type.	Make flexible schedules for volunteers, assemblies, and events to enable parents who work to participate.	Coordinate family-linked homework activities, if students have several teachers.	Offer training to enable parent leaders to serve as representatives of other families, with input from and return of information to all parents.	Inform families of community programs for students, such as mentoring, tutoring, and business partnerships.
Make sure that all information for and from families is clear, usable, and linked to children's success in school.	Review the quality of major communications (newsletters, report cards, conference schedules, and so on).	Organize volunteer work; provide training; match time and talent with school, teacher, and student needs; and recognize efforts so that participants are productive.	Involve families and their children in all important curriculum-related decisions.	Include students (along with parents) in decision-making groups.	Assure equity of opportunities for students and families to participate in community programs or to obtain services.
	Establish clear two-way channels for communications from home to school and from school to home.				Match community contributions with school goals; integrate child and family services with education.

Redefinitions

"Workshop" to mean more than a *meeting* about a topic held at the school building at a particular time. "Workshop" may also mean making information about a topic available in a variety of forms that can be viewed, heard, or read anywhere, any time, in varied forms.

Redefinitions

"Communciations about school programs and student progress" to mean two-way, three-way, and many-way channels of communication that connect schools, families, students, and the community.

Redefinitions

"Volunteer" to mean anyone who supports school goals and children's learning or development in any way, at any place, and at any time—not just during the school day and at the school building

Redefinitions

"Homework" to mean not only work done alone, but also interactive activities shared with others at home or in the community, linking schoolwork to real life.

"Help" at home to mean encouraging, listening, reacting, praising, guiding, monitoring, and discussing—not "teaching" school subjects.

Redefinitions

"Decision-making" to mean a process of partnership, of shared views and actions toward shared goals, not just a power struggle between conflicting ideas.

Parent "leader" to mean a real representative, with opportunities and support to hear from and communicate with other families.

Redefinitions

"Community" to mean not only the neighborhoods where students' homes and schools are located but also any neighborhoods that influence their learning and development.

"Community" rated not only by low or high social or economic qualities, but by strengths and talents to support students, families, and schools.

"Community" means all who are interested in and affected by the quality of education, not just those with children in the schools.

Source: Joyce Epstein, May 1995, "Challenges and Redefinitions for the Six Types of Involvement" from Phi *Delta Kappan,* p. 705. Reprinted by permission of Joyce Epstein.

The theme of school culture is clear in his work: Depending on the context in which one observes a child, one obtains a different view of that child. For example, in one intelligence testing situation (using a test such as the Weschler), the tester (who is Anglo-American) places an object (e.g., a toy airplane) in front of the child (in this case a third- or fourth-grade African American student). The tester says, "Tell me everything you can about this." There is a twelve-second silence, which can be a very long time during an IQ test or in a classroom environment. So the tester then changes the question: "What would you say it looks like?" The child says nothing for eight seconds. When one reviews the transcript and the testing results from such an event, one is likely to conclude that the child lacks critical cognitive and linguistic abilities.

But Labov did not stop there. He looked at the same child in a number of domains. He thought that this outcome might have something to do with the relationship between the African American child and the Anglo-American tester, so he brought in an African American tester from the neighborhood to remove the racial boundary. When he repeated the test, but still with the tester on one side of the table and the child on the other side, the results were not much different. Then Labov did something that is now famous: He removed the trappings of power from the situation. He took the child away from the table, removed the adult, and observed the child interacting with other children on the floor. The child's verbal production increased incredibly. Much like Phillips (1982), who found communicative differences between American Indian students and their school, Labov found significant communicative differences between the various domains of the school itself. In short, if you look at a child in only one situation, you get only one kind of picture.

Moll and Diaz (1986) contributed to this understanding of context specificity. They observed children, not at home and at school, but under different constraints of instruction. The children were enrolled in a bilingual program designed to allow Spanish-speaking children to acquire English as quickly as possible. In this program, the children had two teachers, one for English and another for Spanish. Moll and Diaz videotaped lessons in both settings and asked each teacher to watch the videotapes
of the other. The Spanish-speaking teacher was appalled when she saw the children in the English-speaking teacher's classroom: They were not reading but were instead engaged in drill-and-practice exercises in which very little cognitive activity was taking place. By contrast, in the Spanish-speaking classroom, where the children were being given comprehension activities, they were reading in Spanish. Moll and Diaz discussed this situation with the Spanish-speaking teacher and hypothesized that reading is specific to the domain of language. So they performed

some experiments. They had the children apply the reading comprehension skills they had acquired in Spanish to reading in English. In doing this, by the way, they violated one of the basic tenets of bilingual education: Keep the two languages separate. But when they let the children call upon all the intellectual resources they had available, their progress was remarkable. The students began to comprehend written English very nicely, even though they did not have complete mastery of the language. A bridge between the two cultures was thereby developed in support of the goals of the school.

Gallimore et al.'s (1986) study of the Kamehameha Early Education Program, or KEEP, is another example of how bridges can be built. One recommendation is to allow cultural elements that are relevant to the children to enter the classroom. This is the practice of scaffolding, which was introduced in Chapter 2. Scaffolding enables children to use relevant experiences from the home to move toward the demands of the school. For example, in the KEEP project, teachers incorporated cultural elements into the classroom at the beginning of reading lessons, which were divided into three parts. The first part centered on the children's experiences. Before reading a book, the children talked about their home experiences and things they knew about in the world. Then the teacher made transitions from those experiences to the book and directed the children to read the text. For example, the teacher would say something like, "We are going to read this article. As you read, can you think of three things that the writer says are important about culture?" The students then read the text silently, not aloud, in order to avoid pronunciation difficulties. Now the children have been oriented toward the text. In the end, the children's home experiences are linked with the text reading.

|Scaffolding|

Close discourse analyses of lessons that utilize scaffolding reveal that the questioning structures change during the instruction. In the early part of the lessons, questioning structures are open-ended. Joint responses and joint progressions of narrative are allowed. By the end, however, the lessons very closely follow the traditional format. The children have been slowly guided through the instruction in a very microgenetic way, so they can decide what is important. The teaching is done so that the children's culture, interest, and experiences are preserved.

Tracking and Ability Grouping

Ability grouping is managed by elementary school teachers within classrooms, and tracking distributes students among classrooms, usually in secondary schools. Both of these practices bring together groups of children with similar perceived academic abilities—for example, slow readers versus fast readers,

|Patterns in Student Distribution|

A Community of Learners

Every day, during a one-and-a-half-hour science segment in a self-contained sixth-grade class and in two seventh-grade and one eighth-grade science classrooms, students engage in collaborative research in

Becoming a Responsive Teacher

which they participate in designing their own curriculum. The class is organized into small research groups. Each group is responsible for investigating and writing about one subtopic from a larger content area. For example, different groups chose to study condors, whales, otters, and wolves during a sixth-grade unit on endangered species.

The students conduct their research with the aid of an extended community that includes all members of their own classroom, students and teachers in other project classrooms, research staff and scientists at the University of California at Berkeley, and various experts, such as forest rangers, furriers, and zoo personnel, whose work is related to the students' research. The project provides a core set of resources on environmental science (including books, articles, newspaper and magazine clippings, videotapes, and videodiscs), which the students and teachers supplement with other materials.

As the students gather information, adults guide them in note-taking, outlining, and writing as well as in learning how to read technical material. Adults also intervene when students appear to need help working together on group tasks.

To aid students in their research, the project provides a computer environment based almost entirely on commercially available software. Each classroom contains six or seven Macintosh computers and a laser printer. Students are provided word-processing, spreadsheet, database, and graphics applications; access to a scanner; Internet access; and a computer-based index to the core set of resources (known as a "browser") to help them locate research materials.

An electronic mail package allows students to send messages and requests for help or information to their peers, their teachers, students and teachers in other classrooms, and even to project staff at the university. When appropriate, these questions are forwarded to university scientists who have agreed to be available for occasional consultation.

Once the students have recorded the results of their research, they reassemble into "jigsaw learning groups" composed of one "expert"

Continued   A Community of Learners

from each research group. Students then take turns leading discussions on their areas of expertise, using the materials prepared by their respective research groups.

   This collaborative research approach differs from more traditional approaches to teaching in several ways. The approach intentionally favors depth over breadth and the process of learning over the learning of content only. Given the rate at which knowledge is changing, particularly in the sciences, we believe that a student who merely acquires current knowledge will be inadequately prepared for future demands in school, at work, and as a responsible citizen.

Meeting the Challenge

1. Working with a few of your classmates, draw a diagram of this community of learners from the point of view of one of the students. Draw connecting lines to all the major groups of people the student can call upon during the research process. Draw dashed lines to the research materials and technology available, showing the pathways by which the student would gain access to them. Compare your group's diagram with diagrams drawn by other groups.

2. With your whole class, discuss the extent of organizing, planning, and networking that was required by the educators who established the learning community described previously. What barriers to education are being crossed here? How have some of these interconnections among groups been set up?

3. Develop a list of broad content areas that would be amenable to the process of learning in such a community. For each area, brainstorm with your whole class all the resource groups that could contribute to the learning network.

4. As a teacher of the students described earlier, how comfortable would you be with the hardware and software used daily in your classroom? List the items you would need to learn more about. See if one of your classmates can shed light on your questions.

and high achievers versus low achievers. Many studies (Mirón, 1996; Oakes, 1984a; Rueda and Mehan, 1987) indicate that there is a pattern in the distribution of children among different tracks: children from low-income and minority backgrounds invariably end up in lower tracks, and children from middle- and upper-income backgrounds are in upper tracks. Educational practices are also differentially distributed among these tracks. Students in higher tracks receive challenging educational opportunities; students in lower tracks receive much more practice and drill.

If children were also given equal opportunity to change tracks, this finding would not be quite so troublesome. But children get locked in: If a child is placed in a low-ability group in first grade, he or she will most likely remain there throughout elementary school. If a student is in a vocational track in seventh grade, that student is unlikely to change to a college-preparatory track. Instead of supporting the democratic ideal of a classless society, the school tends to reproduce the divisions within society.

The question is, why do the practices of tracking and ability grouping continue? Most of these activities are organized as practical solutions to very difficult problems: too many children in class, not enough resources, and the existence of distinct levels of student ability. But recent research supports heterogeneity, as opposed to homogeneity, as the basis for grouping students. There is extensive evidence that mixed groupings have a particularly beneficial result for those who need it the most: students from low-income backgrounds who have trouble with school. In Kagan's (1986) review of the literature, study after study shows that children who do not perform well academically succeed best in heterogeneous groups. That idea resonates very well with parents of culturally diverse students but not with middle- and upper-income parents (Oakes, 1989), who think their children will suffer academically under those arrangements. However, research demonstrates that middle- and upper-income children from majority populations are also more likely to succeed in heterogeneous groupings than in homogeneous groupings (Slavin, 1989). That wonderful adage—that the best way to learn something is to teach it—truly does work in practice. When children are involved in the teaching process, they learn as well.

The extent to which tracking and ability grouping have become institutionalized practices is demonstrated by a poignant account related by Trujillo (1989), who was a high school principal. He tells of two counselors, advising two almost identical youngsters in preparation for tenth grade. Both students were Filipino, both had parents with limited English-language skills, and both had nearly identical records and test scores. As Trujillo watched, the first counselor talked the first student and his parents out of the academic program they had originally chosen. He took the youngster

Benefits of Mixing Ability Levels

out of algebra and talked him into another year of remedial math. In the other conversation, however, the second counselor began describing the courses that the second youngster would need when he enrolled in college. The student was trying to avoid taking the harder classes, but the counselor promised that she would meet with him once a week to check on his progress. The father protested, saying, "We are very poor people. College is not one of the goals we have for our child. We could not afford that, and we don't want to deceive him." The counselor replied, "Don't worry about that, we'll get him a scholarship."

Beliefs That Limit Students Both counselors were probably trained in the same program with the same methodology. The techniques and rationale the first counselor used to talk the student out of taking a college-prep curriculum were classic; they would make a beautiful chapter in the counseling textbook. In technique, there was nothing the counselor did wrong, and he could use the test scores to prove that the youngster belonged in the remedial classes. However, whereas the first counselor was still very much part of the belief system he had been taught, the second counselor had moved beyond this system; in short, there seemed to be two belief systems operating. Trujillo (1989) concludes that although the majority of U.S. educators know their subject matter and are fairly well steeped in the appropriate methodologies, they do not understand the students they are teaching: "In other words, the people who do well with children are those who understand them—who don't demean them" (Trujillo, 1989).

Conclusion

Educators must realize that children, all children, come to school motivated to enlarge their worlds. Educators start with the many cultures of students. Educators should not look at them, certainly not initially, as organisms to be molded and regulated. Instead, they should observe their students to determine what they know, what they seek to know, and which of their experiences can be used to fuel the process of enlarging their interest, knowledge, and skills. Educators must not look at their students in terms of their deficits—what they do not know but need to know— for in fact they are rich in assets.

Summary of Major Ideas

1. Students must learn to negotiate the boundaries among the multiple cultures of family, school, and peers. Depending on the nature of the boundary, culturally diverse students may

face great psychological and social consequences when making the transition from one culture to another. Sometimes the psychosocial costs are so great that a boundary becomes a barrier students are not able to cross. A complete understanding of underachievement among minority populations requires a full consideration of the interactions among culture, socialization, and education.

2. Socialization is the process through which prescriptions and prohibitions are transmitted to members of a social group. The family is a major agent of socialization, along with teachers, peers, and the media, especially television. Research shows much diversity in socialization practices across cultures. A child's socialization sets the stage for lifelong patterns of social relations, including those important in schooling.

3. Ecology is the study of the relationships between an organism and its environment. The socialization of children is determined not only by the ecology of the family and the community but also by the broader social ecology, which includes such factors as the urbanization level of the community, the socioeconomic status of the family and community, and societal views about cultural groups. The ecology of the minority family is characterized by its immersion in a hostile educational and community setting. However, many linguistically and culturally diverse families have devised ways of nurturing an appreciation of education and of individual achievement.

4. Ethnic images are people's general beliefs about cultural groups. Research indicates that ethnic images are tenacious in the United States and that people are willing and able to rate others on the basis of their ethnicity. Ethnic images are significant predictors of support for racial integration and desired social distance and for public opinion on affirmative action, school desegregation, and other group-related issues.

5. Personality is a structure that reconciles children's interpreted experiences and emotional states. The social attributes ascribed to the child by others may greatly influence this process of reconciliation and result in a particular sense of ethnic identity. Research shows that children are aware of attitudes toward ethnic differences by the age of four.

6. The cultural systems approach to education considers the organization of a society, specifically the roles and status assigned to cultural groups, to be a major determinant of educational underachievement. This approach suggests that

people's values, perceptions, and social behavior are directly influenced by the social status of the cultural group to which they belong.

7. A voluntary minority group is a population whose members moved voluntarily to the host society. An involuntary minority group is a population whose members were involuntarily incorporated through various means that degrade their status.

8. Members of voluntary and involuntary minority groups may live in the same society and experience similar effects from discrimination and prejudice. Their responses may widely differ, however, depending on five aspects of the cultural model under which they operate: (a) a frame of reference for comparing present status and future possibilities; (b) a folk theory of how to succeed, especially through education; (c) a sense of collective identity; (d) a cultural frame of reference for judging appropriate behavior and affirming group membership and solidarity; and (e) an assessment of the extent to which one may trust members of the dominant group and the institutions they control. Children absorb these cultural models and bring them to bear in their schooling experiences.

9. A focus on ethnic studies alone is not sufficient for addressing the educational needs of culturally diverse students because it is too often based on stereotypes. Educators must instead adopt a broader sociocultural approach to language, culture, and education. They must understand the child, the family and community, the school, and the larger society as constituting an ecological system with interacting elements.

10. Ethnically diverse families have offered valuable suggestions for improving school/family/community partnerships. Among the elements that build such partnerships are the development of parenting, family-school communication, parental participation in school governance, family representation in the schools, and home support for teaching and learning. Also important is the issue of "power" sharing.

11. The cultural arrangements of the school can affect student performance. Instructional strategies such as scaffolding that provide a bridge between home and school can allow culturally diverse children to make a successful transition to school. Tracking and ability grouping, on the other hand, perpetuate cultural barriers and make it more difficult for such students to succeed academically.

Extending Your Experience

1. Study the diagram in Figure 4.1. How might a culturally diverse child's self-concept change as he or she crosses the border between one culture and another? What, specifically, are the psychological costs of crossing a "nonneutral" border? Describe any such experience you may have had. What or whom did you confront while trying to negotiate this border? What, if anything, helped you build a bridge and make the transition?

2. With a small group of your classmates, review the concept of social ecology discussed in this chapter. Why will it be important for you as an educator to understand the environmental context—family, community, and peers—for each student in your classroom? With your group, develop a list of all the possible environmental factors that might affect a student's ability to achieve academically. Think of a male or female student at a particular grade level and be as specific as you can.

3. Examine various media, such as newspapers, magazines, films, and television shows, for portrayals of ethnic images. Bring some of this evidence to class and compare it with material gathered by your classmates. With these data in mind, discuss the implications of research quoted in the chapter indicating that a child's awareness of and attitude toward his or her own ethnicity is formed by age four.

4. Explore the forms of parent/family involvement in a school that you know well. How do you think this school defines *parent involvement?* Is "power" shared between parents and school?

5. In your own words, explain the difference between a voluntary and an involuntary minority status. Read closely the descriptions given in Tables 4.1 through 4.5 and select a contrast between voluntary and involuntary minority status that you find particularly striking. How might this contrast in cultural experience influence a child's academic success?

Resources for Further Study

Print Resources

Anyon, J. (1997). *Ghetto schooling: A political economy of urban educational reform.* New York: Teachers College Press.

Anyon clearly establishes that the economic decline of the inner cities places schools and students in these areas at particular risk. In essence, the broader changes in the economic, social, and political fabric of the inner city create specific and significant challenges for schools. The culture of anger and hopelessness that develops as a result of this situation has to be addressed if urban schools are to succeed or even survive. Although she is optimistic about the future, Anyon paints a picture of inner-city schools that is not bright.

Comer, J. P. (1997). *Waiting for a miracle: Why schools can't solve our problems—and how we can.* New York: Dutton.

This work examines education through an urban sociocultural lens focused specifically on American children. In so doing, it provides a broader perspective that lends itself to the campaign for doing away with the deficit framework that propagates much of the existing negativity used in defining African American children. Comer's book offers a means for counterattacking the negative images often associated with African American youth and their schooling.

Hawley, W. D., and Jackson, A. W. (Eds.). (1995). *Toward a common destiny: Improving race and ethnic relations in America.* San Francisco: Jossey-Bass.

This edited volume is a collection of important pieces that contribute to increasing the positive nature of interactions within race and ethnic relations. The two major parts of the book, which have accompanying explanatory chapters, when combined give us a comprehensive look at how race and ethnic relations influence policy and attitudes. The third section presents the practical means of enriching race and ethnic relations. The fourth and last section focuses on finding a way to create an agenda that would again acknowledge that improved race and ethnic relations would benefit everyone in American society.

Ogbu, J. (1999). *Collective identity and schooling.* Paper presented at the meeting of the Japan Society of Educational Sociology, Tokyo, Japan.

Ogbu critically explores the behaviors among minority groups toward academic achievement. The variation of the behaviors among minority groups is explained by the author as being rooted in socio-historical events. Despite previous discussions that academic success is compromised by differences in language and culture, this author maintains that language and cultural discontinuities do not necessarily lead to academic failure. In fact, the author makes a point of exploring instances in which these discontinuities are stark and yet still lead to positive academic outcomes. The emphasis of this paper is to understand the power and dimensions of a collective identity among minority group members as well as to outline how a collective identity shapes a certain kind of behavior that lends itself to academic success.

Ogbu, J., and Matute-Bianchi, M. E. (1986). Understanding socio-cultural factors: Knowledge, identity, and school adjustment. In Bilingual Education Office, California State Department of Education (Ed.), *Beyond language: Social and cultural factors in schooling language minority students.* Los Angeles: Evaluation, Dissemination, and Assessment Center, California State University (pp. 145–160).

> The central theme of this work examines why minority students continually experience a disproportionate amount of school failure. Why do some minority groups do better than others? What historical and social forces affect the view of education held by some minority groups? Why do such failures persist? The authors present two cases to illustrate minority students' perceptions of the U.S. educational system and their consequent response to their educational opportunities and job outlook.

Soto, L. D. (1997). *Language, culture, and power: Bilingual families and the struggle for quality education.* Albany: State University of New York Press.

> This volume provides a comprehensive case study of Puerto Rican family interaction with the schools. Developed from a set of interviews, the analysis of the struggles these non-English-speaking parents confront in promoting their children's educational needs is instructive to all educators. Of specific relevance is the discussion of parental perceptions of and expectations for their children and the schools that serve them. The parents' critical stance toward the educational system offers important although challenging insights for teachers.

Weis, L. (1988). *Class, race, and gender in American education.* Albany: State University of New York Press.

> School experiences set the tone for how future citizens function in society. The expectations students have about school are influenced by their gender, race, and class. This book discusses, using in-depth ethnographic and statistical data, some of the most heated issues that are at the core of the educational system. It describes the traditional debate between the "culturalists" and the "structuralists," and elaborates on both to enrich and promote discussion between the two camps. The presentation of such different frameworks produces a book full of the tension created by a broad range of perspectives and goals.

Web Resources

Council of the Great City Schools: *http:www.cgcs.org*

> This web site discusses urban education by way of linking home and school to improve and impact school reform and initiatives with the overall goal of increasing community outreach.

Chapter 5
Language and Communication

Focus Questions

- What variables must interact for communication to occur?

- What is metalinguistic awareness?

- How do children develop skills in phonology, vocabulary, grammar, and language pragmatics?

- What are bilingualism and second-language acquisition? What is code switching?

- How is language used as a social instrument, and what are two important sociocultural variables that may affect a child's motivation to learn a second language?

- What are some emerging issues in U.S. bilingual schooling?

- What is a dialect, and how is classroom use of dialect problematical for students in U.S. schools?

- What are the issues surrounding the use of Black English?

> "As the test of what the potter molds is in the furnace; so in his conversation is the test of a man. The fruit of a tree shows the care it has had; so too does a man's speech disclose the bent of his mind."
> —*The Wisdom of Ben Sira 27:4–7*

Place yourself again in Mrs. Tanner's fifth-grade classroom. As we learned in Chapter 1, in the last few years she has begun to teach students who speak a variety of languages in their homes and communities: Spanish, Vietnamese, Russian, Hmong, Chinese, and Farsi. The challenge of effectively communicating—of making meaning—is quite robust in this classroom. Mrs. Tanner has realized that she must understand the cultural context of these students if she is to provide an effective environment for their communication. In essence, she must determine the way to communicate that will most help her reach the teaching and learning goals so integral to her classroom.

Teaching and learning do not begin when students walk into a classroom. On the contrary, these processes are omnipresent in children's worlds. This point is so important that it cannot be overemphasized. If Mrs. Tanner and other teachers in U.S. schools do not build on a child's foundation of previous and non-school learning, then the role of the teacher and the school is merely corrective. At worst, the schools would be trying to subtract the learning experiences a child gains outside of school. As the previous chapters have shown, adding to a child's learning experiences is an objective that is much more conducive to the educational success of culturally diverse students. This chapter will establish a firm basis for the worthiness of this objective by focusing on the communicative aspects of human development as they relate to teaching and learning.

The Nature of Communication

Throughout the ages, politicians, theologians, philosophers, poets, playwrights, comedians, teachers, and social scientists have all relied in their own distinctive ways on the power of the spoken word to convey meaning. Recent interest in **communication** has broadened to a consideration of both verbal and nonverbal systems that enable humans to encode meaning and transmit it to others with some assurance of accurate reception. Scholars who study **language** characterize it as a complex interaction of many

Interaction of Variables

variables, including the verbal signal itself, the one who sends the signal, how and in what environment the signal is sent, the one who receives the signal, and previous experiences the sender and receiver may have had with similar signals.

Let's look at an example of communication in progress. To a naive observer, the interaction between a parent and a young child may seem simple and relatively devoid of meaning. Lots of silly sounds, exaggerated facial expression—what kind of "meaning" could they possibly convey? Upon closer examination, however, this scenario of communication proves to be quite rich and meaningful. An infant's cooing, crying, giggling, and other sounds prepare the parent to receive a signal and interpret its meaning. Anyone who has been around babies understands the difference between "an anger cry" and "a pain cry." Parents learn to decipher what an infant is feeling by paying attention to subtle changes in the sound of the cry. This is communication. The infant can be said to influence the reaction of the parents by sending these signals.

Later, as the growing child learns specifically articulated sounds and combinations of sounds, it seems as if a systematic, rule-governed set of communicative symbols is emerging almost magically. What was once for the infant a simple and idiosyncratic vocabulary, with limited grammatical arrangement, becomes in a matter of a few years an unbelievably large vocabulary with varied syntactical constructions. This is even the case for children who were born with speech or hearing impairments. These children develop alternative, but just as systematic, forms of nonverbal communication.

Making Meaning in School

A naive observer in Mrs. Tanner's classroom may likely note a series of seemingly disconnected communicative acts. In reality, these chunks of communication are so central that they may almost be overlooked. In the course of a day, Mrs. Tanner asks many questions, reads stories, explains science experiments, gives assignments, provides oral and written feedback, and engages in dozens of one-on-one interactions with students. Each time, a complex set of verbal, written, and/or nonverbal transactions is called upon to enhance meaning making—or, in other words, to institute teaching and learning. It is the role of teachers to communicate with students and the role of students to communicate with teachers. Most classroom activity in U.S. schools is founded on this one principle. At the very root of our teaching and learning activity is the understanding that communication must be a prerequisite.

The Development of Language

Learning to communicate may be a child's most impressive accomplishment. Language is a complex set of systems—phonology, vocabulary, grammar, and pragmatics and discourse rules—and each of these systems has its own rules. We shall next examine these domains of communication more closely. Each one is acquired relatively unconsciously by children in the course of use. Each also at some point emerges into consciousness and becomes a topic of conversation for children or a focus for play and problem-solving. Bringing the various domains of communication into conscious awareness is one of the important achievements of schooling. Becoming aware of distinct communicative systems is a necessary development if people are to understand important aspects of their own culture and the culture of others. Being consciously aware of how we use communication, a process called **metalinguistic awareness,** is the foundation of distinguishing diversity within the communicative activities going on around us all the time.

Becoming Aware of Language

Phonology

Knowing a formal communicative system—a language—involves speaking and understanding words. Those words are made up of specific sounds, called syllables, which are the basic units for language production.

Phonology is the study of speech sounds. Much research has been devoted to the development of speech in humans. When infants exposed to English language environments are five to eight months old, they start producing spoken syllables ("ba," "ma," "ga") in the course of their babbling. Open syllables such as "ba" and "ma" are relatively easy to pronounce and thus form the basis for many "baby talk" words (e.g., "mama," "booboo," "peepee"). Words that contain closed syllables (those with a consonant at the end) are harder to pronounce, especially if quite different consonants need to be articulated within one syllable. Thus, young English-speaking children often say "goggie" for "doggie" or "guck" for "truck," because they are not yet able to put such different sounds as /g/ and /d/ or /t/ into one syllable.

Earlier we saw that the United States is home to over one hundred distinct language groups besides English as well as to a variety of dialects. Children exposed to these various languages proceed through similar stages of complex phonological development. Their learning process differs from that of English learners only in the phonological distinctiveness of the language they

Stages of Development

are learning. For example, Spanish-language learners progress through a distinct process of developmental acquisition marked by early acquisition of vowel sounds (Gonzalez, 1991). In contrast, English learners focus early on consonant sounds.

Children's pronunciation of words comes increasingly to resemble adult pronunciation around the ages of three to five years old. However, very young children still do not think of the sounds they are producing in the same ways that adults do. Young children find it difficult to produce rhymes or to segment particular sounds—for example, to say "meat" without the /m/ sound or without the /t/ sound. The reason for this is that when we speak, the articulation of each sound overlaps the articulation of those before and after it. Recognizing an abstract segment of sound such as *m* or *t* requires considerable sophistication in language ability and knowledge about how the phonological system of a language works. Such metalinguistic awareness develops as children grow older.

Three-year-olds can be taught to identify the initial syllables in words fairly consistently. The ability to segment final syllables or to understand the internal structure of words with consonant clusters comes much later. Four-year-olds can judge with very high accuracy whether words rhyme, and many can also produce rhymes. Many educational activities for young children depend extensively on this rhyming ability. Both children and adults enjoy this metalinguistic activity of rhyming. Preschool children can also distinguish accents and may even incorporate the mimicking of dialect into their play.

Rhyming Activities

Vocabulary

After a rather slow start, a child's knowledge of vocabulary grows very rapidly during the preschool period. **Vocabulary** is the sum of words understood and used by an individual in any language group. Children typically acquire their first word at about one year of age. Acquisition of the first 50 words may take several months. Thereafter the process of word acquisition proceeds so blindingly fast that it is impossible to keep accurate records. It has been estimated that children acquire six to ten new words a day between the ages of two and six. Such rapid vocabulary acquisition relies on the child's use of very powerful strategies for guessing what words mean, on his or her considerable willingness to take chances in using new words, and on lots of help from adults and other children in providing information about words and their meanings.

Speed of Word Acquisition

It is important to recognize that the words a child acquires fall into various categories. Words learned early tend to be names for important people ("mama," "papa," "nana") or concrete objects ("socks," "spoon," "bed," "teddy," "cookie," "bottle"); expressions for important social functions ("hi," "bye-bye"); forms of requests ("wanna," "mommy," "mine"); and ways of directing attention ("there," "that," "what that?"). A bit later children begin to acquire verbs that refer to concrete actions: "eat," "sleep," "read," "sing." As they progress through the preschool and elementary school period, though, children increasingly come to use verbs that refer to complex and private cognitive or communicative activities ("think," "wonder," "dream," "tell," "disagree," "deny"); nouns that refer to abstract, superordinate, or affective entities ("thought," "argument," "animal," "furniture," "sadness," "glee"); and other words that have roles in structuring discourse ("because," "but," "however") or representing one's perspective on matters ("hopefully," "doubtfully," "despairingly"). For avid readers in languages with a written tradition (English, Chinese, Japanese, and Spanish, for example), the process of word acquisition continues well into adulthood. In highly oral cultures (Navaho, Zuñi, and Hmong, for example), this same process of vocabulary acquisition continues as adolescents and adults encounter complex historical, religious, and personal accounts.

Categories of Words

It is crucial in talking about vocabulary to acknowledge that children not only acquire new words as they get older but also expand their understanding of words they know. Thus, a Spanish-speaking child might first learn and understand a word like *padrinos* (godparents) in a relatively restricted context, such as the reliable giver of gifts at each birthday. It could take a child several years to learn exactly how *niño* relates to *padrino* (godfather) and *madrina* (godmother), and precisely what sorts of characteristics can be attributed to each term outside of gift giving. In many cultures these individuals play critical roles for children over a lifetime. This is one reason why standard multiple-choice assessments of vocabulary knowledge cannot assess very accurately the full depth of children's vocabulary knowledge.

At some point during the school years, children come to think, wonder, and talk about words themselves and their meanings. As development of metalinguistic awareness continues to expand, children become able to distinguish between a big word ("building") and a word referring to a big thing ("building"). They come to understand that words are arbitrary symbols whose forms have no intrinsic connection to their meanings. Regardless of the language or languages to which they are exposed, all children achieve this truly significant understanding of the symbolic nature of language.

Words as Symbols

Grammar

Grammar is the system of rules implicit in a language that allows words to be arranged with some regularity of structure. Grammar does not necessarily refer to prescriptive grammar ("Don't say 'he don't' or 'I ain't'"). More broadly, it refers to the system of rules by virtue of which we know whether words are nouns or verbs ("the hit" versus "he hit"). Grammar allows English speakers to decide which word specifies the subject, object, and indirect object of a sentence ("John gave Mary an apple") and French and Spanish speakers to distinguish the gender of a noun.

Rules for Interpreting

As soon as children put two words together, they begin to demonstrate what they are learning about the rules of grammar in their native language. Children learning English, for instance, show awareness of word order, or **syntax,** as an important feature of the grammatical system. In English, the sentence pattern subject-verb-object is so common that developing the ability to comprehend and use constructions that deviate from this pattern (passives, such as "The lion was bitten by the flea"; coordinations, such as "I want this and you want that"; and relative clauses, such as "The dog bit the cat that chased the rat") is a lengthy process for children that lasts well into the preschool years. In Spanish, gender and number (e.g., *la muchacha* [the girl] and *los muchachos* [the boys]) are distinct grammatical features. In Chinese, phonological emphasis—the spoken stress on words—marks the grammar in the language.

From normal communicative interactions with adults, children typically acquire the rules of grammar in their native language with little difficulty. Children also normally develop a metalinguistic capacity, displayed when they comment spontaneously on grammatical correctness or respond easily to questions about sentences being "right" or "wrong." Nonetheless, it is hard even for school-age children to attend more seriously to grammatical correctness than to meaning. They are likely to accept as "okay" a sentence such as "The boys is jumping in the lake" and to reject a perfectly grammatical but anomalous sentence such as "Ice cream tastes yucky."

Pragmatics and Discourse Rules

Knowing words, how to pronounce them, what they mean, and how to put them into sentences is only a small part of learning to communicate. Each of these skills depends greatly on the language or languages that are available in the child's environment. Children must also learn how to use language appropriately—

Appropriate Use of Language | how to communicate effectively and to be responsive to the needs of listeners. These skills are closely tied to the child's culture. The term **language pragmatics** refers not only to the rules of the language itself but also to generally accepted notions about appropriate and effective language use. This latter category contains an enormous array of phenomena that are largely cultural in nature. Thus, rules such as "Don't talk with your mouth full" fall under pragmatics, as do rules for politeness that range from saying "please" to avoiding discussion of delicate topics.

Metalinguistic awareness in the domain of pragmatics tends to emerge first in rules for politeness, perhaps because parents initiate many transactions with children that are explicitly pragmatic: "What's the magic word?" or "Don't interrupt, I'm talking on the phone." Young children often violate pragmatic rules that have to do with giving their listeners enough information, but by the age of four or so they do understand clearly that some adults are likely to need more explanation if names of friends or toys are introduced. Unlike grammar, which is mostly acquired by the time children enter school, pragmatic skills, particularly those associated with understanding how to adjust one's language for different audiences, continue to develop throughout the school years.

Pragmatics for Conversation. Most of the oral communication young children experience involves face-to-face conversation with familiar people. Children of preschool age talk with their parents about events in their own and in others' daily lives, such as doing chores, eating, getting dressed, going for walks, and so on. They talk about experiences they have shared with others. As they get older, they increasingly come to talk about unshared events (what happened yesterday or what will happen tomorrow).

Teachers should realize that children do not often realize when they need to supply more information in conversation. Teachers who are fortunate enough to be informed about the general topic are usually more likely to be able to ask questions that fill in missing information. Those who are not so informed must be willing to draw the child out while interpreting and co-constructing miss-

Cultural Differences | ing information. It is easy to see how, if teacher and student do not share similar experiences or similar cultures, their face-to-face communication can be diminished. The concept of conversation and the pragmatic instructions for how it should be carried out are very much culturally determined. In large and authoritarian families (e.g., Mexican American, Appalachian, and American Indian families), children's conversations with adults are usually brief and abrupt. Children learn to listen and to speak very judiciously. A teacher who does not understand this context may mistakenly suspect that such a student is shy or language-delayed.

Pragmatics for Literacy. As children move through school, they become more familiar with written communication. Written language can differ from oral language not only in purpose but also in terms of the intended audience and the relationship between the speaker or writer and the audience. Written and oral language also tend to assign responsibility for effective communication differently. For instance, writers must anticipate the needs of their readers and thus supply or clarify information to avoid confusing them. A speaker, on the other hand, may be directly questioned by the audience if something is not clear. The basic pragmatics for literacy are classically demonstrated in the typical newspaper editorial. The task of the essayist is to make a point clearly and completely and in the process to provide the audience with any background information necessary to understand the point on first reading.

|Responsibility for Clarity|

Many types of oral language use pragmatics similar to those of the editorial—public lectures, for example, or telephone conversations with strangers. And some written forms of expression approximate oral communication in their private, personal, or ambiguous nature—diaries or journals, for example, or poetry. The pragmatic rules governing the sort of effective conversational exchange that the typical preschooler has mastered are only a first step toward the pragmatics of literacy and must be acquired through much oral classroom discourse.

Pragmatics for Different Discourse Situations. As suggested earlier, one important dimension distinguishing the pragmatics of different types of communication is the extent of audience collaboration. Can you expect your listeners to participate actively (asking questions, chiming in with agreements or supportive statements, proposing interpretations and conclusions)? If you can expect such listener involvement, then you do not need to make extensive preparations to ensure that your message is clear.

Expected audience participation is an element of discourse pragmatics that varies across cultures for both oral and written communication. For example, Hawaiian and Athabaskan children have been described as active audience participants, often interrupting enthusiastically when listening to stories (Boggs and Watson-Gegeo, 1991; Scollon and Scollon, 1981). In contrast, in mainstream U.S. culture the storyteller has full responsibility for plot development and performance, and the audience is supposed to be silent until the end. Japanese novelists tend to demand a considerable amount of work from their readers, rarely providing the tidy, wrapped-up conclusion to the plot often expected by

|Audience Expectation|

Western readers. In the United States, teenage girls from working-class backgrounds discuss serious topics by sharing comments with other audience members, who audibly echo or even antici-pate the speaker's points. Girls from middle-class backgrounds, on the other hand, tend to take long and uninterrupted turns pro-ducing what in effect are brief oral editorials on the subject under discussion. Discourse in which responsibility is shared with the audience and discourse in which responsibility rests with the speaker are equally challenging communication skills for children to learn. Practice in the latter skill, in U.S. schools, usually focuses on the types of writing that children are expected to do.

The pragmatics of various discourse forms also differ concern-ing the degree to which background knowledge can be assumed to be shared with the audience. Consider the difference between recounting a harrowing experience to a friend and remembering it with someone who went through it with you. The first account requires considerably more attention to detail and clarity about the participants as well as the order and description of the events. These demands are played out linguistically by reduced use of pronouns (saying a name instead of "she" or "he"), more elaborated use of grammar ("We lost the paddles, and because of

that we went over the falls"), and more explicit background and foreground detail.

An additional dimension of pragmatic complexity is added when the discourse form requires the speaker or writer to presume that background knowledge is not shared when in fact it is. **Classroom Discourse** | This situation emerges in classroom discourse when teachers ask "known-answer" test questions. (Keep in mind that teachers are among the few individuals who ask questions to which they know the answers!) It is also at work when, at sharing time, children are expected to describe objects that they are holding and that the whole class can obviously see.

Giving definitions for common words is a task that taps children's ability to understand that shared knowledge and context must be ignored in such a situation. When asked "What is a clock?" children who assume shared knowledge might point at a clock or say something like "They are like watches, but bigger." Children who are sophisticated in the pragmatics of school discourse, however, tend to avoid responses like these that presume shared knowledge and to respond instead with an answer such as "A clock is a machine that tells time" (Snow, 1991).

Understand the Listener | For children to master pragmatics, they must be able to understand both the listener's perspective and the range of expectations the listener might hold. As members of a culture, we all acquire culture-specific expectations of how interpersonal relationships should be marked linguistically and how information should be packaged for easy communication. Children in the United States have to grasp these culture-specific expectations and move beyond them as they learn to interact in new settings and with different people.

A fundamental challenge for everyone, child or adult, is to understand other people's perspectives and expectations. Part of addressing this challenge is acknowledging that individuals whose cultures are different often have different rules for language use. The specific challenge for any educator is to adapt to diverse communicative needs and expectations in the classroom. This is no easy task. But it is a task that recognizes the crucial importance of effective communication. If it is left undone, the role of the teacher in enhancing the teaching and learning enterprise is substantially compromised.

Bilingualism and Second-Language Acquisition

Let's now contrast what we've learned about the typical pattern of language development among children who speak one language with that of children who speak more than one language. In this section we shall examine how bilingualism and second-language acquisition relate to schooling contexts. In the next section we shall focus on language and schooling in its many shapes and forms. In the rest of this chapter, we shall address issues of teaching and learning as they relate to research and theory developed over the last three decades. We shall see that studies of children's linguistic, cognitive, and social development have dramatically reshaped our view of language variation, multilingualism, and cultural "difference."

As the revealing demographic information cited in Chapter 1 indicates, bilingualism and second-language learning are fast becoming common elements in U.S. classrooms. How are these two attributes of language development defined? **Bilingualism,** which is the ability to speak two languages with equal fluency, occurs when children are exposed to two languages during their early years, usually before they are five. (By contrast, monolingual children are exposed to only one language during these years.) **Second-language acquisition** is a process of language development whereby a child acquires one language first and then is exposed to and required to learn a second language.

Research Focus | Compared with the amount of research focusing on monolingual development, little systematic investigation has been available regarding children who are simultaneously acquiring more than one language during the early part of their lives. Research on this subject, particularly in terms of schooling contexts, has centered independently on three areas of language acquisition of young, multilingual populations:

1. *Linguistic:* The developmental nature of phonology (word sounds), morphology (word formation), and syntax (word order) (Bialystok and Hakuta, 1994)

2. *Cognitive:* Related cognitive aspects of language acquisition (Cummins, 1979; García and McLaughlin, 1995)

3. *Social and communicative:* The social context of language development and its effect on language pragmatics (Zentella, 1997)

We will now review this research and highlight similarities and differences in underlying theoretical concepts. We will also relate these research findings to important schooling issues.

Patterns of Language Development and Cognitive Aspects

It does seem clear from evidence in many societies throughout the world that a child can learn more than one linguistic form. For example, Sorenson (1967) describes the acquisition of three to four languages by young children who live in the northwest region of the Amazon River. The Tukano tribal language serves as the lingua franca (common language of the region), but some twenty-five clearly distinguishable linguistic groups also continue to exist in the region. **Multilingualism** has also been reported within the European community (Baetens Beardsmore, 1982; Skutnabb-Kangas, 1979) and among school-age children in the United States (Skrabanek, 1970; Veltman, 1988; Waggoner, 1984).

Spanish-English Bilingualism

Research into bilingual development in U.S. children, and into Spanish-English language acquisition in particular, yields some common findings. Young children aged two to four do acquire complex morphological, phonological, and syntactic skills for both Spanish and English without any evidence of negative linguistic effects (García, 1983a; Padilla and Liebman, 1975; Valdés, 1996). Children also exhibit a significant ability to produce well-formed and communicative mixed-language utterances, a process referred to as **code switching** (García, 1983a; Huerta, 1977; Padilla and Liebman, 1975). On the topic of code switching, Padilla and Liebman (1975) report:

> The appropriate use of both languages in mixed utterances was evident; that is, correct word order was preserved. For example, there were no occurrences of "raining esta" or "a es baby" [inappropriate grammatical combinations of Spanish and English], but there was evidence for such utterances as "esta raining" and "es a baby" [appropriate grammatical combinations of the two languages]. There was also an absence of the redundancy of unnecessary words which might tend to confuse meaning. (p. 51)

These researchers found that learning two languages simultaneously did not prevent children from understanding more abstract language rules such as those for correct word order or syntax.

Code Switching in Development

García, Maez, and Gonzalez (1979), in a study of Spanish-English bilingual children between the ages of four and six throughout the United States, found regional differences in the relative frequency of code switching. Spanish-English bilingual children from Texas, Arizona, Colorado, and New Mexico showed a higher incidence of switched-language utterances than did such children from California or Illinois, especially at prekindergarten levels. These findings suggest that some children may very well pass through an intermediate developmental stage in which the two languages can merge, before they move to the development of two independent language systems. Research indicates that code switching is a highly expected and normal developmental phenomenon in children exposed to multiple languages. It is not to be taken as evidence of a language disability or "confusion."

The mistakes language learners make have provided researchers with guideposts in understanding the strategies and processes employed during second-language acquisition (Corder, 1967). Dulay and Burt (1974b) studied the errors in the natural speech of 179 children between the ages of five and eight (including a sample of Chicano children in California) who were learning English as a second language. They classified errors as related either to first language (interference errors) or to normal language development (developmental errors). Their analysis indicated that only 4.7 percent of the children's errors could be attributed to first-language interference whereas 87.1 percent of the errors were similar to those made by children learning English as a first language.

Creative Construction   Dulay and Burt (1974b) postulated that a universal "creative construction process" accounts for second-language acquisition. They proposed that the process was creative because no one had modeled the hundreds of types of sentences that children produce when acquiring a second language. The authors suggested that innate mechanisms caused children to use certain strategies to organize linguistic input. They did not claim that they could define the specific nature of the innate mechanisms. They did claim, however, that these mechanisms have certain definable characteristics that cause children to use a limited set of hypotheses to deal with the knowledge they are acquiring. The strategies parallel those identified for first-language acquisition.

Krashen (1981a, 1985) has argued that this process of creative construction is fundamental to second-language acquisition. His thinking is based on two hypotheses about how bilingual children learn language. His "natural order" hypothesis indicates **Unconscious vs. Conscious Learning** that the acquisition of grammatical structures by the second-language learner proceeds in a predictable, "natural" order independent of first-language experiences and/or proficiency. Such acquisition occurs unconsciously, without the learner needing to be concerned with recognizing or using structural rules. Krashen's "monitor" hypothesis suggests that a second language can be learned consciously, however, when the learner has achieved a significant knowledge of structural rules and has the time to apply those rules in a second-language learning situation. The "monitor" hypothesis extends Dulay and Burt's (1974a) concept of creative construction. Krashen concludes, however, that the conscious learning of a second language is not as efficient or functional as a natural acquisition.

Other research has documented a distinct relationship between first-language and second-language acquisition. Ervin-Tripp (1974) conducted a study of 31 English-speaking children between the ages of four and nine who were attending French schools in Geneva. She found that the errors these children made in French, their second language, were a result of their application of the same strategies that they had used in acquiring a first language. Ervin-Tripp described the application of three of these strategies:

1. Overgeneralization

2. Production simplification

3. Loss of sentence medial items (items in the middle of sentences)

In overgeneralization, the American children acquiring French applied the subject-verb-object strategy of English to all French sentences and thus systematically misunderstood French passives. In production simplification, the children resisted using two appropriate French forms if they felt that they both had the same meaning. Finally, pronouns in the middle of French sentences were less often imitated than initial or final pronouns. Ervin-Tripp believed that interference errors occurred only when the second-language learner was forced to generate sentences about semantically difficult material or unfamiliar concepts in the culture of the new language.

Segments of Speech   Through rote memorization, children acquire segments of speech called prefabricated patterns (Hakuta, 1974). Examples of these prefabricated patterns are various renditions of the English verb "to be" (such as "I am," "you are," "he is") and the segments "do you" and "how to" as embedded in questions. These patterns are very useful in communication. Children use them readily without understanding their structure but knowing which particular situations call for which patterns in order to communicate in the target language.

Wong-Fillmore (1976) spent a year observing five Spanish-speaking Chicano children acquiring English naturally, and she noticed the same phenomenon of acquiring segments of speech. The first thing the children did in order to figure out what was being said was to observe the relationship between certain expressions and their situational contexts. They inferred the meaning of certain words, which they began to use as formulaic expressions. (They acquired and used these expressions as analyzed wholes.) The formulaic expressions became the raw material the children used to figure out the structure of the language. Wong-Fillmore provided two examples of how children use first-language acquisition strategies to begin to analyze these expressions: (1) children notice how parts of expressions used by others vary in accordance with changes in the speech situation in which they occur; and (2) children notice which parts of the formulaic expressions are like other utterances in the speech of others. As the children figured out which formulas in their speech could be varied, they were able to "free" the constituents they contained and use them in productive speech.

Children acquiring a second language may depend initially on transfer from the first language and on imitation and rote memorization of the second language. In more practical terms, the less interaction a second-language learner has with native speakers, the more likely it is that transfer from the first language to the second language will occur. As the second language is acquired, many of the strategies that children use to acquire this language seem to be the same as those used in first-language acquisition.

Role of Natural Conversations

Current research suggests that natural communication situations must be provided for second-language acquisition to occur. Regardless of the different emphases of the theories discussed previously, recent theoretical propositions regarding second-language acquisition suggest that through natural conversations the learner receives the necessary input and structures that promote second-language acquisition (August and Hakuta, 1997; Bialystok and Hakuta, 1994; García, 2000).

Recent findings also recognize that the characteristics and circumstances of a particular child can and do influence the rate and quality of second-language development as well as maintenance or loss of the first language (Hakuta and August, 1997). One such characteristic is the child's attitude toward the two languages.

Importance of Attitude

For example, Hakuta and D'Andrea (1992) examined the relationship between English and Spanish proficiency and the language attitudes of Mexican American high school students. They reported that attitudes toward English were *not* related to English-language proficiency while attitudes toward Spanish were indeed related to continued development in that language. This finding strongly suggests that, at least in this population of U.S. bilinguals, a positive or negative attitude toward English is not important for development of English language skills: In other words, you learn English whether you like it or not. But a positive attitude toward Spanish does directly influence the child's continued development of that language and ultimate proficiency in it.

Individual characteristics are not always as important as we might suspect, however. For instance, the age at which an individual learns a second language has always been identified as a key factor in language acquisition. The common belief is that young children can learn a second language faster and more efficiently than older children and adults.

Age Factor— A Myth?

Unfortunately, there is little evidence to support this idea, except for the fact that younger children will have less of an accent in the second language. Although there seems to be a critical age for primary language development, the existence of a similar period for a second language remains a myth (Bialystok and Hakuta, 1994). This suggests that adults are just as capable of learning a second language as young children. Keep in mind, however, that learning a second language may not be easy for everyone: Many individual differences other than age *do* matter. Also, remember that young children are less likely to be able to communicate their difficulties than adults.

To summarize, the research findings with regard to patterns in language acquisition suggest three things:

1. The acquisition of one or two languages seems to follow similar developmental processes. Language learners utilize a consistent set of cognitive hypotheses along with previous experiences with language.

2. The acquisition of more than one language may result in an intermediate phase of language convergence, called *code switching*, that incorporates the attributes of several languages.

3. The acquisition of two languages does not hamper the acquisition of either language, although individual differences in second-language acquisition can be traced to a variety of factors.

New Areas of Emerging Research in U.S. Bilingual Schooling

Authentic Assessment of Second-Language Learners

During the past two decades, teachers of literacy have shifted their practice from a product to a process orientation (Calkins, 1986; Graves, 1994), influenced by a growing body of research about language and literacy learning as well as by their own observations of how children develop as writers. Most educators see this change as positively impacting students' literacy skills, but problems abound in how to document student progress and program effectiveness due to inadequate assessment tools and overreliance on standardized achievement tests, including English and primary-language tests (Wiggins, 1994). One problem is the perceived lack of validity between standardized tests and new, more process-oriented curricula. Many schools now implement authentic assessments, including portfolio assessment, to supplement or replace these tests (Hewitt, 1995; Porter and Cleland, 1995). The use of authentic assessment efforts has developed as a particularly significant tool for instructors in multicultural and multilingual settings.

Teachers in the schools we have studied (García, Casimir, Sun, Wiese, and García, 1999) realize that the qualities of an individual's writing in one or more languages are profoundly influenced by the context in which the writing develops, including the intended purpose and audience. For most writers, and for all developing writers, there is a wide variability from piece to piece. In his landmark text, Graves reflects on the topic of variability, stating, "Writing is a highly idiosyncratic process that varies from day to day" (p. 270). Traditional writing evaluation instruments emphasize language conventions including grammar and spelling. The tasks of organization; development; the establishment of voice, tone, or mood; and audience awareness are overlooked and undervalued. Calkins states that we have "elevated form over content" (Calkins, 1986, p. 14). Proponents of the writing process hold that breaking writing tasks into isolated drills in basic grammar fails to produce students capable of real, substantive writing (Edelsky et al., 1991).

Assessments in Unnatural Conditions

The influences of variability, topic selection, time limitations, demands for conventionality, and one-sample assessments in traditional forms of direct writing assessment are profound. Most direct assessments require students to write from a predetermined prompt, for a specified amount of time, under "test" conditions (Williamson, 1993). Occasionally, the best of these writing assessments will allow for a follow-up session on a subsequent day during which the writers are directed to edit, proofread, and revise their work. Most large-scale assessments do not allow for these limited elements of the writing process to be included or for assessments in languages other than English. In addition, in an effort to equalize the playing field and to adhere to the expectations of a standardized testing paradigm, resource access is prohibited or extremely limited. The assessment requires a decontextualized setting in which to conduct an artificial writing task far removed from the needs, interests, or passions of the writer (Camp, 1993; García, 1994; Moss, 1994b).

Developing New Assessments

These efforts will provide educators, particularly those serving multilingual/multicultural students, with meaningful and consistent writing assessment tools and methods for quantifying data from their classroom observations and from students' portfolios. New assessments are being developed, field-tested, and researched to determine their validity and reliability. Assessment procedures must match classroom practices and current research in order to provide valid and reliable information (Williamson, 1993). According to Wiggins (1994), "an authentic and pedagogically supportive writing assessment would educate students and teachers alike as to the qualities sought in finished products and the processes deemed likely to yield exemplary products" (p. 130).

Negative Effects of Standard Assessment. Frederiksen and Collins (1989) raised concerns over the potential negative effects of some forms of assessment on instructional practice. The purpose of an authentic assessment is to inform instruction in a way consistent with the theoretical constructs of language acquisition theory and writing process theory. Thus, the process is designed to support and enhance the teaching of the writing process. Toward this goal, student writing samples to be assessed by the ALA are taken from student writing that is embedded in a writing process. The context of the writing task is authentic. The pieces to be assessed are real examples of students' work, not samples produced for a test during a 45-minute sitting on a standard topic or prompt. Samples are carefully prompted and are part of a process-to-product interaction.

Uses of Assessment Unique to CLD Students

August and Hakuta (1997) claim that several "uses of assessment are unique to English-language learners and bilingual children." These uses include identifying children whose English proficiency is limited, determining eligibility for placement in specific language programs (e.g., bilingual education or English as a Second Language [ESL]), and monitoring student progress in and readiness to exit from special language-service programs. In addition, tests are used to place culturally and linguistically diverse (CLD) students in categorically specific programs—such as Title I, remedial, or advanced course work—and to monitor them in compliance with state and federal programs. Gonzalez et al. (1996) argue that CLD students tend to be overidentified, underidentified, or misidentified, and that more often than not, CLD students are misidentified as either "culturally and linguistically inferior as well as academically and socially incapable due to their disabling condition" (p. 7) or as children "with mental retardation" (p. 8). As a consequence of being inappropriately diagnosed by certain batteries of tests, CLD students are more likely either to suffer from low self-esteem or to struggle with ill-fitted curricula and programs. To "correct" this situation, Gonzalez et al. argue for assessment that can be administered in a child's native language and validated for the purposes for which the test is used, and for all areas of assessment to be included if a child is suspected of having both a language problem and certain types of learning disabilities. In addition to not addressing special assessment needs and contributing to misdiagnosis, the current methods of assessing CLD students lack an expanded understanding of cognitive, cultural, and psychological development and a solid theoretical model to "translate" this understanding into criteria appropriate for assessing CLD students. Gonzalez et al. propose that to be meaningful, assessments have to have "valid assessment procedures that measure specific aspects of language" (p. 73). They further caution that in order to achieve **construct validity,** the test designers will have to ensure that whatever a

Responsible

language test sets out to evaluate should not only be valid but should also promote learning as it relates to important indicators of second-language proficiency. Otherwise, ill-structured tests or test items might have the negative influence of encouraging fossilization of CLD students' language development.

Recommendations for Authentic Assessment. In writing assessment, standardized multiple-choice tests are especially problematic for measuring children's real ability in their writing development because of the recursive nature of the writing process, which involves multiple steps in a nonsequential way. According to Hughes (1989), "even professional testing institutions are unable to construct indirect tests which measure writing ability accurately" (p. 75). Hughes further proposes that in order for a writing assessment instrument to be an accurate tool for measuring writing ability, three factors should be taken into account:

- The writing task should be "properly representative of the [student] population" and one that "we should expect students to be able to perform."

- The assessment should directly "elicit samples of writing which truly represent the students' ability," and nothing else.

- The samples should be scored reliably.

Gonzalez et al. (1996) have come to the conclusion that in order to best evaluate CLD students, alternative assessment methods such as portfolio assessment, regular observation, anecdotal records, checklists, and performance assessment as "bits of curriculum" should be used.

Reasonable

"Quality Control" for Performance Assessment

Stiggins (1995) suggests that performance assessment needs to have "quality control." He proposes three basic methodological ingredients for sound tests: The assessment system has to have a clearly defined specification of performance to be tested, the testing task or testing exercises should be able to elicit that performance easily, and the design of administration procedures and the scoring process should be sound and reliable. Stiggins further proposes that the criteria for selecting a performance to be tested should be based on judgments about whether this performance is key to academic success and whether it embodies standards that could be naturally applied to classroom tasks. He also emphasizes the importance of **inter-rater reliability** in the scoring process. Unless the process has well-designed scoring guides and specific **holistic rating criteria** that have validity and reliability and can be utilized practically, it will be problematic and unable to accurately and sufficiently assess writing development. Standardized tests tend to be biased against CLD students and may affect them negatively. Performance assessment, on the other hand, seems to have the potential to provide avenues to make measurement more accurate and direct. But we are also cautioned about its possible lack of validity and reliability. Furthermore, there does not seem to be much research regarding writing assessment for CLD students. There are, however, discussions of how to test ESL writing development and how to use native language to test CLD students so that they can understand the task and the test. The previous two points do not consider the following issues, which a sound bilingual writing assessment should be able to address:

- Since assessment can elicit behaviors that are seen as valued in the test, writing assessment should also promote bilingual abilities. In other words, the use of native language should not be seen merely as an aid, but instead should be considered a means and an end of the writing assessment.

- The parallel writing assessments in two languages—English and the student's native language—should specify a similar performance to be evaluated according to equal standards and should use parallel testing procedures, also both in English and in the native language, so that the construct and content validity can be achieved.

- The scoring processes should also be in both languages and have similar scoring guides and guidance.

In response to these concerns, University of California, Berkeley and San Francisco Unified School District colleagues have developed an Authentic Literacy Assessment (ALA) in Spanish, English, and Chinese. The ALA is designed to provide students with carefully developed prompts or topics on which they are required to write. These topics are strategically selected by the teacher, and prewriting activities always precede the writing activity. The ALA assessment processes involve eliminating time limitations, providing access to reference materials, and providing opportunities for rehearsal, limited revision, editing, and proofreading. With this support, the ALA is helpful to the student writer who has had no opportunity to think about what he or she wants to say (or write) in an otherwise constrained setting. In developing the ALA, multiple samples of "real" writing from the same students were assessed, and teacher-defined rubrics were created to score the writing product. The development of rubrics and topics was not completed in a vacuum; rather, teacher input and the examination of actual student writing was and is a natural part of the process. Tables 5.1 and 5.2 provide examples of

Authentic Literacy Assessment

Table 5.1   4th/5th Grade Writing Rubric

	Topic	Organization	Style/Voice	Conventions
6	addresses topic thoroughly and coherently presents/explains topic in interesting/engaging manner	writes a 5-paragraph essay that is well-developed and chronological and has transitional sentences writes well-developed ideas with at least 4 details per paragraph includes an interesting introduction, body, and strong conclusion	demonstrates exceptional control and variation of sentence structure uses thoughtful and appropriate language to engage reader throughout the writing piece includes a variety of literary elements (figurative language, metaphors, simile, alliteration) demonstrates an exceptional sense of audience	*spells* some irregular words correctly and all high-frequency words correctly demonstrates an exceptional command of various *spelling* strategies demonstrates an exceptional command of *capitalization* and *punctuation* (" " ? ! .) *grammar:* few errors in the use of pronouns, adjectives, conjunctions, and adverbial forms
5	addresses topic thoroughly and coherently includes a strong sentence which introduces the topic	organizes ideas into multiple paragraphs well-articulated ideas 3 detail sentences per paragraph	uses varied sentence structure consistently writes complex sentences consistently uses varied and thoughtful vocabulary that enriches description	*spells* some irregular words correctly and all high-frequency words correctly *punctuation:* consistently uses (') *grammar:* few errors in the use of pronouns, adjectives, conjunctions, and adverbial forms
4	addresses topic coherently with several details includes a sentence which introduces the topic	organizes ideas into at least 3 paragraphs includes topic, supporting, and closing sentences at least 3 detail sentences per paragraph	uses varied sentence structure uses some complex vocabulary uses varied word choices uses descriptive language (adverbs, adjectives) includes literary elements (figurative language, metaphors, simile, alliteration) uses language to engage reader demonstrates sense of audience	*spells* some irregular words correctly and all high-frequency words correctly applies *spelling* strategies such as roots, suffixes, prefixes *punctuation:* uses (') and uses (? . ! ") correctly *grammar:* few significant errors in the use of pronouns, adjectives, conjunctions, and adverbial forms

3	addresses topic coherently / develops central idea, / incident, or problem with / supporting details	organizes ideas into at least 2 / paragraphs / includes topic sentence, supporting / sentences, and conclusion / writes paragraphs in correct sequence	uses varied sentence structure / writes complex sentences / may incorporate sense of audience through / vocabulary, description	*spells* most irregular words in an understandable way and / almost all high-frequency words correctly / *punctuation:* few errors in use of (, ') / uses dialogue with appropriate *punctuation* / *grammar:* uses correct plurals for irregular nouns and / correct comparisons (good, better, best) / *grammar:* few significant errors in use of pronouns, adjec- / tives, conjunctions, and adverbial forms
2	expands on topic with / several details, mostly / relevant to the topic / writes detailed descriptions / that support the topic	organizes ideas into at least one / paragraph / includes topic sentence, supporting / sentence, and conclusion / uses some transition words	uses varied sentence structure / may write complex sentences / uses adjectives and may use adverbs / uses varied word choice	uses conventional *spelling* for almost all high-frequency / words / applies varied strategies to *spell* blends, orthographic pat- / terns, contractions, compounds, homophones, and / irregular words / almost always uses appropriate *punctuation and capitali- / zation* at beginning/end of sentences
1	expands on topic with / some details, mostly / relevant to the topic	organizes ideas into at least one / paragraph / may include a topic sentence and / closing sentence / writes in a simple sequence	uses varied sentence structure / writes detailed descriptions of familiar / persons, objects, or places / writes as to not confuse the reader	uses conventional *spelling* for most high-frequency words / applies varied strategies to *spell* some blends, ortho- / graphic patterns, contractions, compounds, homophones / applies varied strategies to *spell* irregular words / few errors in use of *capitalization* / *punctuation:* uses (,) and few errors in use of (? . !) / *grammar:* pays some attention to nouns, pronouns, adjec- / tives, irregular verbs, and adverbial forms

Fairmount Elementary Benchmarks: 4th-Grade score level 3, 5th-Grade score level 5   SFUSD writing standards: 4th-Grade score level 3, 5th-Grade score level 4

Source: "4th/5th Grade Writing Rubric," by Erminda García and Jaime Sandoval, San Francisco Unified School District. Reprinted by permission of the authors.

Table 5.2 Cuarto Grado/Quinto Grado Pauta de Escritura

	Tema	Organización	Estilo/Expresión	Reglas de Gramática
6	se dirige al tema en una manera completa y coherente presenta/explica el tema en una manera interesante y atrayente	escribe una composición de 5 párrafos que está bien desarrollada, sigue una cronología y tiene oraciones de transición desarrolla ideas claramente con por lo menos 4 detalles por párrafo incluye una introducción interesante, el cuerpo y una conclusión precisa	demuestra mando excepcional de varias escturas para formar oraciones usa un vocabulario considerado y variado para atraer al lector incluye una variedad de elementos literarios (metáfora, símil, onomatopeya y personaficación) demuestra mando excepcional del sentido del lector	usa *deletreo* correcto para algunas palabras irregulares y todas las palabras comunes demuestra mando excepcional de varias estrategias de *deletreo* demuestra mando excepcional de mayúsculas y puntuación (" ¿ ? ¡ !.) *gramática*: pocos errores en el uso de pronombres, adjetivos, conjunciones y formas adverbiales
5	se dirige al tema en una manera completa y coherente incluye una oración precisa que introduce al tema	organiza ideas en varios párrafos desarrolla ideas claramente 3 oraciones de detalle en cada párrafo	usa varias estructuras regularmente para formar oraciones escribe oraciones complejas regularmente usa un vocabulario considerado y variado que enriquece descripción	usa *deletreo* correcto para algunas palabras irregulares y todas las palabras comunes *gramática*: pocos errores en el uso de pronombres, adjetivos, conjunciones y formas adverbiales usa los *acentos* según las reglas de acentuación con pocos errores importantes
4	se dirige al tema en una manera completa y coherente incluye una oración que introduce al tema	organiza ideas en por lo menos 3 párrafos incluye una oración principal, oraciones de detalle y una oración final por lo menos 3 oraciones de detalla en cada párrafo	usa varias estructuras para formar oraciones usa in vocabulario complejo y variado usa adverbios y adjetivos incluye elementos literarios (metáfora, símil, onomatopeya y personaficación) usa lenguaje para atraer al lector demuestra sentido del lector	usa *deletreo* correcto para algunas palabras irregulares y todas las palabras comunes utiliza estrategias de *deletreo* como (prefijo, sufijo y raíz) *puntuación:* usa (') y usa (¿ ? ¡ !.) correctamente *gramática*: pocos errores importantes en el uso de pronombres, adjetivos, conjunciones y formas adverbiales

	Contenido/Tema	Organización	Oraciones	Ortografía/Gramática
3	se dirige al tema en una manera coherente con varios detalles · incluye una oración que introduce al tema	organiza ideas en por lo menos 2 párrafos · incluye una oración principal, oraciones de detalle y una oración final · incluye algunas palabras de transición · escribe párrafos según la secuencia correcta	usa varias estructuras para formar oraciones · escribe oraciones complejas · puede que incorpore sentido del autor con vocabulario, descripción	usa *deletreo* correcto para casi todas las palabras irregulares y casi todas las palabras comunes · *puntuación:* pocos errores en el uso de (, ") · utiliza diálogo con *puntuación* apropiada · *gramática:* pocos errors importantes en el uso de pronombres, adjetivos, conjunciones y formas adverbiales · puede que use los *acentos* según las reglas de acentuación
2	detalla sobre el tema con varios detalles, por la mayor parte son pertinentes · escribe descripciones detalladas según el tema	organiza ideas en por lo menos un párrafo · incluye una oración principal, oraciones de detalle y una oración final	usa varias estructuras para formar oraciones · puedo que escriba oraciones complejas · usa adjetivos, puede que use adverbios · usa un vocabulario variado	usa *deletreo* correcto para casi todas las palabras comunes · utiliza una variedad de estrategias para *deletrear* diptongos, patrones ortográficos · pocos errores en el uso de *acentos* en palabras comunes · casi siempre usa *puntuación y mayúsculas* al principio/final de la oración
1	detalla sobre el tema con algunos detalles, por la mayor parte son pertinentes	organiza ideas en por lo menos un párrafo · puede que incluya una oración principal y una oración final · escribe en una secuencia básica	usa varias estructuras para formar oraciones · escribe descripciones detalladas de personas conocidas o lugares o objetos conocidos · escribe para no confundir el lector	usa *deletreo* correcto para la mayoría de las palabras comunes · utiliza una variedad de estrategias para deletrear las palabras irregulares · pocos errores en el uso de mayúsculas · *puntuación:* usa (,) y pocos errores en el uso de (¿ ? ¡ ! .) · *gramática:* pone atención al uso de nombres, pronombres, adjetivos, verbos irregulares y formas adverbiales

Fairmount Elementary Benchmarks: 4th-Grade score level 3, 5th-Grade score level 5   SFUSD writing standards: 4th-Grade score level 3, 5th-Grade score level 4

Source: "Cuarto Grado/Quinto Grado," by Erminda García and Jaime Sandoval, San Francisco Unified School District. Reprinted by permission of the authors.

Table 5.3 Language and Literacy Assessment Rubric, K–12

Oral Language — Upon completing this level, the student:

Level	Item	English	Other Lang.
Fluent L1/Trans. L2	23. Engages/interacts effectively/productively in discussion.	○	○
	22. Produces a full range of grade-appropriate grammatical structures/vocabulary in unfamiliar settings.	○	○
	21. Discusses abstract, academic content/concepts.	○	○
	20. Understands/uses native-speaker cultural references.	○	○
Advanced	19. Communicates ideas/information orally with increasing confidence/sophistication of audiences/purposes.	○	○
	18. Contributes to classroom discussions/responds to questions clearly/debates issues.	○	○
	17. Uses age-appropriate vocabulary.	○	○
	16. Demonstrates understanding of idiomatic expressions and colloquialisms in different registers.	○	○
	15. Communicates in new/unfamiliar settings.	○	○
	14. Critiques a movie/book orally.	○	○

Reading — Upon completing this level, the student:

Level	Item	English	Other Lang.
Fluent L1/Trans. L2	24. Reads/comprehends grade-level text with complex language/vocabulary.	○	○
	23. Reads independently from a wide range of materials while evaluating/analyzing text.	○	○
	22. Uses variety of reading strategies to construct/examine/extend the meaning of diverse materials.	○	○
	21. Actively pursues own reading interests.	○	○
	20. Makes predictions/inferences about readings on all topics including abstract ones.	○	○
Advanced	19. Reads with considerable fluency and comprehension; begins to comprehend highly decontextualized text/complex vocabulary.	○	○
	18. Reads independently; chooses increasingly difficult texts; makes predictions/inferences about readings.	○	○
	17. Expands vocabulary using (translation) dictionary/thesaurus.	○	○
	16. Interacts with text by keeping a reading response journal.	○	○
	15. Reads across variety of genres; identifies features of different reading materials (e.g., theme, plot, characters, genre).	○	○

Writing — Upon completing this level, the student:

Level	Item	English	Other Lang.
Fluent L1/Trans. L2	24. Experiments with variety of writing styles/genres, including fact, fiction, persuasion, comparison.	○	○
	23. Writes expository text that is clear, consistent and organized.	○	○
	22. Identifies a central idea and writes from an organizational plan.	○	○
	21. Uses rich, expressive vocabulary.	○	○
	20. Writes with a strong understanding of conventions of written language.	○	○
	19. Uses writing to get and give information.	○	○
	18. Writes on all topics normally required for grade level.	○	○
Advanced	17. Writes from various points of view, with different purposes/audiences; develops fluency/style/voice.	○	○
	16. Creates several connected paragraphs using appropriate conventions of print.	○	○
	15. Demonstrates variety of vocabulary choice, sentence types, and organization of written discourse.	○	○
	14. Takes accurate notes on new/unfamiliar material.	○	○
	13. Applies the steps in the writing process to writing tasks.	○	○
	12. Uses graphics to present/describe data; writes about the data.	○	○

<table>
<thead>
<tr><th>Intermediate</th><th></th><th></th></tr>
</thead>
</table>

Intermediate

13. Speaks comfortably with peers in small groups. ○ ○
12. Expresses responses in phrases/simple sentences. ○ ○
11. Speaks in class on topic; may lack organization. ○ ○
10. Identifies main topic/details of stories/lectures; retells sequence of events. ○ ○
9. Asks for clarification in different situations. ○ ○
8. Expresses a range of personal needs/preferences. ○ ○
7. Uses a variety of verbal/nonverbal strategies. ○ ○

6. Begins to speak to peers/in some small group situations. ○ ○
5. Makes oral recitations/simple presentations. ○ ○
4. Responds appropriately/thoughtfully/actively to simple commands/questions, through actions or one/two-word phrases. ○ ○
3. Names principal locations/familiar objects. ○ ○
2. Gives basic personal information, expresses personal/safety needs. ○ ○
1. Dramatizes/gestures/draws pictures to show comprehension/needs. ○ ○

Comments

---

14. Constructs meaning from texts containing background knowledge relevant to student's experience. ○
13. Locates/identifies specific facts in a text. ○
12. Chooses appropriate pleasure reading materials independently. ○
11. Uses dictionaries to define words (e.g., maintain a personal dictionary of important new words). ○
10. Recognizes main topic/supporting details of a reading selection, summarizes the selection. ○
9. Reads/follows simple written directions. ○
8. Responds to text in various modes such as drawing, mapping and diagramming. ○

7. Constructs meaning from text through illustrations and other nonprint features. ○
6. Enjoys being read to, demonstrates comprehension/sequencing. ○
5. Reads familiar words and phrases aloud. ○
4. Reads simple narratives of routine behaviors. ○
3. Identifies/associates written symbols, recognizes/identifies letters. ○
2. Demonstrates book sense: tracking/locating cover, author, title/matching pictures to words. ○
1. Follows along in text as story is read aloud. ○

Comments

---

11. Generates ideas for simple stories with awareness of sequence/detail. ○ ○
10. Creates original paragraphs using appropriate conventions of print. ○ ○
9. Writes short answers to questions. ○ ○
8. Uses variety of genres in writing. ○ ○ ○ ○
7. Participates in revising/editing own work. ○ ○

6. Uses some conventions of print including spacing between words, names and letters (e.g., mechanics explicit to language). ○ ○
5. Writes to describe a drawing or illustration. ○ ○
4. Writes statements/questions on familiar topics/on visual prompt. ○ ○
3. Writes primarily about experiences and retells stories written. ○ ○
2. Copies simple text and/or environmental print to communicate. ○ ○
1. Uses invented spelling and familiar words or short phrases. ○ ○

Comments

Beginning

Source: "Becoming a Responsive Teacher: Language and Literary Assessment Rubric," by Erminda García. Reprinted by permission of the author.

Language and Literacy Assessment Rubric

Erminda García
First Grade Teacher
Fairmount Elementary School
San Francisco, CA

The San Francisco Unified School District Language and Literacy Assessment Rubric (LALAR) was created and developed by Erminda García and Jaime Sandoval. It supports teachers in documenting the language-learning stories of their students. The rubric provides teachers with language use descriptors that are grouped together in beginning, intermediate, advanced, and fluent levels. It also allows a teacher to document a student's first language and transitioning skills into second-language levels. This format asks a teacher to document the language use in oral, reading, and writing contexts.

After listening to and observing language use by their students, teachers identifying language descriptors on the LALAR fill in appropriate bubbles and document the current language level of the students. The LALAR then provides the teacher with the next level of language-level descriptors, which can be used to inform instructional decisions around language learning.

The LALARs of individual students will support teachers in documenting the student's language growth in both languages. The LALAR rubrics of a class can be used to help teachers create specific language student groups. The monitoring process that the LALAR reflects has become one of the major components of language review decisions.

Throughout the development of the LALAR, Language Arts Standards and ELD standards for the district were consulted for both type and level of language descriptors. Within the LALAR, teachers will begin to recognize the articulation and consistency of the LALAR, SFUSD Language Arts, and ELD Standards.

It is important to understand that the collection of artifacts, anecdotals, checklists, etc. are used to document language learning on the LALAR. These then become purposeful collections of language learning. Every year these portfolio collections place the LALAR as the centerpiece that gathers the instructional information shared from teacher to teacher.

(Used by permission of the author: Erminda García)

the developed rubrics for fourth and fifth grade in English and Spanish, respectively (See García, Casimir, Sun, Wiese, and García [1999] for details on the ALA.)

In this discussion, I have attempted to articulate the importance of developing and implementing a more authentic assessment of literacy for culturally and linguistically diverse student populations. Drawing upon our own work and observations of effective schooling practices throughout the United States, I list the following set of principles that guided this effort to develop authentic assessments for diverse student populations:

- The assessment process and instrument must be aligned with high standards and instructional activity existent in the classroom, including use of the language(s) in which instruction is given.

- The assessment must maximize the students' experience and ability to demonstrate competencies in several domains.

- The assessment must be ongoing and must be able to demonstrate development/learning over the entire academic year.

- The assessment must be tied to a theoretical and empirical knowledge base and coupled with teacher practice expertise.

- The results and analysis of the assessment must be usable by teachers to inform, adapt, and maximize instruction.

- Wherever possible, students should be able to participate in the development and utilization of the assessment process.

In addition to direct authentic assessments of student work, teacher judgment has been valuable in providing highly useful information about the development of language and literacy. In our own work, researchers and teachers have developed and implemented a very directed student evaluation rubric that depends on teacher evaluation of very specific language and literacy domains. A description and example of the system (the Language and Literacy Assessment Rubric—LALAR) as used in the San Francisco Unified District is provided in the next few pages. (see also Table 5.3 on pp. 200–201).

Two-Way Immersion Programs

The **two-way immersion programs (TWI)** are relatively new in the United States. These programs aim to create bilingual, bicultural students without sacrificing these students' success in school or beyond. Unique among programs, TWI has the dual goal of providing high-quality instruction for language minority students and providing instruction in a second language for English-speaking students. Schools teach children language through content, with teachers adapting their instruction to ensure children's comprehension and using content lessons to convey vocabulary and language structure. Striving for half language minority students and half English-speaking students in each classroom, TWI programs also aim to teach cross-cultural awareness. Programs vary in terms of the amount of time they devote to each language, which grade levels they serve, how much structure they impose for the division of language and curriculum, and which populations they serve. There are two widely adopted models of language division. In the 50:50 model, instruction is given half the day in English and half the day in Spanish throughout the grades. In the 90:10 model, children spend 90 percent of their kindergarten school days using the minority language; that percentage gradually drops to 50 percent by fourth or fifth grade. Currently in the United States there are over 225 TWI programs, and the number is growing quickly (Christian, 1999). Although the vast majority offer instruction in Spanish and English, there are also programs that target Korean, Cantonese, Arabic, French, Japanese, Navajo, Portuguese, and Russian (Christian, 1997).

Goals of Two-Way Immersion

Two-way immersion programs have three major goals: to help language minority children to learn English and achieve success in U.S. schools, to help language majority children learn a foreign language without sacrificing their own success in school, and to promote linguistic and ethnic equity among the students, encouraging children to bridge the gaps between cultures and languages that, unfortunately, divide our society. These goals are naturally interdependent. An English-speaking child who is taught to understand that another language and culture is as equally important as her or his own will be more interested in learning about that culture and in acquiring that language. A minority language child who is given higher school status due to her knowledge of her home language will have more confidence in her ability to learn English. A child who learns the language of her peer is more likely to want to become friends with him, regardless of his racial or ethnic background.

Wallace Lambert (1990) suggests that TWI programs are a perfect resolution to the strange and prevalent dichotomy between foreign language education and bilingual education in U.S. schools. He further maintains that the purpose of "Second Language pedagogy" is to bring "Language Minority families into the American mold, to teach them our national language, to help them wash out as quickly as possible old country ways" (p. 323). On the other hand, he says that "the foreign language approach aims to add refinement and international class to the down-to-earth, eminently practical American character" (p. 324). His clear conclusion: Two-way immersion will improve language teaching for everyone, both second-language learners and foreign-language learners, in the same classroom. However, Valdés(1997) warns practitioners and researchers to beware. Attempting to meet the needs of two such different populations in one program is a dangerous proposition and brings to the fore many questions of power distribution in the classroom and in society. She warns practitioners that when they modify the target language so that majority language students can comprehend it, they may simultaneously be watering down the language for minority language students. There is a difference, Valdés (1997) asserts, between the acquisition of English for minority children and the acquisition of a foreign language for majority children: For minority children, the acquisition of English is expected; for mainstream children, the acquisition of a non-English language is enthusiastically applauded.

As this set of issues continues to receive attention, there is evidence to suggest that TWI is an excellent model for academic achievement for language minority children. It appears to promote English-language learning as well as or better than other special programs designed for language minority children. One hundred percent of Spanish-dominant children in the Key School, a 50:50 TWI school in Arlington County, Virginia, demonstrated oral English fluency by third grade, as shown by the LAS-O Oral English Proficiency measure and classroom observations. Moreover, English writing samples collected from native Spanish speakers in fifth and sixth grade were indistinguishable from those of native English speakers, and all were of high quality (Christian, 1997). In a separate study of four TWI schools following the 90:10 program model in California, it was noted that by fifth grade most students were clearly fluent in English and made good progress in acquiring English reading skills at most school sites (although they did not attain grade-level performance in reading) (Lindholm, 1999).

TWI also appears to encourage achievement in the academic subjects in both English and the minority languages. In a study comparing TWI students with a control population, Christian (1994) showed that third-graders from the Amigos Dual Immersion Program in Cambridge, Massachusetts, outperformed a Spanish-speaking cohort in a more conventional bilingual education program in reading and mathematics in both Spanish and English. In fact, these children performed consistently at or slightly below grade-level norms for children their age, which included English-speaking children. TWI seemed to provide these

Successful Two-Way Immersion Programs

children with the tools they needed to perform well in school assessments in English, even though the majority of their school time had been spent in Spanish instruction. This phenomenon was further demonstrated in a study conducted several years later at the Amigos school. Here, children from fourth through eighth grade were shown to consistently perform at least as well as and often significantly better than control populations on standardized tests in both English and Spanish (Cazabon et al. 1999). In Lindholm's study of four 90:10 schools in California, Spanish bilingual students scored at grade level in mathematics in Spanish and at or below grade level in mathematics in English. Performance in science and social studies was average to very high. Lindholm (1999) notes that these scores should be compared with California's student performance scores in general, which are the lowest of all 50 states; thus, to report that TWI students "were scoring at or above grade level in reading and mathematics means that these students were scoring better than most students in California" (p. 16).

Spanish-speaking children in TWI programs also seem to maintain or improve their oral Spanish proficiency. At the Key School, although only 88 percent of first-grade Spanish-speaking children tested as being fluent in Spanish, Spanish-speaking children in grades two and above all tested as being fluent in Spanish. Christian (1997) asserts that this finding is similar to findings from previous years; even Spanish-dominant students seem to make oral gains in Spanish in these programs (p. 9). California Spanish bilingual students in 90:10 programs also "maintained high levels of proficiency in their first language" (Lindholm, 1999, p. 15). This provides evidence to allay Valdés's fear that TWI programs may water down Spanish-language instruction for minority children.

Two-Way Immersion Results for English-Speaking Children

The evidence concerning English-speaking children is more mixed. It is clear that these students' English skills did not suffer at all from their time spent learning content in another language. English-speaking students in the Amigos program in Cambridge performed comparably with English controls in English reading and English-based mathematics at all grade levels (Christian, 1994). English bilingual students from TWI programs in California "maintained high levels of proficiency in their first language" throughout their years in the program and performed at or above their grade level in English, reading, mathematics, social studies, and science as measured by a nationwide normed standardized test (Lindholm, 1999, p. 18).

Although it does appear that English-speaking children develop strong skills in their second language through their schooling alone, there are gaps in their language knowledge that can probably be attributed to the fact that English, not the target language, is the dominant language in our society. It is also difficult to determine whether their language acquisition is up to par because there is no similar group of children learning a second language with which to compare them; comparing them with Spanish-speaking children learning English, as Valdés (1996) has pointed out, can be confounding. In general, English speakers are not found to have gained strong Spanish oral fluency. Christian's (1994) findings at the Key School indicated that only 50 percent of English-dominant fourth- and fifth-graders demonstrated Spanish fluency (by the SOPR measure and classroom observations), in contrast to 100 percent of Spanish-dominant third graders who demonstrated English fluency. Lindholm (1999) found in her examination of 90:10 programs in California that "while most Spanish bilingual students were clearly fluent in English, many English bilingual students lacked the fluency, vocabulary and grammar to converse entirely in Spanish about a variety of topics" (p. 15).

Therefore, it appears that majority students are certainly not hampered in their progress in English or in academic subjects because they are learning a second language in school. However, it seems that although these students do gain skills in their second language in TWI programs, they do not necessarily gain native-like fluency in it by the time they graduate, and they do not necessarily learn as much of their second language as their Spanish-speaking peers learn of English. Why this difference exists, and how/whether it can be overcome, is not yet clear and is a subject for further research.

Academic English and the Second-Language Learner

Research has suggested that bilingual students in U.S. schools are performing poorly at school because they have not acquired *academic English,* the specific type of English used in reading and writing academic papers and in discussing academic issues (Fillmore and Snow, 1999). Even when their English is adequate for ordinary situations, it is insufficient given the linguistic demands that they face in academic settings (García, 1999).

To acquire English proficiency beyond a very basic level, children have to have access to the language used in written texts; that is, they have to read (August and Hakuta, 1997; Fillmore and Snow, 1999). However, in order to read, they must have more than a basic proficiency in English. Native English speakers generally begin school with basic English proficiency, and if this basic proficiency is augmented through instruction during their early years of schooling, they will be able to access reading fairly easily (Fillmore and Snow, 1999). In contrast, bilingual students have a more difficult time reaching the proficiency level needed to access reading. The books that they are required to access when they begin reading are often already on a level far beyond what they are capable of assessing. As a result of their failure to achieve enough basic proficiency to access reading, these students do not learn to read. Additionally, as a result of their failure to learn to read, these students do not learn to write. By the time many reach middle school, they are often unable to meet the linguistic demands (Snow, Burns, and Griffin, 1998).

Issues involved in teaching academic English have recently received nationwide attention. Most researchers agree that *academic English* refers to the specific types of literacy that students need to achieve academic purposes. Academic literacy tasks include reading abstracts, taking notes on the key ideas presented in lectures, and writing expository and argumentative essays. Fillmore and Snow (1999) report on a recent study of prototype test items for a high school qualifying examination for one of the 23 states that has adopted this required test. Their analysis reveals that students must have competence in academic English to do well on the test. The language used in the test is not different from the language ordinarily used in school textbooks and in academic discussions about science, mathematics, literature, or social studies. To deal with this test successfully, students must do the following:

Academic Literacy

- Summarize texts, using linguistic cues to interpret and infer the writer's intentions and messages

- Analyze texts, assessing the writer's use of language for rhetorical and aesthetic purposes and to express perspective, mood, etc.

- Extract meaning and information from texts and relate it to other ideas and information

- Evaluate evidence and arguments presented in texts and critique the logic of arguments made in them

- Recognize and analyze textual conventions used in various genres for special effect, to trigger background knowledge, or for perlocutionary effect

- Recognize ungrammatical and infelicitous usage in written language and make necessary corrections in grammar, punctuation, and capitalization used in texts

- Use grammatical devices for combining sentences into concise and more effective new ones and use various devices to combine sentences into coherent and cohesive texts

- Compose and write an extended, reasoned piece of writing that is well developed and supported with evidence and details

- Interpret word problems—recognizing that in such contexts, ordinary words may have quite specialized meanings—e.g., that "share equally among them" means to divide a whole into equal parts

- Extract precise information from a written text and devise an appropriate strategy for solving the problem based on the information provided in the text

Academic English serves in a gatekeeping capacity in higher education in the United States. Those students who acquire it are generally able to attain academic success, and those students who do not acquire it generally are not. The basic English language proficiency needed to communicate in everyday situations contributes to the development of academic English, and academic English contributes to general language proficiency. In order to acquire the most advanced English proficiencies underlying the abilities to read, write, speak, and listen in academic situations, students must be able to read and write academic text.

Traditionally, literacy was narrowly defined as the ability to read and write, a skill that involved decoding and encoding. Today, however, most researchers agree that literacy involves not simply deciphering a written text but also understanding what it is about. They take a much broader view of literacy, suggesting that it involves mechanics such as decoding as well as higher-order thinking—conceptualizing, inferring, inventing, testing hypothesis, and thinking critically. These researchers argue that literacy encompasses oral communication skills as well as reading and writing skills (García, 1999).

What Constitutes Academic English?   Academic English is often viewed as a register that encompasses many diverse types of subregisters, representing diverse disciplines and including the language of science, the language of economics, and the language of mathematics. In recent years, there have been many confusing reports concerning what constitutes academic English. This conflicting information has created a difficult situation for teachers who have the daunting task of teaching academic English.

Academic English as a Set of Linguistic Features   One view of academic English prominent in the literature is that it consists of a compilation of a rather narrowly defined range of linguistic features—specifically, language functions and their associated semantic, lexical, and grammatical features (Hamayan and Perlman, 1990). O'Malley (1992) and Valdés (1997) hypothesize, for example, that a small number of language functions characterize academic English. They include seeking information, informing, analyzing, comparing, classifying, predicting, hypothesizing, justifying, persuading, solving problems, synthesizing, and evaluating. Snow, Carcino, Gonzalez, and Schriberg (1987) apply this functional perspective of academic English to mathematics. Their findings are based upon simulated mathematics problem-solving activities among community college students participating in algebra classes. Spanos and his colleagues argue that syntactic features—such as comparatives *(greater than/less than),* logical connectors *(if . . . then, given that),* the passive voice, and specific prepositions—are particular to the language used in mathematics classes. They also identify a limited number of other linguistic features of mathematics language: technical vocabulary (e.g., *additive, inverse, coefficient),* ordinary vocabulary that has different meanings in math, (e.g., *square, power),* fixed expressions (e.g., *least common denominator, negative exponent),* synonyms (e.g., *add, plus,* and *combine),* and mathematical symbols and notations (Snow, Carcino, Gonzalez, and Schriberg, 1987). The National Science Teachers Association (1991) and Chamot and O'Malley (1986) take a similar narrow focus on the functions of academic English. They suggest that in science, academic English functions to formulate hypotheses, propose alternative solutions, describe, classify, infer, interpret data, predict, generalize, and communicate findings. In addition, they argue that science uses nontechnical terms that have unique meanings in a scientific context (e.g., *table, energy)* and that scientific discourse is characterized by a heavy reliance on the passive voice and long noun phrases. Like these researchers, Halliday and Martinez (1993) suggest that the language of science can be characterized by a restricted number of linguistic features—including technical words, special expressions, and grammatical metaphors. Along similar lines, Lempke (1990) undertakes an even more narrow study, showing that the language of science entails a preference for the passive voice.

Such a limited view of academic English as the compilation of a restricted number of discrete linguistic items fails to provide teachers and researchers with enough practical information concerning what it is that students must know if they are to master academic English. Without more detailed information, teachers will have difficulty instructing and assessing emerging academic English effectively. In addition, this type of restricted view of academic English, though interesting and useful to linguists, is not always equally so to teachers. It ignores the traditional terms with which teachers are already familiar (*spelling* and *punctuation,* for example).

In contrast to this very narrow view of academic English is a very broad one. It holds that academic English is any English that

Academic English as Classroom Language

occurs in classroom settings. Researchers accepting this perspective believe that teachers are competent in academic English, use it in the classroom, and teach it through their interactions with children in the classroom. These researchers sometimes conduct extensive discourse analyses of classrooms, suggesting that these analyses reveal the characteristics of academic language (Scarcella, 1999).

Unfortunately, in many classrooms academic literacy rarely, if ever, occurs either in teacher-student interaction of in student-student interaction. This is because in these classrooms interactions are restricted to the basic, more frequently occurring patterns of ordinary language. Children's language learning is affected by teachers' instructional practices (Wong-Fillmore, 1983), and many teachers neither use nor teach academic English.

In the third view prevalent in the research, one advanced by Cummins (1981), scholars attempt to distinguish English acquired in school for academic purposes, which Cummins terms *Cognitive Academic Language Proficiency (CALP)*, from conversational language that is acquired to carry on nonacademic interactions, which Cummins terms *Basic Interpersonal Communicative Skills (BICS)*. Cummins and others who have extended his model (Chamot and O'Malley, 1986; Collier, 1985; Hamayan and Perlman, 1990; O'Malley, 1992) argue that BICS is acquired earlier than CALP since it is easier to acquire. In BICS, meaning is accomplished through the assistance of contextual and paralinguistic cues that help us all make sense of informal, nonacademic interactions. This means that students do not have to depend only on language in order to attain meaning; rather, to attain meaning, they can use a variety of cues, including body language and intonation. These cues are hypothesized to increase the comprehensibility of the input and facilitate language development. CALP, on the other hand, tends to be very context-unspecific: One can read about the intricacies of outer-space travel without traveling there. The words themselves are intended to convey the meaning to the reader.

Although this view of academic English contributes to our understanding of why bilingual students might struggle to acquire it, the view of academic English it presents does not always play out in reality. (For instance, some aspects of BICS are often acquired late.) More importantly, the perspective does not provide teachers with the detailed information that they need to help their students acquire academic English.

Relationship Between Academic and General English. More recently, Scarcella (1999) has suggested that academic English entails multiple, interrelated competencies related to reading,

---

Margin note:

Academic English as Distinct from Conversational English

writing, speaking, and listening. In this perspective, simplified bi-nary explanations of academic English such as the BICS/CALP distinction are rejected. She argues that the features that enable students to use English in everyday situations and in academic situations are acquired at different rates over time; some are eas-ily acquired and some are not. Most features of academic English depend upon the development of basic English proficiency to a large extent, but there are many others (including formulaic ex-pressions and simple word forms and transitional devices) that may depend less on the development of general language profi-ciency. In general, academic English and general English lan-guage proficiency have a symbiotic relationship. A student's acquisition of academic English indicates that his or her general English language proficiency is in the advanced stages because academic English constitutes an important part of the student's general language proficiency, which rests upon the development of general English language proficiency. General English lan-guage proficiency, on the other hand, is viewed as an integral component of academic English, for it is through the acquisition of academic English that general English proficiency is advanced.

In addition, within the various components, some features may be more important than others. For instance, specific lin-guistic *functions* (such as persuading, arguing, and hypothesiz-ing) are more characteristic of academic English than of ordinary English. Also, academic English makes more extensive use of reading and writing while ordinary English makes more extensive use of listening and reading. In addition, Cummins (1981, 1984) points out that academic English, in comparison with ordinary English, is cognitively demanding and relatively decontextual-ized. All students, including those acquiring English as their sec-ond language in a bilingual schooling context, rely on their prior knowledge of words, phraseology, grammar, and pragmatic con-ventions to understand and interpret it. However, perhaps most importantly, academic English requires a much greater mastery of a wider range of linguistic features than ordinary English does. It is important to note that despite these differences, both aca-demic English and ordinary English require proficiency in the same linguistic components: phonological, grammatical, lexical, sociolinguistic, discoursal, and strategic.

In the absence of a consensus regarding notions of academic English and related research regarding its development in bilin-gual schooling circumstances, considerable agreement is begin-ning to emerge concerning the factors that affect its development (see, for example, Snow et al. [1998], García [1999], or Scarcella [1999]). The development of academic English is affected by politi-cal, social, psychological, and linguistic variables. Instruction also has an enormous effect on the acquisition of academic English.

Table 5.4	A Comparison of the Types of Proficiencies Associated with Ordinary English and Academic English (From Scarcella, 1999)

Components of Ordinary English

Components of Academic English

1. **Phonological:** Knowledge of English sounds and the ways sounds are combined, stress and intonation, graphemes, and spelling

   Examples: *ship* versus *sheep* /I/ - /i/
   sheet versus *cheat* /sh/ - /ch/

Knowledge of new phonological features, including stress, intonation, and sound patterns

   Examples: *demography, demographic, cadence, generic, casualty,* and *celerity*

2. **Lexical:** Knowledge of the forms and meanings of words occurring in everyday situations; knowledge of how words are formed with prefixes, roots, and suffixes; the parts of speech of words; and the grammatical constraints governing words

Knowledge of *general words* that are used across academic disciplines (as well as in everyday situations outside of academic settings), *technical words* that are used in specific academic fields, and *nontechnical academic words* that are used across academic fields

3. **Grammatical:** Knowledge of morphemes entailing semantic, syntactic, relational, phonological, and distributional properties; knowledge of syntax; knowledge of simple rules of punctuation

Knowledge that enables students to make sense out of and use the grammatical features (morphological and syntactic) associated with argumentative composition, chronological development, definition, procedural description, and analysis; knowledge of the grammatical co-occurrence restrictions governing words; knowledge of more complex rules of punctuation

4. **Sociolinguistic:** Knowledge that enables ELLs to understand the extent to which sentences are produced and understood appropriately; knowledge of frequently occurring functions and genres

Knowledge of an increased number of language *functions.* The functions include the general ones of ordinary English such as apologizing, complaining and making requests as well as ones that are more common to all academic fields, and technical ones that are associated with specific disciplines; knowledge of an increased number of genres, including expository and argumentative texts

5. **Discoursal:** Knowledge of the basic discourse devices used, for instance, to introduce topics and keep the talk going and for beginning and ending informal types of writing, such as letters and lists

Knowledge of the basic discourse devices; knowledge of the discourse features used in specific academic genres, including such devices as conclusions, transitions and other organizational signals that, in reading, aid in gaining perspectives on what is read, in seeing relationships, and in following logical lines of thought; in writing, these discourse features help ELLs develop their theses and provide smooth transitions between ideas

6. **Strategic:** Knowledge of strategies that may be called into action either to enhance the effectiveness of communication or to compensate for breakdowns in communication due to limiting factors in actual communication or to insufficient competence

Knowledge of cognitive and metacognitive strategies for reading, writing, speaking and listening related to academic contexts—underlining, highlighting, paraphrasing in the margins, outlining, identifying key ideas and using context and word attack strategies to determine meaning

Real-Life Practices That Enhance Literacy Development

In October of his first year of school, a third-grade Hmong child, Se, carefully copies into his journal a few lines of "The Good Morning Song" from the sentence strips his teacher keeps in a pocket chart. The room is filled with other print sources that he could have chosen to copy. The teacher has allowed the children to draw or write on whatever topic they wish. When Se's teacher asks him to tell her about what he's written, he only smiles, for he is not ready to speak in English except for occasional one-word answers, most often given in chorus with other students.

Becoming a Responsive Teacher

This teacher knows she's doing the right thing by immersing her children in print. She's familiar with the work of researchers such as Brian Campbourne who have pointed out that children learning English as a Second Language (ESL) may rely on environmental print as a writing source for their stories or journal entries for a longer period of time than do native English-speaking children. Sometimes ESL children, like young native speakers of English, copy print but don't refer to it when they talk to their teachers about their stories; later, however, they may use their copied words to generate a meaningful message or story. But all children, both ESL and native speakers of English, need a print-enriched classroom.

This teacher has also just begun to allow her students to exercise choice about the topics in their journals and stories. Like many other teachers, she thought that her ESL students, with their very limited knowledge of English, needed topics, frames, or sentences to copy. She and others did not think that their ESL students could go through all the stages of the writing process. But as the teachers at her school have raised their expectations about the language and literacy development their ESL students are capable of, they are finding that these students not only meet those standards but also push them upward.

In a primary-grade classroom, the student teacher asks the ESL children about the kinds of birds that they know. She makes a list of their answers and asks them to listen and look for more kinds of birds to add to the list as she reads them the book *Where's the Green Parrot?* The book's repetitive structure allows children to predict what will happen next and to "read" the story aloud with their teacher.

This student teacher knows the crucial role of linking ESL children's background knowledge and personal experience to the beginning of any literacy event. She also knows that when she does this, she makes it possible for even those children with little English proficiency to construct meaning with her and with their peers as if they were more

Continued   Real-Life Practices That Enhance Literacy Development

proficient in English. Lessons centered on the students' experiences become even more critical when the children are asked to construct meaning in their second language.

This reminds us of how much ESL lessons have changed in terms of materials. We used to think that we needed boxes of special vocabulary- and grammar-controlled materials, with the accompanying dittos. Now those are nowhere to be found at this school. Instead, books—whole books, not excerpts—flood the rooms. Rather than buying basal readers and workbooks, the principal allots each teacher money to purchase trade books, the same children's books that are sold in bookstores. The students have access to attractive, whole books and poems. These sources help ESL students construct meaning by giving them the multiple cues that only authentic children's texts can, such as pictures, complete story grammars, and natural language patterns.

At a high school Working Group on Language and Culture, a teacher examined data on immigrant students' school participation and achievement and found that 25 percent of the students left school after the ninth grade. To address the students' needs and reduce their dropout rate, the group planned and lobbied for funding for an ESL literacy program in which a small number of teachers would work with a small group of students to develop curricula, engage in intensive individual coaching, and track students' achievement. Thus, what had begun as one's teacher observation led to the development of a theoretically sound, clearly articulated, practical program. This program considered the development of academic English—English that would allow students to succeed in the content area of instruction.

Most afternoons children in a combined second- and third-grade classroom may choose to participate in an array of learning centers: dramatic play, art, writing, or math. The talk one hears at these centers—in Hmong, Vietnamese, Spanish, Chinese, and sometimes English, as children from different language groups interact—is rich, rapid, and incessant.

The teacher has purposely organized her classroom so that the students are actively engaged in talking and learning. She knows that recent research indicates that limited-English-proficient children show greater growth in English when they are not in a traditional teacher-directed lesson. As the children are involved with the various classroom learning centers, the teacher circulates, talking with children and noting their language use in anecdotal records that she will add to

Continued   Real-Life Practices That Enhance Literacy Development

their portfolios. She knows that these longitudinal records of observations and interactions give her much more information about her students' language development than any formal language proficiency test could provide.

The teacher comments: "It is true that setting up these conditions for students calls for a dramatic shift away from the curriculum offered them in the past. It essentially calls for a new view of students, of their learning, and of teachers' roles in facilitating that learning. But it also seems to me that teachers and students at this school start with the understanding that there are no barriers to optimizing instruction for students, except perhaps the ones we construct."

Meeting the Challenge

1. Visit a bookstore that has a large collection of children's literature. Spend some time browsing the shelves. Do these books take into account the diverse backgrounds of children in the United States? Write down the name of the author, title, and publisher of the five most interesting books you discover. Bring your notes to class and compile a master list.

Academic English: Conditions for Success

Academic English seems to develop successfully in classroom situations when the following conditions are met:

1. **Teachers provide students with ample exposure to academic English.** Teachers make regular use of classroom activities and assignments that call for students to use academic English. They provide students with extensive practice in the use of academic English in speech and in writing, including its use in meaningful and purposeful academic discussions about texts that the students are using and in writing expository essays.

2. **Teachers get students to attend closely to the features of academic English.** Teachers regularly use classroom activities and assignments that require students to pay particular attention to the features of academic English.

3. **Teachers provide direct, explicit language instruction.** Teachers provide direct, explicit language instruction of

Continued Real-Life Practices That Enhance Literacy Development

2. Experiment with "story time" with your classmates. Bring a children's book written at any grade level to class and read it aloud. When you are a reader, remember to speak clearly and distinctly and to consider your audience. As an audience member while others read aloud, remain attentive to your responses to the story and the reader. During class discussion after all the stories have been read, comment on your experience as a reader and as a listener.

3. What do you think of the concept of "academic" English described in this chapter? What is your attitude toward your own use of academic English? Using one example from a past schooling experience, describe the role that academic English played in your learning process, either positively or negatively.

4. Visit two elementary school classrooms, one that is all English-speaking and one that has a significant number of non-English-speaking students (e.g., an ESL classroom). In each classroom, observe the frequency and quality of social communication, both teacher-student and student-student. Note the structure of each classroom and the opportunities for language acquisition such as reading environmental print, reading aloud, and writing. Record some of the interactions that you find significant and explain why they are or are not supportive of literacy development.

particular features of academic English including instruction in vocabulary (e.g., word formation skills) and in grammar (e.g., specific uses of grammatical rules such as forming tenses).

4. **Teachers provide multiple assessments of ELLs' academic English.** Teachers give learners honest feedback about their English development. They provide valid, reliable, and frequent assessments (including entry placement-level assessment; diagnostic, **formative assessments;** and **summative assessments**) using multiple measures. These measures accomplish the following objectives: (1) They allow teachers to measure their students' developing academic English skills and to tailor their instruction appropriately. (2) They provide parents with information that will help them support their children's learning. (3) They provide instructional information to all students that will help them learn English (adapted from Scarcella, 1999).

Use of Dialects

Along with the multiple languages in use in our society, a great many dialects also exist. A **dialect** is a regional variation of language characterized by distinct grammar, vocabulary, and pronunciation. Between speakers of the same language, different dialects are usually mutually intelligible whereas different languages are mutually unintelligible. However, the dialects of some languages are so different that their speakers cannot understand each other. As the Linguistic Society of America (1997) points out, the Chinese language has two major dialects, Mandarin and Cantonese, which are mutually unintelligible. In contrast, Norwegian and Swedish, which are considered different languages, are mutually intelligible to speakers of each language.

Dialects of English | The English language consists of American, British, Australian, and Canadian dialects. Canadian English is more similar to American English than to British English. Each of these dialects has its own further variations. For instance, in American English there are southern, midland, northern, Boston, Appalachian, Cajun, Black, and Hawaiian dialects (Gleason, 1988). Dialects share most linguistic features with the language on which they are based, but they differ from each other primarily according to the frequency of certain usages. For example, speakers of the Boston dialect pronounce the terminal *r* of words less frequently than do speakers of other American English dialects. To a non-Bostonian, "car" in the Boston dialect may sound like "cah."

Whereas language is associated with a specific national origin or geographic location, dialects tend to be associated with characteristics of the speaker, such as race, gender, age, social class, and geographic region of origin. Only when people change their status or role with respect to these important characteristics do they find it necessary to acquire a new dialect (e.g., in the United States, people who move to the South may acquire a southern dialect). As Harrison (1985) points out, languages are not fixed and isolated entities but rather are collections of repertoires that have appropriate occasions for use, depending on the setting, topic, and social status of the respective speakers and listeners. In most cultures, not all dialects are considered appropriate for all occasions. Because of this, some speakers never have any need to learn more than one dialect in a single language whereas others will need to learn many dialects or languages.

Standard and Nonstandard English | U.S. schooling practices presuppose that Standard English is a vital tool for success in the United States and recognize its increasing prominence as an international language. **Standard English** is the version of English that has the grammar, vocabulary, and pronunciation considered appropriate for most occasions of public discourse and for written communication. It is the "standard" in that its rules for grammar, vocabulary, and pronunciation are taken to be authoritative. Most dialects are "nonstandard," meaning that their rules for sentence structure, word usage, and phonology vary from those of Standard English. Negative attitudes about speech start with the belief that some dialects are linguistically inferior to the standard version of the language. Until quite recently in the United States, any variation from Standard English spoken by children was viewed as a limited and debilitating educational drawback. However, linguistic research (Labov, 1972a) indicates that language variation is a natural reflection of cultural and community differences. People's attitudes toward languages, particularly toward dialects, stem from the social class structure. If some dialects of English are more highly regarded than others, this situation reflects a socially constructed hierarchy that makes deviations from these dialects seem "unnatural, incorrect and inferior" (Thornton, 1981).

Black English

Black English, also referred to as *Black English Vernacular* or *Ebonics,* is the most studied nonstandard American English dialect. It has its roots in African Creole and English but has distinct syntactic, phonological, semantic, and vocabulary rules. Labov (1972b) estimated that 80 percent of the African American population in the United States speaks Black English; he noted that some Puerto Ricans in New York City speak Black English as well as Puerto Rican Spanish. More recent estimates suggest that 60 to 70 percent of the U.S. African American population speaks Black English (Lucas, 1987; Wiley, 1996).

The terms *dialect* and *language* are sufficiently unclear enough to cause much confusion among educators who serve linguistically diverse students. These terms are not even well defined by linguists, although they have learned to live with the ambiguities. In understanding these terms, it helps to recall that everyone grows up speaking a language. If there are noticeable variations in the way the language is spoken by different individuals, we might conclude that they speak different dialects.

Often there is no clear-cut way of distinguishing among different dialects. There are certain criteria, usually based on historical relationships within the language, that are used to make such determinations, but these distinctions are quite arbitrary and depend on the existence of good historical records and sometimes on formal analyses of the written language. Particularly for the spoken languages of today, much arbitrariness enters into decisions about whether the forms of English used by Appalachian

Confusing Terminology

Learning by Talking

Becoming a Responsive Teacher

A crucial aspect of nurturing culturally diverse students is to provide an environment in which they feel safe and comfortable speaking aloud and in which differences of outlook and opinion can be aired and appreciated. One way to achieve this end is to reconfigure class discussion time so that most discussion takes place among the students. This arrangement contrasts with the traditional classroom, where discussion is typically in the form of a teacher-student interaction. In this alternative model, the adult intervenes only as necessary to guide, stimulate, and facilitate student discussions and to support the development of correct concepts. Students no longer direct most of their comments to the teacher, and the teacher steps in only selectively.

Let's look at how this process can work. The first step in developing discussion that teaches effectively is to get all of the students talking about the topic of, for example, a science lesson, in pairs or small groups—expressing opinions or beliefs in an unstructured manner or simply raising questions. Next, the teacher should help the students to listen to others, using the three *rs*: *recognize* someone else's desire to speak, *respect* that person's thought or opinion, and *restate* what has been said to show that you understood. Students should learn that skilled communicators are able to anticipate and address other points of view. Good communicators are also aware that paying careful attention to someone else's view is an important prerequisite for developing a counterargument.

While engaging in speaking and listening, students will also develop thinking skills. They will enhance their ability to

- Evaluate and substantiate opinions by giving reliable sources and using logical arguments and evidence.

- Become critical consumers of information, developing the view that not everything that is published or is stated by an "expert" is necessarily the ultimate truth.

- Think analytically, finding ways to elaborate their own ideas and explanations and to be attuned to the complex considerations and tradeoffs among different points of view.

- Recognize that there is no right or wrong side in many debates.

Continued Learning by Talking

By working with this model, the teacher brings the whole class together from time to time to introduce and clarify important science concepts and to foster development of the thinking skills listed previously. In addition, she or he has the class participate in monthly or bimonthly "dilemma discussions" on complex scientific and environmental issues such as whether oil spills should be cleaned up or allowed to disperse naturally. Also, there can be personally relevant discussions in which students make predictions about their own lives based on what they are learning about the topic.

Meeting the Challenge

1. Select an elementary or high school grade level and develop a series of possible topics on which to base a "learning by talking" curriculum. Keep in mind the diversity of backgrounds that will be represented in your classroom and the different learning issues that will be relevant to your students' grade level. Be sure to build into your plan the opportunity for students to shift the focus or to develop their own topics for discussion.

2. Create some guidelines for language use in your "learning by talking" classroom. Who will get to talk and for how long? How will speakers be recognized? Is interruption permitted? What will your role be? Devise a way to allow your students to have input into this decision-making so they will feel comfortable abiding by the guidelines.

3. When you next spend some time with friends, take a step back and observe the language pragmatics operating. What are the rules everyone seems to be following? What can be said or not said, and how are tone of voice and body language used? What happens when someone breaks a rule? How long does it usually take a newcomer to catch on to the rules? What if he or she is unable to master the pragmatics?

miners, New York City children, and New Orleans hairdressers are distinct dialects. The decision-making process is neither precise nor scientific.

Complicating the problem of identifying dialects are social and political factors. Typically, one dialect comes to be the preferred means of communication in formal institutions such as school, churches, and businesses. According to Wolfram (1993a), this preferred dialect can come to be known as the standard "language" of society, with all other dialects then perceived as failing the test of being a language. Each dialect may have its own well-defined linguistic structures that operate effectively and efficiently in well-recognized circumstances, yet each may still be seen as being inferior to the standard. In fact, the standard dialect does not have a higher linguistic status, only a higher social and political status. A common myth is that the standard is pure whereas dialects are full of errors. Recently, various individuals and organizations in the United States have attempted to correct this misconception as it applies to Black English, as the document in Figure 5.1 shows.

Social and Political Aspects of Dialects

In the classroom and out, the dialect speaker will confront social attitudes toward dialects other than Standard English. For some, the variation in usage may be based on pronunciation and vocabulary (e.g., the Boston dialect). For others, it may also involve syntactic changes (e.g., Black English). A student's use of language may influence his or her chances for success in the classroom and may have important social consequences. Rating children's personality and competence from their dialect alone is both inaccurate and unfair, yet it happens over and over. Williams (1970; cited in Dwyer, 1991) asked teachers to rate the voices of African American, Anglo-American, and Mexican American children. The children whose voices exhibited nonstandard speech were rated as less competent rather than socially different from the children whose voices exhibited a more standard dialect. Cherry (1981) found that teachers were much more supportive, in terms of allowing requests and supplying information, to students who used the standard dialect.

Dialect in School

Harrison (1985) concludes that a dialect can affect the initial judgment about how smart a child is likely to be, how well he or she will fare as a learner, how he or she is grouped for instruction, and how his or her contributions to class will be treated. This judgment, in turn, may affect the child's (1) attitude about herself or himself as a student, (2) willingness to participate in class, and (3) expectations for the results of participation. A child's competence is not easily predicted from dialect, but as Edwards (1981) found, it is more probable that teachers who expect problems from children who speak a dialect will treat those children differently, thereby creating a self-fulfilling prophecy.

Judgments Based on Dialect

| **Figure 5.1** | **Linguistic Society of America: Resolution on Ebonics** |

Whereas there has been a great deal of discussion in the media and among the American public about the 18 December 1996 decision of the Oakland School Board to recognize the language variety spoken by many African American students and to take it into account in teaching Standard English, the Linguistic Society of America [LSA], as a society of scholars engaged in the scientific study of language, hereby resolves to make it known that:

(a) The variety known as "Ebonics, " "African American Vernacular English" (AAVE), and "Vernacular Black English" and by other names is systematic and rule-governed like all natural speech varieties. In fact, all human linguistic systems—spoken, signed, and written—are fundamentally regular. The systematic and expressive nature of the grammar and pronunciation patterns of the African American vernacular has been established by numerous scientific studies over the past thirty years. Characterizations of Ebonics as "slang," "mutant," "lazy," " defective," " ungrammatical," or "broken English" are incorrect and demeaning.

(b) The distinction between "languages" and "dialects" is usually made more on social and political grounds than on purely linguistic ones. For example, different varieties of Chinese are popularly regarded as "dialects," though their speakers cannot understand each other, but speakers of Swedish and Norwegian, which are regarded as separate "languages," generally understand each other. What is important from a linguistic and educational point of view is not whether (AAVE) is called a "language," or a "dialect," but rather that its systematicity be recognized.

(c) As affirmed in the LSA Statement of Language Rights (June 1996), there are individual and group benefits to maintaining vernacular speech varieties and there are scientific and human advantages to linguistic diversity. For those living in the United States there are also benefits in acquiring Standard English, and resources should be made available to all who aspire to mastery of Standard English. The Oakland School Board's commitment to helping students master Standard English is commendable.

(d) There is evidence from Sweden, the United States, and other countries that speakers of other varieties can be aided in their learning of the standard variety by pedagogical approaches which recognize the legitimacy of the other varieties of a language. From this perspective, the Oakland School Board's decision to recognize the vernacular of African American students in teaching them Standard English is linguistically and pedagogically sound.

Chicago, Illinois
January, 1997

"Linguistic Society of America Resolution on Ebonics." January 1997. Reprinted by permission of the Linguistic Society of America.

Consider the example of an African American student who almost missed her opportunity to be class valedictorian at a high school in northern California because of her Mississippi dialect. On the basis of her language, she was initially judged as not being capable of handling college-preparatory courses despite her straight-A record (California Tomorrow, 1997). She was able to overcome this initial assessment and did graduate as the valedictorian only after her parents convinced her teachers to allow her to take the college-preparatory classes. Dialect was similarly perceived as an educational liability for Chicano students in the same high school who spoke a dialect identified as "Calo" or "Spanglish," a mix of Spanish and English that has historical roots in the interaction of English- and Spanish-speaking communities in the Southwest (García, 1993).

Imagine what happens when a student who comes to school with the ability to use five present tenses (as an Ebonics speaker does) or to create meaning by switching from one language to another (as a Calo speaker does) must confront a language that is in some ways less expressive than his or her own yet is more highly valued by the institution. The school's negative view of the student's language can be taken as a personal rebuke. In such situations, language problems are especially likely to develop when students are ridiculed for applying the grammatically consistent rules of their own language. The student who never manages to impress the teacher with "I be good" or "estoy leyendo" is more than likely to withdraw from conversation and ultimately fail to thrive in the classroom. For many educators, the effect can be too easily mistaken for the cause (Wolfram, 1993b).

Learning to Adjust Dialect   Research on code switching does indicate that children learn to use a more standard dialect in the classroom as they grow older. Destefano (1972) recorded the classroom and nonschool speech of African-American children between eight and eleven years old. Their classroom speech appeared to be more formal or careful and to contain a greater frequency of standard features than their nonschool speech. Furthermore, it was reported that in a repetition task, first-graders who spoke Black English responded in Standard English 56 percent of the time. It appears that even the younger children already knew most of the standard forms and were learning to use them in the appropriate contexts. A study conducted by Melmed (1971) revealed that African American third-graders used Standard English 70 percent of the time in school-related tasks.

Lucas (1987) refers to a study of instructional discourse that describes dialect features in predominantly African American classrooms in Washington, D.C. The study reports a developmental progression in the use of dialect from kindergarten through fourth grade to sixth grade. Children in kindergarten are still in the process of learning which situations are appropriate or inappropriate for dialect. By fourth or sixth grade, the learning process is practically complete. Group interviews showed dialect awareness mostly in the fourth and sixth grades.

The Study of Dialect   With regard to the instructional use of dialect and its effects on academic outcomes, few data are presently available. Wolfram (1986; as cited in Dwyer, 1991) proposed that it is possible to introduce students to dialect as a type of language study in its own right. He suggested that the study of dialect would teach an understanding of language variation along with a deeper appreciation for the richness of American dialects. Moreover, he concluded that there is no evidence to suggest that Black English, as a dialect for school-age children, negatively affects academic achievement.

Special Language Minority Populations

Bilingual-Bicultural Education for Deaf Students

The options for language of instruction available to educators of the deaf in the United States have included spoken English, invented representations of English on the hands, written forms of English, American Sign Language (hereafter ASL), or some combination thereof. The current choice for language of instruction advocated by some deaf education researchers and members of the Deaf[1] community is the use of both ASL and written English (e.g., Ahlgren and Hyltenstam, 1994; Mahshie, 1995). Instruction that includes both ASL and written English is commonly referred to as *bilingual-bicultural education.* The bicultural component refers to the inclusion of explicit instruction on the "beliefs, lives, and activities" that are embedded in and unique to the distinct communities of hearing and deaf people (Padden, 1996, p. 87).

I will briefly examine what a bilingual-bicultural model for deaf education entails and relate it to other models that seem optimal for supporting the social and academic development of bilingual children.

Oralism. In the United States, ASL has been in existence for almost two hundred years. During the early half of the nineteenth century, ASL was the primary medium of instruction in educational settings for deaf students. In the mid- to late 1800s, a growing belief that the use of sign language in education interferes with deaf children's learning of English led to the replacement of signed instruction with oral instruction. The official turning point toward oralism[2] occurred at the Second International Congress on Education of the Deaf in Milan in 1880, at which it was declared that "the method of articulation [i.e., speech] should have preference over that of signs in the instruction and education of the deaf and dumb. . . . The convention declares that the pure oral method ought to be preferred" (Gallaudet, 1881, pp. 5–6,

Attempts to Eradicate Sign Language

---

[1]*Deaf* with an uppercase *D* refers to a particular group of deaf people who share a language and a culture. Lowercase *deaf* refers to the audiological condition of not hearing.

[2]*Oralism* refers to instruction that focuses on speech training and lip reading. Under this method, deaf children receive many hours of speech therapy during which they are trained to produce English phonemes and recognize spoken words on the lips. Oral teachers use only spoken English and do not incorporate any form of gestural communication. Children are not allowed to use any form of sign language; rather, they are encouraged to use their speech skills to express themselves and their lip-reading skills to comprehend others.

cited in Jankowski, 1993, p. 6). The result of this declaration was a sweeping eradication of sign language from the classroom and a direct shift to oralism.

The period following the Milan Congress was one of considerable challenge for deaf people. During this time, Alexander Graham Bell led a movement in the United States to prevent the development of a deaf "race" by attempting to impose rules preventing the deaf from marrying one another, preventing the deaf from having children, and prohibiting the use of sign language in public (Hoffmeister, 1990; Jankowski, 1993). Mas (1994) fittingly refers to this era following the Milan Congress as a time of "hearing 'colonialism'" (p. 72). The impact of the Milan Congress was felt worldwide, with many deaf teachers losing their jobs (Bergmann, 1994) and with sign language becoming "pathologized" (Jankowski, 1993, p. 7). During this period of public intolerance of sign language, the Deaf community managed to keep their language alive, albeit only in informal settings.

Total Communication. In the ensuing period of oralism, few deaf successfully acquired spoken English or made strong academic achievements. After nearly one hundred years of oralism, members of the Deaf community began to argue for the inclusion of manual communication in the education of their children (Jankowski, 1993). Starting in the 1960s, some professionals in the United States and elsewhere began to acknowledge the failure of oral methods and began incorporating signs into their instruction of deaf students. What followed was the development of a variety of sign systems used to represent spoken language manually. These artificial systems include vocabulary items from the surrounding community's natural sign language as well as invented signs to represent grammatical morphemes and lexical items unique to the spoken language.

The invention of sign systems contributed to the rise of an instructional approach known as **Total Communication.** Though it has been defined and applied in various ways, the intended conception of Total Communication is the use of multiple communication forms—including signing, fingerspelling, speaking, lip reading and amplification—to provide linguistic input to deaf students based on their communicative needs. In application, though, *Total Communication* has come to mean the practice of signing an artificial sign system while simultaneously speaking— regardless of students' needs. The use of Total Communication became increasingly popular in the 1970s and continues to be the most commonly used method in deaf education in the United States today (Mahshie, 1995).

Though the incorporation of signs into the instruction of deaf children has improved communication between students and teachers, the purported acquisition of language skills in the majority language has not followed. While the United States continues to use artificial sign systems in conjunction with speech, many European countries such as Sweden, Denmark, and the Netherlands have abandoned sign systems in favor of the natural sign language of each country's Deaf community. This shift is the result of linguistic research that demonstrates the inherent limitations of artificial sign systems that attempt to mimic a spoken language along with the linguistic research highlighting the completeness and naturalness of the sign languages used by the deaf. The dissemination of these findings—together with collaboration among deaf adults, parents of deaf children, and educators of the deaf—led to the renewed appreciation of signed language (Bergmann, 1994).

Linguistic Research on Signed Languages

Linguists in the United States, beginning with Braker (1975), showed that American Sign Language is a natural and autonomous language with a complete lexicon and grammar (Wilbur, 1979). Research examining signed English systems in the United States paralleled the European studies, generating findings that these systems are incomplete and unnatural and fail to represent English adequately (e.g., Drasgow, 1993).

Despite parallel efforts, the research findings in the United States have not had the same impact as those in Europe have had. They have been largely ignored or rejected by many educators and parents of the deaf (Mahshie, 1995). Davies (1991) attributes the different outcomes to two important factors, namely governmental support for multilingualism and multiculturalism and a high level of societal multilingualism in Europe. These factors are coupled with a highly centralized school system that applies national standards of educational instruction. The story in the United States is quite the opposite, with the nation as a whole continuing to promote monolingualism (Crawford, 1995). In addition, the United States lacks any cohesive educational strategy, so even if the federal government were to recognize the merits of sign language, local communities would still have the final say regarding how deaf students are taught.

Despite the political and social situations surrounding linguistic minorities in the United States, a bilingual model for the education of deaf students that includes the use of both ASL and English is *slowly* gaining popularity. The pendulum in deaf education is starting to swing back to using ASL as the medium of instruction, as was done 150 years ago. However, as Mahshie (1995) notes, "Widespread implementation of a model that promotes fluency in both the language of the majoity and of the Deaf community would represent a significant departure from current practices in the United States" (p. xviii). A report from Gallaudet's Center for Assessment and Demographic Studies (1992–1993) indicates that most deaf students in the United States are currently educated monolingually—41.1 percent are taught in auditory/aural methods (spoken English only); 56.1 percent are taught in both speech and sign (spoken English accompanied by signs in English word order); 1.9 percent are taught in sign only (Mahshie, 1995, pp. xii–xiv). Furthermore, more than half of the schools serving deaf students have only one or two deaf students, meaning that very few deaf students have regular contact with other deaf children (Ramsey, 1998).

Academic Achievement of Deaf Students

The academic achievement of most deaf students in the current system is alarmingly low. The average deaf person graduates from high school reading at the third- or fourth-grade level. As Lucas (1987) aptly observes, "patterns of depressed English skills and school achievement of deaf children in the United States persist" (Lucas, 1987, cited in Mahshie, 1995, p. xiv). This condition contrasts sharply with the academic achievement of deaf students in European countries, where an improvement in academic outcomes has resulted from the use of natural sign languages for instruction.

The poor reading and writing abilities of most deaf people, together with their low achievement in other academic areas, have led some to conclude that deaf education in the United States is a failure. The lack of academic success of generations of deaf children with normal intellectual capabilities indicates the need for an immediate change in the way deaf education is structured and delivered. For this reason, researchers, educators, and most importantly, the Deaf themselves are taking steps to encourage a change in deaf education, specifically a shift to using ASL as the medium of instruction within a bilingual-bicultural model of education.

Linguistic Necessities for Deaf Children's Cognitive Development

The debate in the United States over the best methods for educating deaf students is now rising in volume. As this debate continues, Grosjean (1996) reminds us that the deaf child has to accomplish a number of things with language:

1. *Communicate with parents and family members as soon as possible.* A hearing child normally acquires language during the very first years of life if he or she is exposed to a language and can perceive it. Language, in turn, is an important means of establishing and solidifying social and personal ties between the child and his or her parents. What is true of the hearing child must also become true of the deaf child. The

child must be able to communicate with his or her parents by means of a natural language as soon, and as fully, as possible. It is through the use of language that much of the parent-child affective bonding takes place.

2. *Develop cognitive abilities in infancy.* Through the use of language, the child develops cognitive abilities that are critical to his or her personal development. Among these abilities are various types of reasoning, abstracting, memorizing, and so on. The total absence of language, the adoption of a non-natural language, or the use of a language that is poorly perceived or known can have major negative consequences on the child's cognitive development.

3. *Acquire world knowledge.* The child will acquire knowledge about the world mainly through language. As he or she communicates with parents, other family members, other children, and other adults, the child will process information about the world. It is also world knowledge that facilitates language comprehension; there is no real language understanding without the support of this knowledge.

4. *Communicate fully with the surrounding world.* The deaf child, like the hearing child, must be able to communicate fully with those who are part of his or her life (parents, brothers and sisters, peers, teachers, various other adults, etc.). Communication must take place at an optimal rate of reception/dissemination of information in a language that is appropriate to the situation. In some cases, it will be sign language; in other cases, it will be the oral language; and sometimes it will be the two languages in alternation.

5. *Acculturate into two worlds.* Through use of language, the deaf child must progressively become a member of both the hearing and the Deaf world. The child must identify, at least in part, with the hearing world, which is almost always the world of his or her parents and family members (90 percent of deaf children have hearing parents). But the child must also come into contact as early as possible with the world of the Deaf, his or her other world. The child must feel comfortable in these two worlds and must be able to identify with each as much as possible.

These issues must be considered in light of other bilingualism and schooling issues and must receive more research and practice attention in the United States. Otherwise, we run the risk of depriving perfectly capable and deserving students of a decent education.

U.S. Indigenous Bilingual Students

Language loss and language revitalization in North America are becoming issues of interest to U.S. bilingual researchers and educators. Kraus (1992) concludes that some 155 indigenous languages are still spoken in the United States. However, he notes that 87 percent of these are close to being lost. The 1990 U.S. Census reports that more than one-third of American Indian and Alaskan Native languages have fewer than one hundred speakers. These languages are made up of 136 different groupings. The Census data reveal that 47 of these languages were spoken in the home by fewer than one hundred persons and that an additional 22 were spoken by fewer than two hundred persons. As Crawford (1995) is quick to observe, this is most likely a very crude measure of indigenous language vitality since it is a self-report measure.

As Sells, Dick, and McCarty (1997) point out, a rapid shift to English is evident even among speakers of the healthiest indigenous languages such as Navajo, whose speakers were historically among the slowest to become bilingual. As late as 1930, 71 percent of Navajos spoke no English, as compared with only 17 percent of all American Indians at the time (U.S. Census Bureau, 1970). The number who speak Navajo in the home remains substantial—148,530 in 1990, or 45 percent of all Native American–language speakers (U.S. Census Bureau, 1993).

Loss of Native Languages

But the percentage of Navajos who speak only English is growing, predictably among those who have migrated from their tribal homeland but also among those who have remained. For Navajos living on the reservation, of those aged five and older, the proportion of English-only speakers rose from 7.2 percent in 1980 to 15 percent in 1990. For those aged 5–17, the increase was even more dramatic: rising from 11.8 percent to 28.4 percent (see Table 5.5). Among school-aged children living on the reservation, the number of monolingual English speakers more than doubled, increasing from 5,103 to 12,207.

As Crawford (1995) concludes, the crisis of the diminishing use of Native American languages can be summarized as follows: "Unless current trends are reversed, and soon, the number of extinctions seems certain to increase. Numerous tongues—perhaps one-third of the total—are on the verge of disappearing along with their last elderly speakers" (p. 28). Native American languages are becoming endangered, as are the attributes that reside in their essence. Shorris (2000) details the tragic consequences thus:

> There are nine different words in Maya for the color blue in the comprehensive Porrúa Spanish Maya Dictionary but just three Spanish translations, leaving six butterflies that can be

Table 5.5	Tribal Population and Home Language Speakers, Age 5 +, Navajo Reservation and Trust Lands (AZ, NM, and UT), 1980–1990					
1980	**Age 5–17**	**%**	**Age 18+**	**%**	**Total**	**%**
Population:	42,121	100.0	65,933	100.0	109,054	100.0
Speak only English:	5,103	11.8	2,713	4.1	7,816	7.2
Speak other language:	38,537	89.4	63,220	95.9	101,777	92.8
1990						
Population:	42,994	100.0	81,301	100.0	124,295	100.0
Speak only English:	12,207	28.4	6,439	7.9	18,646	15.0
Speak other language:	30,787	71.6	74,682	92.1	105,649	85.0

Source: U.S. Department of Commerce, Bureau of the Census, 1989, 1994.

seen only by the Maya, proving beyond doubt that when a language dies six butterflies disappear from the consciousness of the earth. (p. 43)

This set of circumstances did not arise as a result of recent policies and practices. The United States has specifically singled out indigenous-language issues for quite some time. In 1868, a federal effort aimed at a set of treaties signed with American Indians made clear that schools should be established to eliminate "barbaric dialects" and to substitute English for them (Crawford, 1995). These same sentiments and policies continued as the Bureau of Indian Affairs (BIA) established boarding schools and instituted English-only educational curricula. In addition to these policies, the migration of native people to urban areas, the penetration of English via economic efforts, the pervasiveness of the English-language media (particularly video or TV), and the generally positive social status of the English language has further exacerbated these people's language loss (Fishman, 1990).

Causes of Native-Language Loss

Sells, Dick, and McCarty (1997) present a useful analysis of the Navajo language. First, they conclude that the Navajo language is an imperiled language. The reasons for this situation are multifaceted (Fishman, 1990). At the center of these causes is the continued presence of a federal policy aimed at substituting English for Navajo: "The goal of the U.S. effort in Indian affairs is to remove the stumbling blocks of hereditary customs and manners, and language is one of the most important" U.S. Commissioner of Indian Affairs, *Medicine,* 1988, p. 399). Up until recently, schools have represented the single most important institution charged with carrying out this policy. They have been the only

social institution to demand exclusive use of English and to prohibit use of the child's native language (Kari-Swpolsky, 1973;
Crawford, 1995).

But as Sells, Dick, and McCarty (1997) describe, the legacy of
the past has begun to generate proactive resistance to language
assimilation and blatant educational inequities among the
Navajo. This is also the case for the Southwestern Pueblo people,
who are beginning small-scale efforts to revitalize some eight related Tesra languages (Benjamin, Pecos, and Romero, 1997).
Commenting on these efforts, Fishman (1990) appropriately ar-
ticulates the difficulties associated with such endeavors, particularly since schools are influenced by the social and economic
circumstances in which they exist. The tribe itself may wish to restrict the language taught in schools due to the particular language roles prescribed by its culture or religion. The Pueblos, for
example, are not interested in teaching native languages to non-
tribal workers. Interestingly, federal funds for bilingual education
make clear that this manner of formal discrimination is not allowed.

More important than curriculum and pedagogy are school-
based decisions about language that also influence what happens outside of school. At the Navajo Rough Rock School,
bilingual education is organized consciously to revitalize the
Navajo language in the broader community (Holms and Holms,
1994). The schooling activities are meant to reinforce the positive
notions of bilingualism and to hold at a distance the strong
propensity for the students and community to speak only English. The specific intent here is not merely to provide education
but to engage in social engineering aimed at recapturing the utilization of the native language and to restore the well-being of
the Navajo. Initial results from efforts by the Navajo (Dick, 1997)
and Pueblo cultures (Benjamin, Pecor, and Ramero, 1997) in re-
claiming indigenous languages are hopeful. Others, including
Hinton (1994), conclude that limited progress is being made in
retarding the overall phenomenon of language loss among U.S.
indigenous people.

Clearly, as we address issues of bilingualism and schooling in
the United States, this issue will continue to require attention. In
America, with the roots of bilingual education within the domain
of social justice, giving attention to the human, and particularly
to the educational, costs of native-language extinction is crucial.
At the core of this extinction, Fishman (1991) reminds us, is the
issue of "indigenous identity." Cesar Chavez also reminds us that
in the struggle for educational equities in the "United States, "equities are not about equalities but [about] absent dignity." In
essence, bilingual educators in the United States have come to

*Attempts to
Revitalize
Native
American
Languages*

Table 5.6	**Instructional Strategies for Helping Students Become More Effective Communicators**

Instructional Strategies

Issue/Goal	Topics for Class Discussion	Class Demonstrations
Oral communication	Unique functions and appropriate uses of oral communication	Techniques for identifying appropriate uses of oral communication in specific situations
Audience analysis	The role of audience analysis in speech preparation	Techniques for identifying audience characteristics (i.e., motivations, needs, lifestyle objectives) to maximize communication with a specific audience
Language choices	Types, functions, and limitations of language use	Methods to analyze and use effective types of nonverbal communication
Nonverbal communication	The role and limitations of nonverbal communication in face-to-face oral interactions	How to use the most effective language choices for specific audiences
Vocal characteristics and articulation	The role and variables of vocal presentation, including social reactions to different types of vocal presentation	Techniques to enhance the articulation process, particularly in terms of social meanings conveyed to and from others (i.e., standard versus subculture pronunciation usage)
Delivery and style	The range of speaking styles (e.g., formal, conversational) and varied reactions to speaking styles	How to match delivery style to a specific circumstance or social setting
Organization	Audience need for patterned, systematic presentation of information and how organization affects audience perception and comprehension	Techniques to select most effective organizational pattern
Speaker credibility or ethos	The factors that affect a speaker's credibility and image with an audience	Selection of linguistic choices and nonverbal behavior that enhance speaker credibility
Logical and emotional appeals	How logic and emotional appeals can influence the audience	Methods to anticipate audience reactions to specific logical and emotional appeals
Speaking situation	Opportunities and constraints associated with specific types of speaking situations (e.g., interpersonal, intercultural, international)	How to adapt to unique communication requirements of a particular type of speaking situation

(*continued*)

Table 5.6	**Instructional Strategies for Helping Students Become More Effective Communicators (cont.)**	
	Instructional Strategies	
Issue/Goal	Topics for Class Discussion	Class Demonstrations
Oral message construction	Characteristics of effective oral messages (i.e., characteristics that distinguish an oral message from a written message)	How best to construct oral messages
Feedback	The interaction between speaker and audience and how to monitor what is conveyed to and understood by listeners	Methods to monitor how effectively speakers achieve their objectives with an audience

realize that fostering self-worth is a critical element of educating language minority students. Crawford (1995) appropriately points out that language and cultural loss are characteristic of dispersed and disempowered communities, those who may need their language and culture most. Such loss is not a phenomenon of privileged communities.

Conclusion

Humans seek meaning and understanding in every encounter. As educators, we seek to enhance understanding by introducing instructional environments that address our students' desires to make meaning. The environments we create must be structured around the multidimensional aspects of the communicative act and each participant's diverse set of cultural devices for making meaning. Table 5.6 presents a noninclusive set of strategies for educators to use to enhance communication in the classroom. They are offered here as specific practical suggestions that follow directly from the concepts presented in this chapter. Hopefully, they will be a start toward the development of more specific guidelines for constructing effective instructional environments.

The research base and the understandings it has generated clearly show that our students come in many linguistic shapes and forms. We are always faced with the question of how to treat such variation in the classroom. This same research base suggests that educators cannot and should not legislate or regulate the use of language, particularly in the home and in the community. Variation is a phenomenon of the social roots of language and will persist because it feeds into whole sets of alternative identities, purposes, and cultures that speakers find rewarding and valuable. In the classroom, students' language variations should be perceived as linguistic capital that can be utilized to achieve the goals of the schooling process—one of which is to teach a common standard of English. With such an additive response to language variation, we are building upon the language the children already have to help them acquire the language and the subject matter knowledge they need to succeed in school. Language or dialect bashing has no place in a responsive classroom.

Summary of Major Ideas

1. Communication consists of both verbal and nonverbal systems that enable humans to encode meaning and transmit it to others. Language is a complex interaction of many variables, including the verbal signal, the signal sender, the manner and context in which the signal is sent, the signal receiver, and the previous experiences the sender and the receiver may have had with similar signals. Children begin to communicate in infancy and in a matter of a few years develop skills in vocabulary and grammar. Communication is at the core of all teaching and learning activities.

2. Metalinguistic awareness is the conscious awareness of how one uses language. Schooling experiences that increase children's metalinguistic awareness can develop their understanding of their own culture and the cultures of others.

3. Phonology is the study of speech sounds. Infants exposed to environments in which English is spoken begin to produce speech sounds at five to eight months of age. Children in all language groups proceed through similar stages of language development. Spanish-language learners acquire vowel sounds early, and English-language learners focus on consonant sounds early.

4. Vocabulary is the sum of words understood and used by an individual in any language group. Children typically acquire their first word at about age one and then gain vocabulary rapidly between the ages of two and six.

5. Grammar is the system of rules implicit in a language that allows words to be arranged with some regularity of structure. From normal communicative interactions with adults, children typically acquire the rules of grammar in their native language with little difficulty.

6. The term *language pragmatics* refers not only to the rules of a language but also to cultural notions about what is considered appropriate and effective use of the language. Children's knowledge of language pragmatics continues to develop throughout the school years. Among the most important skills in language pragmatics are the ability to be responsive to the needs of listeners and the ability to adjust one's use of language for different audiences.

7. Children must learn the rules of language pragmatics for conversation, for written language, and for different discourse situations. The rules for discourse can vary widely across cultures. School discourse also has its own specific rules.

8. Bilingualism and second-language acquisition are becoming more common among students in U.S. schools. Bilingualism is the ability to speak two languages with equal fluency. Second-language acquisition is a process of language development whereby a child first acquires one language and then is exposed to and required to learn a second language.

9. Research into bilingualism indicates that children between the ages of two and four can acquire skills in both Spanish and English without any evidence of negative linguistic effect. Bilingual children also exhibit code switching as a normal state of language development. Code switching is the production of mixed-language utterances.

10. Research into second-language acquisition indicates that children use cognitive strategies they learned while acquiring their first language to acquire the second. They also rely on rote memorization and exposure to conversation with native speakers of the second language. Individual factors such as motivation are especially important in determining a student's rate of development and proficiency in a second language.

11. Language skills enable children to function and grow in a world of social interactions. Sociocultural variables that can affect an individual's motivation to learn a second language are the learner's attitude toward native speakers of the language and the degree of social distance between the two cultures that the languages represent. Second-language learners need social skills in order to successfully acquire the target language.

12. Second-language learners must acquire the discourse rules of the target language along with the language itself. Research

shows that it is not so much the use of different languages as a discrepancy in language use between the home and the school that constitutes the primary source of confusion for language minority students. The passive language environment of many classrooms may provide linguistically diverse students with only limited opportunities to produce language and to develop more complex language and thinking skills.

13. Authentic assessment can play a critical role in understanding diverse ways to measure achievement that allow for better-informed instruction. Teacher judgments that are strategic and continuous can be utilized to meet this goal.

14. Dialect is a regional variation of language characterized by distinct grammar, vocabulary, and pronunciation. The dialect American English itself has a number of regional dialects. Students who speak a dialect such as Black English may encounter negative judgments about their ability from those who mistakenly believe that a dialect is linguistically inferior to Standard English. Such attitudes can negatively affect a student's self-esteem, willingness to participate in class, and educational expectations. Research shows, however, that children who speak a dialect learn to adjust their speech and switch to more standard usage in school-based contexts.

Extending Your Experience

1. Interview the parent of a child under the age of three. What has he or she discovered firsthand about language development from interacting daily with this child? Formulate your interview questions around the concepts discussed in the text: phonology, vocabulary, grammar, pragmatics, and metalinguistic awareness.

2. Review the text sections on language pragmatics and sociolinguistic conventions. Make a list of social communication rules for language use that you have noticed in your general public interactions with others. Have you ever unintentionally violated such a rule? If so, describe that experience. Now think about the varied communication settings and types of audiences you encounter in a typical day (home, work, school, and so on.) List some of the rules for language pragmatics that operate in each of those settings. Do the rules vary depending on setting and audience? If so, why?

3. Informally survey your classmates in all your current courses and find out how many are bilingual. How many have acquired

a second language (English or other)? Ask them to describe their schooling experiences as speakers of more than one language and record their comments, honoring those who wish to remain anonymous.

4. This chapter describes a good deal of research into language development and use. Why is it important for teachers to attend to the questions asked by educational researchers and to understand their findings? Why is it important for teachers to understand the issues raised by educational theorists?

5. As you learned in this chapter, a child's motivation to learn a second language depends on three things: the child's social skills, the child's attitude toward the second language culture, and the social distance between the two language cultures. Create some teaching strategies for positively addressing these influences on motivations.

6. Ask classmates to articulate ways in which authentic assessments like the ALA can be developed or utilized in the classrooms with which they are familiar.

Resources for Further Study

Print Resources

Beykont, Z. (Ed.). (2000) *Lifting every voice: Pedagogy and politics of bilingualism.* Cambridge, MA: Harvard Education Publishing Group.

> This edited volume is a collection of critical readings that explore the effective practice of bilingualism within various global social contexts that relate to the realms of school and family. This cross section analysis provides a substantive means to identify principles, practices, and conditions that demonstrate bilingualism as ensuring academic success while establishing educational equity.

Bialystok, E., and Hakuta, K. (1994). *In other words: The science and psychology of second-language acquisition.* New York: Basic Books.

> Extending the important earlier work of Hakuta (1986), this volume brings together issues of the theory and research of language development and second-language acquisition. This discussion is interwoven with an examination of topics related to the education of second-language learners. Bialystok and Hakuta develop an important psycholinguistic base for understanding language development, second-language acquisition, and schooling.

García, E. (2000). Bilingualism and schooling in the United States. *International Journal of the Sociology of Language* (in press, expected January 2001).

García's article critically and succintly reviews the cognitive, social, and linguistic nature of bilingualism. In addition, there is a contextual discussion of bilingualism in schools and the ways in which national and state policies of a historical nature are challenged by an ever increasingly diverse student body. Hence, these demographic demands are reasons for contemporary policy solutions that are inclusive and responsive and that legislatively secure educational equity and access to resources. García argues for an understanding of bilingualism that is based on facts grounded in research that speaks to effective theory and practice rather than unsubstantiated myths.

Gleason, J. B. (1988). *The development of language.* Columbus, OH: Merrill.

This book is a collaborative effort targeted primarily at college students. The chapters present various topics and are written by individuals familiar with language theory, research, and practice. Models and theoretical perspectives are also offered. The book provides an insightful perspective on how language development occurs and what forces and issues foster it.

Hakuta, K. (1986). *Mirror of language: The debate on bilingualism.* New York: Basic Books.

This book offers a detailed overview of how bilingual skills are developed and argues for the need to move beyond simplistic research into bilingualism. The overall aim of the book is to dispel myths and misconceptions about bilingualism. It presents pressing issues that will be at the center of bilingual education in the future.

Krashen, S. D., Tse, L., and McQuillan, J. (Eds.). (1998). *Heritage language development.* Culver City, CA: Language Education Associates.

This edited volume explores Heritage Language in terms of advantages and development. Addressing the advantages, the authors discuss the practical benefits of language heritage and the tragic consequences when there is forced absence of it. The development aspect of the book focuses on the dynamic experiences with language heritage such as improvement of student attitude, reading programs, and perceptions. The authors attempt, then, to understand the issue of language use and academic competency.

Piper, T. (1998). *Language and learning: The home and school years* (2nd ed.). Upper Saddle River, NJ: Merrill, an imprint of Prentice-Hall.

This foundations book takes an integrative approach to the ways in which children learn language, the ways in which it is taught, and how these two areas are sometimes at odds. Language acquisition from birth through the school years is tracked by using the experiences of a number of different children to exemplify stages and sequences of development. The overall goal is to understand language development over time and in various contexts. This book addresses the whole language/phonics debate in such a manner that readers are allowed to weigh the evidence and make up their own minds about where they stand in relationship to the debate.

Shorris, E. The last word: Can our small languages be saved? *Harper's, 301,* (1803) 35–43.

Zentella, A. C. (1997). *Growing up bilingual: Puerto Rican children in New York.* Norwood, NJ: Ablex Publishing Corp.
This is the author's most recent contribution to the understanding of multiple-language development in children. This documentation of bilingual children's interaction within their families, neighborhoods, and schools provides a detailed picture of how they live, learn, and communicate in diverse cultures and settings. Although its focus is on the language of the bilingual, the book's broader emphasis is on the multiple roles and relationships that shape that language, particularly for Puerto Rican children in New York City.

Web Resources

Language Minority Research Institute: *http://lmrinet.gse.ucsb.edu/*
This site provides information and links to other web pages that address the needs of limited-English-proficient students.

Chapter 6
Language, Culture, and Cognition

Focus Questions

- What is sociocultural theory, and how does it provide a framework for approaching the education of culturally diverse students?

- How does children's language development relate to their development of higher-order thinking skills?

- What does the general trend in research suggest about the use of intelligence tests?

- What is instructional discourse, and how can it be used to develop students' ability to think and to communicate?

- What part does writing play in a child's symbolic repertoire?

> "It is not the voice which commands the story, it is the ear."
>
> *—Cicero*

As the quotation above suggests—in some ways contradicting ideas presented in the preceding chapter—it is the listener, the receiver of communication, who is the significant player in the communicative act. In its broadest sense, the "ear" represents the intellectual and social attributes of the receiver of communication. Listeners use their language skills, sociocultural background and experiences, and thinking abilities during the process of communication.

How and what the listener attends to represents all of the processes going on in the listener's mind. We saw in Chapter 3 that for humans the process of making meaning is a constructive act. Human cognition, the mental processes we use to acquire knowledge, is complex and multidimensional. Recent developments in cognitive science have shown that the mind includes both "structural" and "representational" aspects (Cole, 1996; Donald, 1991). Over the ages humans have evolved new systems of representation—not just new information but also new ways of thinking. The mind is our storehouse of symbolic reference. It is a library of symbols that are distinctly assembled by our inherited mental "structures" and are also specifically ordered as "representations" of our own personal set of experiences.

Let's look at how this description of the mind as both structural and representational might apply to an educational situation. A new teacher (or a new student, for that matter) encountering the first day of school has prepared herself or himself for the encounter. He or she has called on previous experiences with formal education, on informal family and nonschool experiences in teaching and learning, and on expectations for social interaction and approaches to problem-solving. In short, a variety of experiences recorded and ordered in the "library" of the teacher's or the student's mind are mobilized to prepare for the classroom encounter: How should I behave toward others in the classroom? What language and tone of voice should I use to make my messages understood? What do I want to accomplish? All participants in education call on their own mental libraries to gather their present understandings of the classroom and related experiences and apply them to new classroom experiences.

But what, really, do we mean when we say that the mind is like a library? Compared to the entire world, a library is very small. In the form of books, though, a large part of the world can be represented in that library. This is also true of the human mind: It is physically tiny but can contain representations of anything in the world. The mind is also shaped by what representations of the world are put in it and how those representations are organized (should we put nonfiction on the first floor or on the tenth floor?).

The represented world within our minds is determined both by the mental structures we have inherited and by our own personal experiences and how we tend to order these experiences mentally. Our inherited mental structures are the intellectual faculties that allow us to think and to think in many different ways—by means of formal argument, systematic categorization, induction, deduction, verification, differentiation, quantification, idealization, theoretical synthesis, and so on. But we do not think in a vacuum. We think in a context of our experience, and the world represented in our minds is shaped by that experience. There is an interaction between thinking processes and cultural experiences. We may all possess the thinking skills listed previously, but if our experiences and mental representations of those experiences differ, the results of our thinking will differ. Herein is the basis for recognizing that diversity in experience leads to diversity in thinking. In day-to-day living and in the classroom, the workings of the human mind and the representations of culture are inseparable.

This chapter begins by discussing a theoretical framework for understanding the interaction of language, culture, and cognition as it relates to education. We then examine the problematical notion of "intelligence" and intelligence testing and consider research indicating that multilingualism may be an advantage in cognitive development. In the second half of the chapter we describe elements of teaching that may be particularly effective with culturally diverse students.

The Role of Culture in Cognition

Early theories of teaching and learning focused on the individual learner and were influenced most directly by findings in the field of psychology. Within the last 20 to 30 years, however, scholars trained in such fields as anthropology, sociology, cognitive science, and sociolinguistics have begun to look into the question of

Variables
Affecting
Learning
how thinking processes and cultural experiences interact in schooling situations. The extent of fit or mismatch between home and school cultures provides a dynamic understanding of a wide variety of variables that affect student learning. Researchers in developmental and educational psychology are now devoting increased attention to the social context of learning and to the role of family, peer group, and community in children's school achievement.

During the last decade, many educational theorists have become interested in **sociocultural theory,** an international intellectual movement that brings together the disciplines of psychology, semiotics, education, sociology, and anthropology in what are often referred to as constructivist views of teaching and learning (see Chapter 3). This movement draws on work done by the Russian theorists L. S. Vygotsky and Mikhail Bakhtin, and relates it to the thought of earlier theoreticians and philosophers of education such as William James, John Dewey, C. S. Pierce, and Jean Piaget. The aim is to find a unified way of understanding issues of language, cognition, culture, human development, and teaching and learning. The following sections explore several aspects of this line of thought.

Constructivism and Cognition

As we learned in Chapter 3, constructivism assumes that all knowledge is constructed by using either innate cognitive structures or cognitive structures that are themselves the products of the continued construction of knowledge (Cole, 1996; Davis, Maher, and Noddings, 1990; Noddings, 1973). According to Noddings (1996), constructivists generally agree that

1. All knowledge is constructed.

2. Certain cognitive structures are activated in the process of the construction of knowledge.

3. Cognitive structures themselves are under continual development.

4. Purposive activity brings about the transformation of existing cognitive structures.

5. The environment presses the organism to adapt.

According to this approach, learning can best be described as an activity requiring the construction of knowledge, not the passive reception of new information. More directly, Vygotsky (1956) has provided a conceptual constructivist theory that identifies the developmental level of a child by what the child can do unassisted. Moreover, what the child can do *with* assistance is called the **zone of proximal development (ZPD).** It is within this zone that teaching is important. According to Vygotsky (1956), effective teaching "awakens and rouses to life those functions which are in the stage of maturing, which lie in the zone of proximal development" (p. 278). Teaching, in a constructivist view, is assisted performance, and learning is performance achieved through assistance.

The Function of Teaching

The importance of sociocultural theory and constructivism for education is the proposal that individual learning and social interaction are inextricably connected. Sociocultural theorists and constructivists argue that the psychology of the individual learner is deeply shaped by social interaction—in essence, that both student and teacher are engaged in the process of constructing their minds through social activity. In this view, knowledge is not a given set of fixed ideas that are passed from teacher to student. Rather, knowledge is created in the interaction between teacher and student. Higher-order mental processes, the tendency to look at things in certain ways, and values themselves are produced by shared activity and dialogue (Bakhurst, 1990; D'Andrade, 1995; Rogoff, 1990).

Learning and Social Interaction

To sociocultural theorists our social lives, often considered to be the major products of culture, are also the major ingredients of cognition. Social experience is inseparable from thought. Moment by moment we construct reality. That process of construction, and the understanding it generates, depends on our previous understandings and social experiences.

The focus of sociocultural theory holds particular import for education, partly because education has been a major interest of many of its founding writers, but mostly because educational practice and theory are particularly needful of a unifying theory of teaching and learning. Educators of culturally diverse students will find this theoretical framework helpful because it conceives of learning as an interaction between individual learners and an embedding context. That embedding context may be as immediate as the social environment of the classroom or as indirect as the traditions and institutions that constitute the history of education. Both contexts and many more come into play whenever teachers and students interact. Important contexts for teaching and learning include (1) close, detailed instruction of individual learners; (2) concern for the social organization of classrooms; and (3) a consideration of the cultural attributes of teachers, students, and peers. These contexts interweave, and we can follow their strands to gain a new understanding of the relationships among language, culture, and cognition (Cole, 1995).

The Embedding Context

Language and Culture as Tools of Thought

How do language and culture relate to cognitive development? Recall that human cognition—how and what we know—is a process of mental representation shaped by experience and the structural aspects of our minds. According to Vygotsky, language acquisition is the momentous occasion when internal mental representation and external reality converge. For him, "external reality" is first and foremost cultural: Through the development of language in interpersonal experiences, children begin to construct meaning. In this view, language functions significantly as a tool of thought. As Hamers and Blanc (1989) stated:

> The shared representations and scripts which are basic to language proficiency arise in the interaction between the child and the significant others around him. The representations the child will construct are highly dependent on the shared social representations in his environment. The child will internalize those language functions that are valorized and used with him; it is through the socialization process that he becomes cognizant of functions and representations. (p. 100)

Thus, as children develop their ability to use language, they absorb more and more understanding of social situations and improve their thinking skills. This process in turn allows them to

Mental Frameworks | learn how to control their own actions and thoughts. It is through a culturally bound and socially mediated process of language development that children construct mental frameworks (or **schema**) for perceiving the world around them. If language is a tool of thought, it follows that as children develop more complex thinking skills, the mental representations through which language and culture embody the child's world play a significant role.

If, as Vygotsky proposed, a child's cognitive schema for operating in the world are culturally bound, what are the effects of trying to learn in an environment where the culture of the classroom differs from the culture of the home? Culturally diverse students face the challenge of either accommodating their existing schema or constructing new schema. When the educational focus is on transitioning culturally diverse students to a mainstream culture rather than building on what they already know, the students are forced to change in order to meet the needs of the classroom. As Duquette (1991) concludes:

> Children need to be understood and to express themselves (in the same positive light experienced by other children) in

their own first language, home context and culture. Their minority background brings out the limitations not of the children but of the professionals who are asked to respond to those needs. (p. 98)

Language minority students face a far greater challenge. It is through a child's first language that he or she creates mechanisms for functioning in and perceiving the world. If the culture of the classroom negates a child's first language and accompanying representations of the child's world, it is thus negating the tools the child has used to construct a basic cognitive framework.

Negation of Cognitive Tools

In a discussion of Vygotsky's theory, Diaz and Klinger (1991) outline how language as a tool of thought has major consequences for a child's cognitive development. As language skills develop, a child's cognitive processes become more independent from the directly perceived environment. Through the use of language, children can organize and reconstruct their perceptions in terms of their own goals and intentions. Language development allows the child to act reflectively according to a plan rather than merely on impulse. As their language abilities mature, children can ultimately gain control over their own cognitive processes.

From the perspective of sociocultural theory, cognitive development is reflected by the increasing ability to use language in abstract ways. If the relationship between language and cognitive development operates as Vygotsky and later theorists claim, educational practices that ignore or negatively regard a student's native language and culture could quite possibly have adverse effects on the student's cognitive development. If a student's first language and culture are used only as a means to learn English and mainstream school culture and not to build on previous experiences and representations, then the student's cognitive development could be hindered or interrupted.

A Foundation for Language Proficiency

To further understand the link between language and cognition, various investigators have made the distinction between contextualized and decontextualized language. **Contextualized language** conveys meaning using physical cues such as gestures, intonation, and other concrete representations characteristic of face-to-face communication. **Decontextualized language** relies on more abstract linguistic and cognitive cues that are independent of the communicative context (Duquette, 1991). An example of decontextualized language is a reading assignment in science class. Such an assignment requires the student to construct meaning from a written context only. There is no opportunity to

Abstract Linguistic Cues

observe a physical demonstration of new concepts or to ask questions of others.

As students progress in school, they are increasingly required to use language in an abstract, decontextualized way (reading and writing as opposed to only listening and speaking). Proficiency in decontextualized language is considered to be most indicative of future academic success. In an extensive review of different research, Cummins (1991) shows that a high level of literacy (a decontextualized skill) in the first language is more closely related to development of literacy in the second language than is social communicative competence (a contextualized skill) in the second language. Cummins argues that it takes students much longer to develop decontextualized language and cognitive skills than to develop face-to-face, contextualized language skills. He further states that removing students too soon from educational programs that utilize their native language will lead to their future academic failure (Cummins, 1989). In essence, children use native-language abilities as a tool to construct higher-order thinking processes. Limiting their opportunities to learn in their first language will limit their cognitive growth and related academic achievement.

Learning in the First Language

Because they focus primarily on the oral acquisition of English, current policy and practice regarding the education of culturally and linguistically diverse students are overly simplistic. Such an approach does not take into consideration the complex interweaving of students' cultural, linguistic, and cognitive development. In their study of the possible effects of language on cognitive development, Hakuta, Diaz, and Ferdman (1986) recognize the importance of acknowledging these three major strands in children's development and addressing them in our schools. They conclude that most of the variance in cognitive growth directly relates to the way in which society affects and manipulates cognitive capacities. Therefore, cultural and contextual sensitivity theories that examine the social and cultural aspects of cognitive development will best serve diverse students.

Responsible

An Assessment of Intelligence Testing

Over the last five to seven decades, the educational establishment has been guided by theories that consider the concept of intelligence to be the central factor in learning. **Intelligence** is generally defined as the ability of an individual's mind to perceive, organize, remember, and utilize symbolic information. To its credit, this idea of intelligence attempts to explain (albeit

Concept of Intelligence

somewhat ambiguously) the relationship between the physical aspects of the brain and the human ability to reason and to symbolize. To its discredit, this concept depends extensively on the notion of biological determination (that is, we "inherit" our intelligence) and on the assumption that an individual's intelligence can be validly and reliably assessed through a simple set of test items.

Problems with Intelligence Tests

Historically, culturally diverse children have been negatively affected by this enduring definition of intelligence (García, 1983b). Careful examination of the testing literature has revealed several problems in using the results of intelligence tests to understand the cognitive development of culturally diverse students. Personal, social, and cultural differences among students typically are not accounted for in **psychometrics,** which is the measurement of psychological attributes. Intelligence tests in particular have not adequately assessed the "intelligence" of culturally diverse populations because of language discrepancies, inappropriate test content, and failure to consider diversity in the development of test-scoring strategies. Inherent in this discussion of intelligence testing is the message that explanations of the human mind that rely on the concept of intelligence and on intelligence testing have been educationally misinformed.

Hypothesis of Mental Inferiority

The use of intelligence tests with culturally diverse students and adults has generated much interest because of differences in scores found between this population and normative groups. As early as 1924, Sheldon compared the intelligence of one hundred "white" and one hundred "Mexican" children of the same age and same school environment by administering the Cole-Vicent group intelligence test and then the Stanford-Binet individual intelligence test. Sheldon's results were as follows:

1. The average Mexican child was below the normal development of the average white child by 14 months.

2. In a group comparison, Mexican children had approximately 85 percent of the scored intelligence of their white counterparts.

3. By combining several studies, Sheldon found that Mexican children scored lower than American, English, Hebrew, and Chinese children but higher than American Indian, Slavic, Italian, and Negro children.

4. As chronological age increased, differences in mental age became greater. Sheldon concluded that the average mental age of the Mexican group seemed to have reached its maximum at nine years.

These indicators of lower mental ability among Mexicans seemed to be supported by further research. In 1932, Manuel and Hughes administered the Goodenough Intelligence Test to 440 Mexican and 396 non-Mexican children from the San Antonio public schools. Based on an age and grade comparison, the Mexican children scored in the retarded stage.

The educational hypothesis that Mexicans were mentally inferior began to crumble, however, with such research as the work by Garth, Elson, and Morton (1936). These researchers tested 445 Mexican children between the ages of 8 and 16 on the Pintner Non-Language Intelligence Test and the Otis Classification Test.

Nonverbal Versus Verbal Tests Their aim was to obtain a reliable nonverbal test to ascertain the influence of language and education. Results showed the Mexican children to be inferior to white American children in verbal tests across age and grade. However, on the nonverbal test, their scores were about equal to those of white Americans. The authors suggested that the verbal test could be unfair to the Mexican children.

Despite evidence to the contrary, the hypothesis that some populations were mentally inferior to others continued to prevail. In the 1940s, Altus reported research findings related to racial and bilingual group differences within U.S. Army populations. In an initial study Altus (1945) examined racial and bilingual group differences in trainees' classifications (discharged as inept or kept in the Army) and in mean aptitude test scores. The Wechsler Mental Ability Scale (WMAS) was used to test American Indians, Mexicans, Filipinos, Chinese bilinguals, whites, and Negroes. The results showed that the bilingual groups scored lower than the monolingual groups on all WMAS subtests. In a subsequent study Altus (1948) addressed the issue of group differences in intelligence and the type of test administered. The subject populations used in the study were "Anglos, Negroes, Mexicans, and Indians, who had been classified as illiterate when entering the army." The findings indicated that in the verbal subtest, the "Anglo" and "Negro" populations had higher scores than the "Mexican" and "Indian." However, there were no differences on the nonverbal subtests. Importantly, these data suggested that group inferiority or superiority was in part a consequence of the test used.

Through the subsequent decades, questions of how to assess and interpret individual differences in human intellectual abilities have persisted (for a historical overview, see Laosa, 1978). It **Intelligence as Predetermined** has often been assumed that intelligence is an innate dimension of personal capacity and that it increases at a relatively fixed rate to a level that was predetermined at birth. These notions of fixed intelligence and predetermined potential clearly can have ad-

verse effects on education, employment, and occupational policies and practices since they encourage neglect of intellectual
development. The argument is often made that because intelligence is predetermined, no amount of cultivation can significantly increase it (Laosa, 1978, 1984). Such thinking led
Hernstein and Murray (1994) to the following conclusion:

> The lesson of this chapter is that large proportions of the
> people who exhibit the behaviors and problems that domi-
> nate the nation's social policy agenda have limited cognitive
> ability. Often they are near the definition for mental retarda-
> tion. . . . When the nation seeks to lower unemployment or
> lower the crime rate or induce welfare mothers to get jobs,
> the solutions must be judged by their effectiveness with
> the people most likely to exhibit the problem: the least intel-
> ligent people. (p. 386)

There is no disagreement over the fact that there are differences in the scores of intelligence tests across ethnic groups. It is
also generally agreed that differences among individuals *within*
groups reflect both genetic and environmental influences. However, the disagreements arise over the relative importance of
these two factors and the degree and changeability of inherited
intellectual characteristics.

Effect of Vocabulary

Can ethnic differences in intelligence test scores be explained
by something other than genetics? Laosa (1995) says they can. To
illustrate, he considers the acquisition of vocabulary, which is a
major component of widely used tests of intelligence. According
to Laosa, the differences in ethnic groups' opportunities to learn
the particular vocabulary employed in intelligence tests are sufficient to explain the ethnic variations in test scores, with no need
for genetic analyses. In fact, for group differences to be correctly
measured, "it would seem imperative that . . . we provide . . .
equally detailed data on 'EIPQ,' an Environmental Intelligence
Producing Quotient" (Campbell and Frey, 1970, pp. 456–457). In
other words, it is only when we can assess an individual's "opportunity to learn" the material included on an intelligence test
that we can properly interpret the meaning of that person's test
score.

Social Class and Intelligence Tests

In another significant study, Christian and Livermore (1970)
compared the effects of social class and ethnic origin on intelligence test scores. They divided the group of subjects into two
categories: those with middle-class status and those with lower-
class status. The results indicated that social class was a more important factor than ethnic origin in "intelligence" differences
among children. With this information, important cautions
about test bias began to emerge.

How Two Students Developed Through Collaborative Learning

The Weaker Student: Valuing Not Knowing. Amiri entered school situations expecting failure. He could be heard saying over and over,

"Boy, am I stupid," as he struggled through academic tasks. He assumed he was unable to do whatever was asked of him on his own and therefore sought a great deal of help from both teachers and peers. He did not appear to believe that he had anything of importance to contribute to others, nor did he believe that his participation in activities or discussions was valued. He often engaged in disruptive, attention-seeking activities or just "spaced out." His behavior was consistent with beliefs that intelligence is something you are born with, that he hadn't been given much, and that no amount of effort would change that fact.

Some teachers who had worked with Amiri held a different view of his abilities; they thought he was more able than he himself believed, yet they found themselves at a loss to change his outward behaviors, his low social status in the class, or his apparently poor self-image. But all this began to change when computers were introduced to the classroom. In Amiri's words:

> See, really, when I first started off on computer—it was O.K. because we got to play games. And then I got a little bit serious about it...serious about it around April. At first I didn't really...I was like the dull one...really. I didn't know what was going on.

By the end of the school year, Amiri's school experience was very different from the one he had been used to. He had become an "expert," and the information he had acquired during the previous several months of research was valued by teachers and peers alike. The very expressions of uncertainty that had once marked him as unsuccessful in school were valued in this new environment. Repeated participation in reciprocal teaching groups and large group discussions provided Amiri with ample opportunities for guided practice in new social behaviors, in ways to enter group discussion, and in more successful learning strategies.

Amiri's developing confidence and increasing skills were evidenced by his growing eagerness to participate in large group discussions as well as in the quality of the questions he posed. This extract from a class discussion demonstrates his new thoughtfulness:

Paulette: The bamboo grove is real shady and the pandas is black and white so they sort of blend in.

Continued   How Two Students Developed Through
            Collaborative Learning

Amiri: Why is it that the pandas eat all of the bamboo if they need to be protected? . . . Why would they eat all their, their camouflage?

This previously unsuccessful student came to be appreciated—by others and by himself—for qualities of his mind that his learning environment had enhanced and made visible. Amiri and other students like him found that their willingness to say "I don't know," born of much real-world experience of not knowing, was actually valued here. And, as he reflected at the end of the year, learning was both possible and enjoyable to him: "I'm not going to drop this. . . . I have a lot to learn."

The Stronger Student: Learning to Reflect. Wilson scored in the 98th percentile on standardized tests of achievement in both reading and mathematics. He read voraciously, learned facts quickly, and performed school-related tasks with ease. He was articulate and confident. But Wilson rarely listened to others, did not work well in groups, and preferred finding things out on his own. He most often was heard making declarative statements or directing the activities of his peers. He was sure his way was best and resisted suggestions by others to the contrary. Despite Wilson's high test scores, his inability to reflect interfered with his capacity to be a flexible and responsive learner.

As might be expected, it was difficult for Wilson to participate in a project emphasizing collaborative activity. Would a successful student like Wilson find such a project sufficiently challenging, or would the slower rate of his peers hold him back and frustrate him?

As it turned out, while working with a group, Wilson continued to develop skills and expertise in numerous areas. He learned to listen and to share his knowledge with others, and he began to engage in more flexible and reflective thinking. He also became more open to learning from his peers. In the following segment, Wilson is analyzing the changes in his own thinking and the classroom experiences that stimulated those changes. Later, for the first time, he is seeking clarification of new data rather than holding rigidly to his original point of view:

At first I thought I agreed with Stuart [that pandas are fat because they are indolent] except it really takes a lot of exertion to climb trees. It does. They must burn their energy climbing, because remember, we saw them in that laser disc . . . how the panda was climbing trees to get to the bamboo.

Continued   How Two Students Developed Through
Collaborative Learning

I'm sort of getting two pictures. First you're saying there's
plenty of bamboo, and they sit around and munch it all day, and
then you say that their bamboo is dying off. Can you sort of set me
straight?

Meeting the Challenge

1. Describe your reactions as you read the two previous descriptions
of Amiri and Wilson. Were you surprised by either of these outcomes? Does the underlying teaching approach alluded to here
seem to be "transmitting" or "facilitating"?

2. Do you feel you are more like Amiri or Wilson as a learner? Devise
strategies for broadening the role of social interaction in your own
learning process.

3. Observe a class and record two phenomena: (a) the number of
times that the teacher responds to the way a child learns; and (b)
the number of times the teacher responds to what a child learns.
Describe a teacher response that seemed to be particularly effective for some student.

Test Bias | Recent review of the use of intelligence tests with culturally
and linguistically diverse populations has pinpointed several serious concerns (Figueroa and García, 1994). First, the language
of the test can bias the results, promoting lower scores for non-
English-speaking populations. Second, social class is highly correlated with test performance, which calls into question any
conclusions about intelligence and ethnic background. Third,
the content of the tests is biased toward mainstream U.S. culture.

It seems appropriate to conclude that differences in test performance may be an artifact of the tests themselves or of other
linguistic, psychological, or social factors as yet imperfectly defined. Intelligence tests and the concept of intelligence that underlies them have done and continue to do an educational
disservice to culturally diverse students. The limitations of these
educational "tools" should be recognized, and educators should
be extremely cautious when using them to generalize about
students.

School Reform—Standards-Based Accountability Assessments

Purposes of Assessment

Assessments in standards-based systems serve a number of purposes: guiding instruction, monitoring school and district performance, holding schools accountable for meeting performance goals, and so on. No single instrument can serve all purposes well. Assessment should involve a range of strategies appropriate for making inferences about individual students, classrooms, schools, districts, and states.

In order to provide information on the quality of instruction and to help educators improve teaching and classroom practices, the overwhelming majority of standards-based assessments should be sensitive to effective instruction; that is, they should be able to detect the effects of high-quality teaching. Districts, schools, and teachers should use the results of these assessments to revise their practices to help students improve their performance.

Assessments are essential for measuring the performance of all children. Yet, although 49 percent of children served by Title I are in grades three or lower, the 1994 statute does not require states to establish assessments to be administered before grade three. Without some form of assessment, schools and districts have no way of determining the progress of this large group of students to ensure that they do not fall too far behind.

To measure the performance of young children, teachers should monitor the progress of individual children in grades K–3 at multiple points in time by using direct assessments, portfolios, checklists, and other work-sampling devices. In addition, schools should be accountable for promoting high levels of reading and mathematics performance in primary-grade students. For school accountability in grades one and two, states and districts should gauge school quality through the use of sampling rather than by assessing the performance of every pupil.

Including students with disabilities and English-language learners in assessments also poses significant challenges. Although state policies vary widely, many states exclude large numbers of students with disabilities and English-language learners from assessment mandates. Other states include such students but use measures that may not be appropriate. States and districts should develop clear guidelines for accommodations that permit students with disabilities to participate in assessments administered for accountability purposes. Similarly, states and districts should also develop clear guidelines to accommodate English-language learners in such assessments. Especially important is the need for unambiguous criteria for determining the level of English-language proficiency at which English-language learners will be expected to participate exclusively in English-language assessments. English-language learners should be exempted from assessments only when there is evidence that the assessment, even with accommodations, cannot measure the knowledge or skill of particular students or groups of students.

In an education improvement system, data from assessments provide information that teachers and administrators can use to revise their instructional programs to enable students to meet challenging standards. For that reason, assessment results should be reported so that they indicate the status of student performance as measured against such standards. To ensure accuracy, reports of student performance should include measures of statistical uncertainty, such as a confidence interval or the probability of misclassification. States, districts, and schools should desegregate data to ensure that schools will be accountable for the progress of all children, particularly those with the greatest educational needs.

Responsible

Inappropriate Assessment of Limited-English-Proficient Students

During the National Voluntary Tests debate of the past few years, the U.S. Department of Education has taken a position against appropriate reading assessments for Limited-English-Proficient (LEP) students. The initial proposal called for testing students' reading skills by grade four. However, once the proposal ignited debate over how to test LEP students who may know how to read in their native language (other than English), the U.S. Department of Education narrowed the focus to "reading *in English*" [italics added]. In so doing, the department took the position that it would not support testing in any language other than English.

Proposals for Assessment of LEP Students | As part of the proposed accountability system for ESEA reauthorization (see Chapter 1), the U.S. Department of Education is recommending the administration of a series of mandated assessments for LEP students in Title I and in Title VII:

1. A reading diagnostic assessment would, apparently, be required for all Title I students. It is unclear whether this test could be given to LEP students in their native language.

2. An annual test of English proficiency would be administered to LEP students served by Title I and Title VII.

3. LEP students who have been attending U.S. schools for three years would be required to take the state assessments *in Eng-*

lish, without any accommodation (for purposes of Title I accountability [italics added]).

Detriments of Proposed Assessments

The proposed battery of assessments for LEP student accountability will be more harmful than helpful to these children in accurately assessing their academic progress.

- In the 1994 reauthorization of Title I, we moved away from excessive testing of students, but now the proposed assessments apparently would excessively test only the LEP students. The disparate treatment of these students raises concerns about their civil rights.

- Under the guise of inclusion, the Department of Education would be imposing the inappropriate assessment of LEP students. Requiring assessments in English after students have attended U.S. schools for three years has no basis in sound educational practice. Assessments should be tied to the type of instruction that the children are receiving, not to an arbitrary time limit. Furthermore, prohibiting the use of necessary accommodations is inconsistent with the Standards for Educational and Psychological Testing. The National Assessment of Educational Progress currently allows for the necessary accommodations for LEP students as well as for students with disabilities—another glaring inconsistency with the department's proposal affecting LEP students.

- The inappropriate assessment of LEP students will generate faulty information about their academic performance. For example, an LEP student may be reading at grade level in his or her native language. However, since the reading test is administered in English, the student's reading skills will not be tested; instead, the score will reflect the student's ability to understand English. The assessment results will go into the student's permanent record with the potential for being used to make high-stakes decisions regarding the child's future educational opportunities.

- Under the Department of Education's proposal, accountability for the academic progress of LEP students is narrowly focused on the English language although these children also need to reach academically proficient levels in math, science, and other content areas.

- This misdirected educational goal for LEP students not only promotes limited expectations for those served by Title VII but also distributes these low expectations across all of the ESEA programs, particularly those of Title I.

Social Promotion Provisions Will Also Result in Disadvantages for Limited-English-Proficient Students

The Department of Education and many states have launched initiatives to eliminate social promotion practices in public schools. Efforts to eliminate social promotion permeate existing federal programs through the use of competitive grant criteria and are also a common thread throughout the Department of Education's proposal for ESEA reauthorization. Research points to the serious adverse impact that being retained in the same grade has on students, particularly those at risk of dropping out. Furthermore, the inappropriate use of testing (or the use of a narrow set of achievement indicators) tends to have the greatest negative and disparate impact on ethnic minority students and LEP students. Specifically, the Department of Education's proposals for accountability for LEP students and for the mandatory assessment of LEP students through inappropriate means do not address the issue of social promotion policies. The interrelation of (a) the inappropriate assessment of LEP students and (b) the initiative to end social promotion has yet to be explored. It is an encouraging sign, however, that the House of Representatives, by passing its Title I reauthorization bill, did not heed the department's recommendations about "ending social promotion." Congress should continue to be wary of the imposition of inappropriate assessments.

Some implications of the current proposals include the following:

- LEP students who are inappropriately assessed will likely score poorly. Such scores will become part of their permanent records and may later prove to be harmful to these students.

- The Clinton administration began building, in Title I, an accountability system that could result in moderate to severe financial and programmatic sanctions for schools.

- As schools are pushed further toward prematurely ending social promotion without having the necessary resources in place for early and effective intervention to address educational needs, LEP students may find themselves overrepresented in the population of students retained in grade.

- The findings of the research are clear: Students who have been retained one or more years in the same grade are much more likely to drop out of school. Given that a large number of LEP students are Spanish speakers, this means that the Hispanic dropout rate will only increase.

California's Accountability System Will Create Disadvantages for Limited-English-Proficient Students and Their Schools

I recently felt it necessary to resign my position as a member of California's Public School Accountability Advisory Committee (PSAA), an entity formed by the 1999 legislative action aimed at establishing a comprehensive plan for school-level accountability in the state. Since it had been appointed by the California state superintendent of schools, I was optimistic that this entity, in its role as advisor to the California State Board of Education, could assist in implementing the legislature's and the governor's intent to establish a reliable, valid, and fair set of assessments and a system that would nurture, promote, and hold accountable public schools for the academic achievement of all of California's public school students. The first act of this committee was to adopt a set of guidelines that were aligned with this mission, indicating that the committee must not recommend any assessment or process that was not valid or fair.

We considered the issue of including the SAT 9 academic achievement test scores of limited-English-proficient students in the Academic Performance Index, an index developed for each school which was based on the SAT 9 scores of its students. This index would be used in the accountability system to make decisions regarding rewards or sanctions for the school. The issue was important since some 25 percent (close to 1.5 million) of California's students fall into this category. The committee labored with decisions to include or exclude test scores for limited-English-proficient students—specifically questioning whether the scores should be excluded for a prescribed period of years to allow for English development, whether they should be excluded altogether since the SAT 9 achievement test was not psychometrically appropriate (with neither of these two options meeting prescribed reliability or validity standards for this population), or whether they should be included so that these students would not be left out of the realm of the accountability system. Of critical importance to the committee's deliberations was an analysis of the previous year's SAT 9 scores which compared the response patterns of Limited-English-Proficient students and non-limited-English-proficient students. The comparison indicated that students limited in their English proficiency were scoring at random levels, indicating no understanding of the language of the test item, five to six times more often than students who were not limited in their English proficiency. In short, English language proficiency seemed to be directly related to the test scores of these students, placing them at a substantial disadvantage when their scores were compared with those of their English-proficient peers. This specific California-based SAT 9 data, combined with the psychometric concerns, led the committee to recommend to the California State Board of Education that the scores for these students be excluded from the Academic Performance Index until a reliable, valid, and fair assessment could be put into place. Such an assessment is presently being developed.

The California State Board of Education ignored the committee's recommendation. Specifically, the board's adopted plan for the mandatory assessment of 25 percent of California's students through inappropriate means does not address the issue of implementing a fair accountability policy. These students who are inappropriately assessed will score poorly. Such scores will become a part of their permanent records. These scores will confuse the students, their parents, and the public. Any high-stakes accountability system based on such scores will be fatally flawed and highly disadvantageous for linguistically and culturally diverse students.

Two Aspects of Effective Teaching in Culturally Diverse Classrooms That Focus on Language and Cognition

Since the time of Socrates, educators and philosophers have argued for a kind of teaching that does more than impart knowledge and teach skills. Knowledge and skills are important enough, the argument goes, but true education and real teaching involve far more. They involve, fundamentally, helping students understand, appreciate, and grapple with important ideas while developing a depth of understanding in a wide range of issues.

Goals of Education

Teaching aimed at these important goals is presently most notable for its absence from U.S. classrooms. Goodlad (1984), for example, reports that

> a great deal of what goes on in the classroom is like painting-by-numbers—filling in the colors called for by numbers on the page. . . . [Teachers] ask specific questions calling essentially for students to fill in the blanks: "What is the capital city of Canada?" "What are the principal exports of Japan?" Students rarely turn things around by asking questions. Nor do teachers often give students a chance to romp with an open-ended question such as "What are your views on the quality of television?" (p. 108)

If this portrait is accurate for mainstream American classrooms, it is even more accurate for classrooms in which the students are linguistically and culturally diverse and of low-income backgrounds. Because of the perception that these students fundamentally require drill, review, and redundancy in order to progress academically (Brophy and Good, 1986), their learning opportunities are likely to be excessively weighted toward low-level skills and fact-oriented rather than concept-oriented instruction. As important as skills and knowledge undoubtedly are, no less important are more cognitively demanding learning opportunities that promote, as the philosopher and educator Mortimer Adler (1982) has written, the "enlarged understanding of ideas and values" (p. 23).

With Adler's notion of such an "enlarged understanding" as a goal of education, in the rest of this chapter we shall attempt to consolidate the more theoretical issues of language, culture, and cognition addressed earlier. It is impossible to delineate all the interlocking pieces of this puzzle in this small space. We can make some headway, though. We will examine two recently researched areas that have attended to instructional delivery (the language and discourse of instruction) and the development of literacy. The selection of these two particular areas is not a random one. The basis of enhanced academic productivity for culturally diverse students lies in the manner in which their communicative and cognitive development is organized instructionally in oral and literacy activities (Tharp and Gallimore, 1991). In essence, the way these endeavors are handled in the classroom is highly significant for the student of interest in this book.

Basis for Enhanced Achievement (margin note)

Instructional Discourse

In classrooms throughout the world, but particularly in the United States, daily teaching events are structured around teacher-student dialogues. In one study (García, 1992a), we recorded the following dialogue in a kindergarten classroom with the teacher leading a lesson for several children:

Teacher: Okay, Maria, let's see what we can figure out about the shapes of these blocks.

María: This one's yellow.

Teacher: Sí, yellow is a color, but can you tell me what shape this block is?

María: Todos son amarillos. [They are all yellow.]

Teacher: Sí, but we want to talk about shape. Tú sabes cómo? [You know how?]

María [holding up a triangle]: This one, this one, this one, es amarillo [is yellow].

These sorts of instructional interactions occur repeatedly every day in classrooms. Typically, the teacher asks a question or, as in the preceding example, requests a student response. The student then replies (as with María, not always the way the teacher would prefer). Finally, the teacher evaluates the child's response and may request further elaboration.

Effective **instructional discourse** (as reported by García, 1992a) and the use of **instructional conversation (IC)** (as reported by Tharp and Gallimore, 1988, 1989, 1991) have been demonstrated to be highly relevant to the broader linguistic, cognitive, and academic development of linguistically and culturally diverse children. On the one hand, such conversations are an instructional strategy in that they are designed to promote learning. Yet they are also structured to take advantage of natural and | **Spontaneous Interaction** | spontaneous interactions, free from the didactic characteristics normally associated with formal teaching. Such interactions are interesting and engaging. They center on an idea or a concept. They have a focus that might shift as the discussion evolves but nevertheless remains discernible throughout. They allow for a high level of participation without undue domination by any one individual, particularly the teacher. Students engage in extended discussions—interactions—with the teacher and among themselves.

In instructional discourse, teachers and students are responsive to what others say so that each statement or contribution builds upon, challenges, or extends a previous one. Topics are | **Teacher's Role in Discourse** | picked up, developed, and elaborated. Strategically, the teacher (or discussion leader) presents provocative ideas or experiences and then questions, prods, challenges, coaxes—or keeps quiet. He or she clarifies and instructs when necessary but does so efficiently, without wasting time or words. The teacher assures that the discussion proceeds at an appropriate pace, neither too fast to prohibit the development of ideas nor too slow to lose momentum and interest. The teacher knows when to bear down and draw out a student's ideas and when to ease up, allowing thought and reflection to occur. Perhaps most important, the teacher manages to keep everyone engaged in a substantive and extended interaction, weaving each individual participant's comments into a larger tapestry of talking and thinking.

Such discourse is in many ways similar to interactions that take place outside school between children and adults (e.g., Ochs, Taylor, Rudolph, and Smith, 1989; Rogoff, 1990). These interactions appear to be very important for children's learning and cognitive development in general. For example, Rogoff (1990) notes that middle-class adults tailor their responses to children, "focusing their attention, and expanding and improving the children's contributions." Although not designed to teach in a formal sense, these tailored responses, Rogoff concludes, "appear to support children's advancing linguistic, thinking, and communicative skills" (p. 157).

Elements of Good Classroom Discourse. Moving beyond such general descriptions, what characterizes good classroom discourse? What are its constituent elements? What must teachers know and do in order to implement successfully these types of learning interactions with their students? Working in a low-income, language minority school in California (García, 1989) and building upon earlier work in Hawaii (e.g., Au, 1979; Tharp and Gallimore, 1988), recent research teams comprised of teachers and researchers have attempted to address these questions (see Goldenberg and Gallimore, 1990, 1991b; Goldenberg and Patthey-Chavez, 1991). What has gradually emerged is a more precise description of instructional discourse. As developed by Goldenberg (1992), Table 6.1 compares direct instruction with instructional conversation.

Although these comparisons in no way represent definitive or comprehensive descriptions of direct instruction and instructional discourse, they suggest important distinctions between these two teaching approaches. They are based on very different assumptions about teaching and learning. **Direct instruction**

Table 6.1	Characteristics of Direct Instruction and Instructional Conversation
Direct Instruction	**Instructional conversation**
Teacher models	Teacher facilitates
Exact, specific answers; skill directed	Draw from prior or background knowledge
Easier to evaluate	Many different ideas encouraged
Step-by-step systematic instruction	Build on information provided by students
Teacher-centered	More student involvement
Guided and independent practice following instruction	Establish common foundation of understanding
No extensive discussion	Extensive discussion
Goal is mastery after each step	Fewer black-and-white responses
Check for understanding	Guided understanding

Source: Clarell Goldenberg, *Instructional conversations and their classroom application: Education practice report #2.* National Center for Research on Cultural Diversity and Second Language Learning, University of California, Santa Cruz. Copyright © 1992. Used with permission.

assumes that the teacher acts as a "transmitter," imparting knowledge to the student through modeling and step-by-step instructions. Instructional conversation, on the other hand, views the teacher as more of a "facilitator," building upon the student's existing knowledge. The two approaches imply different roles for the teacher. Instructional conversation emphasizes the teacher's role in facilitating and guiding student learning through extended verbal interactions rather than emphasizing the direct delivery of instruction (Goldenberg, 1992, pp. 5–6).

IC and the "Comfort Zone"

The use of instructional conversation (IC) as a strategy in diverse classrooms is receiving more and more attention. Dalton and Sison (1995) have provided a fruitful analysis of this strategy in middle-school mathematics classrooms. Their work demonstrates how IC can be used to engage students in learning cognitively loaded concepts in geometry. IC always begins with interactions that address individual experiences regarding such concepts without specifically or directly "teaching" them. This approach helps to establish a "comfort zone" for further elaborations that extend beyond the personal experiences. This type of beginning allows all students to participate and develops a scaffold for structuring later conversations related to the instructional theme. It offers the teacher access to students' prior knowledge, including their linguistic and conceptual development.

For example, a teacher who set out to teach the concepts of circumference and diameter began with a discussion of broader issues of space and objects in space, building on the students' knowledge base that was mostly generated by recent motion pictures or TV series. That discussion about space travel and planets, which was conducted in a conversational mode, led into talk about measuring the size of a planet and eventually to the concepts of circumference and diameter:

Teacher: How do you measure a planet?

Edgar: You can't measure a planet.

Teacher: You can't?

Daniel: Yeah.

Teacher: [to Edgar] No?

Luis: Yes you can?

Daniel: You can.

Teacher: How can you?

Luis: You can draw a circle.

Teacher: You can draw a circle? Is that the way to measure a planet?

Luis: Yeah.

Teacher: Explain to me what you mean by that?

Luis: You draw a circle and then you fold it like that?

Teacher: Uh-huh.

Luis: And you make a line in the middle. (Dalton and Sison, 1995, p. 9)

As this very informal conversation shows, IC strategy builds on the existing knowledge of the students, allows the students to engage the teacher and each other in an active way, and therefore leads to the parallel development of language and cognitive/academic content of relevance to the formal educational process.

As the preceding discussion suggests, a primary issue in determining the educational needs of linguistically and culturally diverse children is understanding instructional interaction. Children from different linguistic cultures will use language in ways that reflect their different social environments.

Elements of a Larger Understanding

A comprehensive understanding of instructional interaction must therefore take into consideration the linguistic and cognitive attributes of that interaction. It must consider the child's surrounding environment. Recent data tentatively suggest that social context will determine

1. The specific linguistic and metalinguistic information important for the development of each language

2. The specific rules for social use of each language

3. The roles assigned to each language (García, 1986)

Table 6.2 provides a more fully elaborated vision of instructional discourse in terms of its instructional and conversational elements.

Instructional Discourse for Diverse Students. Tikunoff (1983), in the report of the Significant Bilingual Instructional Features Study (SBIF), also addressed the issue of language use in language minority classrooms. The 58 classrooms observed in the study were located in six school sites throughout the United States, where a variety of non-English languages were spoken. All the classrooms were considered effective on the basis of two criteria: (1) they were nominated by members of four constituencies (teachers, other school personnel, students, and parents), and (2) classroom teachers were found to produce rates of

Table 6.2	**Elements of Elaborated Instructional Discourse**

Instructional Elements

1. Thematic focus.

   The teacher selects a theme or idea to serve as a starting point for focusing the discussion and has a general plan for how the theme will unfold, including how to "chuck" the text to permit optimal exploration of the theme.

2. Activation and use of background and relevant schemata.

   The teacher either "hooks into" or provides students with pertinent background knowledge and relevant schemata necessary for understanding a text. Background knowledge and schemata are then woven into the discussion that follows.

3. Direct teaching.

   When necessary, the teacher provides direct teaching of a skill or concept.

4. Promoting more complex language and expression.

   The teacher elicits more extended student contributions by using a variety of elicitation techniques—e.g., questions, restatements, pauses, and invitations to expand.

5. Promoting bases for statements or positions.

   The teacher promotes students' use of text, pictures, and reasoning to support an argument or position. Without overwhelming students, the teacher probes for the bases of students' statements—e.g., "How do you know?" "What makes you think that?" "Show us where it says _____."

Conversational Elements

6. Fewer "known-answer" questions.

   Much of the discussion centers on questions and answers for which there might be more than one correct answer.

7. Responsivity to student contributions.

   While having an initial plan and maintaining the focus and coherence of the discussion, the teacher is also responsive to students' statements and the opportunities they provide.

8. Connected discourse.

   The discussion is characterized by multiple, interactive, connected turns; succeeding utterances build upon previous ones.

9. A challenging but nonthreatening atmosphere.

   The teacher creates a "zone of proximal development," where a challenging atmosphere is balanced by a positive affective climate. The teacher is more collaborator than evaluator and creates an atmosphere that challenges students and allows them to negotiate and construct the meaning of text.

10. General participation, including self-selected turns.

    The teacher encourages general participation among students. The teacher does not hold exclusive right to determine who talks, and students are encouraged to volunteer or otherwise influence the selection of speaking turns.

Source: Clarell Goldenberg, *Instructional conversations and their classroom application: Education practice report #2.* National Center for Research on Cultural Diversity and Second Language Learning, University of California, Santa Cruz. Copyright © 1992. Used with permission.

academic learning time (a measure of student engagement on academic tasks) as high as or higher than those reported in other research on effective teaching.

Unique Instructional Features

Instructional features found to be unique to the education of language minority students included the use of two languages, special activities for teaching a second language, and teaching practices that took advantage of students' cultural backgrounds. According to the SBIF report, English was used approximately 60 percent of the time. Either the student's native language or a combination of the native language and English was used the rest of the time, with the percentage of English increasing with grade level. An additional significant instructional feature was the particular way in which the two languages were combined. Teachers of limited-English-proficient (LEP) students mediated instruction by using the students' native language and English for instruction, alternating between the two languages whenever necessary to ensure clarity of instruction. Moreover, Tikunoff (1983) reports that students learned the language of instruction when engaged in instructional tasks expressed in that language.

Integrative Approach

This integrative approach to developing English-language skills during ongoing instruction in the regular classroom contrasts with the more traditional procedure of "pull-out," in which LEP students leave the regular instructional setting to receive ESL instruction.

Influence of Classroom Practices

A study performed by Wong-Fillmore, Ammon, McLaughlin, and Ammon (1985) provides a detailed analysis of the influence of classroom practices on the development of oral English in language minority students of Hispanic and Chinese backgrounds. In this study, 17 language minority classrooms (13 third-grade and 4 fourth-grade) served as sites. In these classrooms either the native language and English or only English was used during instruction. The researchers obtained specific measures of English-language production and comprehension over the academic year. In addition, classroom observations documented the character of teacher-student and student-student interaction as well as the organizational features of instruction. These authors reported a series of potentially significant observations:

1. Instructional practices that were related to English-language development depended on the student's initial level of English proficiency. Therefore, instructional practices such as high levels of teacher and peer interaction were more related to enhanced English development for nonproficient speakers of English.

2. The instructional variables that were significant for the students differed. Students of Chinese background seemed to do

best under classroom conditions in which they received independent help on English-language learning and in classrooms in which the instructional style was characterized by teacher-directed instruction. Students of Hispanic background demonstrated enhanced oral English-language development under classroom conditions in which there were more opportunities to interact with English-speaking peers.

In addition, these researchers reported that growth in English-language production and comprehension was related to several attributes of student-teacher interaction. Classrooms in which teachers adjusted the language level of their interaction based on student feedback were more likely to produce overall gains in English-language proficiency. Allowing and encouraging student participation and calling attention to the structure of language while using it were also characterized as instructional features that enhanced language development.

García (1989) examined instructional interaction for linguistically and culturally diverse students under conditions identified as academically successful. Previous research has suggested a potential mismatch between the culture of the home and the culture of the school (Ramirez and Castaneda, 1974). Similarly, research has indicated potential discrepancies in interactional

Effective Instructional Styles

styles (Zentella, 1981). Specifically, García (1990a) examined instructional discourse in "effective" Hispanic classrooms. The study observed and analyzed the instructional styles of "effective" kindergarten, third-grade, and fifth-grade teachers of academically successful Hispanic (bilingual and nonbilingual) students. The results indicated that

1. Teachers tended to provide an instructional initiation often reported in the literature. They elicited student responses but did so at cognitive and linguistic levels of relatively lower order.

2. However, once a teacher had initiated a lesson, students were allowed to take control of the specific lesson topic and were able to invite interaction from fellow students.

Figure 6.1 diagrams the type of instructional discourse identified in this study, or student-dominated discourse as compared with teacher-dominated discourse.

Student-Student Interaction

The finding that teachers were clearly allowing student-student interaction in the child-reply component of instructional discourse was considered significant. That is, the teacher was much more inviting of a student's "call" for peer response once the instructional interaction was set in motion. This finding is particularly important considering what we know about linguistic and

| Figure 6.1 | Lesson Discourse Styles |

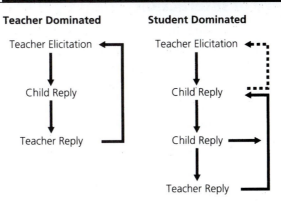

cognitive processes. García (1983b) and Goldenberg (1993) have suggested that discourse strategies that emphasize student-student interaction are important to enhanced linguistic development. Moreover, schooling practices that focus on cooperative child-child instructional strategies are in line with social motives in some Mexican American families. Such a style of instructional discourse would be of linguistic and cultural benefit to Mexican American students (García, 2000).

Student Writing Development

Like oral language, writing is crucial in schooling endeavors. As in all other areas of meaning-making, children first attempt to manipulate written symbols during familiar, manageable activities. Children may continue just to write letters or to use cursive writing (e.g., when writing stories or extended texts in dramatic play) but attempt more precise encoding when writing smaller units, especially names (Ferreiro, 1988; Miramontes, Nadeau, and Commins, 1997). Although such labeling can occur as part of dramatic play, naming is itself an activity of great interest to many young children and one in which they will invest considerable intellectual energy, especially if they are in the company of interested adults and peers.

Naming |

Initially, children's written names do not represent spoken words. Instead, they are letters that belong to certain people or things. That is, rather than trying to encode speech into graphics, children typically make meaningful graphics about what they say (e.g., "This is my Mama's name") (Dyson, 1983). Just as speech helps to organize and elaborate on the meaning of early drawn objects, so too it aids the early writing of names. For children, in

A Tapestry of Interaction

The 32 seventh-graders sit in a large circle on the floor. The teacher, who is sitting on the floor with them, begins:

Becoming a Responsive Teacher

Teacher: What I would like you to do is to look around and call on people to add to what you've said—anything that you left out or that people remember that you haven't said yet. . . .

LaWanda: Is this a thinking lesson?

Teacher: Ah, yes! Exactly. What I'd like you to do is think about your own thinking. That's exactly right.

[LaWanda raises her hand.]

Teacher: Go ahead.

LaWanda [calling on another student]: Elayne, what things does elephants has that is common to otters? Elephants and otters are— what does, what do they have in common?

Elayne: They both get hunted.

LaWanda: And?

Juan: Oh, they both need a lot of space.

LaWanda: What about your animal? The panda and the wolfs?

Marcus: They both need a lot of space. . . .

LaWanda: Is there anything [else] they have in common?

Marcus: They're running out of food.

LaWanda: Their habitats are being destroyed?

Marcus: Yeah. . . .

LaWanda: And the bear group. Is, is, why is your bear becoming extinct? Yolanda?

Yolanda: They kill them for their fur.

Robert: They're used as a food source in China.

LaWanda: I know, you said they're using them for a food source. People eat them, right?

Robert: Right.

Teacher [forgetting to raise her hand]: It sounds like we need to— [LaWanda frowns, doesn't respond. The adult teacher raises her hand.]

[LaWanda calls on the adult teacher formally.]

Teacher: How do you know something is an animal?

LaWanda: Let's start with Juan. What do you think an animal is?

Juan: A creature that roams the earth.

Continued   A Tapestry of Interaction

LaWanda: Valencia?

Valencia: Anything that's alive, and breathing. Like plants aren't really animals. They're alive and everything, but they're not really animals. They can't walk around or do anything. They just sit there.

LaWanda: How do you know something is an animal? Marcus?

Marcus: Anything like mammals, reptiles, amphibians, fish, even a virus are animals.

LaWanda: Can you explain what a virus is?

Marcus: Actually, yes. But I'm sorry, a virus is not a living thing. But animals can be microscopic.

LaWanda: Darius?

Darius: . . . People are animals. Bugs, forest animals, every living thing is an animal. Plants are like animals. Every living thing is an animal. . . .

LaWanda: I have a question. You say almost everything is an animal. Why do you say that?

Kaylan: Not human beings.

Darius: Every human being is an animal.

LaWanda: Which way do you mean? 'Cause of behavior?

Darius: Because they're living things, and living things are animals.

Teacher: Let's think about this for a minute. It sounds like everybody would agree that all animals are living things. Turning that around, are all living things animals? What living things are not animals?

LaWanda: [to teacher] Did you raise your hand? [To Chakita, who had gone to get a dictionary] Say it.

Chakita: [reading from dictionary] *Animal . . . any living being that can move about by itself, has sense organs, and does not make its own food as plants do.*

Meeting the Challenge

1. Reflect on your own experience as a student in U.S. elementary and secondary school classrooms. Does it match the version of American education portrayed previously? If not, how does it differ, and what is the significance of that difference? What are these students being encouraged to learn that you may not have been?

2. Is this transcript an example of instructional discourse or direct instruction? Point out moments of interaction that suggest one or the other. Use Tables 6.1 and 6.2 for reference.

Continued   A Tapestry of Interaction

3. As the teacher of a fourth-grade class, devise a list of open-ended questions for discussion (versus fill-in-the-blank or known-answer questions). You may select any content field, such as language arts, math, science, social studies, and so on.

4. Develop a writing activity to engage the students portrayed in the preceding transcript. Be sure to take into consideration the emphasis put on social interaction in this classroom.

fact, names are types of objects; they belong to people and things (Ferreiro and Teberosky, 1982).

Many publications describe for teachers the "developmental stages of writing," which progress from child scribbles to invented spelling. It is important to remind ourselves that these sorts of observations about children's writing are based on attention to superficial manifestations of development, not to the complicated process of representation. There is no linear progression in cognitive development, nor in the development of oral and written language. Development is linked in complex ways to the whole of children's symbolic repertoires. Its evolution involves shifts of function, symbolic form, and social give-and-take as children explore and gradually control new ways to organize and to represent their world and to interact with other people about that world.

Symbolic Repertoires

Putting writing in its symbolic place—seeing its emergence within the student's total symbolic repertoire—suggests, first, that in the early years children need many opportunities to use the arts freely: to draw, play, dance, and sing. For young children, the most accessible media are those that most directly capture the movements of their own bodies, the sounds of their own voices, and the images made by their own hands as lines, curves, and colors take form on paper. This teaching strategy requires a knowledge base of the child's language and culture.

First-grade teacher Karen Gallas (1991) describes an instructional unit on insects and their life cycles, beautifully detailing how drawing, painting, music, movement, drama, poetry, and storytelling, "separately and together, became part of [the children's] total repertoire as learners" (p. 42). In a classroom in which cultural, social, and language barriers might have kept children apart, use of the arts allowed individuals many avenues for learning, expression, and communication. Some children sketched insects, focusing on visual details, while others drama-tized the life cycle of an insect, using their bodies to capture the changing shapes of life. Still others drew grass as seen from the perspective of an insect. New intelligences, in Gardner's (1985) sense, were visible as children forged new understandings through colorful images and felt movements, understandings that will surely enrich each child's later experience with print as a reader and a writer.

The curious world and the students themselves should be the center of the curriculum, not the "steps" in writing or reading. In-deed, making literacy the center of the curriculum may prevent **Literacy as a Tool** reading and writing from becoming the dynamic, colorful intel-lectual and social tools they should be. Teachers must help con-nect print with the liveliness of students' use of other symbolic forms. In a series of books on her own classroom life with chil-dren, Paley (e.g., 1981, 1986) has illustrated how elementary stu-dents can collaboratively transform themes in their own lives into dictated texts, elaborated texts, and dramas. For many stu-dents, dictated words did not sufficiently represent the action, and they needed to share the action through media of their own voices and movements. Transforming their own texts into dra-mas allows students and teachers opportunities to find words for unarticulated ideas and previously unknown cultural representa-tions of those ideas.

Children's interweaving of language, culture, and thinking does pose developmental challenges, since eventually children must differentiate and gain control over the unique interactive **Importance of Reflection** powers of these domains. Therefore, it is important to talk to stu-dents about their expressive efforts and in this way to help them reflect upon their development. Indeed, many educators con-sider spending such reflective moments with a student dis-cussing his or her ways of talking, playing, and writing to be an important means of supporting the student's development. What aspects of a student's imagined world are in the pictures? the print? in dramatized action? Which are still unarticulated, wait-ing for an interested other to help give them shape? At the same time, students must be allowed to remain in charge of their own intentions (Genishi and Dyson, 1984). Children feel no compul-sion to put into written words the meanings they express through acting and talking. Their differentiation and control of these var-ied media are a gradual developmental process, one we can nur-ture but cannot force.

In summary, the complexity of development is linked to the **Control of Written Symbols** whole of children's symbolic repertoire. Unlike oral language, written language involves the use of a deliberately controlled sys-tem of symbols to mediate activity. An adult or an older student writing a letter is substituting written communication for the opportunity to speak in person to another individual. A student, however, who says she is pretending to write a letter may not be using written language to mediate her activity. To use Halliday's (1973) terms, the student may be showing an awareness of the interactional function of literacy, but the letter is fulfilling an imaginary as much as an interactional function. For some students whose native language is not written, such an act is quite revolutionary. It is more prop than mediator. To understand truly how development occurs, it would be necessary to understand how the child attempts to write the letter, the role of letter writing in the child's social activity, the role of other media in the accomplishment of the letter writing, and how the child's interaction with other people and with other media changes over time as writing is transformed from primarily a prop to a mediator.

Both to understand and to foster written language development, we must view that development within the particularities of children's social lives. Indeed, we as adult writers may turn to media that seem to fit most comfortably the initial contours of our ideas before struggling to craft those ideas within the linear confines of print: We may draw, map, make gestures in the air, or even scrawl conversational language across a page. Written language emerges most strongly when it is firmly embedded within the supportive symbolic sea of gestures, pictures, and talk—that is, put simply, when it is embedded in our cultures.

Conclusion

This chapter has attempted to highlight theory and related educational practices that provide a broad understanding of issues of importance to the schooling of diverse student populations: language, culture, and cognition. As indicated, the knowledge base in this area continues to expand, and it is in no way to be considered comprehensive as yet. Also, it would be an error to conclude that the data and theory that have emerged have been used as a primary basis in determining the educational treatment of these students. Too often, the education of these students has been determined instead by "political" variables (Hakuta and García, 1989). However, we can identify possible program and policy implications derived from research and theory highlighted by the foregoing discussion and by other previous reviews, such as August and García (1988); August and Hakuta (1997); Cazden (1988); Goldenberg and Gallimore (1991a); García (2000); and Tharp (1989). This research suggests the following:

1. One major goal regarding the education of culturally diverse students should be the development of the full repertoire of language, literacy, and cognitive skills.

2. For non-English speakers, time spent learning the native language is not time lost in developing cognitive and academic skills. Children can best become cognitively competent by building on previous language and cultural experiences and representations.

3. There is no cognitive cost to the development of multilingualism in children. Very possibly, bilingualism can enhance children's thinking skills.

4. Education programs should be flexible enough to adjust to individual and cultural differences among children, particularly in the development of expected cognitive literacy domains.

We have seen that the linguistic, cognitive, and social character of the child develop simultaneously and that linguistic, cognitive, and social development are interrelated. Cognitive factors may act to influence linguistic and social development. Linguistic development (the ability to operate within the structural and pragmatic aspects of languages) may in turn act to influence social and potential cognitive functioning. The development of social competence directly influences the acquisition of linguistic and cognitive repertoires.

Figure 6.2 presents a model of the interactions among language, cognition, and culture as children develop. This interactive model is not meant to provide a definitive description of human development but rather simply to reflect the integrated nature of linguistic, social, and cognitive factors in learning. Changes in each of these domains may be attributed to changes in other domains, and in turn may further alter the character of

Figure 6.2   A General Integrative Model of Language, Cognition, and Culture

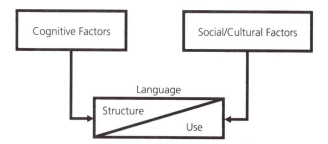

the individual child. This and other similar conceptualizations of integrated development should guide our instructional efforts for all children, but they are particularly important as a foundation for enhancing the cognitive development of our diverse student populations.

Summary of Major Ideas

1. The human mind is a library of symbols shaped by inherited mental structures and by representations of the world that come from our own individual experiences. The cognitive processes by which we acquire knowledge develop in conjunction with language background and sociocultural factors. To be effective, teaching and learning practices must consider the interactions of language, culture, and cognition.

2. Sociocultural theory is an international intellectual movement that draws on ideas from psychology, semiotics, education, sociology, and anthropology in what has been called a constructivist perspective. Recent work in this area seeks a unified way of understanding language, cognition, culture, human development, teaching, and learning. Proponents of this theoretical perspective claim that the psychology of the individual learner is deeply shaped by social activity and that knowledge is always constructed in a social context. In this view, learning occurs in an interaction between individuals and an embedding context.

3. Because children use language in a sociocultural context to construct meaning, language and culture function as significant tools for cognitive development. Children whose language and culture do not match those of the schools are usually forced to adjust their schema (their mental frameworks for understanding the world) or to construct new schema. Such negation of a child's language and culture also negates the child's cognitive tools and can seriously hinder cognitive development.

4. Contextualized language relies on more abstract linguistic and cognitive cues. Proficiency in the use of decontextualized language takes longer to achieve and is usually considered indicative of academic success. Limiting opportunities for children to learn in their first language may prevent them from developing the proficiency in decontextualized language required for academic achievement and for literacy.

5. Intelligence is generally defined as the ability of an individual's mind to acquire and apply knowledge. The traditional notion of intelligence presumes that it is an inherited intellectual capacity that can be measured by a test. Research into test bias over the past few decades has identified serious concerns about using intelligence tests to determine the intellectual capacity of culturally diverse students.

6. Recent accountability systems that utilize tests that do not meet strict test development and test use guidelines may place linguistically and culturally diverse students and their schools at a disadvantage.

7. Effective teaching in culturally diverse classrooms involves organizing oral and literacy activities that develop students' communicative and cognitive abilities. Instructional discourse, or instructional conversation, is a teaching strategy that emphasizes discussion in the classroom. In contrast to the didactic character of most formal teaching, it is structured to take advantage of natural and spontaneous interactions between teacher and students and among students.

8. In direct instruction as an approach to teaching and learning, the teacher transmits knowledge to students through modeling and step-by-step instructions. In instructional conversation, the teacher acts as a facilitator, building on students' existing knowledge and guiding learning.

9. Children from different language cultures will use language in ways that reflect their different social environments. Research indicates that effective instruction of language minority students includes the use of two languages in the classroom, special activities for teaching a second language, and teaching practices that take advantage of students' cultural backgrounds. Discourse strategies that emphasize student-student interactions rather than solely teacher-student interactions may also enhance linguistic development.

10. As with the use of oral language, students' development in the use of written language is likewise tied to language and sociocultural factors. Unlike the use of oral language, however, using written language requires children to control a highly abstract system of symbols. To help children develop literacy as a social and intellectual tool, teachers must connect the student's use of print with other, more concrete symbolic forms such as physical movement and oral language.

Extending Your Experience

1. Describe the approaches used by a teacher who is a "transmitter" and a teacher who is a "facilitator" and explain how these approaches differ. Have you had both types of teachers in your student career? Select two teachers who adopted contrasting approaches and describe your experience as a learner with each one. Remember to consider "teachers" you may have had outside the formal school environment, such as music or art instructors and sports coaches.

2. As this chapter points out, sociocultural theorists argue that knowledge is not a fixed set of ideas passed on from teacher to student but is instead created in the social interaction between teacher and student. What do you make of this claim? Do you agree or disagree? Note down the reasons for your position and discuss them in class.

3. Interview a psychology professor on your campus or a few friends who are majoring in psychology. Ask them to define the term *cognition* for you and to explain what they have learned about this concept. Then ask them to do the same with the term *intelligence.* Only after you have recorded all their comments, refer to a dictionary or encyclopedia and note the definitions given there. Report the results of your investigation to your classmates.

4. This chapter quotes research showing that children use their ability in their first language as a tool in learning how to think. What are the implications of this research for the education of language minority students, whose first language is not English?

5. What do you consider to be the goals of education? List at least three and be prepared to discuss them in class.

6. What patterns of social interaction do you expect to encounter in your own educational experiences? Think back over your past and present classroom experiences as a learner. Would you characterize your interactions as mainly teacher-student or student-student? Has this pattern of interaction shaped how and what you learn? In what way?

Resources for Further Study

Print Resources

Baca, L., and Cervantes, H. T. (Eds.). (1998). *The bilingual special education interface* (3rd ed.). Upper Saddle River, NJ: Merrill.

Baca and Cervantes provide the most current information regarding bilingual education. This is a primary resource for educators interested in knowing about the most effective teaching practices, current legislation, and concepts as well as the frameworks related to bilingual education. The main objective of this book is to show that it is possible to educate students better in bilingual education classes.

Collier, V. (1995). Acquiring a second language for school. In National Clearinghouse for Bilingual Education (Ed.), *Directions in Language and Education, 1*(4). [Online]. Available: National Clearinghouse for Bilingual Education, Washington, DC, at *http://www.ncbe.gwu.edu/.*

This article details ongoing research related to the complexities associated with second-language acquisition in education contexts. The author elaborates on the thesis that the acquisition of a second language in schools is not merely a linguistic enterprise. Instead, it involves cognitive "loads" that are related to content learning in science, mathematics, and so on. With this form of second-language acquisition, students need extended periods of time as well as structural experiences in order to achieve a high level of proficiency.

Diaz, R. M., and Klinger, C. (1991). Towards an explanatory model of the interaction between bilingualism and cognitive development. In E. Bialystok (Ed.), *Language processing in bilingual children* (pp. 140–185). New York: Cambridge University Press.

This article is part of a volume that reports research into basic processes in language acquisition and use for bilingual students. The aim of the book is to describe the acquisition and development of a second language and to explain how such processes affect language awareness. In particular, the authors revisit the old issue of the impact bilingualism has on intelligence. Ultimately, they conclude that in order to substantiate the relationship, more detailed research needs to be done. The theoretical foundation for this essay is directly associated with Vygotsky's work, with a minor twist.

Duquette, G. (1991). Cultural processing and minority language children with needs and special needs. In G. Duquette and L. Malave (Eds.), *Language, culture, and cognition* (pp. 115–135). Philadelphia: Multilingual Matters.

This publication is a collection of recent research findings on topics that have generated more discussion of bilingualism and multiculturalism. Presenting an array of perspectives, the work lacks in-depth discussion of any single topic but does provide up-and-coming concepts and instructional approaches in the education of language minority students. Seventeen chapters are divided into three areas that deal with the cognitive process, the nature and role of language in culture, and aspects of teaching and learning. Taken together, all of these essays critically analyze and interpret how bilinguals acquire knowledge and develop academically.

Gonzalez, V. (Ed.). (1999). *Language and cognitive development in second language learning: Educational implications for children and adults.* Boston: Allyn and Bacon.

> This comprehensive volume discusses the issue of second-language learning by using a multidimensional perspective. This book focuses on philosophical and theoretical models and issues related to cognitive and language development. It also provides some discussion on alternative assessment related to language minority children.

Tharp, R., and Gallimore, R. (1988). *Rousing minds to life: Teaching, learning, and schooling in social context.* Cambridge: Cambridge University Press.

> This book is considered a new and important contribution to the arena of multicultural education. It offers an improved model to advance the teaching and learning process. Using Vygotsky's theory, the authors present a series of educational concepts and discuss their impact and development in everyday interaction. One chapter examines the theory of teaching and the development of skills to improve teaching. The book centers mainly on the Kamehameha Elementary Education Program (KEEP) and explains how theory and practice developed this project into an exemplary model. It emphasizes the importance of education to society and stresses that the connection between theory and practice must be strengthened to ensure that future generations of students receive the best education possible.

Web Resources

National Center for Research on Cultural Diversity and Second Language Learning (NCRCDSLL): *http://www.cal.org/cal/html/ncrcdsll.htm*

> This web site offers the most current information related to effective teaching and learning and alternative assessments for language minority students.

National Clearinghouse of Bilingual Education: *http://www.ncbe.gwu.edu*

> Funded by the U.S. Department of Education, Office of Bilingual Education and Minority Language Affairs (*http://www.ed.gov/offices/OBEMLA*), and operated by The George Washington University Graduate School of Education and Human Development, Center for the Study of Language and Education, in Washington, DC, this web site brings together research and practice in an organized and accessible manner. It is a clearinghouse of information specific to research, classroom instruction, student assessment, teacher training, program development, and grant applications. The NCBE (National Clearing-

house for Bilingual Education) web site also offers an online library that contains over three hundred full-length articles, reports, guides, and other documents on topics related to school reform, student diversity, language, parental and family involvement, and instruction. Supplementing this information are resources that are available from teachers and administrators, such as lesson plans and discussions regarding practices. The web site serves as a link to other web sites that would also be helpful in your search.

Intercultural E-Mail Classroom Connections (IECC): *http://www. stolaf.edu/network/iecc*

For students in K–12 and college.

Part Three
The Educational Response

Whereas Parts One and Two of this book focused on the context and roots of diversity in American schools, Part Three centers on the practical side of teaching and learning.

Chapter 7 addresses the current system of professional preparation and assessment, outlines recent changes in teacher-preparation programs, and traces the dimensions that define what it is to be an "effective teacher." In addition to discussing school reform, Chapter 8 offers an in-depth examination of "effective" schools and instructional practices, including specific case studies. Chapter 9 begins with this author's account of his own schooling, using it to introduce a discussion of school improvement, especially middle school and high school efforts in literacy, mathematics, and English language development. Particular attention is paid to the issue of college preparation.

Chapter 7
The Effective Teacher: Preparation, Assessment, and Characteristics

Focus Questions

- How are teachers of culturally and linguistically diverse students currently prepared in the United States, and what institutions are responsible for assessing their competence?

- What are the patterns in state credentialing available for teachers of bilingual education and English as a Second Language?

- What are some of the competencies, roles, and responsibilities of effective teachers of language minority students?

- How has the connoisseur model been implemented in at least one local school district to further the professional development of inservice teachers?

- What types knowledge, skill, disposition, and affect characterize effective teachers?

- How can schools and classrooms adopt useful assessment strategies to serve culturally and linguistically diverse students?

> "You are the giver of a lifelong gift. An impulse; an enduring tool; a prolific engine called learning. The infectious transfer of enthusiasm."
>
> —F. X. Trujillo

A typical teacher, looking at the students in the classroom, sees a picture much different from the classroom of her or his childhood. Today one in three children nationwide is from an ethnic or racial minority group, one in seven speaks a language other than English at home, and one in 15 was born outside the United States. The linguistic and cultural diversity of America's school population has increased dramatically during the past two decades, and it is expected to increase even more in the future. The concept of "minority" group will soon become obsolete because no group will be in a majority status.

Educating children from immigrant and ethnic minority group families is a major concern of school systems across the country. Please remember that for many of these children, American education is not a successful experience. Whereas one-tenth of non-Hispanic Anglo-American students leave school without a diploma, one-fourth of African Americans, one-third of Hispanics, one-half of Native Americans, and two-thirds of immigrant students drop out of school.

Confronted with this dismal reality, teachers, administrators, and parents urge each other to do something different—change teaching methods, adopt new curricula, allocate more funding. Such actions might be needed, but they all will be meaningless unless we begin to think differently about these students. In order to educate them, we must first educate ourselves about who they are and what they need to succeed. Thinking differently involves viewing these students in new ways that may contradict conventional notions.

As this country and the world shrink communicatively, economically, and culturally, our diversity becomes more visible and harder to hide. But it always has been and always will be there. Our schools will need to address it more than they have in the past, and of specific importance will be how our teachers, administrators, and parents help us address it successfully. Please recall that at the core of this success are two pivotal values for any professional serving a growing culturally diverse population:

To honor diversity is to honor the social complexity in which we live—to give integrity to the individual and to where he or she comes from.

To unify is absolutely necessary, but to insist upon it without embracing diversity is to destroy that which will allow us to unite—individual and collective dignity.

This chapter discusses effective teachers. We assume that who does the teaching is of major importance regardless of the educational model being implemented. We will extend our understanding of this basic idea by cautiously but directly addressing the development, assessment, and specific attributes of "effective" teachers who serve diverse student populations. We will look closely at credentialing policies and analyze their political and empirical underpinnings. We will also examine the attributes of effective principals to see how these school leaders help establish a fruitful setting for teaching and learning. The overall purpose of this chapter is to suggest ways of enhancing the education of culturally diverse students by focusing on the educational professionals who serve them every day.

The Current System of Professional Preparation and Assessment

Professional preparation and assessment of teachers who serve culturally diverse students are problematic, complex, and cumbersome processes. It is an area ripe for criticism. A variety of programmatic efforts have been developed in response to the growing number of culturally diverse students in the U.S. schools, but it has become evident that professional preparation, particularly for teachers, has not kept pace with the demand for educational personnel who are specifically trained to implement these new programs. The following discussion provides an overview of the preparation and credentialing of educators and builds a foundation for understanding the relevant issues.

Teachers Are Professionals   In our society, teaching is considered a profession. A **profession** is characterized by two general features (Friedson, 1986): (1) acquisition of knowledge obtained through formal educational endeavors and (2) an orientation toward serving the needs of the public, with particular emphasis on an ethical, altruistic concern for the client. Practices for preparing and judging the competence of professionals have always been embedded in a local time and place, in line with generally accepted concepts and purposes—the profession's Zeitgeist. Thus, educational endeavors and assessments of professional educators, usually called teaching credentials, develop in concert with the general intellectual and ethical climate and needs of the time (McGahie, 1991).

Our present concerns about teaching credentials are derived from the ethical considerations of our time and the pressing need to prepare competent teachers to serve diverse student populations. As it stands, the training and assessment of educators are functions performed by the states or by professional societies, or by some combination of these institutions. Typically, the focus is

Types of Assessment on assessing either (1) the individual as a preprofessional (usually through an examination such as the National Teaching Exam) before allowing him or her to enter the profession or (2) the professional institutions and programs that produce teaching professionals (the National Council of American Teacher Educators [NCATE] Reviews are an example of such a review by an association, and the California Commission on Teaching Credentialing Program Reviews are an example of state-authorized reviews). In some cases, both individual and program reviews are required. Although presently not fully implemented, a national effort to certify teachers is under serious development.

Professional Credentialing of Teachers

It is important to note that professional preparation for teachers of linguistically and culturally diverse students is a relatively new enterprise. Not until the mid-1960s did substantial educational initiatives exist in this specialized arena, and not until 1974 did the U.S. Congress authorize resources for institutions of higher education to use in teacher education (August and García, 1988). The recent nature of this innovation, much like similar developments in the field of special education, has spawned many new programs in teacher preparation that are still struggling to establish themselves alongside long-standing programs in elementary and secondary education. These new programs tend to have a more complicated content with a more multidisciplinary perspective. Such teacher-preparation programs must be concerned not only with subject matter and pedagogy but also much more directly with language, culture, and instructional practices.

Need for Bilingual Teachers The 1980–1982 Teachers Language Skills Survey identified the need for 100,000 bilingual teachers in the U.S. schools. This figure was based on the number of schools in which limited-English-proficient students from one language background were sufficiently concentrated to make bilingual programs feasible. Compare this finding with reality: In 1982, there were an estimated 27,000 to 32,000 bilingual teachers, which means 68,000 to

73,000 more were needed. Statistics from 1998 reveal that older teachers are retiring early, newer teachers are less qualified to teach, and students who begin teacher-education programs often do not complete them. These are just three factors of many that are creating a serious teacher shortage. In terms of exact figures, there are 5 million unqualified teachers presently in the classroom. According to the 2008 projections made by the U.S. Department of Education, after steady increases, "880,000 untrained teachers will be teaching more than 13 million students" (NCES, 2000, p. 2). Yet over 3 million children in the United States coming to their first day of school are from homes in which English is not the primary language. As is the case with the preparation and credentialing of "regular" teachers, the credentialing of teachers whose main function is the education of linguistically and culturally diverse students is quite variable.

Availability of Credentials   Twenty-five states and territories presently offer no professional credentialing for teachers of culturally diverse students. Half of the country does not produce a specific teaching credential, even though 20 percent of U.S. students might require such specially prepared teachers. It is not coincidental that those states least affected as yet by increases in the population of language minority students are in this group. Keep in mind that all states require some type of certification of teaching professionals in the public schools.

California, Florida, Illinois, New York, New Jersey, and Texas are home to almost two-thirds of this nation's language minority students. In these states, teacher credentialing in bilingual education, language development, and ESL or in some other related area is available. Four of these six states now mandate professional credentialing (California, Illinois, New Jersey, and Texas).

Uneven Progress   Therefore, in states that are greatly affected by growing numbers of language minority students, concern for professional teaching standards is developing, but the progress has been uneven. Because of the segregation of language minority students, state school systems often do not feel the full impact of these students. Linguistically and culturally diverse students, for example, tend to be concentrated in a few school districts within the state, and even though their academic presence is felt strongly by these individual districts, this same pressure is not exerted statewide.

Even for those 25 states that either mandate or permit credentialing for teachers of culturally and linguistically diverse students, the present modes of assessment are highly problematic. Present methods of professional assessment can be criticized in several ways (McGahie, 1991; Shimberg, 1983; Sternberg and Wagner, 1986):

1. Professional competence evaluations usually address only a narrow range of practice situations.

2. Professional competence evaluations are biased toward assessing formally acquired knowledge rather than what the teacher can do in a classroom.

3. Almost no attention is given to the "disposition," "affective," and "commitment" domains of teacher behavior, which have been identified as being as significant as content-knowledge and practice skills (Pease-Alvarez, Espinoza, and García, 1991).

We also know that professional assessment instruments can be subject to severe violations of reliability and validity (Berk, 1986; Feldt and Brennan, 1989).

According to McGahie (1991), teacher assessment continues to operate within the **connoisseur model** of professional assessment, which presumes that (1) not all professional practices can be quantified, (2) a professional problem or question may have more than one answer, and (3) practicing teachers are the most effective evaluators of teachers in training. As the need for more teachers who can effectively serve diverse student populations grows, the need to develop and assess the competence of these professionals will be of critical importance.

Connoisseur Model

Recommended Competencies for Teachers of Linguistically Diverse Students

Methods of assessment aside, what skills should teachers of linguistically and culturally diverse students have? All teacher-preparation programs must identify as the desired goal of their efforts some set of performance competencies imparted to teachers. The literature abounds with numerous listings of such competencies (Collier, 1985; National Association of Bilingual Education, 1992; National Board of Professional Teaching Standards, 1996). The most detailed is presented by Chu and Levy (1988). Their list of competencies is derived from a review of federally and nonfederally supported teacher-preparation programs presently operating within U.S. universities. It focuses on some 34 intercultural competencies, no small number, that serve as a foundation for the success of a well-prepared teacher of linguistically diverse students. These competencies cover the instructor's knowledge in three areas: educational theory, social trends, and classroom strategies.

Lists of Competencies

The most widely distributed list of teacher competencies to be used for credentialing was developed and published in 1984 by

the National Association of State Directors of Teacher Education and Certification (NASDTEC). That list, presented in an abbreviated format in Table 7.1, resulted from combining previous competency lists developed by the Center for Applied Linguistics in 1974 and the Teachers of English to Speakers of Other Languages Association in 1975. Although not as comprehensive as the Chu and Levy (1988) list, it has served as a cornerstone of teacher preparation programs and credentialing analysis in the United States.

State Handbook | Recently, states and school districts have begun to articulate the expected roles and responsibilities of teachers of language minority students. One such effort is the handbook of the New Jersey State Board of Education (1991), which is summarized next.

Role of Bilingual Teachers. According to the New Jersey State Board of Education (1999), the bilingual teacher should

- Help to identify limited-English-proficient students

- Communicate with other teachers in planning for the teaching of bilingual programs that meet the needs of eligible students

- Communicate with ESL and other teachers in planning for the bilingual-program students in ESL and special subject areas

- Provide input in areas covered by pupil personnel services

- Apply current research findings regarding the education of children from diverse cultural and linguistic backgrounds

Table 7.1	**NASDTEC Certification Standards: Competencies Required for Teachers of Language Minority Students***

In Bilingual/Multicultural Education (B/M ED)

Possible University Offerings

1. Proficiency in L1 (primary language) and L2 (secondary language) for effective teaching

Foreign language and English department courses

2. Knowledge of history and cultures of L1 and L2 speakers

Cross-cultural studies, multicultural education (ME), history and civilization, literature, ethnic studies

3. Historical, philosophical, and legal bases for B/M ED and related research

Foundations of Bilingual Education (BE) (or Introduction to BE)

4. Organizational models for programs and classrooms in B/M ED

Foundations of BE

5. L2 methods of teaching (including ESL methodology)

Methods of teaching a second language

6. Communication with students, parents, and others in culturally and linguistically different communities

Cross-cultural studies, ME, school/community relations

7. Differences between L1 and L2; language and dialect differences across geographic regions, ethnic groups, social levels

Sociolinguistics, bilingualism

In English for Speakers of Other Languages

Possible University Offerings

1. Nature of language, language varieties, structure of English language

General linguistics; English phonology, morphology, and syntax

2. Demonstrated proficiency in spoken and written English

English department courses

3. Demonstrated proficiency in a second language

Foreign language courses

4. L1 and L2 acquisition process

Language acquisition

5. Effects of sociocultural variables on language learning

Language acquisition, ME, cross-cultural studies, sociolinguistics

6. Language assessment, program development, implementation, and evaluation

Language assessment, program development, and evaluation

*Supplemental to the standards required for *all* teachers
Source: National Association of State Directors of Teacher Education and Certification, 1984.

- Develop language proficiency in the native language of the students enrolled in the program and in English

- Have knowledge of techniques, strategies, and materials that aid teaching in the two languages

- Structure the use of the two languages to systematically make the transition from the native language to English

- Select activities and materials for classroom use that indicate an understanding of the developmental level of the students

- Help students to identify similarities and differences for successful interaction in a cross-cultural setting

- Provide experiences that encourage positive student self-concept

- Promote and understand the supportive role and responsibilities of parents/guardians and explain the bilingual program to them

Role of ESL Teachers. The handbook of the New Jersey State Board of Education (1999) states that the ESL teacher should

- Help identify limited-English-proficient students

- Participate with administrators in designing an ESL program that meets the needs of eligible students

- Communicate with other teachers in planning for the teaching of the ESL student in the bilingual or English-only classroom

- Demonstrate awareness of current trends in ESL and bilingual education

- Demonstrate proficiency in English commensurate with the role of a language model

- Use English as the principal medium of instruction in the areas of pronunciation, listening, comprehension, speaking, structure, reading, and writing

- Select activities and materials for ESL use that indicate an understanding of the language-proficiency level of the students

- Express interest in and have an understanding of the native culture of the students

- Provide experiences that encourage positive student self-concept

- Promote and understand the supportive role and responsibilities of parents/guardians and explain the ESL program to them

Preparing teachers of culturally and linguistically diverse students remains an innovative process. Assessment and credentialing of these teachers are new areas of research inquiry. We have no time-tested methods and specific educational results to direct us. The connoisseur model, however, holds great promise.

Changes in Teacher-Preparation Programs

Developing Programs

Leighton, Hightower, and Wrigley (1993) provide a well-articulated overview of teacher-preparation programs for individuals with a particular interest in serving linguistically and culturally diverse students. In general, many of these programs are still in the development stages. None has the mature position or the national visibility that comes with long-standing status (Delpit, 1995; Grant and Secada, 1990; Ladsen-Billings, 1994). Most programs designed for training teachers of culturally and linguistically diverse students are built around research findings that point to effective instructional strategies. Few of the people running these programs have thoroughly analyzed their own training efforts (August and Hakuta, 1997). Almost all these programs of teacher preparation, however, do address the issues of content integration, knowledge construction, prejudice reduction, equity, and empowerment of the school community (Banks, 1993b; Ladson-Billings, 1994).

Factors to Address

According to Delpit (1995), five factors must be addressed in preparing teachers of culturally and linguistically diverse students:

1. Issues of power enacted in the classroom

2. Codes or rules for participating in power

3. Realization that the rules of power are those of the individuals in power

4. Clarification of the rules of power to those who do not have power

5. Recognition that those in power are the least aware of power and that those without power are most aware of it

Simply put, if teachers continue to be prepared as they were in the past, the power will remain in exactly the same places, which very likely will mean that the status quo will be maintained and that culturally and linguistically diverse students will suffer the consequences.

Shift to Site-based Training

Because of the need for changes in the way teachers of culturally and linguistically diverse students are prepared, the recent trend has been to withdraw many of the training activities from the standard "college of education" framework, in which a prospective teacher typically takes theory courses from professors and then does supervised teaching at a school site. Instead, the new programs have moved a greater proportion of teacher preparation to the school site itself (Leighton, Russo, and Hightower, 1993; Milk, Mercado, and Sapiens, 1992). For example, Calderón (1994) reports on a large-scale effort to train teachers in bilingual settings. Professors teach in the school in which the student teachers are working so that the student teachers receive most of their own instruction at the school site. The professors attempt to make direct connections between daily classroom activity and the conceptual understandings that are usually discussed in formal teacher-preparation courses. Similarly, the Latino Teacher Education Project (Genzuk and Hentschke, 1992) has developed a school-based program to train paraeducators, individuals from the school community who are initially hired as instructional aides. In Los Angeles, this program is an example of the "grow-your-own" philosophy. Besides allowing members of the target community to move from the status of nonprofessional instructor to professional teacher, the program preserves and makes use of their expertise in the local cultures and languages. It also promotes stability in the local teaching force.

| *Training at the School Site* |

Similarly, local school districts have implemented extensive professional development programs for existing teachers to increase the linguistic expertise of their teaching personnel. One such program, in Denver, exemplifies such professional development activity. This urban district, which serves a diverse population of Hispanic, African American, and Southeast Asian students, determined that its needs could be partially met by the professional development of its existing teaching staff. The plan had several key features:

| *Denver Inservice Program* |

1. The program developers believed that teachers needed both theoretical grounding and opportunities to apply theory practically in instructional settings.

2. External consultants with expertise would work collaboratively with a cadre of local teachers over an extended period (four to six years).

3. A local group of teachers demonstrating enhanced expertise would provide mentor support to their colleagues.

4. Development of new mentor groups at individual school sites would ensure the systematic augmentation of expertise throughout the district.

The school district also developed its own credentialing requirements since state requirements were not responsive to the local

Results
of Denver
Program
needs. Over five hundred district teachers participated in this preparation from the mid-1980s through the late 1980s. Significant gains in service delivery to Denver's growing population of diverse students have been documented. A corps of one hundred mentor teachers, specifically available to train their colleagues, provides formal preparation experiences, classroom demonstrations, local site networking, and curricular leadership. These experts, or connoisseurs, also evaluate new teaching professionals.

Similarly, in California local school districts can now implement their own "intern" teacher-education programs using an institution of higher education as a partner. This training initiative places the focus on the school district rather than on the institution of higher education. Like the Denver program and the movement toward site-based training of student teachers, the California intern programs offer a way of blending theoretical learning and direct teaching experience.

Local Expertise
What was born out of great necessity in Denver may give us insight into the appropriate development of teaching professionals. First, in the examples we have been looking at, professional development takes on a localized flavor that reflects the diversity of students and programs in the school district. Second, a corps of expert teachers who can serve in an evaluative capacity develops over time. Local knowledge of educational needs is cultivated in experts who in turn evaluate the professional expertise of their colleagues.

Benefits
of Teacher
Support
Significantly, professional development also relates to teacher burnout. **Burnout** is physical or emotional exhaustion, most often caused by a great deal of stress experienced over a long period of time. It is particularly apparent in teachers whose major responsibility is serving highly diverse student populations (Calderón, 1991). Recent studies have made it very clear that ongoing support, particularly through the first few years of teaching, is crucial to instructors. Calderón (1991) has displayed these data in graphic form. Figures 7.1 and 7.2 portray the cycles of teacher engagement with the profession, with and without the presence of ongoing support in the form of professional development. As the figures show, all teachers experience anticipation, disillusionment, reenergizing, and periods of reflection. But only those with ongoing professional development support experience substantive growth without "termination," that is, withdrawal from the profession.

The alternative form of teacher preparation and district-level professional development, credentialing, and support that took shape in Denver was born of immediate needs that could not be met through more typical teacher-preparation pathways or state

Figure 7.1   Self-Reported Efficacy in First Year of Teaching, for Teachers Without Support System

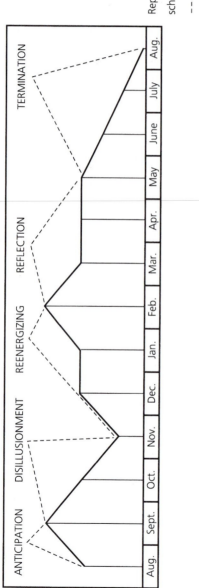

Reported each month of the school year.

– – – – – – Veteran Teacher

———— First-year Teacher

Figure 7.2   Self-Reported Efficacy in First Year of Teaching, for Teachers with Support System

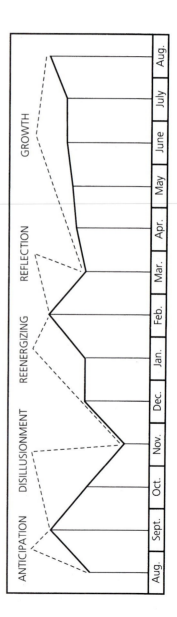

credentialing standards. It demonstrates a useful and highly responsive solution to a problem many school districts face with respect to serving culturally and linguistically diverse student populations. This alternative form of local preparation, ongoing support, and credentialing could be appropriate for enhancing the effectiveness of most educational professionals. Specifically, though, it is worthy of particular attention in the field at a time when effective teachers are needed more than ever.

Characteristics of Effective Teachers of Culturally and Linguistically Diverse Students

Chapter 1 described research reports that have attempted to identify the qualities of effective teachers who serve culturally diverse student populations (Dwyer, 1991; Ladsen-Billings, 1994; Villegas, 1991; Villegas et al., 1995). This research emphasis is related to the broader interest in identifying "exemplary" characteristics for teachers in general (Reynolds and Elias, 1991). To go beyond these generalizations, we shall explore the research that has attempted to document empirically the attributes of "good" teachers. The studies are few, but they begin to provide a set of standards that may be useful in preparing and evaluating teachers of culturally diverse students. The purpose of this discussion is not to suggest that all "good" teachers must be like the ones described here. Instead, we shall examine this information in order to see if we may use it to better understand the needs of students.

Tikunoff (1983), in his analysis of the Significant Bilingual Instructional Features (SBIF) study, reports commonalties in the "exemplary" teacher's response to classroom organization and instruction. As we saw in Chapter 6, the 58 teachers observed in this study represented six sites and spoke a variety of non-English languages (Spanish, Chinese, Vietnamese, Hmong, Navaho, and Hopi). All classes were considered "effective" on two criteria: (1) teachers were nominated by other teachers and school personnel, students, and parents; and (2) their teaching behaviors produced rates of academic learning time as high as or higher than rates reported in other research on effective teaching.

Attributes of Effective Teachers   An initial set of instructional features identified as characteristic of effective teachers of diverse student populations pertains to the organization and delivery of instruction:

1. Successful teachers specify both task outcomes and what students must do to accomplish tasks. In addition, teachers communicate high expectations for students in terms of learning and a sense of efficacy in terms of their own ability to teach.

2. Successful teachers of diverse students, not unlike effective teachers in general, use "active teaching" behaviors found to be related to increased student performance on academic tests of achievement in reading and mathematics. These teaching behaviors include (a) communicating clearly when giving directions, specifying tasks, and presenting new information; (b) obtaining and maintaining students' engagement in instructional tasks by pacing instruction appropriately, promoting involvement, and communicating their expectations for students' success in completing tasks; (c) monitoring students' progress; and (d) providing immediate feedback whenever required regarding students' success.

3. Successful teachers of limited-English-proficient (LEP) students mediate instruction for them by using the students' native language and English for instruction, alternating between the two languages whenever necessary to ensure clarity of instruction. Although they use this type of language switching, these teachers do not translate directly from one language to another.

Recent research (García, 1992b, 2000; Ladsen-Billings, 1994; Villegas, 1991) has focused on teachers who were consistently identified at the level of the school site and the district as "effective." In classrooms studied by García (1992b, 2000), approximately 50 to 70 percent of the students were non-English-speakers, and the remaining English-speaking students represented several ethnic groups. For the purpose of discussion, we can divide the findings of these studies of teacher attributes into four distinct but interlocking domains: (1) knowledge, (2) skills, (3) disposition, and (4) affect.

Knowledge

Effective teachers held the prerequisite state teacher credentials and had graduated from programs with specific emphasis on multicultural and/or bilingual education. They had an average of 7.1 years of experience as teachers of culturally diverse students. These were not novice teachers. They reported that they routinely participated in staff development efforts, either taking courses or attending workshops on teaching techniques they wanted to implement in their classrooms. Some of the workshops were sponsored by the school or district and were mandatory. These teachers also participated in courses that they sought out and financed on their own, some related to language development and others related to pedagogy and curriculum.

Experienced Teachers

These teachers were knowledgeable and articulate with regard to the instructional philosophies that guided them. They communicated these philosophies coherently in their interviews. They never hesitated to explain why they were using a specific instructional technique and usually couched these explanations in terms of how they saw their role with regard to teaching and how students learn. Principals and parents also commented on the ability of these teachers to communicate the rationales for their instructional techniques. One principal commented, "She's always able to defend her work with her students. When I first came here, I didn't agree with all that she was doing, and sometimes I still do not agree. But she always helps me understand why she is doing what she is doing. I respect her for that. She is not a 'recipe teacher'" (García, 1992a, p. 134).

Coherent
Teaching
Philosophy

One parent commented about her child's journal writing: "I didn't understand why she was letting _____ make all these spelling mistakes. It annoyed me. During the teacher-parent conference, she showed me the progress _____ was making. His spelling was getting better without taking a spelling test every week. I was surprised. She knows what she's doing" (Pease-Alvarez et al., 1991, p. 356). A parent concerned about his daughter's lack of English competency indicated:

> Me explicó que aprendiendo en español le va a ayudar a mi hija hablar mejor el inglés. Dice bien, porque mi hijo que vino conmigo de México, hablando y escribiendo en español, aprendió el inglés muy facil. [She explained that my daughter's learning of Spanish would help her learn English. She was right, because my son knew more Spanish when he came to the U.S. and he learned English easily.] (García, 1992a, p. 133)

Moreover, these teachers seemed to be quite competent in the content areas. For example, the upper elementary teachers who were instructing students in fractions had a solid and confident understanding of fractions. They did not seem to be only "one step ahead of the students."

Skills

Despite their differing perspectives, the teachers demonstrated specific instructional skills. Bilingual teachers used English and Spanish in highly communicative ways, speaking to students with varying degrees of Spanish and English proficiency in a communicative style requiring significant language switching. Direct translation from one language to another was a rarity, but utilization of language switching in contexts that required it was common.

Variations existed among these exemplary teachers, of course, but each had developed a particular set of instructional skills that, they indicated, led to their own effectiveness:

1. *Teachers had adopted an experimental stance toward instruction.* Along with many of their colleagues, these exemplary teachers had abandoned a strictly skills-oriented approach to instruction. To varying degrees they had organized instruction in their classes so that children focused first on what was meaningful to them. Teachers in the early grades used an approach to reading instruction that treated specific skills in the context of extended pieces of text (e.g., an entire book, passage, or paragraph). They initiated shared reading experiences by reading to and with children from an enlarged book, pointing to each word as they read. Because most of these books relied on a recurring pattern (e.g., a repeating syntactical construction, rhyming words, repetitions), children who could not read words in isolation were able to predict words and entire constructions when participating in choral reading activities. With time, teachers encouraged students to focus on individual words, sound-letter correspondences, and syntactic constructions. The teacher also encouraged children to rely on other cuing systems as they predicted and confirmed what they had read as a group or individually.

These teachers utilized a thematic curriculum. Science and social studies themes were often integrated across a variety of subject areas. Once a theme was determined, usually in consultation with students, the teachers planned instruction around a series of activities that focused on that theme. For example, a unit on dinosaurs included reading books about dinosaurs, categorizing and graphing different kinds of dinosaurs, visiting a museum that featured dinosaur exhibits, writing stories or poems about a favorite dinosaur, and speculating on the events that led to the dinosaurs' disappearance. In another example, a student in a third-grade classroom suggested that the theme address "the stuff in the field that makes my little brother sick" (García, 1992b, p. 137). The teacher then developed a four-week unit that engaged students in understanding pesticide use, which is a relevant topic for the children of migrant farm workers.

Despite the use of instructional strategies that depart from traditional skills-based approaches to curriculum and instruction, these teachers did sometimes structure learning around individual skills or discrete components. It was not

Focus on the Meaningful

Thematic Curriculum

uncommon for a teacher to form an ad hoc group of students needing special help with particular academic skills. Interestingly, the teachers reported that they devoted a week or two toward preparing students for standardized tests. During this time they taught skills that would be tested and administered practice tests. One teacher related, "I don't like testing. But we have to do it. I teach my kids how to mark the bubbles, and I make sure that they take their time. We practice test-taking" (García, 1992, p. 131).

2. *Teachers provided opportunities for active learning.* A good portion of class time was organized around a series of learning activities that children pursued either independently or with others. During science and math, children worked in small groups doing a variety of hands-on activities designed to support their understanding of a particular concept (e.g., classification, estimation, place value) or subject (e.g., oceanography, dinosaurs).

Each teacher's commitment to active learning was revealed by the consistent use of a studio or workshop format for literacy instruction. Instead of teaching students about reading and writing, teachers organized their program so that students actively read and wrote. Real reading and writing took place in the context of a literature-based reading program and during regularly scheduled times when students wrote in their journals on topics of their own choosing, with teachers reliably responding to their entries. There was also time for students to engage in writer's workshop, during which they generated their own topics and wrote, revised, edited, and published their finished writings for a larger audience. Like published authors, they shared their writing with others and often received input that helped them revise and improve upon what they had written. For example, one teacher commented, "These kids produce their own reading material and they take it home to share it with their parents. It's real good stuff. I help a little, but it's the kids that help each other the most" (Pease-Alvarez et al., 1991. p. 351).

Learning by Doing

3. *Teachers encouraged collaborative and cooperative interactions among students.* These teachers organized instruction so that students spent time working together on a wide range of instructional activities. Primary-grade teachers structured their day so that students worked on group and individual activities (e.g., graphing, journal writing, science projects) in small, heterogeneous groups. Students who worked in small groups on their own art project, journal, or experiment did not

Student Collaboration

Becoming a Responsive Teacher

A Successful Practitioner in Math

Kay Toliver's math program has been celebrated—and for good reason. She teaches at Harlem Tech Middle School—15% Afro-American, 85% Hispanic, and located in a poor New York City neighborhood. Yet her teaching strategies exemplify those recently recommended by the National Council of Teachers of Mathematics.

Toliver, who is not a textbook fan, makes math interdisciplinary. Her students constantly hypothesize and engage in hands-on activities. In one activity, they constructed two paper bridges, one made of quadrilaterals and the other of triangles, and found that the triangle was better suited as a building block. Toliver's students also create and illustrate math problems based on their own lives. For example: "There are two fire escapes on the outside of the building. If one is rusted and opens twice as slowly as the other, which opens in 7.4 seconds, how long will it take the rusted one to open?"

Toliver prefers authentic assessment methods to conventional testing. Her students have been asked to form a pentagon from any combination of six pattern-block pieces which included a square, an equilateral triangle, a rectangle, a trapezoid, a parallelogram, and a rhombus. They then had to determine the sum of the interior angles of the pentagon and explain how they arrived at their answer.

Not surprisingly, many of Toliver's students have gone on to prestigious schools, such as the Bronx High School of Science, and to college and vocational schools.

Source: David Hill, "Overnight sensation," *Teacher Magazine,* March 1993, pp. 23–27.

Meeting the Challenge

1. Develop two interdisciplinary math activities, one for an elementary-level classroom and one for a secondary-level classroom. Assume that your students are culturally and linguistically diverse. Include a collaborative aspect.

2. Contact the National Council of Teachers of Mathematics by letter, telephone, or Internet (*http://www.nctm.org/*). Ask a representative of the organization how you might view the material referred to in the preceding selection regarding the strategies the council recommends for teaching math. Share any information with your classmates.

necessarily interact with other members of their group. Teachers explained that students, particularly those who did not share the same dominant language, often ignored one another during these kinds of group activities. They felt that cross-cultural interactions were much more likely to take place when students were obliged to work together to complete a single task. Middle-grade teachers followed this same collaborative approach.

Disposition

A person's **disposition** is his or her usual temperament and frame of mind. We can describe the following attributes of effective teachers as constituting disposition because no other category seems relevant. The individual characteristics of these

Personal | teachers explain their success as professionals. For instance, they
Commitment | were highly dedicated. They reported working very hard, getting to school first and being the last to leave, working weekends, and sometimes feeling completely overworked. They reported spending close to $2,000 of their own resources to modify the classroom and obtain the materials their students needed. They indicated that they saw themselves as "creative," "resourceful," "committed," "energetic," "persistent," and "collaborative." They sought assistance from their colleagues and were ready to provide as much assistance as they received.

Although these teachers felt that they were effective, they were not complacent. They reported that they continued to change their instructional practices and in some cases their instructional

Change | philosophies over the years. These teachers reported undergoing great change in their approach to learning and instruction—of having "shifted paradigms." For example, teachers who once advocated skills-based and authoritarian modes of instruction such as DISTAR (a prescriptive reading program) were now considering and experimenting with child-centered approaches. Teachers felt that they enjoyed a certain degree of autonomy in their school. They felt free to implement change. In recent years, when they have wanted to institute a new classroom approach, they have presented a carefully thought-out rationale and eventually enlisted the principal's support.

The changes these teachers were involved in affected other classrooms as well as their own. With other teachers, they have worked to eliminate ability grouping across subject areas. They were involved in individual and group efforts to improve the quality of education at the school and district level. In short, these teachers were highly committed to improving themselves and the services to students in general.

Above all, they were highly confident, and even a bit "cocky," regarding their instructional abilities, as the following comments indicate:

> "I have changed my own view on how students learn—we need to understand learning does not occur in bits and pieces. Why do teachers still insist on teaching that way?"

> "I know what I am doing is good for kids. Some of my colleagues say I work too hard—I say they do not work hard enough. Not that they are lazy, they just don't seem to understand how important it is to do this job right."

> "I know my kids are doing well, all of them. I would rather keep them with me all day than send them to someone who is supposed to help them in their 'special' needs but doesn't help them at all." (García, 1992a; Pease-Alvarez et al., 1991)

Affect

The term **affect** is used in psychology to refer to people's feelings and emotions as distinguished from their thoughts and actions. The emotional energy these teachers bring to their work contributes to their effectiveness. These teachers felt strongly that classroom practices that reflect the cultural and linguistic background of minority students are important ways of enhancing student self-esteem. They recognized that part of their job was to provide the kind of cultural and linguistic validation that is missing in the larger society, which more often deprecates minority cultures and languages. According to teachers working with Latino students, learning Spanish and learning about Latino culture benefits Anglo-American students as well as Latino students. In their eyes, people who learn a second language tend to be more sensitive to other cultures. Like other teachers, these teachers felt that multicultural awareness enriched their students' lives.

These teachers had high expectations for all their students:

High Expectations |

> "No *'pobrecito'* [poor child] syndrome here—I want all my students to learn and I know they can learn even though they may come from very poor families and may live under 'tough' conditions. I can have them do their homework here and I can even get them a tutor—an older student—if they need it. I understand that their parents may not be able to help them at home. That's no excuse for them not learning." (García, 1992a, p. 133)

In many respects, these teachers portrayed themselves as being quite demanding, taking no excuses from students for not accomplishing assigned work and willing to be "tough" on those students who were "messing around."

Most significant was the teachers' affinity for their students:

"These students are like my very own children."

"I love these children like my own. I know that parents expect me to look after their kids and to let them know if they are in trouble."

"When I walk into that classroom, I know we are a family and we're going to be together a whole year. . . . I try to emphasize first that we are a family here. . . . I tell my students, "You're like brothers and sisters," and some students even call me *Mom* or *Tía* [Aunt]. It's just like being at home here." (García, 1992a, p. 133)

Each teacher spoke of the importance of strong and caring relationships among class members and particularly between the teacher and the students. They felt that such relationships provided students with a safe environment that was conducive to learning.

Parent Trust | Parents also reported a similar feeling. They referred to the teachers in the interviews as extended family members—someone to be trusted, respected, and honored for service to their children. These teachers were often invited to *bautismos* (baptisms), *bodas* (weddings), *fiestas de cumpleaños* (birthday celebrations), soccer games, and family barbecues. And they attended such occasions, reporting that such participation was inherently rewarding and instructive with regard to their own personal and professional lives. Parents commented during interviews:

"La señorita _____, le tengo mucha confianza, quiero que mi niño la respete como a mí." [Ms. _____, I trust her, my son respects her as he does me.]

"Nunca se larga mi niña de ella, se porta como mi hermana, siempre le puedo hablar y me gusta mucho ayudarle." [My daughter stays close to her, she is like my sister, I can always talk to her and I like to help her.]

Parent Journals | "I know my son is well cared for in her class, I never worry—she even calls me when he does something good." (García, 1992a, p. 137)

One very innovative process that our research has reported involves the extension of the interactive journal that we had seen utilized in communication between teachers and students at various grade levels. This particular activity involves the teacher's communicating on a weekly basis with the parents or family members of students in her or his classroom. As one teacher in our study described them:

> Parent journals have become interactive informers of [each student's] family's lives, experiences, and expectations regarding their child's schooling. They have informed what I teach and why. In turn, they [have allowed] me, on a continuous and informal basis, to tell my families about who I am [and] why I am teaching what I am teaching and to answer questions regarding personal and educational issues that are always on my students' parents' or caretakers' minds. Too often we as teachers have little time or space to attend to those we serve in this way. The weekly, interactive, informal writing back and forth provides that safe space and time.

Another teacher described the journals in an even more expansive manner:

> It is our responsibility to acknowledge parents whose oral language has become the resource to their child's literacy learning. When my students' parents were not able to write, I called and took notes in the parent journal. And, in several cases siblings became the writers of the parent entry, with my questions requiring them to "engage" the family in the response.

Very specifically, as we have seen them implemented, parent/family journals are notebooks filled with entries containing the weekly interactions between a teacher and a student's family member; sometimes this is a parent, a grandparent, an older sibling, or even a close friend whom the family designates as the appropriate respondent. Students are asked to take the notebooks home each week and to return them within a few days. They are asked to have a family member respond to the teacher through the journals, much as they would respond to their teacher through their own classroom interactive journals. The key to their success seems to be the teacher's and the family member's willingness to respond authentically and reliably during this conversation.

Value of Journals | In an effort to assess empirically the value of this resource to both parents and teachers, we asked parents and teachers to respond to a short survey regarding the use of these journals. In this elementary school setting, all 21 teachers began using the journals at the beginning of the year, and 19 of the 21 reported continuing their use until the end of the academic year. Similarly, 82 percent of the parents or family members who had been asked to participate in the journal interaction did so throughout the year. On a more qualitative basis, both teachers and parents made highly positive responses to survey questions regarding the value of the exercise. Almost all of the parents responding to the survey, some 70 percent, indicated a deep appreciation of the teachers for allowing them the opportunity to communicate in this way. One parent made her feelings very clear in an example of the kind of open-ended response that could be given in the survey: "I really appreciate the way we have come to know my daughter's teacher—her goals, her personal interest in my child, and the way we talk about the things that matter in my life and hers. It is so much better than those teacher conferences that I go to."

The results of this brief analysis suggest that this interactive tool assists teachers in establishing a partnership between home and school that enhances the student's achievement. At the same time, the parent journal allows teachers to learn about and become more responsive to the varied cultural and linguistic spheres that their students inhabit beyond the confines of classrooms and schools. The parent journal appears to

- Establish a direct way for families to become active participants in their children's schooling

- Stimulate authentic and purposeful communication between families and teachers on a continuous basis

- Encourage reflective communication by parents and teachers as each considers the learning and teaching contexts of the students

- Provide an open-ended format that can lead to unexpected insights about the cultural and social resources that a child or family member can bring to the schooling process

- Generate yet another venue for valuing literacy both inside and outside the classroom

The "Being a Responsive Teacher" feature suggests a way to begin using such journals. Please consider using them.

In summary, the teachers who are considered effective for culturally and linguistically diverse students are highly experienced, not novices to teaching or to the instruction of these students. They are skilled in communication with students, parents, and

How Do I Implement Interactive Parent/ Family-Teacher Journals?

Becoming a Responsive Teacher

- Establish the purpose of the journals with parents. This can be done at a short meeting during which you can present some ideas of what they might write about. Alternatively, you can write a short note on the front page of the notebook establishing the journal's purpose and "ground rules." (Mine state that the language used, topic, and amount of writing done are their choices and that the writing mechanics of my entries should not be considered as I will not be evaluating theirs.)

- Establish what day of the week the journals will be sent home with the students and when they should be returned. They should be dated and sent home as the "parent homework" for one night. (Mine go home on Thursdays and are returned on Friday morning. I give a reminder on Monday for those that did not make it back.)

- Follow the parent/family responses. Let them lead the discussion by answering their questions and commenting on their ideas as well as by asking meaningful questions. A journal becomes interactive through the conversations that are enriched by the quality of the questions and comments that are shared. (I often end my entries with a question that focuses on literacy as I respond to their questions.)

- The parent/family-teacher journals belong to the families. The richness of the dialogues as well as the personal nature of the entries becomes the means by which teachers assure families that the journals will be theirs at the end of the school year. (I have borrowed the following examples with the families' permission, and these families continued to remind me of that permission!)

administrative supervisors. They think about and communicate their own instructional philosophies. They work hard to understand the community, families, and students whom they serve, and they incorporate into the curriculum attributes of the local culture. They have adopted instructional methods that are student centered, collaborative, and process oriented—no "worksheet" curriculum was found. They are dedicated hard workers who collaborate with colleagues and continue to be involved in personal and professional growth activities. Most significantly,

Examples of Parent/Family-Teacher Interactive Journals

Para La Familia de Francisco,

Espero que les va gustar escribir on este Diario. Así nos podemos comunicar de varios temas, hacer preguntas, etc.

Yo puedo ver que Francisco escribe y habla en las dos idiomas. Es muy callado pero empieza a hablar y participar con más confianza, ¿Como es que Francisco es tan bilingüe?

Escribemé. Parte de Sra. García

Translated:

To Francisco's Family,

I am hoping that you will like writing in this journal. We can use this journal to communicate on a variety of themes, to ask and answer questions, etc.

I have noticed that Francisco speaks and writes in both languages. Although he has been shy in the past, he now speaks and participates more confidently. How is it that Francisco is so bilingual?

Write back, Mrs. García

* * *

Dear Armondo's Family,

This is our interactive journal. I will write to you each week and ask you to write back on Thursday night. We can write about anything.

So far I have learned lots about San Francisco. I just moved here three months ago. And I love Fairmount School—the kids are great. Armondo writes about "buffed" guys—how come? What do you as a family do together?

Write back, Mrs. García

these teachers care deeply for and personally connect with their students. They are advocates: Having "adopted" their students, they watch out for their students' welfare while at the same time challenging them with high expectations and refusing to accept the *"pobrecito"* syndrome.

Effective Teaching and Learning

As we learned in Chapter 3, there are certain elements of teaching practices that increase the likelihood that culturally and linguistically diverse students can be academically successful (see

Table 3.1). We shall now explore particular key questions that can serve as starting points for developing useful strategies for teachers.

Effective Learning Environments   August and Hakuta (1997, p. 171) provide a comprehensive review of schools and classrooms in which linguistically and culturally diverse populations achieve high academic performance. These settings have been found to share the following attributes:

- A supportive schoolwide climate
- School leadership
- A customized learning environment
- Articulation and coordination within and between schools
- Use of native language and culture in instruction
- A balanced curriculum that includes both basic and higher-order skills
- Explicit skills instruction
- Opportunities for student-directed instruction
- Use of instructional strategies that enhance understanding
- Opportunities for practice
- Systematic student assessment
- Staff development
- Home and parent involvement

The following section draws on these concepts in order to develop several key questions that we need to ask when examining schools' efforts.

The Key Questions

We can begin with the core issue of student engagement in the classroom. The literature on language acquisition and effective instruction for language minority students indicates that students are much more likely to be engaged learners in environments in which the curriculum and teaching approaches build on the diversity of the students and teachers (Pease-Alvarez et al., 1991; Wong-Fillmore, 1991). Further, teachers should have a **Student Engagement** close connection to, or at least a familiarity with, the home communities of their students. This connection allows the teachers to develop practices that reflect the kinds of experiences on which the students can construct an understanding of complex ideas and new concepts (Pease-Alvarez et al., 1991). In addition, culturally and linguistically diverse students can experience engaged learning only when they have the time to interact with each other and with the adults in the school community. Such interactions improve the students' social and communication skills and create a "safe" environment in which to learn. Finally, assessments of the students' progress in learning various subjects, developing conceptual understandings, and acquiring particular skills need to be aligned with the established curricular and instructional goals. To be a true gauge of the quality of the learning environment, these assessments must involve all students. In other words, if linguistically and culturally diverse students are systematically left out of regular schoolwide or classroom assessments, the results of such efforts cannot begin to address all of the learning that goes on in a school—or, more importantly, the areas to which further attention should be devoted. With these elements in mind, we can pose our first key question:

How are language, culture, and student diversity incorporated into instruction, curriculum, and assessment practices?

Professional Development

Very closely related to the issue of engaged student learning is the matter of professional development. As noted, teachers and other professionals who work with students with diverse backgrounds are called upon to bring many skills, strategies, and insights into their classrooms. A concern arises with regard to how their teaching strategies are developed and shared within (and beyond) the learning environment. It is thus appropriate to ask:

What resources, experiences, and structures contribute to the professional development of the school community; and how are they related to student achievement?

In addition to concerning ourselves with teaching practices and the classroom environment as support mechanisms for academic success among culturally diverse students, we must also

Schoolwide Vision

focus on practices that affect the entire school. These include the development of (1) a schoolwide vision that celebrates cultural diversity and that is aimed at optimizing the learning opportunities for all students (Pease-Alvarez et al., 1991), and (2) relationships and structural features of the school that facilitate active participation across all sectors of the school community, again with the goal of high academic performance. To further our understanding of these elements as they operate in schools with large populations of culturally and linguistically diverse students, it is also important to know:

How are the school's visions and missions alive in each instructor's teaching and values, and how are they articulated for and to each teacher?

Power Relationships | Finally, with respect to the broader organizational context (Delpit, 1995; Ladsen-Billings, 1994), the research suggests asking:

How do power relationships in the educational and local community as well as in the larger society become embedded in the classroom? What prevailing norms and underlying beliefs shape the roles, expectations, and standards in classroom instruction?

The Principal's Role in Effective Schooling

Just as our earlier discussion focused on the effective teacher, this section will use similar data to analyze the administrative leadership of schools that have proved effective for linguistically and culturally diverse students (García, 1997). It is no small task

"Exemplary" Administrators | to identify the exemplary principal, a process that involves interviewing and observing these individuals along with teachers and parents to obtain a more comprehensive perspective. It is not my intent to suggest that all "good" principals must be like the ones described here. Instead, I want to describe carefully the attributes of these individuals so that others may use this information to serve highly diverse constituencies more effectively.

The following discussion is based on data derived from selected elementary and middle school principals in eight schools in California and Arizona. All these principals had been consistently identified at the school and district level as "exemplary" professionals, and their schools had been recognized for serving linguistically and culturally diverse students effectively (for specific selection criteria, see García, 1997). Approximately 50 to 70 percent of their students were Spanish-dominant speakers; the remainder were dominant in English or another language (Vietnamese, Hmong, and/or Cantonese). The findings with regard to professional attributes were divided into three distinct but interlocking domains: integrity, responsibility, and affect.

Integrity

The principals in this study were all bilingual and biliterate in English and Spanish. They had the prerequisite state credentials and had graduated from specific administrative programs after serving as teachers for three or four years. They had an average of 4.1 years (range 1.4–8.1 years) of teaching experience in schools with bilingual or second-language educational interventions. Therefore, these were relatively inexperienced professionals, with limited background as either teachers or principals. Many had been thrust into administrative roles because they had worked with diverse student populations, even though that experience may not have been extensive. As one superintendent said of one of the principals, "We needed her to help us in that principalship. I had no other candidate who could better understand this community."

Aspects of Integrity | However, these principals were perceived as individuals with high integrity: honest, dedicated, hard-working, professional. They reported participating in professional development activities that they sought out and financed on their own, some related to Spanish-language development and others directly related to management, assessment, and educational practice.

Articulateness | These principals were quite knowledgeable and articulate with regard to the district and local school philosophy, missions, and goals, which they communicated quite coherently in their interviews. Teachers and parents also commented on the principals' abilities to deal effectively with the district office. One teacher commented, "He's always able to defend our work to the superintendent and the board. I respect him for that." Speaking about the principal's reactions to her child's disciplinary problems, a parent remarked, "I can count on him defending my son. He is fair and will make sure _____ is not mistreated." On the basis of such relationships, the principals had achieved a high degree of autonomy and respect from district administrators, teachers, and parents. One school board member indicated, "Someone is in the driver's seat."

Despite such positive characteristics, these principals were not always aware of the teachers' philosophical or theoretical positions. Nor were they the intellectual leaders found among the principals described in other research on "effective schools."

Building Respect | Overall, however, these principals were able to build on their limited experience and professional knowledge to construct a respect from the parent, teaching, and educational community. This seemed to come from the perception that the principal was hard-working and sincere. The principals themselves reported working, on average, 55–60 hours per week, most of that time at the school.

These effective principals were also self-critical, never satisfied that they were doing enough. They never hesitated to ask themselves why the school was using specific curriculum or instructional techniques. They looked more to teaching colleagues than to other administrators for support, and they themselves organized and sustained support networks—but usually with teachers rather than with other administrators.

Responsibility

Responsible

The principals whom we studied had realized that in the present climate of school-targeted reform, students and parents have a right to expect schools to deliver on their charge of preparing the next generation of workers and citizens and that the public in general has a right to expect progress in return for their tax investments. It is correct for the state and local districts to focus on such accountability. However, these school leaders displayed a keen interest in being more directly *responsible* for their schools' documentation of student performance and for the use of this documentation to inform instruction of their students. The usual standardized testing programs that are used for accountability purposes fall short in meeting the responsibility index to which these principals referred.

A full-fledged and appropriate evaluation system in these schools focused on the following:

- *A fair and technically sound assessment system.* To account for student differences and subject-matter variation, multiple measures of performance were used, including those that relied on independent student performance or work as well as those that relied on teachers' judgments about that performance or work. These measures incorporated accommodations for non-English-proficient students, students with special needs, and very young students. Student performance assessments measured what the schools directly incorporated into their curricula, not generic skills included in some off-the-shelf assessments.

- *Adequate preparation for the assessments.* For any student evaluations to be meaningful, students must have prior instruction in the evaluation area. In order for student learning to reach desired achievement levels, instruction must improve. That requires investment in teacher development and curriculum. It also means that instruction must be focused on the standards for learning that also guide the assessments. Schools must also have time to develop instruction aimed at helping students achieve the standards before students are judged as being successful or failing. The principals made sure that time was made available for teacher consultation, for professional development, and for debriefing on the student assessments themselves. In addition, students in the upper grades were themselves engaged in the development, implementation, and discussion of the assessments that they were given. As one principal put it, "students were not just 'victims' of or 'noninterested bystanders' of the assessment process."

- *Appropriate uses of assessments.* Assessments need to inform a number of decisions, including teacher plans for individual students, school curriculum designs, and teacher professional development needs as well as decisions about what to do when students' school performances lag—high-stakes decisions about grade retention, graduation, and other matters that directly influence the future educational circumstances of individual students or groups of students. Different tests are needed for different purposes; there is no such thing as an all-purpose assessment.

- *Responsibility for all.* In these schools, principals and teachers were sure to disaggregate student performance indicators in order to be better informed about how groups of students were performing. Disaggregation of data by gender, ethnic group, race, and English-language proficiency helped the entire school community understand how *all* students were doing.

In short, these principals acted on their perceived need to invest resources and time in the *responsibility* system. This system recognizes that there are differences in the ways in which students demonstrate competence and that ignoring this fact also ignores a well-documented variable in making student assessments valid, reliable, fair, and useful for encouraging student achievement.

Affect

Much like the teachers in their schools, these principals felt strongly that their school practices must reflect the cultural and linguistic background of the students. They reported that part of their job was to provide the kind of cultural and linguistic validation that was missing in the local community, where minority culture and language were deprecated. In their eyes, people who learned a second language tended to be more sensitive to other cultures. They felt that being bilingual and bicultural enriched their students' lives.

The principals also had high expectations for all their students. No Excuses | In many respects, just like the effective teachers described earlier, these professionals portrayed themselves as strict, unwilling to accept excuses from students, and willing to be firm with students who were misbehaving.

Most significant were the feelings the principals had toward those whom they served: "I know that parents expect me to look after their kids and to let them know if they are in trouble," said one. Another noted, "Some students even call me *tio* [uncle]. It's just like being at home here." Each principal spoke of the importance of strong and caring relationships among themselves and those whom they served. Almost all indicated an interest in remaining at the school, even though they expected that they might be asked to take an "easier" assignment. They also said that they "liked" the community and the parents.

Caring Relationships

Parents also reported similar feelings about the principals, referring to them as extended family members, people to be trusted, respected, and honored. The principals were often invited to soccer and baseball games and family get-togethers. And they attended such occasions, reporting that such participation was inherently rewarding and instructive both personally and professionally. Parents commented: "Al señor _____, le tengo mucha confianza, quiero que mi niño lo respete como a mí"; "I know my son is well cared for at school, I never worry—I want my son to respect him just as he respects me."

This discussion has focused on the attributes of principals who are considered effective among linguistically and culturally diverse students. Much like the teachers in these effective schools, these individuals are highly committed, although they do not always have prior administrative experience. They are highly skilled in communicating with students, parents, and administrative supervisors. They are able to articulate their schools' goals clearly. They work hard to understand the community, families, and students they serve, and they incorporate into the school aspects of the local culture. They collaborate with teacher colleagues and continue to be involved in personal and professional growth activities. Most significantly, these professionals implement systems of responsibility for the students whom they serve. They are their students' advocates; having "adopted" them, the principals both look out for them and challenge them.

Conclusion

It seems clear that culturally and linguistically diverse students—often referred to en masse as "at risk" students—can indeed be served effectively by schools and educational professionals. Schools must develop educational structures and processes that consider both the general attributes of effective schooling practices and the specific attributes of effective teachers (Carter and Chatfield, 1986; García, 1988, 1992a; Tikunoff, 1983). Although the training of such teachers is in a developmental period, and further clarifying research is needed, it is clearly not in its infancy. A serious body of literature that examines instructional practices and organization, and their effects, is emerging.

The preparation of teaching innovators is a challenge for university, federal, state, and local educational agencies. The needs are great, and the production of competent professionals has lagged. Teacher organizations, credentialing bodies, and universities have responded with a new array of competencies, guidelines, and professional evaluation tools. The most often utilized professional evaluation tool is the connoisseur model of professional assessment. Like other assessment methods, the connoisseur model is not yet sufficiently reliable or valid enough to use at a statewide level. It has been employed with some success, however, at the level of the individual school district, using locally derived credentials. This district-level credentialing process is an alternative worthy of serious consideration. The challenge for all those engaged in the preparation, assessment, and credentialing of linguistically and culturally diverse teachers is to consider the rapidly expanding research literature, to evaluate its implications critically, and to apply it in educational contexts with the help of locally developed connoisseurs.

Summary of Major Ideas

1. A profession is characterized by (a) acquisition of knowledge obtained through formal education and (b) an orientation toward serving the needs of the public, with an emphasis on ethical and altruistic concern for the client. The professional preparation of teachers has not kept pace with the educational needs of culturally and linguistically diverse students in the United States.

2. At present, educators are prepared and assessed by state agencies, by professional societies, or by both. Assessment may focus on the individual preservice teacher through a test such as the National Teaching Exam or on the programs that prepare teachers through state or association reviews. The professional credentials that teachers are required to have reflect the general intellectual and ethical climate and needs of the time.

3. Not until 1974 did the U.S. Congress provide institutions of higher education with resources for use in preparing teachers of culturally and linguistically diverse children. The 1980–1982

Teachers Language Skills Survey estimated that whereas 100,000 trained bilingual teachers were needed in U.S. schools, barely a third of this number were available. The survey also reported that only 40 percent of teachers assigned to teach English as a Second Language had been formally prepared to do so. In 1994, there was an estimated national shortage of some 175,000 teachers of language minority students.

4. As of 1998, 25 states and U.S. territories offered no professional credentialing for teachers of bilingual education or ESL. Less than one-third of the states required schools to provide services to limited-English-proficient students, even in such places as California, Florida, and New York, which are greatly affected by growing numbers of language minority students.

5. Present methods of professionally assessing teachers are limited and are often unreliable and invalid. The connoisseur method of assessment, by which experienced practitioners evaluate the effectiveness of teachers in training, is not sufficiently developed for use on a statewide level.

6. Performance competencies expected for teachers of culturally and linguistically diverse students cover the instructor's knowledge of (a) educational theory, (b) social trends, and (c) classroom strategies. In 1984, the National Association of State Directors of Teacher Education and Certification (NASDTEC) developed a list of competencies to be used for certifying teachers of language minority students. Some states, such as New Jersey, have detailed the roles and responsibilities of these teachers in published handbooks.

7. Although teacher-preparation programs for linguistically and culturally diverse students are still in the developmental stage, the recent trend has been to conduct most training at the school rather than at a university or college. Other programs have encouraged members of the local community to be hired and trained as education professionals.

8. All teachers experience anticipation, disillusionment, reenergizing, and periods of reflection. Burnout is exhaustion caused by stress experienced over a long period of time and is prevalent among teachers who serve highly diverse student populations. Burnout may cause even good teachers to leave the profession. Research shows that first-year teachers can resist the effects of burnout and experience substantive growth if they are provided with ongoing support in the form of professional development.

9. Effective teachers of diverse student populations organize and deliver instruction in a characteristic way. They specify task outcomes and communicate high expectations for students. They use "active teaching" behaviors. Effective teachers of LEP students switch back and forth between the students' first language and English without directly translating.

10. Effective teachers have also been found to have specific attributes in the domains of knowledge, skill, disposition, and affect. Disposition is a person's usual temperament and frame of mind, and affect is a person's feelings and emotions as distinguished from thoughts and actions. These effective teachers were highly experienced and skilled at communicating with students, parents, and administrators. They used student-centered, collaborative, and process-oriented instructional methods. They were dedicated to their own personal and professional growth. They personally connected with and advocated for their students.

11. Effective principals, like effective teachers, are highly committed to the diverse students they serve. Although they are not always experienced administratively, they communicate well with students, parents, and administrative supervisors and work hard to understand the community, families, and students they serve. Most importantly, they develop and implement assessment systems that are built upon the responsibility they require for themselves.

Extending Your Experience

1. Effective teachers have a deep commitment to the educational enterprise. Ask yourself and two other colleagues (a new teacher and a seasoned teacher) the following questions: Why did you choose teaching as a profession? Why are you now a teacher? Will you remain in teaching for the next five years? Why or why not?

2. Write to or explore the web site of the National Clearinghouse for Bilingual Education at the U.S. Department of Education. Find out what information and services it provides that would be of interest to teachers of culturally and linguistically diverse children. In particular, compile a list of inservice training available through state education departments or local school districts.

3. In your local school district, who are the educators who might be called on to serve as mentors, or connoisseurs, in a training

and assessment program for teachers of culturally diverse students? How would you go about identifying these experts and learning what they do to provide their students with an effective education?

4. This chapter describes the characteristics of effective teachers of culturally and linguistically diverse students according to four areas: knowledge, skills, disposition, and affect. How would you rank these areas in terms of importance? Write each one as a heading on a sheet of paper and take an inventory of yourself. Can you identify your own strengths and weaknesses in these four areas?

5. Working with a group of your classmates, design a series of questions to be used to interview candidates for a teaching position in an elementary or secondary school with a large population of linguistically and culturally diverse students. Base your interview questions on the four areas of teacher characteristics discussed in the chapter.

6. Interview one or two elementary or secondary school principals about their experience with student accountability measures—the state's, the district's, and their own. Share your findings with your classmates, respecting the principal's anonymity, if necessary. What is your own assessment of these systems?

Resources for Further Study

Print Resources

Davis, D., Davis, T., and Leppo, M. (1999). *First class teachers speak out.* Washington, DC: Sallie Mae Education Institute.

The Sallie Mae First-Class Teacher program presents findings from 1,200 mail surveys and 37 extensive telephone interviews with teachers in this report. Its goal is to understand teachers' thinking regarding effective teaching strategies, issues of assessment and state standards, class size, and the role of administrators in terms of providing professional development and supporting collaborative activities as well as ensuring school safety.

Davis, D., Davis, T., and Leppo, M. (1999). *A first class look at teaching.* Washington, DC: Sallie Mae Education Institute.

Supported by the Sallie Mae First-Class Teacher Program, this report presents responses to 1,200 mail surveys from teachers on their teaching experiences, with the intended goal of improving the quality of education at the elementary and secondary levels. The report focuses attention on such topics as teacher preparation, professional development, student teachers' experiences with teaching mentors, and future plans in teaching. It also offers advice from these instructors that is vital for keeping teachers committed to teaching.

Freedman, S. Warshauer. (1994). *Exchanging writing, exchanging cultures: Lessons in school reform from the United States and Great Britain.* Cambridge, MA: Harvard University Press.

The author matches four middle schools and high schools in the United States with schools in London that share similar educational concerns. The London schools are model schools that give reason for a thorough reconsideration of the goals and objectives that U.S. educators have for their students regarding literacy. Specific focus is given to the educational policies and structures that have been instituted in these British schools. This comparative study encourages classroom teachers, policymakers, and school reformers to reevaluate their current methods of teaching writing.

Kreinberg, N., and Nathan, H. (1991). *Teachers' voices, teachers' wisdom: Seven adventurous teachers think aloud.* Berkeley, CA: EQUALS, Lawrence Hall of Science, University of California at Berkeley.

This book offers an insight into teaching from a teacher's perspective. This is an opportunity for readers to appreciate the complexity, struggles, and victories of teaching. Specifically, the book focuses on the ways in which teachers think about themselves in terms of their relationships with their students, their own teacher preparation, and their teaching careers. Essentially, this book shows how these beliefs guide and define teaching practices.

Pease-Alvarez, C., Espinoza, P., and García, E. (1991). Effective instruction for language minority students: An early childhood case study. *Early Childhood Research Quarterly, 6*(3), 347–363.

The authors offer a descriptive analysis of two teachers in order to illustrate effective instructional perspectives and practices. Such effective practices are quoted from large-scale studies. The two teachers' experiences demonstrate how to educate language minority students. The teachers' personal, professional, and educational goals provide the reader with insight into how language and culture can become an integral part of the classroom along with innovative perspectives, effective instructional practices, and different philosophies.

Villegas, A. M. (1991). *Culturally responsive pedagogy for the 1990s and beyond.* Princeton: Educational Testing Service.

The author's main goal is to identify the most current and significant literature dealing with promising instructional practices for minority students. The document reviews the most current thinking on minority students. A number of authorities from different disciplinary perspectives such as anthropology, sociology, linguistics, sociolinguistics, psychology, psycholinguistics, and curriculum and instruction were invited to provide input.

Chapter 8
Effective Instruction of Liguistically and Culturally Diverse Children

Focus Questions

- What are some of the characteristics of elementary schools that effectively serve culturally and linguistically diverse students?

- What are some of the characteristics of high schools that effectively serve culturally and linguistically diverse students?

- How radically must schools be transformed in order to educate all of our students?

- How will acknowledgment of linguistic, sociocultural, and cognitive factors in children's development bring about change in educational practices?

- What classroom strategies have been identified as being effective for enabling language minority students to achieve academically?

- Why are authentic assessments important to effective schooling? Give some examples of their use.

> "Knowledge is not something separate and self-sufficing, but it is involved in the process by which life is sustained and evolved."
> —*John Dewey*

It seems only appropriate to begin our discussion of effective instructional practices by addressing the previous statement by one of this country's most renowned educators, John Dewey. Too often the greatest purpose of our schools is perceived to be the "dispensing" of knowledge. Dewey, however, reminds us that knowledge cannot be dispensed. It must be constructed, reconstructed, and located in our own individual ways of living. It is more a process than an entity, something that maintains us while simultaneously transforming us.

Today's teachers face numerous challenges. To begin with, a teacher must interact with many students, each with unique learning biographies, interests, strengths, and experiences. Schools exist, at least in part, to provide an opportunity for students to encounter ways of knowing and doing that they would not likely meet out of school. Under these conditions, it seems essential that the teacher give careful thought and preparation—both material and intellectual—to the creation of instructional events. Dewey (1916) recommends instruction that engages the interest of students so that each is enabled to meet the challenges and make meaningful, on his or her own terms, the "educational" material available in that milieu. Only then can the school, the classroom, and the teacher "step back and follow the student's lead" (Dewey, 1916, p. 19).

As the U.S. population continues to diversify racially and ethnically, particularly among school-age children, the nature of schooling must reflect this significant demographic transformation. Schools today are being asked not simply to improve their functioning but also to adapt to new populations, new societal expectations, and new intellectual and employment demands. Our next generation of young people, and ethnic and racial minority children in particular, will continue to be vulnerable if our schools do not successfully complete the required metamorphosis. The future lies in understanding how a diverse population, one with many individuals at risk for underachievement, can attain social, educational, and employment competence. As always, the new ideas, the energy, and the resources for our society's future reside in our youth.

We have seen that educational vulnerability is a historical reality for culturally and linguistically diverse students in the United States. The phrase "culturally and linguistically diverse" is a relatively new educational term that does not fully portray the stunning diversity among the populations it labels. Recent educational leaders, such as former U.S. Secretary of Education Richard Riley, have concluded that populations identified as such have been perceived by the majority of society as linguistically, cognitively, socially, and educationally inferior (Riley, 1994). This perception has given rise to a variety of social and educational programs that have attempted to eliminate these "inferior" characteristics (August and Hakuta, 1997). Meanwhile, linguistically and culturally diverse populations continue to struggle to attain educational success.

Recent educational research and associated instructional practices have revealed the nature of educational vulnerability as it relates to language, culture, and cognition. In the following section we shall review some of the theoretical underpinnings of new educational strategies. We then will look at research into characteristics of effective schools and effective instructional practices. Particular emphasis will be placed on how an instructionally responsive stance can lead to a more productive educational future for culturally diverse student populations.

A Theoretical Framework: Two Divergent Views

Before we examine effective schools and instructional practices, let's go back a few chapters and review the theoretical base available to us. Recall from Chapter 3 that at one end of the continuum of educational theory, educators argue that addressing the academic underachievement of linguistically and culturally diverse populations requires a deeper understanding of the interaction between a student's home and school cultures (Tharp, 1989). These theorists claim that educational failure can be explained by the "culture clash" between home and school. Alternatively, other theorists state that the academic failure of any student rests on the failure of instructional personnel to implement the principles of teaching and learning that we know "work."

In any sincere attempt to address the educational circumstances of students, these theoretical positions need not be

Both Theories Are Useful | incompatible. In fact, both positions offer a more informed perspective on the effective and efficient education of all students.

Making distinctions among theories is a necessary starting point in our discussion of instructional practices that might enhance education for historically unsuccessful student populations. The continued failure of past and present schooling practices to serve these students effectively is highly significant. The rest of this chapter describes the extent to which schools and schooling practices must change in order to reverse this failure.

Characteristics of Effective Schools

Within the last 25 years, researchers have compiled a considerable body of data on effective school practices. A review of the accumulated data identifies the following characteristics of effective schools (Purkey and Smith, 1985):

Administrative leadership: Effective principals are actively engaged in curriculum planning, staff development, and instructional issues.

Teacher expectations: Teachers maintain high achievement expectations for all students.

Emphasis on basic skills: There is a deliberate focus on reading, writing, math, and language arts.

School climate: An orderly, safe environment conducive to teaching and learning is maintained.

Regular feedback: Continual feedback on academic progress is provided to students and parents.

Edmonds (1979) contributed to the emerging picture of effective schools, particularly with regard to "minority" students. He

Variables in Schools | identified two groups of variables—organizational and structural variables, and process variables—that together define the climate and culture of the school. Organizational and structural variables include the following:

School site management: School leadership and staff have considerable autonomy in determining the exact means by which they address the problem of increasing academic performance.

Instructional leadership: The principal initiates and maintains procedures for improving achievement.

Curriculum planning and organization: In elementary schools, the curriculum has a clear focus on the acquisition of basic skills. Instruction takes into consideration students' linguistic and cultural attributes across grade levels and throughout the entire curriculum.

Staff development: This variable is essential to change and consists of a schoolwide program closely related to the instructional program. This activity is crucial in schools serving language minority students.

Parent support and involvement: Support from parents is essential to the success of any educational program for language minority students.

Schoolwide recognition of academic success: Recognition of student achievement is reflected in the school's activities.

District support: Financial and administrative support is fundamental to change and to the maintenance of effective schools.

Edmonds (1979a) defined *process variables* as factors that sustain a productive school climate. He identified four process variables:

Collaborative planning and collegial relationships: Teachers and administrators work together to implement change.

A sense of community: A feeling of belonging contributes to reduced alienation and increased student achievement.

Clear goals and high expectations: These are commonly shared. A focus on those tasks deemed most important allows the school to direct its resources and shape its functioning toward the realization of goals.

Order and discipline: These help to maintain the seriousness and purpose with which the school approaches its task.

Carter and Chatfield (1986, p. 224) report similar attributes present in effective elementary schools serving Mexican American, African American, and Asian students in California. Their analyses suggest that processes, not structures, of pedagogy, administrative arrangements, and classroom organization are most closely linked to effectiveness. Carter and Chatfield describe an effective school for language minority students as a well-functioning total system producing a school social climate that promotes positive outcomes. They broke their analysis into two parts:

1. Specific characteristics crucial to the development of effective schooling and thus to a positive school climate, such as a safe and orderly school environment and positive leadership, usually from the formal leaders (administrators, principals, and curriculum specialists). Also important was common agreement on a strong academic orientation—that is, clearly stated academic goals, objectives, and plans—and well-functioning methods to monitor school input and student outcomes.

2. A positive school social climate that includes high staff expectations for children and the instructional program; a strong demand for academic performance; denial of the cultural-deprivation argument and the stereotypes that support it; high staff morale, consisting of strong internal support, consensus building, job satisfaction, feelings of personal efficacy, belief that the system works, a sense of ownership, well-defined roles and responsibilities, and practices that reflect the policy that resources are best expended on people rather than on educational software and hardware.

Much like Edmonds (1979) and Purkey and Smith (1985), Carter and Chatfield (1986) examined the attributes of schools that selectively promoted achievement of immigrant students. Table 8.1 identifies factors that will facilitate teaching and learning with respect to immigrant students.

These findings correspond with those of other recent studies of the effectiveness of programs specifically designed for diverse populations. California Tomorrow (1995, p. 8), in a study of early childhood care in California, concluded that the following principles guided quality childcare across a variety of settings that serve a growing community of linguistically and culturally diverse families:

1. Supporting the development of ethnic identity and nonracist attitudes among children.

2. Building on the cultures of families and promoting cross-cultural understanding among children.

3. Fostering the preservation of children's home languages and encouraging bilingualism among all children.

4. Engaging in ongoing reflection and dialogue.

After reviewing the literature on multicultural early childhood education and interviewing experts in the field, Cohen and Pompa (1994) came to the same conclusion, noting that universal notions of "developmentally appropriate" approaches must be revised to recognize the more specific "culturally appropriate developmental" issues.

A state-mandated study of exemplary schools serving California's linguistically and culturally diverse students indicated that several key attributes were common in such settings. These key attributes included the following:

1. *Flexibility:* Adapting to the diversity of languages, mobility, and nonschool needs of these students and their families.

| Table 8.1 | **Reconceptualizing of Responsive Schools for Immigrant Students** |

Reconceptualizing of Learners as . . .	**Implications for Immigrant Students**
Active constructors of knowledge	• Supports and values learning through various means, thus acknowledging different styles • Reduces reliance on language as the medium for learning • Conflicts with the views of many other cultures, which hold that learners take in what teachers deliver • May require more language use and cultural knowledge than some immigrants have attained
Collaborators	• Promotes language use in the classroom • Promotes cross-cultural learning and communication • Is consistent with learning strategies in cultures with a collective orientation, which traditional U.S. competitive learning is not • May require more language use and cultural knowledge than some immigrants have attained • Requires cross-cultural sensitivity for all involved
Decision makers	• Draws on strengths of students who play decision-making roles • Conflicts with collective orientation in emphasizing individual will, action, and responsibility • May conflict with adolescent roles in other cultures
Communities	• Encourages everyone to learn about immigrant students and families in order to integrate them into the community • Requires personalization of schooling
Learner centered	• Encourages everyone to learn about immigrant students and families in order to design schooling with learners at the center • Requires personalization of schooling
Part of a larger situational and chronological context	• Encourages schools to find ways to engage immigrant families in schooling • Brings together multiple providers of service and assistance for immigrant families • May eventually lead schools to provide assistance for immigrant students as they move beyond high school into work and higher education
Mediators between home culture and mainstream culture	• Makes information about U.S. culture and schooling accessible to immigrant students • Shows immigrant students that their cultures and experiences are valued • Gives immigrant students access to academic knowledge and abilities

Source: Adapted from T. Lucas, *Into, Through, and Beyond Secondary School: Critical Transitions for Immigrant Youth.* Washington, DC and McHenry, IL: Center for Applied Linguistics and Delta Systems, 1997, pp. 58–59. Reprinted by permission from Tamara Lucas.

2. *Coordination:* Utilizing sometimes scarce and diverse resources, such as federal and state funds and local community organizations, in highly coordinated ways to achieve academic goals.

3. *Cultural validation:* Validating students' culture by incorporating materials and discussions that build on the linguistic and cultural aspects of the community.

4. *Shared vision:* Uniting the principal, staff, parents, and community behind a common, coherent sense of who the students are and what they hope to accomplish (Berman, 1992a).

Three more recent analyses of exemplary schools that serve high percentages of linguistically and culturally diverse students are worthy of mention. The first is a series of studies in five urban and suburban school districts in various regions of the United States that focused on the variables that determine whether students achieve academic success in a second language (Collier, 1995). These studies included some 42,000 students per school year over an 8- to 12-year period for each school district. Three key factors were reported as significant in producing academic success for students in the schools studied:

Key Factors | 1. Complex cognitive instruction in the students' first language for as long as possible and in the second language for part of the school day.

2. Use of current approaches to teaching academic curriculum in both the primary language and secondary language through active discovery and cognitively complex learning.

3. Such changes in the sociocultural context of schooling as integrating English speakers, implementing additive bilingual instructional goals, and encouraging positive minority/majority relations (Thomas and Collier, 1995b).

Another recent set of studies focused on selected schools in which highly diverse and poor student populations demonstrated academic success. These schools were subjected to intensive site-by-site study in order to identify the attributes that related to the effectiveness of each school and those that were common to all (McLeod, 1996). Schools in Texas, Illinois, California, and Massachusetts were particularly successful in achieving high academic outcomes with a diverse set of students. They shared the following goals for ensuring high-quality teaching:

1. *Foster English acquisition and the development of mature literacy.* Schools utilized students' native-language abilities to

develop literacy expertise that was then transferred to English literacy development at high levels.

2. *Deliver grade-level content.* Challenging academic work was introduced along with the goal of learning English. Teachers organized lessons to deliver grade-level instruction through a variety of native-language, ESL, or **sheltered English** activities—specifically designed academic instruction in English that maximizes nonverbal instructional communication, combining content with English-language learning goals.

3. *Organize instruction in innovative ways.* Examples of innovations included developing "schools-within-schools" to deal more responsively with the diverse language needs of the students, forming "families" of students who stayed together for major parts of a middle-school day, creating "continuum classes" in which teachers remained with their students for two to three years in order to become more familiar with and respond to their diversity, and continually grouping students more flexibly in order to accommodate their native- and second-language developmental differences.

4. *Protect and extend instructional time.* Schools utilize after-school programs, supportive computer-based instruction, and voluntary Saturday and summer schools to multiply the opportunities for students to learn. Not surprisingly, a majority of the students took advantage of these voluntary extensions. Care was taken, however, not to allow teachers' auxiliary responsibilities to erode the daily instructional time.

5. *Expand teachers' roles and responsibilities.* Teachers were given much greater roles in instructional and curricular decision-making in order to ensure cross-grade articulation and coordination. Teachers in these schools became full co-partners with the administrators. They devised more authentic writing, math, and related assessment tools that could inform instruction.

6. *Address students' social and emotional needs.* These schools were located in low-income neighborhoods and served poor families. Therefore, they adopted a proactive stance with regard to community issues. For example, in one school an after-school activity aimed at families, and particularly at issues of alcohol and drug abuse, family violence, health care, and related needs, brought the school staff together with social service agencies. Similar instances of family counseling and direct medical care were arranged at other sites.

7. *Involve parents in their children's education.* Some of these schools were magnet schools; parents had chosen to send

their children there. In such sites, parent involvement was part of the contract, and it included participating in school committees, assisting with school programs, helping on student field trips, and the like. In nonmagnet schools, parent outreach services were an integral part of the school operation. In all cases, regular communication in the various languages of the home occurred. Parent participation in governance of the school was a common attribute, although highly variable.

In a third recent analysis—a more intensive case study of two elementary schools and one middle school—Miramontes, Nadeau, and Commins (1997) detailed the development of exemplary school attributes, emphasizing the link between decision-making (who decides what and how instruction is implemented) and effective programs. Over a period of several years these schools, where as many as five languages were represented, earned local, state, and national recognition for their academic success with their extremely linguistically and culturally diverse student bodies. Table 8.2 lists the basic premises that Miramontes, Nadeau, and Commins identified as keys to the schools' effective programs.

The research described previously offers a quick set of checklists for assessing what "good" schools should be like. Whereas these examinations are based on "what is," other educational reformers have pointed us in the direction of "what ought to be." For example, Berman (1992a, 1996) offers us a view that portrays the ideal schooling transformation, as outlined in Table 8.3.

In summary, effective instructional strategies recognize that learning is rooted in sharing expertise and experiences through multiple avenues of communication. They also recognize that any attempt to address the needs of linguistically and culturally diverse students in a deficit or "subtractive" mode is counterproductive. Instead, educators add to the rich core of cognitive, linguistic, academic, and cultural understanding and skills that these students bring with them. Each one of us can assist in the development of instructional practices that more fully explore the issues raised here.

Marginal notes: Link to Decision-Making; Transforming Schools

The National School Reform Perspective

Recent policy statements regarding the challenges of educating a linguistically and culturally diverse student population reinforce this charge to all of us working in the field. The National Council of Teachers of English and the International Reading Association (1996, p. 3), in their enunciation of standards for English language arts, state:

Marginal note: Policy Statements

Table 8.2	**Basic Premises of Effective School Reform**

Premise 1. Active learning. Knowledge is best acquired when learners actively participate in meaningful activities that are constructive in nature and appropriate to their level of development.

Premise 2. The primary language foundation. The more comprehensive the use of the primary language, the greater the potential for linguistically diverse students to be academically successful. There are always ways to nurture the primary language regardless of school resources.

Premise 3. The quality of primary language use. There is a difference between a token use of the primary language in instruction and its full development as a foundation for thinking and learning.

Premise 4. Strategies for second-language development. Second-language development creates an added dimension to instructional decision-making. Instruction must reflect specific strategies designed to meet the needs of second-language learners.

Premise 5. Contexts for second-language development. Second-language instruction must be organized to provide students the time, experiences, and opportunities they need to fully develop language proficiency. This requires a range of social and academic contexts in which both language and content are emphasized.

Premise 6. First- and-second-language environments. Bilingual academic proficiency requires that clear, distinct, and meaning-enriched contexts for each language be created during instructional time.

Premise 7. Transitions and redesignations. Decisions regarding transition to formal second-language reading and redesignations that exit students from programs cannot be made arbitrarily.

Premise 8. Instructional assessment. Instructional assessment must be based on students' first- and second-language development, rather than on grade level or predetermined criteria. An appropriate assessment plan should address language and literacy development, as well as content knowledge.

Premise 9. Parents and community. Parents and community need to play a major role in the learning and schooling of their children.

Premise 10. Planning for cross-cultural interactions. Instruction must be organized to help students understand and respect themselves and their own culture as well as the cultures of the broader society. Planned cross-cultural interactions are an essential component of programs for all students.

Premise 11. Socio-cultural and political implications. Socio-cultural factors and political context must be considered in making decisions regarding every aspect of program planning.

Premise 12. Teachers as decision-makers. Teachers are decision makers. As part of a learning community they are all equally responsible for decisions regarding the instructional program for linguistically diverse students.

Table 8.2, "Basic Premises of Effective School Reform," from O. B. Miramontes, A. Nadeau, and N. L. Commins, *Restructuring Schools for Linguistic Diversity: Linking Decision Making to Effective Programs* (New York: Teachers College Press, © 1997 by Teachers College, Columbia University. All rights reserved.), pp. 37–38.

Table 8.3	Schooling Transformation: What Is Versus What Ought to Be

CURRENT SYSTEM: School as Learning Environment	**NEW SCHOOL DESIGN: School as Community of Learners**
Passive. Instruction relies on teacher as dispenser of known knowledge and student as consumer and is based on abstract modes of learning.	**Engaged.** Instruction relies on guided inquiry and conversations with teacher as mentor providing assistance to enable students to perform authentic tasks that they could not otherwise do by themselves; teachers create multiple learning activities and "group" for diverse learning styles, and students engage in self-regulated performance activities with clear goals and measures of performance.
Age-based groups and tracking. Classes and students are grouped by "ability" and/or tracks at age levels.	**Developmental.** Students would be organized in (cognitive and affective) developmentally appropriate groupings, rather than age-specific grades, and classes would be heterogeneous within development groups; students would work in smaller, fluid groups within classes, and act as coaches as well as performers.
Abstract curriculum. Curriculum based on abstract categorizations and driven by college entry requirements and standardized tests.	**Thematic and integrated curriculum.** Curriculum designed by teachers and students together and based on themes and projects that relate to student experiences and interests.
Unclear and/or irrelevant standards. Standards largely defined by college course entry requirements and vary greatly and idiosyncratically for students.	**Performance-based standards and assessments.** Standards defined and redefined by the broader community with a focus on authentic outcomes and indicators.
Affectively neutral. Pseudo "business" environment, professionals charged with producing academic goals.	**Affectively engaged.** Professional "care" for the students, to celebrate and embrace them, and for the intellectual well-being of the institution.

Source: Paul Berman, *The Status of Bilingual Education in California.* Copyright © 1992. Used with permission.

Students develop an understanding of and respect for diversity in language use, patterns, and dialects across cultures, ethnic groups, geographic regions, and social roles.

Students whose first language is not English make use of their first language to develop competency in the English language arts and to develop understanding of content across the curriculum.

Celebrating our shared beliefs and traditions is not enough; we also need to honor that which is distinctive in the many groups that make up our nation.

The National Association for the Education of Young Children (1997, p. 12) echoes these same concerns in its position statement:

Early childhood educators can best help linguistically and culturally diverse children and their families by acknowledging and responding to the importance of the child's home language and culture. Administrative support for bilingualism as a goal is necessary within the educational setting. Educational practices should focus on educating children toward the "school culture" while preserving and respecting the diversity of the home language and culture that each child brings to the early learning setting.

Lastly, the U.S. Department of Education has issued a set of principles that are meant to guide states and local school districts as they consider systemic reform of practices and knowledge regarding the education of linguistically and culturally diverse students (see Table 8.4).

Through all these efforts, schools are being asked to transform themselves into institutions that actively engage learners in a diverse community. They must be cognizant of the fluidity of human development, focused on a thematically integrated curriculum, responsive to performance-based standards and assessments,

Table 8.4	**Guiding Principles**

Principle #1. Limited English proficient students are held to the same high expectations of learning established for all students.

Principle #2. Limited English proficient students develop full productive and receptive proficiencies in English in the domains of listening, speaking, reading, and writing, consistent with expectations for all students.

Principle #3. Limited English proficient students reach challenging content and performance standards in all content areas, including reading and language arts, mathematics, social studies, science, the fine arts, health, and physical education, consistent with those for all students.

Principle #4. Limited English proficient students receive instruction that builds on their previous education and cognitive abilities and that reflects their language proficiency levels.

Principle #5. Limited English proficient students are evaluated with appropriate and valid assessments that are aligned with state and local standards and that take into account the language acquisition stages and cultural backgrounds of the students.

Principle #6. The academic success of limited English proficient students is a responsibility shared by all educators, the family, and the community.

Source: The George Washington University Center for Equity and Excellence in Education, *Promoting Excellence: Ensuring Academic Services for Limited English Proficient Students,* 1996, Arlington, VA: Evaluation Assistance Center East.

and staffed with highly professional and caring personnel. Although this is a tall order, such an envisioned transformation drives home the point that the schools of the future will not only need to do a better job but will also need to change radically.

Effective Instructional Practices

Socialization |
Instructional reform is a necessary element of radical change in our schools. Given the notion that schools, like families, directly or indirectly socialize children as much as they formally teach them (Spindler, 1955), the development of academic competence may be related to academic socialization (Trueba, 1987). Ethnographic studies and case studies (Au and Jordan, 1981; Diaz, Moll, and Mehan, 1986; Duran, 1983; Erickson, 1987; Moll, 1988; Tharp and Gallimore, 1988; Trueba, 1988b) have reported a significant relationship between instruction that is congruent with a student's culture and that child's academic success.

Successful Techniques |
For example, Gallimore and Tharp (1989) have carefully described the educational program developed for native Hawaiians. These programs utilize gender-relevant cooperative education procedures that match the gender roles in this population: boys and girls work together in small groups. Similar cooperative education structures are utilized effectively in Navaho classrooms: boys are grouped together, and girls are grouped together (Tharp, 1989). Moll (1988) has also described successful cooperative techniques used with Hispanic students in southwestern U.S. schools. He concludes that such cooperative social structures directly "match" specific Hispanic family values and practices. Furthering the notion of Academic English discussed in Chapter 5 of this book, other sociolinguistic studies have shown that the language of the classroom—or academic discourse—is a highly specialized code that students need to learn and "is not simply a transparent medium through which the academic curriculum is transmitted" (Mehan, 1979, p. 124). From this perspective, schooling involves not only cognitive development and the acquisition of knowledge but socialization as well (Spindler, 1974, 1982).

Interaction of Factors |
The understanding that cognitive development and socialization are paired leads to several important implications for the education of culturally and linguistically diverse children. Language and culture, and their accompanying values, are acquired in the home and community environment. Children come to school with some knowledge about language, how it works and how it is used, and learn higher-level cognitive and metalinguistic skills as they engage in socially meaningful activities. Children's development and learning are best understood as the interaction of linguistic, sociocultural, and cognitive factors.

An Effective Teacher's Reflections, in Her Own Voice

Cup of coffee in one hand and my journal in the other, I sit down to write my reflections. It is 7:30 a.m., and my bilingual first-grade class will start in half an hour. I flip to yesterday's page and recall how well our learning logs are going and how unsure I had been about their use. I also jot a short comment about how well Sammy is approximating in his phonetic guesses in reading and writing, something I also was not sure about just 24 hours ago. In fact, just eight years ago I was unsure about a lot of my teaching because of the paradigm shift that I was going through. That isn't true now because of the knowledge and practice I have acquired through professional reading, peer discussion groups, risk-taking, time, and reflection.

Becoming a Responsive Teacher

Today I look around, and I see a classroom filled with print, print that is chosen for its functional use; print that often reflects what we are currently learning and hope to learn, print that belongs to children in process of becoming literate community members. Today the children are immersed in a print-filled classroom that identifies our theme, dinosaurs. The brainstorm charts include the titles "What We Know" and "What We Want to Learn" about dinosaurs. One vocabulary chart in particular will be used to classify dinosaur words or put them in ABC order. In the book corner there is a minimum of 100 books, with at least 20 authored by the children. Lists around the room remind us of our schedules, what we need to order or who will be visiting our classrooms. I stop and look at a chart that lists the books we have already read during our dinosaur theme. We also have noted whether they inform us with scientific facts or teach us about literature. The condition of immersion supports children's reading and writing as well as collections of their knowledge.

The student-centered feeling in my classroom comes from children bringing themselves and their world into our collaborative learning. Their language, background, experiences, and interests, what they know and what they want to learn, are continually shared. On the first day of school we shared what we wanted to learn in first grade and why. These themes then became the curriculum, and my role became one of orchestrating grade-level objectives, instructional strategies, and the content of the theme.

When my students write in interactive journals, they highlight for me this condition of student-centeredness. They share their lives, what they know or are not sure about. Children write about the visit they had with their grandparents or what they hope Mommy will buy for them on Saturday or why the doctor can't help their little sister get better. I respond to each child about his or her written entry with both

Continued   An Effective Teacher's Reflections, in Her Own Voice

written and oral discourse. We read together my response, and the child then responds orally to my questions or comments. A student-centered condition reflects that children have ownership of their learning.

As an instructional strategy, interactive journals allow me to demonstrate literacy on a very individual basis. I demonstrate that oral language is meaningful, that written language uses a phonetic system, and that what they write (initially strings of letters) is important to me. During interactive journal writing, I sit next to each child, and we read, write, speak, and listen to each other. Demonstration informs children as to how I do it and informs me as to how they do. Through thinking aloud during my demonstrations, I try to communicate why and how they might make better approximations in their learning.

Approximation is a condition that allows children to take risks in all areas of literacy. I see approximations in their writing pieces that are in their learning logs, journal entries, and narrative first drafts. I hear approximations in their reading and their personal response to literature as well as in their oral discussions about their learning. These approximations include the quality of being close to as well as knowing what is almost exact. These approximations help to inform my instruction so that I am able to plan for optimal learning.

I have organized my classroom in four distinct areas. These areas call for children to actively participate in social organizations that promote specific types of engagement. The main area of the classroom places children in desks that are in foursomes, allowing children to actively participate in cooperative structures quickly. It also produces lots of talk. The discourse that is shared might be about the content of the theme or about constructing meaning from one language to another.

Near the front of the room is a small area where I teach to four small groups, one group each half hour. The active participation that occurs during this strategy comes in part from the nature of the text we use for literacy lessons: whole texts. This morning I will be teaching about sequencing within a wordless book strategy. Even the wordless book has a complete story to be told, and therefore it supports the students as they construct with me a written text to accompany the story in pictures. Another lesson I will teach today begins with a whole poem which the children learned through repeated choral reading. During this shared reading lesson, I will focus on rhyming words and their smaller parts, called short vowels.

Wholeness is a condition that also lies within theme work and literature conversations. A theme cycle begins with the whole class sharing

Continued   An Effective Teacher's Reflections, in Her Own Voice

thematic knowledge, moving into smaller groups to share and gain specific information, and returning to the whole to share new learning and initiate a new theme cycle. Within a literature conversation, I or a student reads the whole book; then in small groups or pairs we share personal connections as well as our thoughts on literature elements such as plot and setting.

Across the room, eight to ten children are able to sit around a long rectangular table and participate in the writing process. Children choose their own topics, share what they are writing, and ask for support in content and mechanics from each other at the writing table. Around the room there are centers that are organized by theme, ABC awareness, bilingual use, listening, and/or art. Two children work at each center in pairs. These pairs were created so that children could demonstrate to each other language, knowledge, social skills, and/or work habits. Active participation as a condition occurs more often when the condition of choice is also present.

Choice happens in my classroom individually and collaboratively. In both interactive journals and during the author's cycle children choose the topic, amount, genre, and even language (Spanish or English) of their written work. During DEAR [Drop Everything and Read] Time, children choose what book or books they will read. In theme work they often choose what they will research and what group they will join. At the listening center children choose what form (such as story map, word web, or character profile) they will use to share their connections to the book with the rest of the class.

When children see the authentic purpose for the choices they are making, they become more involved in their learning. The purpose must go beyond the classroom and beyond covering the skills of first grade. Again, the organization of my classroom supports children in real-life uses of language and literacy: Children engage in talk in large groups, small groups (teacher-directed), groups of four (peer talk at the desk groups), and one-on-one (centers). The organization also helps them in the real-life task of selecting which kind of talk is most functional. If students choose to author a book about their younger brother and his adventures, they realize they will go through the same process that real authors do. The narrative text will call for teaching and learning opportunities, but the authenticity lies in the sharing of the published book with an audience. Much of the written work that my children write is shared with others for response.

Response helps children to understand their work better through the reflections of others. These reflections assist children in their oral and written performance. In the Author's Chair phase of writing, my

Continued   An Effective Teacher's Reflections, in Her Own Voice

children read their first draft to an audience that understands that they are to listen for story line or informational facts. If students in the audience are unable to construct meaning during Author's Chair, they need to ask the author for support and then assist him or her with words or ideas that support meaning. During editing, both peers and I will help with mechanics such as spelling or punctuation. This type of response helps to create the condition of community.

The community of co-learners that my students and I belong to has common interests and commitment to working together. I often find this condition hard to describe, but it is one you can feel and observe in a very short time. What is often mentioned by visitors to our classroom is the ownership that the children have of their classroom, how they participate in its management, and their interest in sharing their community with others.

As I sit here and complete my reflections, I am surprised that I have not mentioned the condition called expectations. In fact, this condition is the one I bring to my classroom and can be the most important one for my children. It is also the one condition that teachers control through what they believe their children are able to do. Can all the children learn to read and write in my classroom? Yes, and so they will. Once, a long time ago, I expected that only one group of children in my classroom would read at grade level, that another group would almost achieve that level, and that the third group would just get through one small book. Expectations or lack of expectations are often influenced by social and economic factors that we note about our children (such as being poor, having no books at home, or having no one to help at home). Our lack of understanding of the linguistic or cultural diversity that our children bring to our classrooms also influences the expectations that we set for our children. This condition is also of interest because my peers set expectations for themselves, as I do each school year. I have never failed to meet the expectations I have set for myself and would guess that very few others have failed to meet theirs. Yet I often hear about how expectations had to be lowered so that students could feel successful in learning. Holding high expectations for all learners not only calls for trust in the learner but also for creating conditions for optimal learning in every classroom.

It's 7:55 a.m., my coffee is cold, and the children will arrive in five minutes. As I look through my written reflections, I wonder what my colleagues think about these conditions creating optimal learning for all children?

Source: Erminda García, Alianza School, Watsonville, CA. Used by permission of the author.

Continued   An Effective Teacher's Reflections, in Her Own Voice

Meeting the Challenge

1. According to this teacher, what are the conditions that create optimal learning for all children? Identify as many as you can, using the teacher's own wording.

2. If you could sit and talk with this teacher for a while, what questions would you ask? Describe what you think would be your areas of agreement or disagreement regarding the methods and goals of education.

3. Experiment with interactive journal writing in class. Go back through this book and select a topic that you still have questions about. Write a page or two of reflection as a journal entry. Now exchange journals with a classmate, write a response, and exchange journals once again.

These conclusions can be directly supported by recent research that documents instructionally effective practices with linguistically and culturally diverse students in selected schools around the United States (August and Hakuta, 1997; California Tomorrow, 1995 ; Cohen and Pompa, 1994 ; Faltis and Hudleson, 1997; Fashola, Slavin, Calderón, and Duran, 1997; McLeod, 1996; Miramontes et al., 1997; Romo, 1999; Rose, 1995; U.S. Department of Education, 2000). These descriptive studies identified specific schools and classrooms that served linguistically and culturally diverse students well. Using the case study approach, the researchers looked at instructional practices in preschool, elementary school, and high school classrooms. They interviewed teachers, principals, parents, and students and conducted specific classroom observations that assessed the dynamics of the instructional process. We shall now examine two of these studies: the SBIF study and the García and related studies.

The SBIF Study

In Chapter 7 we described the Significant Bilingual Instructional Features (SBIF) study performed by Tikunoff (1983) in order to identify attributes of exemplary teaching approaches. The SBIF findings can be divided into two parts: instructional features common to language minority and majority classrooms and instructional features unique to language minority classrooms. As we saw in Chapter 7, this study of 58 "effective" classrooms identified the following set of instructional features:

SBIF Findings | **1.** Task outcomes were clearly specified for students.

2. "Active teaching" behaviors were utilized extensively to (a) maintain students' engagement in tasks by pacing instruction appropriately and promoting involvement, (b) monitor students' progress, and (c) provide immediate feedback to students.

Effective instructional features specific to limited-English-proficient (LEP) students of Hispanic background included the use of two languages, special activities for teaching a second language, and instructional practices that took advantage of the students' culture.

Use of Language | The SBIF study reported that English was used approximately 60 percent of the time, and that the native language **(L1)** or a combination of L1 and the second language **(L2)** was used the rest of the time. The percentage of English used increased with grade level. The two languages were often combined in one of the following ways:

1. Instructors alternated between the students' native language and English whenever necessary to ensure clarity. They switched languages but rarely translated directly from one language to another.

2. Students developed English-language skills during ongoing instruction in the regular classroom rather than in a separate ESL classroom.

Language Switching | Of interest is the finding that bilingual instruction was characterized by the use of both the native language and English in classroom interactions. This language switching seemed to directly assist in clarifying instructional discourse. However, Wong-Fillmore and Valadez (1985) have suggested that language switching may be detrimental to second-language acquisition if too much translation is encouraged. In a study of a concurrent bilingual instructional model, Milk (1986) reports that a non-translation concurrent approach yielded functional language-switching discourse patterns similar to those found for separation instructional models. Students in the study followed a language choice rule ("Speak to the speaker in the language in which you are addressed") in a discourse situation that included 47.5 percent Spanish use and 57.5 percent English use. Such data suggest further that instructional discourse should concentrate on clarity and that clarity can be enhanced through the use of the students' native language.

The SBIF study also reports that incorporating aspects of the LEP students' home culture can promote engagement in instructional tasks and contribute to a feeling of trust between children and their teachers. The SBIF researchers found three ways in which home and community culture was incorporated into classroom life: (1) cultural referents in both verbal and nonverbal forms were used to communicate instructional and institutional demands, (2) instruction was organized to build upon rules of discourse from the home culture, and (3) values and norms of the home culture were respected equally with those of the school.

The García and Related Studies

In recent research on Mexican American elementary school children, García (1988, 1991d, 1997) reported several related instructional strategies utilized in "effective" schools. Students at these schools, which were nominated for the study by teachers of language minority students, scored at or above the national average on standardized measures of academic achievement in Spanish and/or English. This research characterized instruction in the effective classrooms as follows:

1. Students were instructed primarily in small groups, and academic-related discourse was encouraged among students throughout the day. Teachers rarely utilized large-group instruction or more individualized (e.g., mimeographed worksheets) instructional activities. The most common activity across classes involved small groups of students working on assigned academic tasks with intermittent assistance by the teacher.

2. Teachers tended to initiate instruction by eliciting student responses at relatively lower cognitive and linguistic levels. They then allowed students to control the discourse and to invite participation from peers. These invited interactions often occurred at higher cognitive and linguistic levels.

Of particular relevance are intensive case studies of elementary and middle schools (Freeman and Freeman, 1997; García, 1988, 1992a; García and Stein, 1996; Heath and Mangiola, 1991; Henderson and Landesman, 1992; Miramontes et al., 1997; Moll, 1988; Pease-Alvarez and García, 1991; Secada, 1996). The results of these studies are summarized next according to several instructional categories that were empirically relevant. Much like the attributes of effective teaching discussed in Chapter 7, the attributes described are not to be construed as necessary for the effective instruction of linguistically and culturally diverse students. Instead, they are offered as an example of how instructional environments can be structured to serve diversity.

High Levels of Communication. In the classrooms studied, functional communication between teacher and students and among fellow students was emphasized more than might be expected in a regular classroom. Teachers were constantly checking with students to verify the clarity of assignments and the students' roles in those assignments. Classrooms were characterized by a high, sometimes even noisy, level of communication that stressed student collaboration on small-group projects organized around learning centers. This organization minimized individualized work tasks such as worksheet exercises and provided a very informal, familylike social setting in which the teacher either worked with a small group of students (never larger than eight and at times as small as one) or traveled about the room assisting individuals or small groups of students as they worked on their projects. Large-group instruction was rare and was usually confined to start-up activities in the morning.

Informal Setting

Integrated and Thematic Curriculum. Significantly, the instruction of basic skills and academic content was consistently organized around thematic units. In the majority of classrooms studied, the students actually selected the themes in consultation with the teacher, either through direct voting or some related negotiation process. The teacher's responsibility was to ensure that the instruction revolving around the chosen themes covered the school district's content- and skill-related goals and objectives for that grade level.

The theme approach allowed teachers to integrate academic content with the development of basic skills. The major thrust in these classrooms was the appropriation of knowledge centered on chosen themes, with the understanding that students would necessarily develop basic skills as a means to appropriate this knowledge. Students became "experts" in thematic domains while also acquiring the requisite academic skills. Henderson and Landesman (1992) provide an excellent example of this approach as used by middle-school mathematics teachers, who worked closely with their colleagues in language arts, science, and social studies to construct thematic lessons across these disciplines.

*Benefits
of Theme
Approach*

Interactive Cross-Age Tutoring. A common occurrence in exemplary classrooms was the use of older students as tutors for younger students (August and Hakuta, 1997; Heath and Mangiola, 1991). These student tutors usually were able to communicate in the younger students' native language, even if the teacher could not do so. Literacy experiences—working with students in reading and analyzing a story, assisting them with the writing process, and participating in interactive journals—were among the more typical activities of the tutors, although specific math and science tutoring also took place. This interactive cross-age tutoring had the benefits of providing more instructional assistance for the teacher, allowing for the use and development of more first- and second-language lesson activities in small groups

Students Tutoring

Interactive Journals: An Example of Responsive Pedagogy

In *Interactive Journals,* students write about what is important to them. They share their life stories and their burning interests. In return, teachers are able to say to their students through their oral and written responses, "What goes on in your life is important to me." *Interactive Journal* writing also promotes the development of written conventions through written demonstration by teachers as they respond to the students' entries. Furthermore, the emphasis on the message (and not the mechanics) encourages students to take more risks with their writing topics and skills (in the language they choose). *Interactive Journals* in which students write and teachers respond on a daily basis create a developmental record of writing progress (Flores and García, 1984; García, 1996).

Recommended Procedures:

1. The *Interactive Journals* procedure has at least three basic parts: (a) the student draws and writes; (b) a teacher/paraprofessional/parent volunteer or peer responds with a written question about the student's entry; and (c) the student answers the question either orally or in written form.

2. Before beginning this instructional strategy, it is helpful to demonstrate the three basic parts of the interaction. In a large format such as an overhead transparency or a chart, write the date, brainstorm a topic out loud, [and] draw and then vocalize the words as you write your entry. Then, if possible, ask another teacher or parent to write a written question to your entry. Finally, orally respond to the question.

with native speakers, and supplementing the academic experiences of the student tutors.

Collaborative Learning. Reported analyses of instructional events in literacy and math, along with analyses of actual literacy products (dialogue journals, learning logs, writing workshop publications, etc.) and math products (learning logs, homework, surveys, etc.), indicate that teachers in Latino language minority classrooms organized instruction in such a way that students were required to interact with each other utilizing collaborative

Student Discourse | learning techniques. It was during student-student interactions

3. Ask students to follow the same procedures that you have demonstrated. As they finish their entries, students bring them to [you] for a response in the form of a question. Students in turn orally or in written form answer [your] question.

For emergent readers and writers: When students bring you a journal entry that you cannot read (i.e., it is scribbled or in letter string form), simply ask them to "read" it to you. As you respond with a written question, be sure [to] vocalize as you write so that the students can understand the question and respond to you.

For independent readers and writers: Experiment with buddy journals. Pair students up with a buddy (either randomly or by allowing students to suggest their top choices for a writing partner, with you making the final decision) and ask them to write to each other. Teachers occasionally collect and respond to the journals to provide both a model of writing and to monitor students' progress.

Reminders:

- Students, not teachers, choose topics for [the language and] journal entries.
- Students receive a response each time they write.
- During journal time, teachers write in their own journals and ask a student to respond.

Adapted from Barbara Flores and Erminda García, "A Collaborative Learning and Teaching Experience Using Journal Writing," *NABE: The Journal for the National Association for Bilingual Education, 8,* no. 2 (Winter 1984). Reprinted by permission of the National Association of Bilingual Education.

that most linguistic discourse of a higher cognitive order was observed (García, 1988, 1992a). Students asked each other hard questions and challenged each other's answers more readily than they did in interactions with the teacher. Moreover, students were more likely to seek assistance from other students and were successful in obtaining it. Specific techniques, such as "think-pair-share," "four corners," and "heads together," which have been well articulated by Kagan (1993), were commonly utilized.

Language and Literacy. In classes with Spanish speakers, lower-grade teachers used both Spanish and English as the language

of instruction whereas upper-grade teachers utilized mostly English. However, students were allowed to use either language. With regard to the literacy development of Spanish-speaking students, observations revealed the following:

• Students progressed systematically from writing in the native language in the early grades to writing in English in the later grades.

• Students' writing in English emerged at or above their grade level of writing in Spanish.

• Students' writing in English was highly conventional, contained few spelling or grammatical errors, and showed systematic use of invented spelling.

• Students made the transformation from Spanish to English themselves, without any pressure from the teacher to do so.

Freeman and Freeman (1997) have provided a detailed analysis of native-language reading processes, particularly in Spanish, that is relevant to all literacy programs with an initial focus on the student's native language. They have developed a very useful checklist for assessing effective reading instruction (see Table 8.5). Too often, students are moved from native-language reading into English reading without attention to the level of their reading effectiveness in their native language. The "reading cost" to students in such circumstances can be severe since they are

"Reading Cost" |

Table 8.5	Checklist for Effective Reading Instruction

1. Do students value themselves as readers and do they value reading?
2. Do teachers read frequently to students for a wide variety of genres?
3. Do students see teachers engaged in reading for pleasure as well as for information?
4. Do students have a wide variety of reading materials to choose from and time to read?
5. Do students make good choices and read a variety of genres for authentic purposes?
6. Do students regard reading as meaning making at all times?
7. Are students efficient readers? That is, do they make a balanced use of all three cueing systems?
8. Are students efficient readers? That is, do they make a minimal use of cues to construct meaning?
9. Do students have opportunities to talk about what they have read, making connections between the reading and their own experiences?
10. Do students revise their individual understandings of texts in response to the comments of classmates?
11. Is there evidence that students' writing is influenced by what they read?
12. Are students provided with appropriate strategy lessons if they experience difficulties in their reading?

Reprinted from *Teaching Reading and Writing in Spanish in the Bilingual Classroom* by Yvonne S. Freeman and David E. Freeman. Copyright © 1997 by Yvonne S. Freeman and David E. Freeman. Published by Heinemann, a division of Reed Elsevier, Inc., Portsmouth, NH. Reprinted by permission of the publisher.

not able to transfer their instructional gains in reading from one language to the other.

Making Instruction Understandable

Strategies that assist in making instruction more understandable include (1) simplifying but not artificially restricting language structures (using shorter sentences, unambiguous terminology, etc.); (2) contextualizing both oral and written texts with pictures, charts, diagrams, and realia; (3) providing for repeated access to ideas and vocabulary; and (4) creating interactive structures that allow for both comprehension and the need to act on and talk about content (Becijos, 1997). The key is not to depend solely on lecture (words) and text to provide meaning. Instead, a mix of drawings, visuals, demonstrations, and collaborative interaction should be woven into the lesson. Meaning-based lessons that are designed to maximize comprehensibility can serve a wide range of language-learning needs. They are helpful instructional methods for all students but are particularly useful to second-language learners. With such an approach, the focus is not on learning English but on learning content *and* English.

For example, Ms. Otero, who uses a sheltered English technique, arrives at class with her lecture notes. She also brings a box full of equipment, including many bowls, a small hot plate, and a bag of ice cubes. Ms. Otero writes "Three States of Matter: Solid, Liquid, Gas" on the board. Underneath each word she adds a drawing to represent the concept and illustrate its molecular structure. As Ms. Otero lectures, she melts ice and then boils water, and under the respective drawings on the board she writes "ice," "water," and "steam." She also assigns students a portion of the text to read. Rather than answering the questions in the text, they work in pairs to write their own comprehension questions about the passage to ask their peers. As students begin to read the text, Ms. Otero sits down with a group of four beginning ESL students to review the main ideas and prepare them to participate in the next day's lesson. She also shows them that they are to copy the drawings of the three molecular structures into their science journals and add labels.

Growing Practice Support for a Responsive Pedagogy

A Research Base

To illustrate some of the points made in this chapter, we can look at a series of classroom and school "snapshots." These are based on reports from research and demonstration programs, most of which were funded by the U.S. Department of Education. The snapshots come directly from specific reports, from site visits, and from the *Directory of Two-Way Bilingual Programs in the United States* (Christian and Whitcher, 1995). These snapshots provide a picture of a developing empirical base that supports a new vision of educational programming for a linguistically and culturally diverse population (García and Stein, 1996).

Three Unusual "R's"

Watsonville, California. In Erminda García's third-grade classroom at Alianza School in Watsonville, California, students are asked at the very outset of the academic year to consider the thematic study of the "Three R's: Resourcefulness, Responsibility, and Respectfulness." In essence, they are asked to study how they can become resourceful, responsible, and respectful in relationship to each other and to what they have to accomplish in their classroom. In this regard, the languages of the students (Spanish and English) are immediately identified as resources, and the children articulate the ways in which these and other resources (parents, family, books, computers, etc.) can be used to enhance their academic pursuits. This discussion, coupled with the question "What do we want to learn?" helps the students see both where they need to go academically and what resources are available to get them there.

To promote the sharing of students' language resources, Ms. García organizes the desks so that the children face each other in groups of four. Even in whole-group instruction, children are paired for interactive discussion. Students select from Spanish and English resources, often using one another for assistance in choosing those materials. The knowledge they acquire is displayed in published works, in brainstorming charts, and in posted student products; examples of learning are always put on display in whatever language that learning was accomplished. Students also keep individual learning logs and participate in daily interactive journal communication with selected peers using their language of choice—sometimes their native English or Spanish, and other times their second language. Similarly, learning logs and dialogue journals are shared with parents and other family members.

In such circumstances, students and parents are asked to share each other's language resources and related expertise. This approach emphasizes using language as a learning tool rather than learning a language. Although the latter is achieved through the former, language continues to be viewed as a *resource* for learning.

Chicago. Sixth-graders in Chicago's Interamerican Magnet School, a K–8 school where all instruction is in both Spanish and English, cluster in small groups for a Writer's Workshop. The teacher asks them to write sentences using these words: *unintelligibly, committee, prop, rambunctious, intention, loyalist, instinctively, elaborated, defiantly,* and *daintily.* Students discuss the assignment among themselves and write sentences in their journals in either Spanish or English. Then a first-grade class enters, and the younger students pair up with the older ones; each pair has an English- and a Spanish-speaker. The older students read stories they have written to the younger ones. The first-graders have an endless supply of questions and really push the sixth-graders to explain and elaborate on what they have written. In the last part of the class, the teachers ask the students to focus on what they like and dislike about the stories.

Pairing Older and Younger Students

The sixth-grade teacher has thus created a learning environment that is distinct from that of the traditional classroom. Here students assume responsibility for their learning, serve as resources for one another, get feedback on their work from an audience, and engage in teaching younger children. This level of interaction did not happen by accident; at this school the pedagogical approaches have been designed to support students' active participation in their own learning process.

Use of Themes

The teachers often develop their curriculum around themes that are drawn from the culture of the Americas. For example, the fourth-grade teachers developed a social studies unit on Mayan civilization. As part of this unit, classes visited the Field Museum in Chicago to see an exhibit on Mayan culture, architecture, and religion. Teachers used this theme to integrate the studies across curriculum areas. In social studies, students explored the geographic spread of the Mayan civilization as well as its religious and cultural traditions. In science, they studied Mayan agriculture and architecture. In language arts, students wrote about the Mayans. Using such thematic instruction allows students to see the natural connections among traditional disciplines. At the same time, linking those themes to cultures allows students to learn about their own backgrounds and those of their fellow students.

Los Angeles. Korean- and English-speaking kindergarten children in Los Angeles's Denker School concentrate on language-rich arts and design activities. The classroom talking fits the task at hand. Four students at one instructional center make posters of city scenes and cutouts and pasted models of houses, cars, buildings, streets, parks, and schools for an upcoming parent conference. On this day, everything, including all the talk, is in Korean. The English speakers have learned some Korean vocabulary and struggle to put these words into sentences; their Korean-speaking friends help them out.

Using Korean |

After 20 minutes or so, each group changes tables and takes up the next task. The tasks are cumulative; as the children move from site to site, they add to what others have already done at the site. One group now takes up Korean letters and words to spell out the days of the week and the calendar for the month of February on a poster. Another builds intricate mobiles and other room decorations. Students at a third table read large-print storybooks with the teacher. These books focus on school and neighborhood themes that correspond with the themes of the instructional centers. The children begin the reading, with each one taking a page. The teacher becomes involved only rarely to keep the children on track and to answer questions. An instructional assistant and several parent volunteers help at some of the instructional centers. Groups of parents meet on evenings and weekends to learn either English or Korean as a second language.

These children are strongly devoted to their tasks. They rarely get distracted. They move from table to table when the time to switch tasks arrives, and they are truly engaged in their activities. The project director tells of recently talking to some of the Korean children who had no idea that Korean is a minority language in the United States: they had assumed it was of equal importance to English because the students at their school speak both languages.

Milwaukee. Milwaukee's Fratney Elementary School has gone a step further than the Denker School: the whole school is conducted in Spanish and English. One day all subjects are taught in Spanish; the next day everything is in English. Half of the students are from English-speaking backgrounds, and half are from Spanish-speaking backgrounds. They serve as peer coaches and tutors to one another; the languages have equal status in the learning enterprise. However, the languages are not mixed. The students are truly immersed; they have to rely on their inner strength, their memory, and each other. Thus, they actually produce the languages rather than merely absorbing them. Each month a schoolwide theme emerges that has a classroom focus, and it is tied to field trips, hall displays, assemblies, library exhibits, mapping exercises, and interviews with community members (Wood, 1992).

A School in Two Languages

Arlington, Virginia. Upon entering Key Elementary School in Arlington, Virginia, you feel the pulse of the learning process. Clusters of classes are located in a pod matrix. In this arrangement, students can move easily back and forth from learning centers in the classroom to activity centers in the oval-shaped pods that encircle the classroom clusters. On a Spanish day, you hear only Spanish; on an English day, only English. As the learning is going on, the students are adding to their home experience, not deleting it. They are being encouraged to communicate with their parents and grandparents, not to ignore them or put them down for being immigrants.

Activity Centers

San Clemente, California. Parents and grandparents turn out in significant numbers during parents' night at the Las Palmas Elementary School's two-way program in San Clemente, California. More than 80 percent of the Spanish- and English-speaking parents of the kindergarten and first-grade students attend. In some cases, divorced or separated parents are both present. Most of the questions the parents ask the teachers and the principal are concerned with trying to ensure that a similar two-way program will be available when their children move on to middle school. One mother reports that her child already feels in command of English and Spanish and wants to know about the possibility of studying a third language, maybe Chinese.

A Two-Way Program

The parents break into discussion groups in their native languages and begin a few curricular exercises with the teachers that help explain how content is taught in the classroom. Discussion topics include how to strengthen their children's homework and study habits and particularly how the school and parents can work together as closely as possible. In addition,

A Letter Home

The following letter was written by a student in a new program integrating linguistically and culturally diverse students with the general school population:

Becoming a Responsive Teacher

Dear Mom and Dad,

Please read all of the theme assignments for the last two quarters in my portfolio. The folder should be set up so that the pieces for the "Coming of Age in the '90s" theme are on the left and the assignments for the "Gangs" theme are on the right. I would like you to read the writing for the activities I have done about these themes.

When you read my folder, I am asking that you take the time to answer, in a letter back to me, a few questions:

1. What assignment in my portfolio tells you the most about my schoolwork?

2. What do you see as strengths in my writing?

3. What do you see as the areas that need improvement?

4. What suggestions do you have that might aid my growth as a student?

Thank you very much for investing your time in my theme portfolio.

Sincerely,

Meeting the Challenge

1. In addition to the letter response previously requested, what other activities might increase parental involvement in children's education?

2. Explain why it is important for parents to understand the challenges their children face in school.

some of the English-speaking parents are learning Spanish, while many of the Spanish-speakers are in ESL classes. At the end of the evening, all the parents regroup and plan future activities, and they all promise to keep coming to the bimonthly meetings.

Dearborn, Michigan. Arab parents and community members in Dearborn, Michigan, attest to their satisfaction with the Arabic-English bilingualism in the local public schools. Several parents say that they had sent their children to private Arabic-language evening or weekend schools but were not seeing their children develop full proficiency. They preferred the school program because it taught students to grasp both Arabic and English. Some of the parents were longtime Michigan residents whose children spoke English as their first language. They were extremely happy that their children could now communicate with relatives, visit the parents' home country, master Arabic as a future career enhancer, and participate more fully in community and religious services. They talk about outreach programs to the newest arrivals: students from Iraq and Yemen. They work with the school system's outreach workers to make the newcomers feel welcome and to deal with issues like the chaperoning of female students and the wearing of native dress.

Parent Satisfaction

Artesia, California. The Elliot School in Artesia, California, uses a series of devices to assess the literacy, numeracy, and other content skills of its students. About a third of these students are Portuguese LEP students whose parents or grandparents immigrated from the Azore Islands following devastating earthquakes in the late 1950s. Although performance-based assessment is the norm in this school, student achievement is described in other ways in its Portuguese-English two-way program. The students' reading performance, for example, is assessed along a continuum ranging from "emerging reader" to "expert leader." Even the term *emerging reader* gives a positive connotation to the direction of learning. A "native leader report card," on which comments about various types of student performance can be written, has also been developed so that parents can become fully involved in their children's learning. In addition, the school has recently been able to obtain a steady supply of literature from Portugal. At times in the past, the school had to buy Spanish books and manually insert Portuguese spellings.

Unique Assessment Measures

Conclusion

The research described in this chapter addresses several significant practical questions about effective academic environments for linguistically and culturally diverse students:

1. *Did native language instruction play a role in providing effective instruction?* The schools in these studies considered instruction in the students' native language a key component of academic success in the early grades (K–3).

2. *Was there one best curriculum?* No common curriculum was identified in these studies. However, a well-trained instruc-

tional staff that is capable of implementing an integrated, student-centered curriculum in which literacy is pervasive in all aspects of instruction was consistently observed across grade levels. Basal readers were utilized sparingly and usually only as resource material.

3. *What instructional strategies were effective?* Teachers consistently organized instruction so as to ensure collaborative learning in small, heterogeneous groups. Group academic activities required a high degree of student-student interaction. Individual instructional activity was limited, as was individual competition as an ingredient of classroom motivation.

4. *Who were the major players in effective schooling?* School administrators and parents played important roles, but teachers were the key. They gained the confidence of their peers and supervisors. They worked to organize instruction, create new instructional environments, assess effectiveness, and advocate for their students. They were proud of their students but consistently demanding. They rejected any notion of academic, linguistic, cultural, or intellectual inferiority in their students.

These features of effective classrooms for linguistically and culturally diverse students support, above all, the need for the establishment of an interactive, student-centered learning context. In other words, effective instructional staff recognize that academic learning has its roots in processes of social interaction. The practices identified here as effective have also been affirmed by recent educational intervention research aimed at restructuring education for these students (August and Hakuta, 1997). The convergence of findings from this new empirical research generates the following set of specific guidelines:

- Any curriculum, including one for diverse children, must address all categories of learning goals (cognitive and academic, advanced as well as basic). We should not lower our expectations for these students; they, too, need to be intellectually challenged.

- The more linguistically and culturally diverse the children, the more closely teachers must relate academic content to the children's own environment and experience.

- The more diverse the children, the more integrated the curriculum should be. That is, multiple content areas (e.g., math, science, social studies) and language learning activities should all be centered around a single theme. Children should have opportunities to study a topic in depth and to apply a variety of skills acquired in home, community, and school contexts.

- The more diverse the children, the greater the need for active rather than passive endeavors, particularly informal social activities such as group projects in which students are allowed flexibility in their participation with the teacher and other students.

- The more diverse the children, the more important it is to offer them opportunities to apply what they are learning in a meaningful context. Curriculum can be made meaningful in a number of creative ways. Science and math skills can be effectively applied, for example, through hands-on, interactive activities that allow students to explore issues of significance in their lives, such as an investigation of the quality of the local water supply.

In conclusion, recent research indicates that schools can effectively serve linguistically and culturally diverse students. These students can achieve academically at levels at or above the national norm. Instructional strategies that serve them best acknowledge, respect, and build upon the language and culture of their home. Teachers play the most critical role in students' academic success, and students become important partners with teachers in the teaching and learning enterprise. Although much more research is required, we are not without a knowledge base that can make a difference.

Summary of Major Ideas

1. As American educator John Dewey claimed, knowledge is not a thing to be dispensed but rather a process of construction and reconstruction that allows us to live and to grow. Schooling practices in the United States must begin to reflect this understanding of knowledge and to adapt to new populations of students and new societal expectations. If it does not, the educational vulnerability of culturally diverse students, with their accompanying loss in employment competence, will continue.

2. Some theorists claim that educational failure can be explained by a "clash" between the student's home and school cultures. Others claim that academic underachievement is caused by educators' failure to use principles of teaching and learning that have been proved to be effective with students. Both these theoretical perspectives are useful in identifying instructional practices that might enhance education for culturally diverse students.

3. Research indicates that effective schools focus on making improvements according to the following organizational and

structural variables: autonomy in school-site management, instructional leadership from the principal, curriculum that considers students' cultural and linguistic attributes, staff development, parent support and involvement, recognition of student success, and district support. Effective schools also attend to the following process variables: flexibility, collaborative planning and collegial relationships, validation of the students' cultures, a sense of community, clear goals and high expectations, and order and discipline.

4. Case studies show that schools that effectively serve a diverse student population promote literacy, deliver grade-level content, organize instruction innovatively, protect and extend instructional time, expand teachers' roles and responsibilities, address students' social and emotional needs, and involve parents in their children's education.

5. Proponents of education reform claim that U.S. schools generally encourage passive learning, age-based groupings and tracking, abstract curriculum, unclear and irrelevant standards, and neutral affect. These reformers state that schools must be transformed to constitute a community of learners that emphasizes active engagement, developmentally appropriate heterogeneous groupings, thematic and integrated curriculum, performance-based standards and assessments, and care for students.

6. For children, development and learning occur as a result of interactions among linguistic, sociocultural, and cognitive factors. Effective instruction of diverse student populations is additive rather than subtractive; that is, it recognizes the importance of adding to the rich cultural understandings and skills these students bring with them.

7. Research into instructional practices has shown that high levels of communication between teacher and students can be especially effective, as can the use of a thematic curriculum and collaborative, small-group instruction. Students who work together in small groups tend to participate in linguistic discourse of a higher cognitive order. LEP students are more successful if both the native language and English are used for instruction. Sheltered English, or specifically designed academic instruction in English that combines content with the learning of English, has proved to be especially productive.

8. Recent research has provided an increasing body of empirical evidence that supports the new vision of a pedagogy that is responsive to the needs of culturally and linguistically diverse students and their families.

Extending Your Experience

1. Much of the research cited in this text indicates that culturally and linguistically diverse children learn higher-level cognitive skills best in a social context—by talking and writing, reading and listening. What do these findings imply for the way classrooms are organized? for the role of teachers?

2. Explain the difference between active and passive learning activities. Give an example of a passive learning task typical of a traditional, teacher-centered classroom and then describe a way to transform it into an active, student-centered activity.

3. Plan an integrated curriculum for a school of linguistically and culturally diverse children. Together with a few of your classmates, decide on the grade levels and demographic makeup of your students. Each one of you could design a single facet of the curriculum and then, acting as a collaborative team of teachers, assemble these facets into a whole. Specify the learning materials you will use, such as books, music, physical objects, resource people, and so on. Remember the importance of student-student interaction and try to apply some of the research findings discussed throughout this text. Present your curriculum plan to the class.

4. Create a class book titled "Why Teach?" Ask each member of your class to contribute a single sheet of paper on which he or she personally answers this question, in writing or in any other graphic form. Make sure your classmates use black ink, so that their contributions will be legible for duplicating. Bind enough copies for everyone in class, including your instructor, and distribute them.

Resources for Further Study

Print Resources

Carter, T. P., and Chatfield, M. L. (1986). Effective bilingual schools: Implications for policy and practice. *American Journal of Education, 95*(1), 200–234.

> The authors describe the relationship between bilingual programs and effective schools. They argue that all students, including LEP students, can succeed in an academic environment that is always striving to improve learning. This approach must be planned, organized, and sustained, and the guidelines for improvement must be part of the school's structure in order to be effective. Actions that promote support across departments, including bilingual programs, produce high levels of student achievement.

Cloud, N., Genesee, F., and Hamayan, E. (2000). *Dual language instruction: A handbook for enriched education.* Boston: Heinle and Heinle.

> Intended for K–12 teachers, policymakers, and other educational professionals, this handbook discusses dual language instruction in three sections: instructional process, applications and resources, and references and resource materials. This book provides a thorough overview of existing issues such as program development and implementation, teaching literacy, teaching content, assessment, and advocacy related to dual language instruction.

Figueroa, R., and Hernandez, S. (2000). *Testing Hispanic students in the United States: Technical and policy issues.* Washington, DC: The President's Advisory Commission on Educational Excellence for Hispanic Americans.

> This report reinforces the standards-based movement in regard to better educating Hispanic children by recognizing that limited resources combined with students' limited fluency in English result in a combination that produces academic failure. This work maintains that standardized tests do not accommodate student needs or serve as appropriate assessment instruments. Aside from highlighting the grave educational circumstances resulting from the use of these standardized exams, this report also discusses what can be done to change existing methods that incorrectly measure student achievement.

García, E., Casimir, M., Sun Irminger, A., Wiese, A., and García, E. (1999). Authentic literacy assessment (ALA) development: An instruction based assessment that is responsive to linguistic and cultural diversity. *Educators for Urban Minorities, 1,* 51–60.

> The authors present an instrument that assesses student progress and program effectiveness. The instrument discussed in this report is the result of a collaboration between teachers and researchers who want to be responsive to the multilingual and multicultural contexts in which standards of competency must be assessed.

The George Washington University Center for Equity and Excellence in Education. (1996). *Promoting excellence: Ensuring academic success of limited English proficient students.* Arlington, VA: Evaluation Assistance Center East.

> Based in the contexts of practice and policy, this resource highlights principles of learning and teaching that are considered to be key foundations required to create optimal learning conditions for all children.

Miramontes, O., Nadeau, A., and Commins, N. L. (1997). *Restructuring schools for linguistic diversity: Linking decision making to effective programs.* New York: Teachers College Press.

> Due to the sheer number of increasingly diverse student populations attending schools in the United States, these authors suggest that following models and implementing them in a decontextualized manner

can have an adverse academic effect on students. Instead, the authors suggest that decisions about how best to meet the needs of a culturally and linguistically diverse student body require that educators be mindful and respectful of their students. A universal application of a model neglects the backgrounds and skills of a specific student body and disempowers the efforts of the existing educational community.

Purkey, S. C., and Smith, M. S. (1983). Effective schools: A review. *Elementary School Journal, 83,* 52–78.

This article presents an extensive review of literature and case studies that focus on ways of making schools more effective. The authors offer a series of characteristics to use to improve the learning environment and make it more conducive to knowledge transmission. Schools, they argue, are not solitary entities but rather an integral part of a social system with diverse cultures. For change to occur, educators must reexamine institutions and priorities to provide the best education possible for all students. Additional questions and issues are raised to further the discussion of promoting effective schools.

Tharp, R. G. (1989). Psychocultural variables and k constants: Effects on teaching and learning in schools. *American Psychologist, 44,* 349–359.

The literate and cognitive activities in schooling are deeply connected to the psychocultural teachings and learning processes developed in the student's home and community. Psychocultural variables are also responsible for the sharp differences in school achievement shown by members of different cultural groups. All cultures bring different variables to the academic field, and schools must not only recognize but also embrace these variables to promote diversity and academic growth. The author offers some recommendations as to how schools can adapt and how the environment of the classroom may be improved. The author also suggests research questions that must be answered to advance school reform.

U.S. Department of Education and The White House Initiative on Educational Excellence for Hispanic Americans. (1999). *What works for Latino youth.* Washington, DC: Author.

This is a directory of programs that work with Latino youth and that have been recognized as being effective. The directory provides a description of and the contact information for the programs. It is intended to be a resource for businesses, policymakers, community-based organizations, schools, universities, and other individuals or agencies that have a vested interest in helping Latino youth prosper educationally.

Web Resources

The White House Initiative on Educational Excellence for Hispanic Americans: *www.ed.gov/offices/OIIA/Hispanic*

This is a primary web site for accessing information about the most current pertinent issues confronting Hispanic Americans in the

United States. Moreover, this site offers a general statistical profile of patterns of Hispanic American students' achievement from primary through postsecondary levels of education.

Video Resources

Profile of Effective Bilingual Teaching—First Grade (1995). 40 minutes.

> The teacher in this videotape demonstrates how she goes about creating a classroom community in a bilingual classroom. We see children actively participate in achieving the class's goals and objectives, which are outlined by Mrs. García but proposed by the students. This is a student-centered classroom in which there is visual evidence that meaning and purpose are threaded throughout the curriculum. The teaching strategies shown in this videotape are effective because the teacher understands that academic success happens when student knowledge is joined with book knowledge. This videotape allows educators to see that teaching is about understanding the community from which students come, about understanding that students are not "empty vessels," and about recognizing that good teaching is a combination of theory, practice, and common sense.

Profile of Effective Bilingual Teaching—Kindergarten (1995). 40 minutes.

> Mrs. Espinoza, the teacher, is shown working with kindergarteners in literature circles. The power of the literature circles is apparent when this teacher asks students to turn to their neighbors and try to predict what will happen next in the reading of the book. In this classroom we see the benefits of having a print-rich environment and well-thought-out teaching strategies that access the students' strengths and use them as an additional resource for building literacy skills.

The media distributor for these videotapes can be reached at the following address:

Center for Applied Linguistics/CREDE
4646 40th Street NW
Washington, DC 20016–1859
202-362-0700
http://www.cal.org/

Chapter 9
Educational Approaches at the Middle and Secondary School Level

Focus Questions

- What special challenges do middle and high schools face in attempting to serve diverse populations?

- What types of instructional strategies for serving diverse students might these schools implement?

- What organizational issues are important to consider in efforts to serve underachieving adolescents?

- How can Specially Designed Academic Instruction in English (SDAIE) be helpful to a responsive teacher?

> "For students, dropping out forecloses a lifetime
> of opportunities—and makes it far more likely that our
> children will be less successful academically."
>
> —U.S. Department of Education, 1998

Both my own experience and recent research indicate that students like me—those who do not fit into the "typical American" model—are at particular risk at the secondary level (Lucas, 1997; Olsen, 1997; Romo and Falbo, 1996). For that reason I will devote this chapter to detailed discussion of the schooling of culturally diverse adolescents. I'd like to begin with an account of some of my own experiences as a youngster and as an adult. This very personal case study will set the stage for an examination of some important research on educational practices at the middle school and secondary level.

Then and Now: A Personal Rendition of What Works

It is a very common phenomenon: I always know the question is coming when I address an audience regarding the research on effective educational intervention for linguistically and culturally diverse students. It usually comes from a "nonminority" individual, but not always. The negative implication of the question is one that we are all aware of—the "yes, but" attitude. It's as if the person had not been listening but instead had been thinking up a way to counter the point he or she believed the speaker was making.

A Typical Question | The question goes something like this: "Yes, but how do you account for your own academic success? You are Latino, from a large and poor family, you did not speak English, and yet here you are, a product of a system you have strongly suggested must change to meet the needs of individuals just like you." Sometimes the question is accompanied by the description of a relative's experience, usually the questioner's grandfather or grandmother, who came to this country in poverty, did not speak English, and has left a legacy of economic and educational success among his or her progeny.

This is a difficult situation for me because it requires me to think of my own grandfather, father, mother, sisters, brothers, cousins, nephews, and nieces and to think about the unforgivable lack of educational opportunity that they experienced. It makes me feel as if someone is using my academic success to point the "blame" for the absence of others' achievement at each of my family members and collectively at my entire family and similar families. Imbedded in this question is the predominant American belief that the individual is master of his or her destiny. Success is accordingly attributable to individual characteristics, particularly native intelligence, talent, and motivation. Should I then not see this question as applauding my own individual intelligence, talent, and motivation? Not at all. Instead, it reflects a superficial understanding of academic success in this country generally and for our culturally diverse students specifically.

Understanding Academic Success

My first reaction each time the question is asked is to attribute my success to "luck." How else *could* I react? In a family that included brothers and sisters and sixty or so cousins (one of my aunts had 18 children, including three sets of twins), I am the only one to have graduated from college. Five attended a college (four of these attended a community college), but none except myself ever graduated. In fact, more than sixty percent of the family cohort never graduated from high school, with many never finishing the tenth grade.

All the members of the cohort were born, like our parents and grandparents, in the southwestern and western United States. We all attended schools in these areas, some public and some private. Was I so smart and so motivated and so different from the rest of my family that I have succeeded where they failed? Absolutely not. I have brothers, sisters, and cousins who I know are "smarter" than I am. I grew up with these individuals, saw them articulate and solve complex intellectual problems, and watched them succeed in challenging circumstances. I saw first-hand the high motivation, hard work, goal-setting, analysis, and "stick-to-it-iveness" that are often associated with success in any endeavor. In short, I am about as talented as the rest of my family cohort—I'm not even in the upper 10 percent in terms of native physical or intellectual talent. Nor am I more motivated or more hardworking than most of them. Was I just lucky? Luck is but one legitimate explanation for my success. I would like to think that more than luck was responsible.

The Foundation of Family

The roots of my success began in a family that valued education. My father, a poor and humble man who taught himself to read by using the Spanish Bible (remind you of Abraham Lincoln?), said to all of us, *"La educación nunca te la pueden quitar"* (No one can take away what you have learned). This was a profound insight from a head of a household who had been asked to move his family when he couldn't pay the rent, had lost much of what he owned during the Great Depression, and had worked primarily as a farm laborer in situations that were, for the most part, completely out of his control—sometimes there was work and sometimes there wasn't. He understood, as did my mother, aunts, and uncles, that it was what we learned—our education—that was the key to our future economic and social well-being. That fact was unquestionable. My father and mother made certain we all attended that first day of school at the age of six (I remember arriving with my Big Chief tablet and pencil in hand) and gave us the *consejo* (advice), *"Portate bien"* (Behave yourself and make us proud).

For me and the rest of my family, this belief in education was a very sound foundation. It was not, however, what would be called an academic foundation. My parents did not read to me; in fact, my mother never learned to read and write at all. I did not have the opportunity to "see the world." We had no vacations, no travel, no museum visits, and only limited access to the mass media (we had a radio that worked sporadically but was never fixed since there was no Spanish-language programming). My playmates, for the most part, were my many cousins, and each of us was socialized in the same linguistic and cultural environment until we went to school. Even after we went to school, our social and economic dependence on the family minimized our interactions with other students and their families. We were insulated, but we were safe and secure. We knew who our friends were, and we knew where to go for help—to our nuclear and extended families. But even under such safe and nurturing circumstances, most children in my family did not succeed educationally.

What was important about this upbringing, then, was not the specific roots of educational preparation but instead the broader understanding that education was crucial, that hard work was important, and that respect for adults who could show you the way, particularly our own elders and schoolteachers, was natural. My uncles were wonderful storytellers who could weave wonderful lessons about life from their own experiences, handed-down proverbs (*dichos* or *consejos*), and religious teachings. As young children we gathered around these individuals as they shared these tales among themselves, knowing fully well that we were all listening. It never seemed like a directed lesson in life, ethics, or the literacy of the oral tradition, but we all learned a great deal. In addition, we learned by watching and doing. When you are poor, every able hand is a resource; we all had chores from the earliest age that I can remember. We were told to "watch, then do." We were never provided a verbal or written description of our assigned tasks. And we were never rewarded socially or economically for accomplishing those tasks. The clear expectation was that you would do those things assigned to you, work hard while doing them, and understand that you would do them well or do them again. All this would appear to have set the stage for my being a good student.

It was neither all good luck nor individual talent nor motivation that allowed me to achieve educationally; nor was it all bad luck and lack of talent and motivation that led many of my family and friends to fail educationally. It was a strong family infrastructure, combined with the efforts of school personnel who saw the potential and resources in me and who adapted their pedagogy, curriculum, and expectations to address my own circumstances—along with, of course, a little bit of luck—that enabled me to succeed.

As educators, we can't do much about luck, and we can only remotely influence family infrastructure. But we can adapt our pedagogy, curriculum, and expectations so that *all* students can in fact succeed educationally. The remainder of this chapter focuses on educational endeavors that demonstrate the reality of this conclusion. We will examine how the components that helped me are leading to academic success for millions of other students like me. Some of these programs are ones that I have had the honor of studying personally while others I have only admired from a distance. All make it evident that students like me need not experience academic failure.

The Genesis of Project Theme

It was right after the release of our "effective schools" research (García, 1991c) that a local middle school principal issued the following public challenge: "Well, that's all very interesting. But I'm not sure we can *change* our school. We are not doing well and we want to do better. How do we change? Maybe you ought to come out and help us to become an 'effective' school rather than studying those that have already attained their goal."

I couldn't answer his question, but how could I refuse his challenge? Here was a principal who had an interest in developing effective schooling for a highly linguistically and culturally diverse student population, and he was giving me an opportunity to answer that important question of how one moves from ineffective schooling to effective schooling. Of course, we called a meeting immediately to discuss this!

First Steps in an Intervention | And our activities soon went beyond the stage of meetings. The principal, Carlos García, now a superintendent of a large and

diverse school district, invited me and a group of my university colleagues to his school to speak to the teachers. On the day of our visit, an announcement was read over the public address system: "Dr. Gene García and a group of his colleagues will be in the library after school today to discuss a possible intervention at this school based on his research." I learned later that the principal had also put notices in the mailboxes of the thirty or so teachers. Mr. García could not attend the meeting because a student crisis had arisen, but some nine teachers joined us in the library. I lectured to the group a bit about the research we had done, and we discussed the possibilities of working in the school. Two teachers, after politely indicating their lack of interest, left. The remaining group decided to meet one more time to consider our offer. These teachers also said they would ask around to see if other teachers were interested in joining us. About two weeks later I held another meeting that was attended by eight teachers, six from the first group and two new recruits. (Unfortunately Mr. García again had a scheduling conflict and could not be present.) At this meeting, we decided to give our proposed intervention a try. We named it *Project Theme.*

Project Theme: Principles and Strategies

Our team of eight teachers, four university faculty members, and two graduate students agreed that Project Theme would be guided by a number of principles that our review of the literature had demonstrated to be effective in promoting literacy, mathematics learning, and English-language development for linguistically and culturally diverse students. Some of our principles were the same ones listed in the conclusion for Chapter 8 (see pages 353–355). In addition, we noted the following:

- The more diverse the students, the more likely it is that excessive practice and drill that focus only on skill development will endanger their willingness to use those skills.

- In general, the more the curriculum emphasizes *performance goals* rather than *learning goals* of relevance to the students, the more likely it is that they will distance themselves from the school. Performance goals rely on pressure to get the right answer whereas learning goals emphasize how much one can learn.

Intervention Strategies   Because Project Theme was ultimately concerned with students learning how to learn, particular significance was assigned to the following strategies, again drawn from effective schooling research. These strategies support the development of both basic skills and higher-order linguistic and cognitive processes, and they use linguistic, analytical, cognitive, and metacognitive processing to maximize academic learning:

Strategy 1: Use of thematic, integrated curriculum so that academic objectives are achieved through content-integrated instruction

Strategy 2: Emphasis on small-group activities incorporating heterogeneous language grouping and peer tutoring and emphasizing higher-order linguistic and cognitive processes (in which learning proceeds from the concrete to the presentational to the symbolic)

Strategy 3: Emphasis on literacy activities such as interactive journals, silent reading followed by small-group discussion, interactive literature study, individual- and group-authored literature, and mathematics logs

Strategy 4: Use of cooperative learning strategies emphasizing the systematic participation of each student in processing curriculum materials

Strategy 5: Documentation of interpersonal inequities related to gender differences among middle school students, with a focus on strategies that foster equal-status interactions and support effective learning in general

The project reorganized the seventh-grade instructional environment of 110 students at the school. Specifically, an instructional intervention was implemented for two heterogeneous groups of approximately 30 students each. One group was made up of English-only (EO) and reclassified bilingual (Spanish and English) students. All the instruction for this group was conducted in English. The second group included EO and fluent-English-proficiency (FEP) students, along with higher-level LEP students who were already in transitional English reading or near that level. For this group the instruction was bilingual. In both groups, the students were with the same classmates for four of the school's six periods. During the other two periods, they were integrated with students from the rest of the school for physical education and an elective.

Integrated Thematic Curriculum The eight teachers worked with the university faculty to implement an interdisciplinary, collaborative curriculum for these two groups of theme students. The content-area subjects taught were reading, English, science, mathematics, and social studies (science was taught for one semester and social studies for the other). A comparison group was established, consisting of 48 students in the regular middle school program who were matched with the Project Theme group on measures of academic achievement. Students in the comparison group changed classes throughout the day; in their six nonintegrated content-area subjects, they experienced six different combinations of classmates.

Recall that the theme students were heterogeneously grouped in two strands, one bilingual and one English-only, in which they remained through math, reading, language arts, and social studies/science. Within the first week of school, Project Theme's instruction began using the Olympics as the first unit. With that theme as a springboard, the four content areas were taught. The teachers met in order to share their individual areas of curriculum focus and to integrate lessons across the curriculum.

Team Meetings The teachers and the university faculty met weekly during lunch to update one another and to share pertinent information, such as the need for resources and materials, student involvement, the theme's progress, assessment scheduling, classroom visitations, collective field trips, and parent meetings.

The overflow of business and actual instructional/collaborative planning time was handled during a monthly **release-time meeting.** The school staff and university faculty met to review teaching issues, share assessment data, solve problems, plan cross-content lessons, and basically expand on, in depth, the actual mechanics of the project.

The tasks of organizing the meetings and facilitating project business were handled by the project's half-time site coordinator, who also taught one of the classes in the two strands. It was the coordinator who maintained communication between the university and the school, planned field trips, scheduled substitutes, ordered materials, disseminated information, arranged instructional support, dealt with problems, and served as the project's contact person.

At the end of the project's second theme, the fine arts, a parents' potluck dinner with student presentations took place. This provided an opportunity to involve parents and further inform them about the project. The staff was available to explain Project Theme's rationale and to answer questions. The students described their theme classes and shared completed projects.

Specific Activities of Project Theme

Implementing changes in instruction within the complexities of a school site is no small matter. The success of such a program requires the augmentation and reconstruction of various activities that already form the core of the school:

1. Professional development for teachers

2. Assessment practices

3. Enhancement of students' academic learning

4. Improvement of students' self-esteem

The project, in a very direct and highly collaborative mode, attempted to address each of these issues, as the following sections will explain.

Professional Development for Teachers. Project Theme addressed professional development in a number of ways:

Methods of Professional Development

- Project teachers participated in preservice and inservice training activities in LEP-effective instructional strategies, particularly those related to cooperative learning, peer tutoring, literacy as a sociopsycholinguistic phenomenon, and the cognitive foundations of literacy, mathematics, and science. This was accomplished at a week-long institute held at the university and in two preservice workshops.

- Project teachers met monthly to go over the implementation of instructional strategies.

- Project teachers observed each other's classrooms and discussed their observations.

Assessment Practices. Project Theme developed a strategy for assessment of students' progress as well as a strategy for assessment of the program itself. The key assessment features included these:

- Theme students were pretested in September/October using the California Test of Basic Skills (CTBS) and the Spanish Assessment of Basic Education (SABE). Later in the academic year they were posttested. The comparison group of 48 students was also pretested and posttested.

Collaborating on Assessment

- Project teachers and research team members collaborated in the development and implementation of specific academic assessment strategies.

- Previous effective schooling measures were reviewed, assessed, and used to develop a specific assessment of the instructional character of the program.

- Members of the team participated in training relevant to assessment techniques, including student, parent, and teacher interview techniques. Then team members applied these techniques in interviews with students, parents, and teachers.

Enhancement of Students' Academic Learning. Specific steps were taken to enhance academic learning for all the students in the project:

Groups and Themes

- Theme students were placed in collaborative learning groups intended to maximize effective communication and learning. These groups were characterized by academic heterogeneity and by an orientation toward positive interdependence.

- Theme students participated in a core-integrated curriculum that promoted increased opportunities for language and literacy development and integrated content-related instruction. The integrated instruction was organized around the following themes: (1) the Olympics, (2) the fine arts (popular music, art, and fashion), (3) the ocean, (4) crime and nonviolence, (5) careers, (6) gender, (7) AIDS, and (8) ethnic identity. Students and teachers together selected these themes.

Improvement of Students' Self-Esteem. In addition to academic learning, the cultivation of students' self-esteem was considered vital to the success of the program, and Project Theme used the following strategies to foster good self-images among the students:

Building a Good Self-Image

- Theme students were recognized for both their individual achievements and their contributions to group products.

- Theme students worked in cooperative learning structures— particularly the "Tribes" process—to develop skills in leadership and cooperation.

- Theme students in cooperative groups discussed specific situational conflicts and utilized problem-solving skills to determine solutions.

- Teachers implemented programs that recognized student improvement and success across a range of abilities.

- Teachers integrated lessons that promoted understanding and appreciation of individual and cultural differences.

The Results of Project Theme

The pretesting and posttesting for both the Project Theme students and the comparison group focused on the areas of language, reading, writing, and mathematics. In addition, survey and interview data regarding the students' academic self-concept and social identity were gathered. (Besides gathering the data when students were in middle school, researchers also conducted interviews at the end of the students' sophomore year in high school.) Moreover, parents were interviewed regarding their social identities and their perceptions of schooling. The results can be grouped in the following specific areas:

1. Academic achievement in language, reading, and writing

2. Ethnographic data on students' self-concepts

3. Social identity of students and parents

4. Math achievement, attitudes, and self-concepts

5. Long-term effects of the project

These five areas are discussed in detail in the following sections.

Academic Achievement in Language, Reading, and Writing

To examine the effects of the instructional intervention in the domains of language, reading, and writing, academic achievement measures in English and Spanish were obtained during the spring semester. For English-only and bilingual students in the theme group and the comparison group, six subtests of the English version of the CTBS along with seven subtests of the English version of the Language Assessment Scales Reading/Writing (LAS) were used. The CTBS subtests were (1) Vocabulary, (2) Language Mechanics, (3) Reading Comprehension, (4) Reading Total, (5) Language Expression, and (6) Language Expression Total. The LAS subtests included (1) Synonyms, (2) Fluency, (3) Antonyms,

(4) Mechanics and Usage, (5) Reading for Information, (6) What's Happening, and (7) Let's Write. For LAS subtests 1 to 5, students were given multiple-choice items while for subtests 6 and 7 they were required to write a description of a scene that was depicted, create a description of their own scene, or both. In addition, bilingual students were administered the vocabulary and reading subtests of the SABE.

Test Results | On each subtest, the English-only theme students received higher scores than the bilingual theme students. More important, however, the bilingual theme group did not differ significantly from the English-only comparison group on any of the subtests. The students in the bilingual theme group had originally been identified by their need for further academic development. As noted earlier, the group included both English-dominant and Spanish-dominant students, and they were taught in bilingual classrooms. It was striking that this group did not differ in academic achievement from a group of English-only students in the regular curriculum.

In other respects, the theme groups consistently performed higher than their comparison counterparts. This was particularly true for bilingual students. On six of the seven Language Assessment Scale (LAS) subtests, bilingual theme students scored significantly higher than bilingual comparison students. Of particular interest were the significant differences found between these groups in the sixth and seventh subtests, which measure written-language ability. Moreover, on the two SABE subtests, the scores of the bilingual theme group were higher than those of the bilingual comparison group, though this difference was not statistically significant on the vocabulary subtest. Similarly, English-only theme students significantly outscored English-only comparison students on four of the six CTBS subtests (Vocabulary, Language Expression, Language Expression Total, and Reading Comprehension).

In summary, the results consistently show higher achievement among the theme students, for both the bilingual and the English-only groups.

Ethnographic Data on Students' Self-Concepts

Several themes relating to students' self-concepts emerged from the participant classroom observations, student interviews, and teacher interviews. These themes may be categorized in the following four domains: (1) ethnic identity, (2) positive self-esteem, (3) future aspirations, and (4) academic strategies and perceptions about schooling. Let's examine each of these domains in turn.

Ethnic Identity. *Students of Mexican origin and Anglo-American origin did not use a wide range of ethnic labels when referring to themselves and other students.* When we asked students to identify the different types of students at the school in terms of specific ethnic labels commonly heard in the community, they usually used only a few terms: "Mexican," "Mexican American," and "American." Very few students were familiar with the term "Chicano." When asked what distinguished individuals within the generic category of "Mexican," they talked in terms of language ability, physical appearance, and country of birth. One Anglo-American girl discussed differences among Project Theme students in terms of those "who are bilingual and those who are straight." Most of the Mexican-origin students were familiar with other ethnic labels (e.g., "Cholo," "Pocho") but did not feel they applied to the Mexican-origin student population at the school. When asked to categorize themselves, students of Mexican origin most frequently chose "Mexican" or "Mexican American." The most commonly used ethnic labels for the Anglo-American students among both groups were "white," "American," and occasionally "Anglo."

Ethnic Labels |

Most of the Project Theme students stressed commonalities among people, especially among the groups in the school. They gave responses such as "It doesn't matter if you're Mexican or American; people are people." This is not to say that the students did not perceive differences among students at their school or even among categories of students. However, the distinguishing features they used did not necessarily reflect differences in ethnic identification. When asked to identify different groups in school, without any prompts for ethnicity, all but two students distinguished students in other ways (e.g., athletes versus nerds, popular versus not popular, good students versus bad students).

Positive Self-Esteem. *Students of Mexican descent exhibited a positive sense of self and expressed pride in their Mexican heritage.* In a variety of contexts, students expressed pride in being Mexican, giving examples of holidays and other special occasions when they felt particularly proud. At this point, we are not sure in what specific ways, if any, this ethnic pride was linked to a positive sense of self, to a particular ethnic label, to positive attitudes toward Spanish-English bilingualism, or to other social experiences in the school, family, and community.

Ethnic Self-Image |

We were particularly interested in finding out if any of the Mexican-descent students wanted to change places with any of the Anglo-American students in the class or in the school, especially those who were identified as being popular, attractive, and/or high academic achievers. However, very few of the Mexican

Ethnic Identity: Who Am I?

We observed that a handful of students, girls in particular, appeared to exhibit a certain amount of tension in discussing specific ethnic labels carrying a negative connotation (e.g., "Cholo"), especially if these labels indicated behaviors that could be linked to ethnic identity. One girl in the bilingual theme group discussed how she had changed in the last year. She described how just a year before she had been an "angel," someone who did her homework regularly, listened to her mother, did what her older brother told her to do. "Now, my friends have changed me: I now dresses differently, don't do my school work, gets into fights with family members, things like that." She concluded that this was both "good" and "bad." It is "good" that she no longer allows her over-bearing brother to boss her around but "bad" that she talks back to her mother and that her work is lagging.

In many ways her description of herself contradicts the impression conveyed by her grades and her teachers' perceptions of her as a student. By these standards, she appears to be one of the stronger students in the program.

American students we interviewed expressed any desire to switch places with anyone else, and in fact, they were frequently surprised that such a question would even be asked. "Why would I want to do that?" was a typical response. "I like being me."

We also asked the students to identify which, if any, aspects of their physical appearance they would change. Here there were some important gender differences, especially among some of the darker-skinned Mexican American girls. Although the boys, with several exceptions, did not identify any changes they would make in their physical appearance, many of the girls said they would change the shape of their nose, remove freckles, and/or lighten the color of their hair or skin. This preliminary finding bears more careful scrutiny, especially as the girls mature and go on to high school. Furthermore, it will be important to explore in greater detail any relationship between elements of ethnic awareness—both positive and negative—and feelings of self-worth and confidence in one's appearance, especially among the Mexican-descent girls.

Future Aspirations. *All students, regardless of ethnicity, aspired to professional careers.* All the Project Theme students were interested in pursuing a profession. The survey data indicate that the most commonly chosen categories were law (45.7 percent), medicine (40.6 percent), and the arts (over 30 percent). When presented with a choice of careers, students often identified a range of possibilities that included professional as well as service-related jobs. For example, one student expressed interest in becoming a scientist, mechanic, doctor, waitress, photographer, and beautician.

Visions of the Future | *Finishing high school and/or college was in everyone's future plans, and the students linked schooling to future success.* The students believed that a college education was needed in order to get a "good" job, although they thought they could get an "adequate" job—such as mechanic or beautician—with a high school diploma. Moreover, everyone reported that their parents' views were similar. With very few exceptions, all students said that their parents would be moderately to greatly upset if they quit school before high school graduation. Some talked about how their parents expressed their options in very realistic terms: working in the fields versus something better. For them, the "something better" meant an occupation that could be attained by staying in school and going on to college. The survey data revealed one distinction between Anglo-American and Mexican-descent students: Mexican-descent students were evenly divided in terms of planning to pursue two years of college or four years while Anglo-American students overwhelmingly favored finishing four years of college.

This leads us to another point. Despite their aspirations, *students of Mexican descent lacked specific instrumental knowledge on how to prepare for the careers they wanted to pursue.* It was

---

Aspirations: Who Will I Become?

Among the Mexican-descent students, there was no interest in becoming a farm worker or cannery worker, the jobs that were commonly held by their parents. They were aware of the difficulties of these occupations, as revealed in the following comments:

"*A mi no me gusta trabajar en el campo porque asi aprende uno como se cansan los padres para mantenernos y comprarnos lo que queremos.*"

"If I played professional football, I wouldn't have to work as hard as my parents. They sweat for hours working in the fields. I wouldn't like that."

Career Options: What About College?

Among those Mexican-origin students who did have some idea about the demands of a college education, its pursuit was seen as a potentially very difficult struggle. One girl identified the obstacles in her way: "getting pregnant and poor grades." Money was also frequently reported as a major barrier. As one girl noted, "You need lots of money to learn in college." This is not to say that these students think college is an impossible dream, but they do believe that it entails a great deal of hard work above and beyond the rigors of the academic requirements. Several students explicitly stated that if they worked hard enough, they would make it to and through college, citing as examples the experiences of a cousin, aunt, older sibling, or close family friend.

clear from our interviews that although these students knew that college was a prerequisite for many of the professions they were interested in, they did not have specific knowledge about the types of postsecondary education that were available, the different credentials and opportunities each might offer, and the number of years required to complete particular levels of training. This is in marked contrast to many of the Anglo-American students we interviewed, who had a much clearer, although sometimes inaccurate, picture of the differences between a community college and a four-year institution. Most of the Anglo-American students understood the connection between higher-status occupations (e.g., teaching, nursing, architecture) and the need to complete at least four years of college. In contrast, many of the Mexican-descent students felt that a two-year education at the local community college would be sufficient to enter these occupations. One Mexican American girl said that to be a doctor, "You have to have five years of something before you can get out of the university." Very few of these students knew the names of colleges other than one or two of the local community colleges, and none knew where to obtain this information. Many assumed that this information would be presented to them at some later point in their education. During these discussions we became aware of the extent to which these students conceptualized the pursuit of a college education as something one sets out to acquire in much the same way that one purchases an expensive car or other concrete object. What is lacking in their comments is any substantive knowledge of the instrumental behaviors, attitudes, motivations, orientations, and scholastic achievements required.

The research also probed the students' beliefs about the role of bilingualism in their desired careers. *Students of Mexican descent felt that being bilingual and biliterate would contribute to their future success.* These students frequently expressed very positive attitudes about bilingual ability. They believed that knowing Spanish and English would benefit them in terms of future job opportunities. Frequently, students gave examples of specific work situations, possibly derived from their own experiences, in which a bilingual employee was able to assist a monolingual speaker. According to our survey data, the perception of this advantage was also held by half of the non-Mexican-descent students. On the whole, Mexican-descent students were eager to maintain or improve their Spanish-language skills by continuing to take classes in Spanish.

Academic Strategies and Perceptions About Schooling. *Doing homework and listening and behaving in class were the attributes students most often linked to success in school.* When we asked students to describe how one becomes a good student, they responded in ways like these: "by doing my homework and listening in class," "by paying attention to the teacher and doing all the work," "by not messing around and getting your work in on time." They felt that being quiet in class was also important.

Attributes of a Good Student | Given a choice among several attributes of a successful student, 50 percent of our sample ($N = 30$) felt that completing schoolwork was the most important attribute. When asked to identify a successful student in their class or describe someone whom they considered to be a good student, they invariably named or described someone who did his or her homework and was well behaved. When we asked them how they thought they could improve their own academic performance, nearly all said that they should do their work, listen in class, and pay attention to the teacher.

Nevertheless, *the students were not challenged by their schoolwork.* In our interviews, as well as in many—but not all—of our observations of actual classroom sessions, students exhibited little enthusiasm or genuine engagement in their classes. Only 15 percent of the students felt that their schoolwork was too hard. Moreover, the majority wished that their classes were more interesting.

Social Identity of Students and Parents

Social identity is an intriguing and complex phenomenon. It is both a social *product,* emerging out of biological, social, and cultural influences, and a social *force,* emanating from the created social product to guide an individual's choices in behavior.

Identity research with people of Mexican descent has focused almost exclusively on ethnic identity, or the sense of oneself as a member of an ethnic group. However, although ethnic identity is undeniably significant, it is not the only critical dimension of one's social identity. Few studies have investigated such potentially important nonethnic dimensions of social identity as occupation, race, family, religion, and language. In one study that did examine this issue, adolescents living in inner-city Detroit chose to describe themselves by using a nonethnic label rather than an ethnic category.

In Project Theme we examined the social identities of the seventh-graders and their parents by administering a measure of social identity that included race, class, family, and ethnicity. By comparing the differences and similarities in the social identification of parents and their offspring, we can form an empirical basis for how social identity, including ethnic identity, is transmitted from one generation to another.

Table 9.1 profiles the social, economic, and linguistic background of theme students and their parents. Note the difference in language choices between parents and students. With these basic characteristics in mind, what would you expect to find in the survey data about social identities?

As it turns out, the data indicate both similarities and differences in the social identities of parents and their children. Both parents and children had a familial dimension (that includes gender) to their social identities (e.g., sibling, daughter/son, mother/father,

Table 9.1	Social, Economic, and Linguistic Background of Project Theme Students and Their Parents	
Mexican-descent students		87
Anglo-American students		23
Students language choice for interview:		
Spanish		31
English		56
Parents' language choice for interview:		
Spanish		77
English		23
Family income:		
$2,000–$10,999		21%
$11,000–$24,999		53%
$25,000–$34,999		12%
$40,000 and above		14%
Parents' education level (average)		6.5 years
Parents' marital status		88% married

Generational
Differences wife/husband, *comadre/compadre*). For parents, there was a strong religious dimension (e.g., Catholic, Christian, religious person) that was not present in their offspring. As might be expected, whereas parents identified with their occupations (e.g., family breadwinner, farm worker), their children did not. The greatest divergence between parents and children was in the manifestation of their ethnicity. Whereas the ethnic dimension of social identity for parents included such labels as "Mexican" and "Hispanic," for their children it included "Mexican American," "American of Mexican descent," "U.S. citizen," "Mexican," and "American." *Thus, these adolescents had not yet formed a clear ethnic identity for themselves. Students of this age group are in the formative stages of the development of the identifiers that society uses for them and that they are likely to adopt for themselves later in their lives.*

Math Achievement, Attitudes, and Self-Concepts

In our study we also addressed the general problem of underachievement in mathematics among Hispanic students as well as their underrepresentation in high school classes that are prerequisite to educational and occupational opportunities in science and technology. The multifaceted intervention involved thematic integration of mathematics content across the curriculum. This approach broadly engaged students in gathering, processing, representing, and communicating about quantitative concepts. Since traditional approaches to instruction for Hispanic students tend to emphasize computation more than meaning, we hypothesized that students exposed to such thematic instruction would perform better than comparison subjects on a test of mathematical concepts and applications. We expected no achievement differences in computational skills. The data supported both of these hypotheses.

Attitudes
Toward Math A secondary function of this aspect of the research was to obtain baseline data on attitudes toward mathematics in order to examine similarities and differences between the National Assessment of Educational Progress (NAEP) sample and our sample. Preliminary analysis of these data indicate that theme students expressed more positive feelings toward mathematics than either the Anglo-American or the Hispanic students in the NAEP sample. To a greater extent than students in the NAEP sample, they also considered themselves to be good at mathematics and expected to work in an area requiring mathematics when they left school. The implications of such findings when juxtaposed with the students' overall low performances in mathematics were puzzling.

A final purpose of this research was to test for changes in motivational self-perceptions regarding mathematics through the academic year and to examine the relationship of self-perceptions to instructional outcomes. Contrary to our earlier assumptions, females reported more positive math self-concept than males on these measures. The influence of self-perception variables on learning outcomes in mathematics was examined as well. Results indicate that the best predictor of math achievement was a positive math self-concept rather than a generally positive self-concept.

Long-Term Effects of the Project

Three years after we completed Project Theme, we conducted a follow-up study to measure the following variables among both the theme and the comparison students: (1) future aspirations, (2) academic performance as measured by course grades, and (3) perceptions of middle school. Data were obtained by means of a self-administered survey that included the following questions:

What is your grade-point average?

Was your middle school a good institution?

Did you receive excellent grades in middle school?

Did you find the subjects in middle school to be very interesting?

Did middle school teachers help you develop interest?

Did middle school teachers help you plan for future goals?

Did middle school teachers like you?

Did you hate your middle school?

What are your future plans?

Do high school teachers help you plan for the future?

Do high school teachers like you?

Do you feel comfortable at your high school?

Do you get along well with other students in high school?

In the follow-up study the questionnaire was submitted to the former theme and comparison students enrolled at Watsonville High School who were able to attend the one-afternoon session near the end of the academic year. Thirty-eight students participated, 21 from the theme group and 17 from the comparison group. Students completing the survey were not told that its purpose was to assess the effects of any particular program.

Impact of
Project Theme

The survey revealed that Project Theme had a significant effect on grades, with approximately 70 percent of the grades of the theme group being *above average* and about 75 percent of the grades of the comparison group being *below average*. Although this is a self-report indicator, we have some confidence in the finding because students were clear about the confidentiality of their responses. Also, 65 percent of the theme students thought of their middle school as a good institution, whereas only 40 percent of the comparison group reported such a perception. Moreover, 80 percent of the theme students described their middle school subjects as interesting, as opposed to 30 percent of the comparison students.

In addition, teachers were perceived by the theme students as providing greater inspiration. Some 85 percent of this group agreed that teachers helped them develop interest, versus only 47 percent of the comparison students. Also, 57 percent of the theme students indicated that teachers had helped them plan for the future, as opposed to 40 percent of the comparison students. The implementation of this project also created a significant difference in the students' future aspirations. About 85 percent of the theme students indicated a strong desire to go on to college, whereas only 69 percent of the comparison students expressed this desire.

In summary, the follow-up study indicated a consistent pattern of outcomes related to grades, perceptions of middle school, and future aspirations that dramatically favors the theme students.

The Conclusion of Research on Project Theme

Project Theme brought middle school teachers and university faculty together in a redesign of seventh-grade instructional organization. This redesign was based on recent empirical work that identified components of instruction and curriculum that proved to be effective with linguistically and culturally diverse students. It was also based on recent theoretical formulations that are of general relevance in enhancing academic learning.

Theme students were part of an educational experience that kept them together for the majority of their school day. This experience included participation in small, heterogeneously structured learning groups. Instruction focused on jointly determined themes that integrated reading, language arts, math, science, and social studies. The academic outcomes of these theme students were compared with the outcomes of a group of students who participated in the same school's typical seventh-grade organization: seven independently taught, homogeneously leveled classes with limited curriculum integration and a more traditional, whole-group instructional approach.

Lessons of Project Theme

The implementation of the project required extensive rethinking of the existing middle school organization by teachers, administrators, and participating university faculty. Moreover, the restructuring that took place required wide-ranging collaboration, especially by the teachers. These teachers reported that without the time the project allowed them to meet and plan, the program would not have been possible. In addition, they stated that the on-site coordinator played a key role in bringing them together and in ensuring that the specific objectives were always at the forefront of the project activity. Recall that the teachers had at least one release-time meeting each four to six weeks and that they also met on a weekly basis during lunch. The coordinator, who had the time to meet individually with teachers and university faculty, was a key resource person with regard to finding and developing theme-related curriculum material. In sum, the project could not have been implemented without the additional release time provided for teachers and the presence of an effective on-site coordinator.

The results of the project are clearly positive. That is, the data show consistently more positive academic outcomes for the theme students as compared with those of students in the school's conventional program. Most notably, comparative analyses in reading comprehension, vocabulary, language mechanics, and language expression in English significantly favored the theme students. Similar results were found on Spanish measures.

Constraints of Project Theme

Although these empirical results are promising, we should identify two important constraints of the study. First, the study was a voluntary effort by a group of self-selected and particularly motivated teachers and university faculty. Second, we could not identify specific causal links between the intervention subcomponents and the dependent variables. For example, were the improvements on language and reading tests "caused" by the theme structure, by the cooperative learning methods, by the efforts to bolster students' self-concepts, by any other individual components of the program—or by all of these components in combination? For these reasons, among others, the results of the study are difficult to interpret in detail. It does seem appropriate, however, to conclude that the findings suggest a set of school and classroom restructuring alternatives that may provide enhanced educational success for a population of educationally vulnerable students. The teachers, parents, and students of Project Theme echo this conclusion.

Rethinking, Rebuilding, and Engaging Change at the High School Level

California is a microcosm of the peculiar state of affairs concerning the high school experiences of linguistically and culturally diverse students. A recent study of California high schools indicated that "California is generating 50,000–75,000 non-completers (students who go to high school but never finish), just about the same number as students who become eligible for the University of California system" (Minicucci and Olsen, 1992). The number of Latinos graduating from high school in 1995 was reported to be 60,000, but only 2,000, fewer than 4 percent, actually found their way to the University of California. These figures are just one sign of the complicated and often neglected educational circumstances of minority high school students. Recently, researchers, educators, and many others have begun to voice their concern about these California students, whose language and diversity should be viewed as an advantage for the future and not a liability for the present (Hurtado, Figueroa, and García, 1996).

Minicucci and Olsen (1992) direct our attention to four areas that directly affect the education of linguistically and culturally diverse and immigrant high school students in California and elsewhere:

- Overt conflict, violence, and tension

- Status quo of separations (both social and institutional)

- Conflict students feel when caught between two worlds and when a world around them requires assimilation for acceptance

- The ability of secondary schools to address these issues and design appropriate interventions

These recent findings undeniably require additional study. Lucas, Henze, and Donato (1990) provide a useful summary of research on the effective instruction of minority populations in general and of immigrant students in particular (see Table 9.2). This work has yielded conceptual understandings and empirical findings that could be included in a practical, multifaceted instructional plan to enhance the academic learning of such students at the high school level.

A substantial impediment for many students is tracking, a practice that directs students into low-, regular-, or high-achieving groups (Oakes, 1984a). Although tracking may begin as early as elementary school, it is most often initiated at the junior high

Table 9.2	Attributes of High Schools That Promote the Achievement of Language Minority Students

1. Value is placed on the students' languages and cultures by:
   * Treating students as individuals, not as members of a group
   * Learning about students' cultures
   * Learning students' languages
   * Hiring bilingual staff with cultural backgrounds similar to the students'
   * Encouraging students to develop their primary language skills
   * Allowing students to speak their primary languages
   * Offering advanced as well as lower division content courses in the students' primary languages
   * Instituting extracurricular activities that will attract language minority (LM) students

2. High expectations of language minority students are made concrete by:
   * Hiring minority staff in leadership positions to act as role models
   * Providing a special program to prepare LM students for college
   * Offering advanced and honors bilingual/sheltered English classes in the content areas
   * Making it possible for students to exit ESL programs quickly
   * Challenging students in class and providing guidance to help them meet the challenge
   * Providing counseling assistance (in the primary language if necessary) to help students apply to college and fill out scholarship and grant forms
   * Inviting college representatives and minority graduates who are in college to speak
   * Working with parents to gain their support for students going to college
   * Recognizing students for doing well

3. School leaders make the education of language minority students a priority. These leaders:
   * Hold high expectations for LM students
   * Are knowledgeable of instructional and curricular approaches to teaching LM students and communicate this knowledge to staff
   * Take a strong leadership role in strengthening curriculum and instruction for all students, including LM students
   * Are often bilingual minority group members themselves
   * Hire teachers who are bilingual and/or trained in methods for teaching LM students

4. Staff development is explicitly designed to help teachers and staff serve language minority students more effectively. Schools and school districts:
   * Offer incentives and compensation so that the school staff will take advantage of available staff development programs
   * Provide staff development for teachers and other school staff in:
       effective instructional approaches to teaching LM students, e.g., cooperative learning methods, sheltered English, and reading and writing in the content areas
       principles of second language acquisition
       the cultural backgrounds and experiences of the students
       the languages of the students
       cross-cultural communication
       cross-cultural counseling

5. A variety of courses and programs for language minority students is offered.
   * Include courses in English as a second language and primary language instruction (both literacy and advanced placement) and bilingual and sheltered English courses in content areas.
   * Make sure that the course offerings for LM students do not limit their choices or place them in low level classes. Offer advanced as well as basic courses taught through bilingual and sheltered English methods.

Table 9.2	**Attributes of High Schools That Promote the Achievement of Language Minority Students (cont.)**

- Keep class size small (20–25) in order to maximize interaction.
- Establish academic support programs that help LM students make the transition from ESL and bilingual classes to mainstream classes and prepare them to go to college.

6. A counseling program gives special attention to language minority students through counselors who:
   - Speak the students' languages and are of the same or similar cultural backgrounds
   - Are informed about post-secondary educational opportunities for LM students
   - Believe in, emphasize, and monitor the academic success of LM students

7. Parents of language minority students are encouraged to become involved in their children's education. Schools can provide and encourage:
   - Staff who can speak the parents' languages
   - On-campus ESL classes for parents
   - Monthly parent nights
   - Parent involvement with counselors in the planning of their children's course schedules
   - Neighborhood meetings with school staff
   - Early morning meetings with parents
   - Telephone contacts to check on absent students

8. School staff members share a strong commitment to empowering language minority students through education. This commitment is made concrete through staff who:
   - Give extra time to work with LM students
   - Take part in a political process that challenges the status quo
   - Request training of various sorts to help them become more effective
   - Reach out to students in ways that go beyond their job requirements, for example, by sponsoring extracurricular activities
   - Participate in community activities in which they act as advocates for Latinos and other minorities

Source: Tamara Lucas, Rosemary Henze, and Ruben Donato, "Promoting the Success of Latino Language Minority Students: An Exploratory Study of Six High Schools," *Harvard Educational Review, 60* (3), pp. 315–340. Copyright © 1990 by the President and Fellows of Harvard College. All rights reserved.

Pitfalls of Tracking

school level. By high school, tracking is vividly established, and class assignments often are driven by perceptions (accurate or inaccurate) of the student's level of academic achievement. Once minority students are placed in a track identified as being for low achievers, their opportunities for academic success are significantly limited (Oakes, 1984a). Putting a student in a remedial class automatically increases his or her chances of being enrolled in another remedial class. Such a student receives a less effective education because remedial courses do not expose students to a challenging curriculum. In most cases, in fact, the teachers assigned to remedial classrooms with low-income and linguistically diverse students are teachers who have no expertise in language acquisition and development and no particular cultural sensitivity. In other words, the students who are most in need of high-quality instruction and experienced teachers instead get the opposite (Finley, 1984; Haycock and Navarro, 1988).

As many researchers have pointed out, "most American high schools still have a long way to go to substantially improve the engagement and achievement of their students" (National Center of Effective Secondary Schools, 1991, p. 19). Yet in their efforts to "improve" the quality of education, high schools often seem to forget the most vulnerable groups in their ranks. It is for the forgotten students that we must create robust academic programs with the flexibility to combine research, theory, and practice into an agenda of change. The following section describes one such effort at the high school level. Known as Project AVANCE, it took place in California, a state that, as we have seen, serves as an important microcosm of our nation's educational system.

Project AVANCE

Project AVANCE (the Spanish word for "advance") incorporated alternative instructional strategies that are demonstrably effective in advancing the linguistic minority student's literacy, mathematics, and English-language skills. Ultimately, AVANCE's aim was to promote "students learning how to learn." The project's specific instructional strategies included the following:

AVANCE's Strategies

- Use of a thematic, integrated curriculum, with academic objectives that were achieved through content-integrated instruction

- Emphasis on small-group activities incorporating heterogeneous language grouping and peer tutoring, and emphasizing higher-order linguistic and cognitive processes (in which learning proceeds from the concrete to the representational to the symbolic)

- Emphasis on literacy activities such as interactive journals, silent reading followed by small-group discussion, interactive literature study, individual- and group-authored literature, and mathematics logs

- Use of cooperative learning strategies that emphasized the systematic participation of each student in processing curriculum materials

- Documentation of interpersonal inequities related to ethnic and gender differences and implementation of strategies to foster equity

These strategies were consistent with techniques that the California Department of Education (1990) had already identified for use in its high school curriculum frameworks:

1. *Language arts and reading:* Reading Situations, Anticipating the Reading, Reading Process, Initial Response, Discussion, Written Interpretation, Reflections on the Reading Experience

2. *Mathematics:* Free Response Questions, Mathematical Investigations, Portfolios

3. *Science:* Performance Tasks, Open-Ended Questions, Student Portfolios

4. *Social studies:* Portfolios of Student Work, Performance Assessment (including oral presentations, drama, debates, group collaborations, student-assessor dialogues, etc.), Writing Tasks, Integrated Assessment (incorporating more than one technique and interdisciplinary skills in a complex task that demands higher-order cognition)

Reorganizing the Structure of the School

Like many of the other projects discussed in this book, AVANCE was based on a good deal of theoretical work in language development and effective schooling. Such theoretical foundations often suggest that typically underserved students can succeed academically if instructional strategies that emphasize cooperative learning, student-generated themes, and close staff networking are woven into the existing academic framework of the institution with relatively minor changes. Yet modifications that on the surface seem quite simple or minor can be very difficult to fulfill, especially if they challenge "seldom-questioned regularities of school culture" (Oakes, 1992, p. 5). The AVANCE intervention was not immune to this problem. Let's examine the way AVANCE was set up.

The intervention at the high school was designed to benefit 60 students, who were divided into two heterogeneous groups of approximately 30 students each. Both groups were made up of English-only, reclassified bilingual (Spanish and English), and ESL students. Students were selected only if teachers, counselors, or classmates considered them to be "high-motivation" students.

Building the | A team of seven teachers, one counselor, and university re-
Framework | searchers worked collaboratively to plan and implement the curriculum. The content-area subjects were English, science, mathematics, and social science (world civics was taught for one

semester and health studies for the other). The two groups of students were integrated with the rest of the student body for two periods: physical education and an elective class.

The comparison group was made up of 60 randomly selected students in the regular high school curriculum. As these students changed classes throughout the day, they experienced six combinations of classmates in six different, nonintegrated content areas.

An office at the high school was established where the team met weekly to discuss, share, update, and relate pertinent information. The agenda for the meeting included discussions on the theme's progress, classroom visitations, budget, meetings, and data collection. The organization of meetings and related on-site business was delegated to AVANCE's part-time coordinator, who also taught four classes. The coordinator's main responsibilities were to schedule meetings, order materials, arrange instructional support, and deal with any logistical problems.

Project teachers participated in workshops specifically related

**Preparing
Teachers**

to culturally and linguistically diverse children. These workshops, created by the National Center for Santa Cruz, included presentations by prominent researchers in the field who shared their research findings as well as demonstrations, classroom videos, and hands-on activities. Other preparatory events for the teachers included the following:

- The teachers and the school's principal visited the site of Project Theme to observe the classrooms and discuss the program with the instructors.

- Two leading educators conducted a workshop to address specific concerns and field questions about thematic teaching.

- Teachers planned a series of five monthly meetings to discuss and plan the curriculum and structure of the program.

- Teachers attended a three-day summer conference to share and plan their individual areas of curriculum focus within the overall program theme and to integrate lessons across the curriculum. Here they also chose "Community" as their first thematic unit, which they implemented during the first week of school.

- Students and teachers participated on a one-day tour and workshop on science and technology at UC Santa Cruz.

Outcomes of the AVANCE Intervention

To assess AVANCE's reforms, teachers were interviewed and classrooms observed. In one sense, teachers were the judges and jury regarding the program's effectiveness in challenging the traditional delivery of education. Often their evaluations brought to the fore dimensions that had never been discussed during the planning of the intervention.

Course Standards and Evaluation. Teachers in this study wanted simultaneously to retain the standards required for students to enter college preparatory courses and to meet the needs of the students who were performing slightly below those academic levels. They discussed this issue extensively, considering both course content and student assessment. Although the majority of the teachers used the student-centered content of AVANCE, one teacher at times felt a need to alter the content to allow the less academically prepared students to participate effectively. The teachers were, however, unwilling to "water down" the curriculum for any student, and they made their commitment to this principle eminently clear.

A major change occurred in the teachers' attitude toward performance-based—sometimes called authentic—assessment of the students' academic achievement. One teacher stated:

> "When you say, 'Evaluation,' I say, 'Grade.' I have what I hope to be a wide variety of activities. I evaluate their portfolio, their lab binder or lab notebook, exams, unit test, quiz, lab work, and their self-evaluation. I grade on a participate/not participate basis. If I have an exam which is in English (all exams are in English), I would allow students to do other things to make up for points they missed in the test."

Teachers' Reactions | This attitude carried over to the manner in which teachers viewed their own performance as teachers. As one person said, "Not only do I have to cover what I'm required and they'll be tested on, but I have to cover the themes." It was also apparent in the curriculum shift from strictly "book" academics to "everyday-life" academics:

> "[One way in which I changed the test reflects] what people do in real life. For example, in my ESL class on library skills I phrase all questions [like this]: 'What would be the first thing you would do if you were interested in electronics at the library?' The test [in this class] mimics a real-life process of being able to get a book."

One factor that was expected to have an impact on the AVANCE project was the scarcity of Spanish-language minority students who could meet the academic challenge in the way that the teachers required. Considering the current state of education, some teachers felt that AVANCE recruited and received students who were willing to face the academic rigors but were not fully prepared to deal with the academic consequences. In fact, the teachers generally agreed that their students with a strong knowledge of English benefited the most from the intervention because they could participate fully in an academic environment that was unlike a mainstream classroom. Despite this potential problem, an English teacher stated:

> "I would be willing to say that I would put my English I class against any other group at [this school] in the CORE pieces of work. Pick any other English teacher. Give a multiple-choice test. They'd do O.K. Those who have English will come out stronger."

During the program, teachers appeared enthusiastic about the manner in which academics could be used to communicate with parents. There was an air of optimism when teachers realized that their academic curriculum could also help to establish a dialogue among parents, students, and teachers.

Student-Generated Themes. A major challenge teachers encountered was the notion of allowing students to participate actively in defining the curriculum. The first challenge arose when teachers questioned how to forge a comprehensive academic partnership between teachers and students while simultaneously embracing the community. In other words, the issue was how to continue to deliver the mandated, districtwide curriculum effectively and weave into it the new theme-centered agenda. Particular attention was given to the composition of the student body: the students in this program, who were either members of groups with low socioeconomic status or recent immigrants, had been given the least amount of academic support and were perceived as unwilling to work academically. With initial hesitation, the teachers embraced the concept of allowing student input. Once the first theme had been selected, they welcomed the partnership. As one teacher put it,

> "Having student-generated themes formalized student input for curriculum [because] they create the theme, [and] we [teachers] let them imagine what they want to study. They write the curriculum at the start of the six-week unit. From assignment to assessment, they are more involved."

Student Input | The formation of this partnership became one of the more successful aspects of the program. It allowed students to nominate their top three interests as themes. These ideas were analyzed to determine which one was the most popular, best used available resources, and could be woven into the mandated curriculum. In some instances, themes were discussed and then expanded to cover a broader range of issues and provide more leeway to include the mandated curriculum.

One theme that required little expansion was "Gangs." The English teacher incorporated *Romeo and Juliet* into this unit. In mathematics, the curriculum centered on the number of Hispanics in prisons, and students drew the connections among Hispanics, gangs, and prison. In science, students studied gangs from the perspective of animal behavior, including social grouping and territoriality.

As the program progressed, teachers realized that the student-teacher partnership that had originally been envisioned as problematic and difficult to implement became one of the best means of promoting student participation, input, and academic responsibility.

Staff Networking. At the outset of AVANCE, teachers were made aware that they were free to inquire, suggest, or constructively

Teacher Camaraderie criticize as the program moved forward. This unique opportunity to discuss students, curriculum, and decisions that affected their own academic environments gave the teachers a sense of professional growth and camaraderie. As one said, "I've gotten to know some of the teachers in the program very well. You don't really get to know people in other departments. It's affected us as teachers. *We* can share things in the future around campus."

In a traditional school organization, most teachers felt, the lack of opportunity to interact with teachers from other departments restricts the development of a collective consciousness. "An issue on the positive side," said one teacher about the project, "is that we've been able to communicate between the teachers on a daily or weekly basis. It's pretty evident if a student is not [himself or herself]. We work together on understanding some of that behavior."

Effective Strategies and Practices. A major aim of AVANCE was to implement effective instructional strategies that promoted an integrated curriculum and student interaction. The same English, math, and science content was included, but it was taught

Alternative Classroom Techniques with a different approach. The new method required more hands-on activities, language-proficiency grouping, and gestures and drama, as these examples from teachers illustrate:

> "[I] put notes on the board or the overhead; explaining or rephrasing of texts; doing symbols or pictures of concepts. I did more close activities; I tried to work in a tutorial second period."

> "I use the same palette of tools [found in traditional classrooms but]…in different combinations…[such as] prior knowledge—saying, 'You are the content of the course,'

Using Instructional Conversations for Content-Area Learning

Becoming a Responsive Teacher

As we saw in Chapter 6, it is common during the early phase of an instructional conversation (IC) for middle school teachers and students to converse about a broad range of topics, particularly individual experience and background knowledge. In this way, teachers develop a comfort zone that encourages all students to share. For language minority students, talking with peers and teacher means an opportunity to express language with native speakers of both the language of the home and the language of instruction. For teachers, student talk is a rich source of information about students' life experiences and funds of knowledge, a basis for relationship, and an occasion for authentic assessment. In conversation, student talk reveals students' language proficiency in the languages of home and of instruction.

In early IC conversation, what appears to be divergent—even desultory—discussion is important preparation for scaffolding later conversation to intended IC themes. The teacher used a photograph from a familiar television series, "Star Trek," as a stimulus for students to talk about space, a topic used in the regular class. In the conversation, students moved the topic to talk about stars.

Edgar: They have like holes in them. Like . . . [he moves his hands in a curved motion]

Teacher: They have like holes in the planet. "Holes in the planet," does anybody know what else we can call that ?

Edgar: *Pozos.* [Holes.] [Another student, Concha, giggles.]

Edgar: Shooting stars.

Teacher: Shooting stars? Is that another name for the holes in the planet? Does anyone know what those . . .

Edgar: Shooting stars are like stars, but they go shoo [hand gesture] really fast and when you see them, you can make a wish.

In this excerpt, the students participated comfortably in English, with one response in Spanish, giving the teacher a sense of their proficiency when conversing on a general topic. Following the direction of students' talk about stars, the teacher encouraged students' participation using prompts, restatements, and probes.

Luis: The black hole.

Teacher: Do you know what the black hole is? Can you explain that to everybody in the group?

Luis: It is a round thing, and it has a lot of stars.

Continued   Using Instructional Conversations
for Content-Area Learning

Teacher: It is a round thing. [Turns and writes on board.] So you're saying that the black hole is something . . .

Concha: I don't really care.

Teacher: . . . that is round [Luis and Concha laugh] and it has, what else
did you say?

Luis: Stars.

In this excerpt, the teacher pressed students to use language to express what they know, while ignoring an inappropriate response.
Without interrupting the IC, she heard one student's attitude toward
the topic. She and the other students modeled constructive social interaction that comprises appropriate IC talk. For students with little
experience of conversation on an academic content topic, the ordinary conversational quality of early IC is familiar, attractive, and an
occasion to model conversation conventions.

As the excerpts show, the students' conversation was at an everyday
level and included an instance of Spanish-language use. The students
used incomplete utterances and gestures to convey meaning. The
teacher demonstrated prompting, questioning, and restating student
utterances. In the following excerpt, the teacher continues to probe
students' background knowledge about planets and draw every student into participation in the conversation.

Teacher: Yeah, and we also talked about some other characteristics. We
talked about colors and sometimes some planets have rings around
them, right?

Luis: Just Saturn has it, only Saturn? [He looks up at a poster.]

Teacher: I don't know, does only Saturn have a ring around it?

Daniel: Yeah.

Teacher [to Daniel]: Yeah?

Luis: They're all right there. Look. [Points up. Everyone is looking up
at the wall poster.]

Edgar: Yeah, I think, huh?

Concha: Yeah, only Saturn.

Teacher [to Concha]: Only Saturn? [Concha nods.]

The teacher tracked the conversation by listing space- and math-
related terms on a chart. The list became another visual aid for
reviewing the course of conversation and for transitioning conversation to math topics—in this case, measurement.

Continued   Using Instructional Conversations
                for Content-Area Learning

Teacher: When we look up here, do we see any words, on our list that we made, that have to do with math?

Luis: Yeah.

Teacher: Like what?

Luis: Star Trek.

Concha: Saturn.

Teacher: Star Trek?

Luis: Like in the movies, like in . . . ?

Teacher: What does that have to do with math?

Luis: Mmm, on the machines, the computers that they have on the *Enterprise*, like they measure stuff.

Teacher: They measure stuff? With their computers, okay. Yeah, so the computers on a starship would help you measure, like measure what? What sort of things?

Luis: Planets.

Using Luis's speculation about measuring planets, the teacher hooked onto a mathematics topic. Luis's answer, "planets," was an opportunity to bridge the conversation to measurement.

The first IC yielded abundant information about students' language proficiency, content knowledge, and conversational skills. The majority of the students participated competently at a general or everyday level, while one, Concha, was extremely reticent. The teacher accepted all student responses nonjudgmentally, including inappropriate contributions, treating them as genuine attempts to contribute to the conversation.

From "Enacting instructional conversations with Spanish-speaking students in middle school mathematics" by S. Dalton and J. Simon, p. 8–9. © 1995. Reprinted by permission of the National Center for Research on Cultural Diversity and Second Language Learning and the authors.

telling them my job will change [the text] rather than looking at [the] text as school, looking at their experience as the source of knowledge."

Specially Designed Academic Instruction in English (SDAIE). Of particular significance for non-Spanish-speaking teachers in AVANCE was the use of Specially Designed Academic Instruction in English (SDAIE) techniques (Becijos, 1997). These strategies attempt to minimize the use of English as the primary mode of

Continued   Using Instructional Conversations
              for Content-Area Learning

Meeting the Challenge

1. Instructional engagement is particularly important in moving older
   students from what they know or understand toward new concepts
   and understandings.

   A. Consider introducing a new scientific concept to students. How
   would you introduce the concept to ensure student engagement?

   B. Do the same for a mathematics or social science concept (the
   concept of "ego" in psychology or the "depression/recession"
   cycles in economics are always good ones).

2. In the preceding dialogues, where would you have responded differently as the teacher? Why?

3. Student engagement in the learning process does not always involve communicative acts. Think of some examples of student engagement that are like these. How can they be enlisted to help other
   forms of student engagement like the ones depicted previously?

delivering content-based instruction while tapping the existing
knowledge base of the students. By using SDAIE techniques,
teachers can enable students to do the following:

Benefits of SDAIE

1. Present their own abilities that do not depend only on English
   proficiency (for example, by making material representations
   or using pictures to portray a science concept)

2. Connect their real-world experiences to the subject under
   study (for example, by beginning with fiction the students
   have read in their primary language or analyzing biological
   phenomena present in their own lives)

3. Utilize their talents not normally interjected into academic
   content learning (for example, by incorporating music or
   drama into instruction)

4. Seek and receive support from their peers (for example, by
   working on group projects or community-based data-
   gathering)

5. Utilize diverse ways to focus on and analyze the assigned material (for example, by using journals and learning logs, **quickwrites,** or graphic organizers)

6. Connect content-area material through thematic units (for example, by presenting an interdisciplinary organization of the material in a theme)

Table 9.3 outlines how SDAIE strategies can be used to engage students in reading texts.

Learning from Project AVANCE

Project AVANCE attempted to realize the vision of creating a program specifically to give linguistically and culturally diverse students access to the content curriculum in their high schools and to expand their language skills. Principles developed by researchers and theoretical frameworks of "what works" for Hispanic students were closely examined and translated into actual practice. The collaborative team wanted to learn not only new instructional skills but also the theoretical perspectives with which such "effective" skills could be developed. The team established guidelines for a "tailored" program capable of improving the academic and social opportunities of all the participating students. The lengthy team discussions touched on the social, educational, racial, psychological, and structural changes needed to serve these students effectively. Some of the most salient issues the team considered were as follows:

Theory into Practice

1. The recruitment of students who met the requirements established by the team (grades, self-esteem, etc.)

2. The implementation of effective instructional methods to deliver a strong academic curriculum for students with limited English skills

3. Reliance on the suggestions provided by work conducted in elementary and junior high schools

4. The impact the program might have on the educational and social lives of the students

5. The positive and negative elements of the intervention

6. The most appropriate means of spending the limited financial resources the team received

The fact that the AVANCE team was able to conceptualize, create, and implement this project at a high school allows the researchers to offer various thoughts about its process and outcomes:

| **Table 9.3** | **SDAIE Techniques for Promoting Interactive Reading** |

Activities for Accessing a Text

1. Read portions aloud as an introduction.
2. Use guest speakers as classroom resources and to provide background experience.
3. Incorporate journal writing, quickwrites, or discussion about similar situations so that students can personally relate to the material.
4. Provide overviews and synopses for students; tell students they needn't understand every word of what they are going to read to still understand the main points.
5. Study vocabulary in context; students may keep vocabulary notebooks.
6. Provide background for students, such as information on the author, historical facts, or dates.
7. Use films, filmstrips, or recordings to evoke an interest in the material.
8. Use graphic organizers to help with vocabulary, upcoming concepts, or background information.

Activities for Addressing a Text

1. Explore text in depth; for example, study the implications of crucial quotations.
2. Use oral presentations; for example, present a scene from a literary work dramatically.
3. Let students take on the role of one of the characters or important figures from the text in written or oral work.
4. Have students keep reading logs to record quotations they like, to relate ideas to their own experience, and to make predictions.
5. Have students visualize the text artistically through illustrations, collages, charts, diagrams, time lines, and the like.
6. Establish collaborative groups for students to explore the work together.
7. Independently develop questions on the text to use in group or class discussion.
8. Evaluate the learning process and integrate it with students' prior knowledge.

Activities for Students to Select

1. Use parallel readings to illustrate common concepts and themes.
2. Create games or presentations relating to the reading.
3. Write and perform a play or reader's theater based on the reading.
4. Make connections to happenings in the news or in the students' lives.
5. Interview other students or adults relating to a topic introduced in the reading.
6. Research a topic of interest relating to the reading.
7. Write a letter, story, sequel, or poem on the topic of the reading.
8. Create a poster, mural, collage, or other artistic representations of the theme.
9. Relate the information to other content areas.
10. Use technology to represent the text; for example, create an audio- or videotape, or use the computer.

Source: Adapted from J. Becijos, *SDAIE: Strategies for Teachers of English Learners* (Bonita, CA: Torch Publications, 1997), p. 37.

Lessons of
AVANCE

1. With minimal administrative support, teachers can organize, create, and reorganize within a school's framework to improve the educational environment for students.

2. Allowing new teaching techniques and organizational methods into the classroom can enhance the learning of both teachers and students.

3. Educational change at the high school level must take into account volatile issues (for example, plans after high school and inter- and intragroup relations) that can affect the students on a daily basis.

4. Regardless of students' English-language knowledge, they will respond positively when they are academically challenged.

5. The means by which teachers meet to discuss their students must be significantly updated.

6. Hispanic students at the high school level must be provided with a challenging and integrated curriculum in order to optimize their opportunities to succeed in life.

Programs That Work to Enhance College Participation

Programs to enable minority students to participate more in higher education have evolved during recent decades, tending to become more comprehensive and to address more subtle obstacles to academic, social, and economic advancement. DeAcosta (1996) describes the history of such programs as beginning with meeting needs for financial aid, moving on to the improvement of students' academic skills (such as focusing on language arts and strengthening college prep curriculum), to attending to psychological and social factors (e.g., adding academic and career counseling) and to helping students negotiate the institutional culture of college. She and others (Gándara and Maxwell, 1998) identified the common characteristics of successful programs: sensitivity to individual students, to student cultures, and to the institution where the program is located; proactive interventions; focus on acceleration; enriched learning; small class size; and partnering with students' families and community.

Review of
Successful
Programs

This review of successful programs looks first at efforts to increase student access to higher education. These educational efforts are becoming more important as affirmative action programs are being eliminated throughout the United States (Wilson, 1999). The key barriers for culturally and linguistically diverse students to overcome seem to cluster around several domains: lack of information, counseling, and advisement; academic tracking in low-level course work; test requirements; course-taking patterns; underprepared teachers; low aspirations, expectations, and motivations; and the cost of higher education (PACE, 1997). We will employ a helpful typology utilized in a recent study of outreach programs performed by PACE (Policy Analysis for California Education) (1997) to describe programmatic effects. *Student-centered outreach* refers to predominantly academic development programs (and sometimes includes financial aid). *School-centered outreach* includes teacher development, recruitment and retention, and scholarship programs. Some programs combine features of both categories, but regardless of their orientation, their focus is on removing obstacles to participation in higher education. This section highlights programs that are student centered or student and school centered.

Student-Centered Programs

Early Outreach Partnerships by Colleges and Universities. The first of the system-wide outreach programs in California, the Early Academic Outreach Program (EAOP), began in 1976. Similar programs of early outreach, however, can be found throughout U.S. public universities as the schools attempt to recruit and prepare students for their institutions and for higher education in general. These outreach programs typically serve seventh- through twelfth-graders, enrolling thousands of students nationwide. Every teacher should know about the local, regional, or state efforts that can benefit her or his students. Although high school counselors are aware of these programs, many students never see the connection between the program's features and their own academic futures. However, teachers can play a strategic role in helping them make this connection. These programs have evolved to include academic skill development, motivational activities, and parent involvement activities (College Board, 1999). Nearly half of African American, Latino, and Native American graduating seniors in these programs continue with postsecondary education. This is impressive since the nationwide average of high school graduates from these groups who continue with postsecondary education after completing high school is fewer than 25 percent.

MESA. The Math, Engineering, and Science Achievement (MESA) program provides an academic enrichment program for precollege students at elementary schools, junior high schools, and senior high schools. A new effort, the Mathematics, Engineering, Science, and Agriculture Achievement (MESA2) program, introduces rural precollege students to high-tech opportunities in agriculture.

Founded in 1970, MESA has organized 20 centers that serve 13,857 students from 259 schools at all levels in California. In addition, seven other states have joined with California's program to form MESA USA. The main elements of the MESA model include academic enrichment, group study, academic and financial aid advising, career exploration, parent involvement, and teacher training. For the latter element (which stretches beyond the original student-centered focus), MESA offers training opportunities for its advisers, those math and science teachers who work with MESA students. MESA provides a three-day annual training institute so that advisers can learn new teaching techniques and hands-on activities. Companies and foundations have funded other MESA regional training opportunities. Many training sessions call for attendees to train other teachers, including non-MESA educators.

MESA high school seniors average a 3.13 GPA, compared with the statewide average of 2.78. They average a combined score of 903 on the SAT, which is comparable to the national average scores of all groups and much higher than the average scores of African Americans or Hispanics. These students complete physics, for example, at double the rate that students statewide do. Most impressive are the numbers of college-bound MESA graduates: 97 percent go on to college (75 percent of whom enroll at four-year colleges). Culturally and linguistically diverse students make up approximately 75 percent of the precollege MESA enrollment.

School-Centered Programs

AVID: Untracking Students. The AVID (Advancement Via Individual Determination) program was developed as an alternative to compensatory education and remedial tracking for underachieving high school students, especially those from ethnic and linguistic minority backgrounds. Mary Catherine Swanson, a member of the English Department, introduced the idea of untracking underachieving students to San Diego in 1980 at Clairemont High School, a predominately white school. *Untracking* became a way to educate minority students bused to Clairemont from predominantly ethnic minority schools in Southeast San Diego under a court-ordered desegregation decree. Unwilling to segregate African American and Latino students into a separate, compensatory curriculum, Swanson and the Clairemont faculty placed the bused students who had high test scores but low grades in regular college preparatory classes. In addition, these students were provided with special mentoring through an elective class. The AVID program soon spread beyond Clairemont

High School: by 1997, more than five hundred secondary schools in eight states and the U.S. Department of Defense Dependents Schools overseas had introduced AVID programs.

AVID: Eligibility | Those eligible for the AVID program are high school students who are members of low-income, ethnic, or linguistic minorities and who have average to high achievement test scores but whose grades average C. Once these high-potential, underachieving students have been identified and selected by AVID coordinators, their parents are contacted. Those parents who agree to support their children's participation in the AVID program sign contracts to authorize their enrollment.

The previously underachieving students who have been placed in college prep classes are not left to sink or swim. AVID arranges a system of supports to assist students in making the transition from low-track to high-track high school classes. Among the most visible supports in the AVID untracking program is a special elective class that meets for one academic period a day, 180 days a year, for three or four years. In addition to a classroom teacher, college tutors assist these students on a 7:1 student-to-tutor ratio.

AVID: Weekly Plan | AVID provides a basic plan for weekly instructional activities within the program's classrooms. Two school days are designated as tutorial days. On these days students work in small groups with the assistance of a tutor. On two other days, writing as a tool for learning is emphasized. On these days students engage in a variety of writing activities, including writing essays for their English, social studies, science, and history classes. Other important activities that occur within the classroom include instruction in note-taking, test-taking, and study strategies. One day a week, usually Friday, is a "motivational day." On these days guest speakers are invited to address the class or field trips to colleges are scheduled. By teaching these academic study techniques and exposing students to higher educational opportunities, AVID gives them explicit instruction in the implicit or "hidden" curriculum of the high school. In terms discussed earlier in this chapter, AVID provides Hispanic students with some of the "capital" at school that is similar to the capital that more economically advantaged parents give to their children at home.

AVID: Socialization | Institutional support of the students augments this explicit socialization process. AVID coordinators help remove impediments to students' academic achievement by intervening on their behalf with high school teachers, administrators, and college admissions officers. AVID also connects its students to social networks, thereby again increasing the amount of social capital available to them. If schools and their agents act collectively in a deliberate, intensive, and explicit fashion to generate a socialization process that produces the same sorts of strategies and resources available in privileged homes and institutions, then, working-class and minority youth can enjoy those same advantages.

Peer-group relations also support untracking. Participation in AVID publicly marks the students' group identity. Their notebooks clearly display the AVID logo, as does the AVID classroom that is used for lunch, social gatherings, and academic instruction. Within the social space demarcated for them, AVID students form new, academically oriented friendships and develop academic identities. The time that students spend together on field trips to colleges, in collaborative study groups, and in informal discussions with college tutors and guest speakers from local colleges and businesses also facilitates this process.

AVID: Results | From 1990 to 1992, the AVID program was studied in eight San Diego high schools to see whether previously underachieving students from low-income ethnic and linguistic minority backgrounds who had been placed in college-bound courses with high-achieving students had benefited academically and socially from the experience (Mehan, Villanueva, Hubbard, and Lintz, 1996). During the study period, 1,053 students who had participated for three years in the AVID untracking experiment graduated from 14 high schools in the San Diego City Schools (SDCS) system. During those same years, 288 additional students started the program but left after completing one year or less. Two hundred and forty-eight of the three-year AVID students and 146 of the one-year AVID students were interviewed.

Of the 248 primarily Hispanic students who "graduated" from AVID who were interviewed, 120 (48 percent) reported going on to attend four-year colleges, 99 (40 percent) reported going on to attend two-year colleges, and the remaining 29 students (12 percent) said they were working or doing other things. These outcomes are particularly impressive given that fewer than 20 percent of California's Hispanic high school graduates during the same years went on to attend a college or university. Of specific importance, 43 percent of the three-year AVID students went on to attend a four-year college. Nationally, this figure is 29 percent (Nora, Rendon, and Cuadraz, 1999). Therefore, in AVID, we find a program providing academic and social supports that significantly influence Hispanic students' college attendance. AVID addresses the highly tracked conditions that these students would ordinarily face and it alters the academic and social high school experiences of these students with highly positive results.

High School Puente. *Puente* means "bridge" in Spanish; the Puente Project was conceived of as a bridge from one segment of education to another. The High School Puente Project is an outgrowth of Puente's successful community college program, which was initiated at Chabot College in Hayward, California, in 1981 to address the problem of the low transfer rate of Hispanic students to four-year colleges and universities. The program combines innovative teaching and counseling methods with community involvement to provide a focused, supportive, and culturally sensitive learning environment to foster student success. The academic focus is on the development of critical analysis and writing skills, areas in which Latino students consistently underachieve. Since 1981, the program has expanded to 38 community colleges throughout California.

Puente: Goals | The High School Puente Project began in 1993 with a four-year pilot program to be tested in 18 California schools. The goal of High School Puente is to increase the number of Hispanics graduating from high school and enrolling in college. At each pilot high school, Puente students, who represent a wide range of skill and motivation levels, are enrolled in a Puente college prepatory English class for their ninth and tenth grades. The course is taught by a Puente-trained English teacher and integrates community-based writing, portfolio assessment, and Latino-authored literature into the regular core curriculum. The Puente counselor works closely with the Puente students and their parents to ensure that the students are enrolled in college prep courses and that the parents have the information they need to support their children's academic progress. In addition, a community mentor liaison (CML) both recruits mentors from the community to work directly with students and seeks resources from the business and professional communities to help support the program.

Puente: Relationships | The High School Puente model is "front-ended" in its resource allocations. Students are placed in the Puente classroom for the first two years of high school with the hope that this placement will provide the foundation to mainstream them successfully into the core college preparatory English classes. Counselors work most intensively with the students during these first two years, and the assigned mentor is also asked to maintain a relationship with the students during these years. It would be ideal, though not required, if the mentoring relationship could last longer than two years, but to date most have not. Hence, adults associated with the Puente program carefully monitor the first two critical years of high school. In subsequent years, students are encouraged to maintain the relationship with their Puente counselor, and when possible, also with the Puente teacher. In addition, the Puente Club is an avenue for maintaining the Puente connection. The counselor—and, in some cases, the teacher—works to maintain the club and its activities in an attempt to preserve the integrity of the Puente group and to encourage the students to support each other. Another strategy used by counselors to monitor the Puente students is to group them into one or more classes during their junior and senior years where the counselor can maintain contact with them and can organize activities through a single visit to the classroom. The design of the program emphasizes a strong start in the first two years, with continued counseling and monitoring of students in the final two years of high school.

The Puente intervention has three major components: instructional, counseling, and mentoring. Associated with each component is a cluster of activities and interventions.

Instructional Component. The instructional component consists of a two-year class in which students are enrolled during ninth and tenth grades. The class is composed entirely of the heterogeneous Puente cohort of 30 students. A specially trained Puente teacher focuses on intensive process writing instruction, the interweaving of acclaimed Latino literature into the regular ninth- and tenth-grade literature curriculum, and training and experience in the use of writing portfolios so that students may learn to critique their own writing, assess their progress, and establish their own high performance standards.

Each year that they are in the program, Puente teachers receive several weeks of training in Hispanic literature and cultural awareness, process writing, heterogeneous classroom instruction, and portfolio assessment. A portion of this training is provided during summer vacation, but an important element of the staff development is also continual contact and training throughout the school year. These sessions are of shorter duration than the summer program and occur at frequent intervals during the year, either on site or regionally, generally for one or two days at a time. The importance of these sessions is seen not only in their role as a means of providing continuous instruction for teachers (and counselors and community mentor liaisons) but also as a means of monitoring implementation of the program and allowing local staff to disseminate more broadly practices that have been developed at the site level.

Puente: Teacher Training

Students generally are required to write daily, in journals and in other forms; they also must maintain their own writing portfolios and assist fellow students in their writing. Their English courses cover the regular English curriculum as well as the Latino literature component. The Puente class also serves as an important forum for cultural discussions as well as for frequent presentations and conversations about colleges, careers, and personal aspirations.

Mentoring Component. The counseling component provides oversight of the Puente student's high school program, assuring that the student will be placed in college preparatory classes, that any deficiencies will be quickly noted and addressed, and that the student will be supplied with the information necessary to prepare himself or herself for postsecondary education. Counselors also participate in some Puente classroom activities to integrate themselves into the daily activities of the Puente students. These activities may include a planned writing experience, a session on university admission requirements (known as "a through f" in the California system), or some other focused activity. Counselors also arrange for college visits and other field trips and for parent and mentor meetings and events; most oversee the Puente Club, an extramural club where students get together for social events that support their college preparatory activities (e.g., plan for car washes and bake sales in order to support a field trip).

Puente: Function of Counselors

Counseling Component. The mentoring component is coordinated by a Community Mentor Liaison (CML), who seeks out appropriate mentors from the community for the students, trains them, and then matches these mentors with students in the program. The CML also works with the counselor to arrange appropriate activities for the students and mentors and then monitors these relationships. Mentors are encouraged to maintain relationships with the students for a minimum of two years, during which the goal is to meet with students at least monthly, either individually or in groups. Mentors are also urged to meet with the students' families, preferably in the family home in order to learn more about the student. Ensuring that these meetings occur regularly and that they are productive and satisfying for both mentor and student is a labor-intensive activity.

Puente: Mentoring Relationships and Tasks

In addition to locating, training, and monitoring mentors, the CML is also charged with a more vaguely defined community relations role—making presentations to local community groups and raising the profile of Puente in order to encourage greater community participation in the program by eliciting donations, resources, and volunteers to serve as mentors. For example, the CML may find companies that are willing to sponsor field trips, site visits, or even internships for Puente students. Some of these companies may be willing to make cash or in-kind contributions to Puente activities. However, the primary role of the CML is the rather arduous task of locating and training Hispanic professionals to mentor and serve as role models for high school students.

Puente: Results   The results of High School Puente are impressive (Gándara, Larson, Rumberger, and Mehan, 1998). At the end of their junior year, Puente students were significantly ahead of the control group in the number of college preparatory courses taken and in terms of their academic success (GPA attained). A constant increase in GPA generally characterized Puente students in later grades while the reverse was true for non-Puente control group students. In addition, 95 percent of Puente students felt confident that they knew what was necessary to apply to college; fewer than 33 percent of non-Puente students reported this same confidence. Also, by the twelfth grade, 91 percent of Puente students had taken the necessary college entrance exams while only 35 percent of the non-Puente students had done so. By twelfth grade, 53 percent of Puente students had actually completed applications to four-year colleges while only 25 percent of the non-Puente students had done so. The college matriculation rate was also double for Puente students.

In short, Puente students are more likely than non-Puente students to stay in school and to remain at the same school. They take and pass more college preparatory curses than non-Puente students do, their attitudes toward school are significantly more positive, their preparation for making college applications is stronger, their aspirations are higher, and they are more eager to be identified as "good students." Because we know that willingness to put forth effort makes the greatest difference in long-term academic success (Gándara, 1995), the reported willingness of Puente students to give up other things in favor of school and their openness to readily identify themselves as good students are especially compelling evidence that Puente can make a long-term difference in the lives of these students. A more positive attitude toward schooling combined with enhanced preparation for college would appear to be providing the Puente students with a substantial advantage as they look toward their futures (Gándara, 1997).

Implications for Intervention Programs

The findings of the programs discussed previously and those reviewed by others (Gándara and Jolly, 1999; Hope and Rendon, 1996) have several implications for programs that seek to enhance Hispanic students' academic achievement and move them successfully up the educational ladder:

- The evidence points to the critical importance of interventions that are consistent, intensive, and well articulated from grade to grade and that provide consistent monitoring of students throughout the secondary years. There is no point at which it appears safe to let down one's guard (Mehan et al., 1998). Students growing up in risky environments remain at risk throughout adolescence, even when they may appear to be on track. Sustaining educational gains requires that the intervention be maintained.

- All the programs attribute much of their success to the fact that at least one adult in the school setting takes personal responsibility for each student in the program. This adult may be a teacher, counselor, social worker, or mentor, but he or she must know and understand the student and his or her family situation and be ready and able to intervene on the student's behalf. Adolescence is not too late a period in which to make a substantial difference in students' lives; even the highest-risk low-income youth can be educationally engaged and can dramatically improve their achievement if provided with a comprehensive program that involves caring adult advocates.

- These programs have designed intervention components that address the issue of locating students in supportive peer groups that reinforce achievement-oriented behavior. It is essential that students receive consistent messages about the importance of staying in school and doing well. The effects of programs are strengthened when students band together to support a shared achievement ideology.

- The findings point to the need for increased time to achieve high academic goals. These findings are consistent with Puente's focus on providing supportive resources for students outside of school hours. Even before considering modifying or improving the quality of classroom practices, it seems necessary to increase the amount of time that previously low-achieving students spend on math, science, literature, and history. In effect, this is the approach that the highly celebrated Garfield High School teacher Jaime Escalante took with his previously underachieving Hispanic calculus students. Although he was rightfully applauded for his charismatic motivational efforts, one cannot overlook the fact that Escalante exponentially increased the number of hours, days, and weeks that his students spent in the classroom. Instead of spending 180 hours in business or consumer math during one academic year, his students spent three times that amount each year in advanced math courses (Escalante and Dirmann, 1980).

- Puente relied extensively on heterogeneous, collaborative grouping practices. Cooperative learning, the classroom practice of grouping students heterogeneously for the purpose of accomplishing tasks collaboratively, seems to help underachieving students improve their classroom performance while also helping high-achieving students maintain theirs.

- The successes of these programs have been built on sensitivity to the particular circumstances of the students' families and the creation of strategic places for students to interact in the school. The personal connections, however, must be predicated on honoring the cultural and linguistic practices of the students' homes. These programs have shown that parents can be recruited, if given respect and care, as powerful allies for enhancing the educational outcomes of their children and, by virtue of promoting the aspirations and achievements of significant numbers of students, for strengthening the schools which they attend.

Conclusion

This chapter has traveled a route from an individual assessment of "what works" for a student to a broader discussion of effectiveness issues and case studies that document effective instruction in middle school and high school. This route and the stops along the way provide detailed insights into the development and implementation of educational interventions in schools that serve diverse student bodies. These are instances that my own experiences and research suggest are valuable. Understanding the efforts described in this chapter will help us address the underachievement so often experienced by the diverse students in our middle and secondary schools.

It is important here to offer my thanks to the teachers, administrators, students, and parents at the sites in which these studies took place. Their contribution to our understanding of effective schooling has been significant. In particular, the teachers in these studies played a major role in making the educational programs work. I cannot say enough about their hard work, instructional skills, and personal commitment to serving as advocates for these students. It was as if the students were the teachers' own children. Such commitment to advocacy is very difficult to measure and quite impossible to teach. Yet in each of the case studies in this chapter, such unflagging dedication of the teachers was present in major proportions. It reminds me, as it did my colleagues, that effective schooling is a social enterprise conducted by individuals who care about one another, respect what they bring to the enterprise, and then go forward together. The ability to create such an enterprise is the key to the future success of educational professionals working with linguistically and culturally diverse students, their families, and their communities.

Summary of Major Ideas

1. Students who do not fit the "typical American" model are at particular risk at the secondary school level. However, they can achieve academic success if teachers are able and willing to adapt their pedagogy, curriculum, and expectations to the particular circumstances of such students.

2. Specific interventions such as Project Theme have been effective in promoting academic achievement in reading, language, writing, and mathematics among linguistically and culturally diverse students in middle school. Teachers' professional development and students' self-esteem and future aspirations are also enhanced by such programs.

3. Strategies that have been particularly effective in improving the academic learning of linguistically and culturally diverse students include the use of thematically integrated curricula, heterogeneous small groups, literacy activities, cooperative learning, and interactions that foster equal status and support effective learning.

4. Language-minority high school students are an especially neglected population in terms of education. Research has identified the following attributes of high schools that promote the academic achievement of such students: placing value on their language and culture, having high expectations for such students, making their education a school priority, training staff to serve them more effectively, offering them a variety of courses and programs, developing a counseling program that gives special attention to their needs, involving parents in their education, and having staff who are strongly committed to empowering these students through education.

5. Tracking, or the practice of directing students into low-, regular-, or high-achieving groups, can be especially detrimental for minority students. Once such students enter a track designated for low achievers, their chances for academic success are significantly limited.

6. In order to serve the linguistically and culturally diverse students in our high schools, we need to create robust academic programs that combine research, theory, and practice in an agenda of change. AVANCE is one such program that has successfully incorporated alternative instructional strategies to advance the linguistic minority student's literacy, mathematics, and English-language skills.

7. A commitment to maintaining high academic standards for all students, a willingness to involve students in the process of curriculum definition, the establishment of an open network for staff communication, and the use of Specially Designed Academic Instruction in English (SDAIE) are some of the strategies that have proved most effective in projects such as AVANCE. Central to the success of such a program is a collaborative team that is willing and able to conceptualize, create, and implement its guidelines and goals.

8. Programs like AVID and Puente have made significant strides in preparing more students for college. Every teacher should know about their successes.

Extending Your Experience

Your assignment is to assess in a critical and comprehensive manner the attributes of ethnic difference within two populations—*your family* and *one minority group* residing in your area (e.g., African American, Hispanic, Native American, Asian, etc.). These projects will require the clear consent of the informants involved and should include interviews, analysis, and a written report incorporating the following areas:

A. Description of informant (include yourself as an informant)
   1. Age, sex, self-identified ethnicity
   2. Family attributes (over three generations)
      (a) Work
      (b) Education (with an emphasis on secondary schooling)
      (c) Social status

B. Language history (over three generations)

C. Values (over three generations)
   1. Work
   2. Family
   3. Education (with emphasis on secondary schooling)
   4. Success/failure

D. Other cultural attributes

   Examples: social attributes (competition, sharing, groupings, etc.), sex roles, rites of passage, etc. (with particular emphasis on adolescence)

E. Future prospects for cultural maintenance/change

Share these reports with your colleagues so you can compare and contrast findings. Keep in mind that such sharing should maintain the highest levels of confidentiality regarding your informants. This suggested exercise should reveal in some detail the complexities over generations of "culture" and "culture change" that are particular to adolescence.

Resources for Further Study

Gándara, P. (1995). *Over the ivy walls: The educational mobility of low-income Chicanos.* Albany: State University of New York Press.

Focusing on the generational differences between two cohorts of Chicana doctoral students, Gándara examines the differences in their educational experiences. The reader gets a real sense of how students make decisions and negotiate life circumstances. She highlights experiences that shed light on strategies that are not acounted for in current models of academic achievement.

Gándara, P., and Bial, D. (1999). *Paving the way to higher education: K–12 intervention programs for underrepresented youth.* (Unpublished).

The authors identify the challenges that are potential obstacles that can prohibit minority students from succeeding in schools. They connect this discussion with the most current literature related to educational achievement and attempt to draw some conclusions about why these challenges continue to be problematic. As a way to alleviate the challenges, the authors focus on 13 academic programs that work for youth.

Gándara, P., and Maxwell-Joy, J. (1999). *Priming the pump: Strategies for increasing the achievement of underrepresented minority undergraduates.* New York: College Board Publications.

The authors identify higher education programs and strategies that can help to improve the representation of minorities in higher education, specifically at the undergraduate level.

Hawley, W. D., and Jackson, A. W. (Eds.) (1995). *Toward a common destiny.* San Francisco: Jossey-Bass.

This edited volume provides a comprehensive assessment of research on ethnic relations in the United States. Of particular interest are the issues of ethnic identity formation, group membership during adolescence, and the influence this identity has on school experiences. The book offers much more than a theoretical treatment of issues such as race, class, national identity, and group formation. The authors provide specific in-depth studies and analyses of direct importance to education.

Lucas, T. (1997). *Into, through, and beyond secondary schools: Critical transitions for immigrant youths.* New York: National

Center for Restructuring Education, Schools, and Teaching, Teachers College, Columbia University.

Lucas provides a comprehensive overview of the immigrant experience in the United States and its relationship to schooling. Immigrant students' lives are best understood as a set of critical transitions: from one schooling system to another, from complex micro- and macrosocieties to yet others. Focusing on secondary school transitions, this volume identifies four major attributes from recent research on immigrant students and highlights findings from excellent secondary schools. Specific examples are a major contribution of this volume.

Miller, L. S. (1995). *An American imperative: Accelerating minority educational advancement.* New Haven: Yale University Press.

The primary aim of this book is to have leaders and professionals in government, education, business, foundations, and the media think about what they can do collaboratively to resolve the educational crisis of minority students. Miller takes a very systemic approach to reducing the educational gap. That is, accountability is seen as a simultaneous event that has a long-term life span and involves the assistance of a variety of social institutions. Effectiveness is determined by the collaboration of efforts committed to improving the academic status of minority students.

National Task Force on Minority High Achievement. (1999). *Reaching the top: A report on the National Task Force on Minority High Achievement.* New York: College Board Publications.

The task force offers a set of recommendations and programs that work to rectify the gap in educational outcomes that continues to exist. Particular attention is paid to understanding the notion of achievement and its importance. Without some concerted effort to ensure the success of minority students, there will inevitably be economic and social consequences that will impact the lives of all citizens.

Orfield, G., and Miller, E. (Eds.). (1998). *Chilling admissions: The affirmative action crisis and the search for alternatives.* Cambridge, MA: Harvard Education Publishing Group.

This edited volume looks at the negative effects of anti–affirmative action policies. There is a real sense that less diversity on campus sacrifices the potential for an enriched educational experience for college students in general. Moving beyond the traditional debates and solutions, this book offers alternative paradigms that can reduce the hostility on many college campuses while still subscribing to the goals and objectives that characterize affirmative action.

Romo, H., and Falbo, T. (1996). *Latino high school graduation: Defying the odds.* Austin: University of Texas Press.

Paradoxically, while 35 percent of Latino students in the United States drop out of school, larger *absolute* numbers of Latino students are graduating from high school than ever before. Documenting the educational experience of one hundred students in an Austin high school, the authors identify the various obstacles and support strategies that the students encounter, and offer the following recommendations for school reform: (1) put the learning of students first, (2) clarify scholastic standards, (3) eliminate programs that lead to student failure, (4) reward participation in schoolwork, (5) emphasize hard work, (6) make school accessible, and (7) create clear pathways to outcomes.

Wilson, W. J. (1999). *The bridge over the racial divide: Rising inequality and coalition politics.* New York: Russell Sage Foundation.

William Julius Wilson campaigns for the formation of grassroots multiracial coalitions as a way for the economy to begin to take care of all citizens. Without these coalitions, there will continue to be a disparity in the distribution of monetary, social, and political wealth in our nation. He contends that a united front that stresses commonalities rather than differences, an alliance across race and class lines, specifically among the poor and the middle class, can vastly improve current conditions and generate policy solutions, alleviating the social, economic, and political ailments that are a constant part of these people's everyday realities.

Glossary

acculturation The process by which the members of a society are taught the elements of the society's culture.

act psychology A model for human cognitive processes that focuses on the assertion that the mental functions of perceiving, remembering, and organizing—ultimately knowing—are all acts of consumption.

affect A term used in psychology to refer to people's feelings and emotions as distinguished from their thoughts and actions.

Americanization *Assimilation* as it is practiced in the United States. See *assimilation.*

assimilation An approach to acculturation that seeks to merge small ethnically and linguistically diverse communities into a single dominant national institutional structure and culture.

bilingualism The ability to speak two languages with equal fluency.

Black English The most studied nonstandard American English dialect. Although its roots lie in African Creole and English, Black English has its own distinct syntactic, phonological, semantic, and vocabulary rules.

burnout Physical or emotional exhaustion, most often caused by a great deal of stress experienced over a long period of time.

code switching The production of mixed language utterances.

cohort rates report A report, compiled over a given time period, that describes what happens to a single group of students.

communication A combination of verbal and nonverbal systems that enables humans to encode meaning and transmit it to others.

connoisseur model A method of teacher assessment that allows experienced and knowledgable educators to train and judge other educators.

construct validity A measure of the extent to which individual items test what they are supposed to test.

constructivist perspective The belief that, for humans, knowing is the result of continual building and rebuilding.

contextualized language Language that conveys meaning using physical cues such as gestures, intonation, and other concrete representations characteristic of face-to-face communication.

cultural capital The notion, grounded in an economic perspective, that knowledge and ideas are a means of symbolic wealth that can be used to gain access to or maintain the use of resources. Thus, a primary way of building cultural capital is through education.

cultural systems approach The approach to education that considers the organization of a society, specifically the roles and status assigned to cultural groups within it, to be a major determinant of educational underachievement. Also known as *institutional racism, perceived labor market explanation, secondary cultural systems theory,* and *structural inequality.*

culture A system of values, beliefs, notions about acceptable and unacceptable behavior, and other socially constructed ideas characteristic of a society or a subgroup within a society.

culture concept A term defined by Edward Tylor in 1871 as "that complex whole which includes knowledge, belief, art, law, morals, custom, and other capabilities and habits acquired by man as a member of society."

curriculum The area of schooling that addresses the content of instruction.

decontextualized language Language that relies on abstract linguistic and cognitive cues that are independent of the communicative context.

dialect A regional variation of language characterized by distinct grammar, vocabulary, and pronunciation.

direct instruction A teaching strategy wherein the teacher transmits knowledge to students through modeling and step-by-step instructions.

disposition An individual's usual temperament and frame of mind.

distributive model of culture A model that implies that each individual's portion of the culture differs in some ways from that of any other individual.

double immersion A program whose goal is to produce a student population that is bilingual and bicultural.

ecology The study of the relationships between an organism and its environment.

ethnic A general term used to refer to groups of people who are differentiated by race, religion, nationality, and/or region of origin.

ethnic images A term used to designate general beliefs that people have about the characteristics and attributes of a cultural group.

event rates report A report, compiled within a single year, that gives the percentage of students who left high school without finishing work toward a diploma.

formative assessment A diagnostic tool that is used to identify areas of weakness in learning skills so that remedial action can be taken.

grammar The system of rules implicit in a language that allows words to be arranged with some regularity of structure.

group-oriented concept of culture The use of attributes that are shared by all individuals in a group to define culture.

holistic rating criteria A method of obtaining a score on a test, or a test item, that results from an overall judgment of performance using specified criteria.

individual-oriented concept of culture The use of individual attributes to identify participants of a culture.

inservice preparation Professional training for teachers who are already working in a classroom.

institutional racism See *cultural systems approach*.

instructional conversation (IC) Conversation that allows the student to engage the teacher and other students in an active way, thus leading to the parallel development of language and cognitive/academic content of relevance to the formal education process.

instructional discourse A teaching strategy that emphasizes discussion in the classroom.

intelligence The ability of an individual's mind to acquire and apply knowledge.

inter-rater reliability The consistency of rater judgments evaluating the work or performance of people.

L1 Term that refers to the primary language most often used in the student's home.

L2 Term often used to identify the student's nonprimary language, usually referred to as the language of schooling.

language The use by human beings of voice sounds, written symbols, and hand signals to communicate thoughts and feelings. For the purposes of this text, *language* is a complex interaction of many variables, including the verbal signal, the signal sender, the manner and context in which the signal is sent, the signal receiver, and previous experiences the sender and the receiver may have had with similar signals.

language minority student A student characterized by substantive participation in a non-English-speaking social environment who has acquired the normal communicative abilities of that social environment and is exposed to an English-speaking environment on a regular basis only during the formal school process.

language pragmatics The rules of a language as well as the cultural notions about what is considered appropriate and effective use of the language.

limited-English-proficient (LEP) A student identified as nonproficient in English based on (a) the use of a language other than English at home, (b) an English-language assessment performed by the school, and (c) low academic performance in English.

magnet school A school whose purpose is to attract a highly diverse set of students around a thematically designed curriculum that is multilingual and multicultural.

May 25 memorandum A memorandum issued by the U.S. Department of Health, Education, and Welfare in 1970 that clarified the mandate of the 1964 Civil Rights Act with respect to non-English-speaking populations of students.

meta analysis A method of analyzing and summarizing large numbers of research studies.

metalinguistic awareness The conscious awareness of how one uses language.

minority A group that is subordinate to another dominant group and that is subject to a negative power relationship.

modal grade level The academic level considered normal for students of a particular age.

multicultural education A curriculum whose content educates students on the contribution of more than one culture.

multilingualism The ability to speak three or more languages with equal fluency.

new immigrant A term that refers to an immigrant who is more or less educated than native-born Americans. Oftentimes this immigrant population is disproportionately comprised of people from several east and south Asian nations, whereas in previous years Europe was the source of large-scale emigration. These new immigrants are part of a more globalized economy, which may not necessarily offer them upward mobility.

participant-structured demand In education, the demands of instruction that are imposed on children by the organization of the learning environment itself.

participant structures In communication, the rules that govern who speaks when.

perceived labor market explanation See *cultural systems approach.*

personality The pattern of the character, behavioral, mental, and emotional traits of an individual. In education, the personality is a structure that reconciles a child's interpreted experiences with his or her emotional states.

phonology The study of speech sounds.

profession A job characterized by (1) the acquisition of knowledge obtained through formal education; and (2) an orientation toward serving the needs of the public, with an emphasis on ethical and altruistic concern for the client.

psychometrics The measurement of psychological attributes.

quickwrites A story or essay written by a student within a specific time frame. The writing is guided by a set of questions.

release-time meeting A meeting, usually three hours in length and scheduled during the school day, when teachers work collaboratively, often developing lessons together or observing each other. Substitute teachers are scheduled to teach classes during this time.

scaffolding An educational practice that provides support for children as they move between disparate home and school cultures.

schema A mental framework for perceiving the world.

secondary cultural systems theory See *cultural systems approach.*

second-language acquisition A process of language development whereby a child first acquires one language and then is exposed to and required to learn a second language.

sheltered English A varied set of instructional techniques that recognize that the student is not a primary speaker of English and that the teacher is not proficient in the student's primary language. These techniques maximize nonverbal instructional communication (e.g., the use of visual/demonstration strategies) that combines content (e.g., math, science, and social studies) and English-language-learning goals.

social distance The relationship between two cultures, determined in part by their relative status.

socialization The process through which prescriptions (ideas about what one should do) and prohibitions (ideas about what one should not do) are transmitted to members of the social group.

sociocultural theory An international intellectual movement that brings together the disciplines of psychology, semiotics, education, sociology, and anthropology.

Standard English The version of English that has the grammar, vocabulary, and pronunciation considered appropriate for most occasions of public discourse and for written communication.

status rates report A report, compiled at any point in time, that gives the percentage of the population of a given age range who either have not finished high school or are not enrolled.

structural inequality theory See *cultural systems approach*.

summative assessment A type of evaluation represented by terminal tests and examinations that are administered at the end of a course of training.

syntax The feature of a grammatical system having to do with word order.

transitional bilingual education The program that provides language minority students of Spanish-speaking backgrounds with a transition from early-grade instruction with Spanish emphasis to later-grade instruction with English emphasis and eventually to English-only instruction.

vocabulary The sum of words understood and used by an individual in any language group.

zone of proximal development (ZPD) A term defined by Tharp and Gallimore (1988) as "the distance between the actual development level as determined by individual problem solving and the level of potential development as determined through problem solving under adult guidance or in collaboration with more capable peers."

References

Abi-Nader, J. (1990a). A house for my mother: Motivating Hispanic high school students. *Anthropology and Education Quarterly, 21*(1), 41–58.

———. (1990b, April). *Helping minority high school students redefine their self-image through culturally sensitive instruction.* Paper presented at the annual meeting of the American Educational Research Association, Boston.

Ahlgren, I., and Hyltenstam, K. (Eds.). (1994). *Bilingualism in deaf education.* Hamburg : Signum.

Alder, M. (1982). *The paideia proposal: An educational manifesto.* New York: Macmillan.

Allport, G. (1954). *The nature of prejudice.* Reading, MA: Addison-Wesley.

Altus, W. (1945). Racial and bilingual group differences in predictability on mean aptitude test scores in an army special training center. *Psychological Bulletin, 42*, 310–320.

———. (1948). A note on group differences in intelligence and the type of test employed. *Journal of Consulting Psychology, 12*, 194–196.

Appleton, C. (1983). *Cultural pluralism in education: Theoretical foundations.* New York: Longman.

Aronowitz, S., and Giroux, H. A. (1991). *Postmodern education: Politics, culture and social criticism.* Minneapolis: University of Minnesota Press.

Au, K. (1979). Using the experience-text-relationship method with minority children. *Reading Teacher, 32*, 677–679.

Au, K., and Jordan, C. (1981). Teaching reading to Hawaiian children: Finding a culturally appropriate solution. In H. Trueba, G. Guthrie, and K. Au (Eds.), *Culture and the bilingual classroom: Studies in classroom ethnography* (pp. 139–152). Rowley, MA: Newbury House.

August, D., and García, E. (1988). *Language minority education in the United States: Research, policy, and practice.* Chicago: Charles C. Thomas.

August, D., and Hakuta, K. (1997). *Improving schooling for language-minority children: A research agenda.* Washington, DC: National Council Research.

Baca, L., and Cervantes, H. T. (Eds.). (1998). *The bilingual special education interface* (3rd ed.). Upper Saddle River, NJ: Merrill.

Baden, B., and Maehr, M. (1986). Conforming culture with culture: A perspective for designing schools for children of diverse sociocultural backgrounds. In R. Feldman (Ed.), *The social psychology of education* (pp. 289–309). Cambridge, MA: Harvard University Press.

Baetens Beardsmore, H. (1982). *Bilingualism: Basic principles.* Clevedon, UK: Tieto.

Bakhurst, D. (1990). *Consciousness and revolution in Soviet philosophy: From the Bolsheviks to Evald Ilyenkov.* Cambridge, UK: Cambridge University Press.

Banks, J. (1981). *Multiethnic education: Theory and practice.* Boston: Allyn and Bacon.

———. (1982). Educating minority youths: An inventory of current theory. *Education and Urban Society, 15*(1), 88–103.

———. (1993a). Multicultural education as an academic discipline: Goals for the 21st century. *Multicultural Education, 1*(3), 8–11.

———. (1993b). Multicultural education: Development, dimensions, and challenges. *Phi Delta Kappan, 75*(1), 22–28.

———. (1993c). The canon debate, knowledge construction, and multicultural education. *Educational Researcher, 22*(5), 4–14.

Banks, J., and Banks, C. A. (1995). *Handbook of research on multicultural education.* New York: Macmillan.

Barker, R. L. (1975). Implementing performance/competency-based teacher education: A view from the state level. *Journal of Industrial Teacher Education,12*(4) 22–28.

Beauf, J. (1977). Development of ethnic awareness in Native American children. *Developmental Psychology, 13*, 244–256.

Becijos, J. (1997). *SDAIE: Strategies for teachers of English learners.* Bonita, CA: Torch.

Bell, D. A. (1980). A reassessment of racial balance remedies–I. *Phi Delta Kappan, 62*(3), 177–179.

Bell, D., Kasschau, P., and Zellman, G. (1976). *Delivering services to elderly members of minority groups: A critical review of the literature.* Santa Monica, CA: Rand Corporation.

Benjamin, R., Pecos, R., and Romero, M. E. (1997). Language revitalization efforts in the Pueblo of Cochiti: Becoming "literate" in an oral society. In N. H. Hornberger (Ed.), *Indigenous literacies in the Americas: Language planning from the bottom up.* Berlin and New York: Mouton de Gruyter.

Ben-Zeev, S. (1977). The influence of bilingualism on cognitive strategy and cognitive development. *Child Development, 48*, 1009–1018.

Bergmann, R. (1994). Teaching sign language as the mother tongue in the education of deaf children in Denmark. In I. Ahlgrean and K. Hyltenstam (Eds.), *Bilingualism in deaf education, Stockholm, Sweden* (International Studies on Sign Language and Communication of the Deaf, Vol. 27). Hamburg: Signum Press.

Berk, R. A. (1986). *Performance assessment: Methods and applications.* Baltimore, MD: Johns Hopkins University Press.

Berman, P. (1992a). *Meeting the challenge of language diversity: An evaluation of California programs for pupils with limited proficiency in English.* Paper presented at a meeting of the American Educational Research Association.

———. (1992b). *The status of bilingual education in California.* Berkeley, CA: Paul Berman and Associates.

———. (1996). *High performance learning communities: Proposal to the U.S. Department of Education.* Emeryville, CA: Research, Policy, and Practice Associates.

Bernstein, B. (1971). A sociolinguistic approach to socialization with some reference to educability. In B. Bernstein (Ed.), *Class, codes, and control: Theoretical studies towards a sociology of language* (pp. 146–171). London: Routledge and Kegan Paul.

Beykont, Z. (Ed.). (2000). *Lifting every voice: Pedagogy and politics of bilingualism.* Cambridge, MA: Harvard Education Publishing Group.

Bialystok, E., and Hakuta, K. (1994). *In other words: The science and psychology of second-language acquisition.* New York: Basic Books.

Bigler, E. (1999). *American conversations: Puerto Ricans, white ethics, and multicultural education.* Philadelphia: Temple University Press.

Bilingual Education Act, Pub. L. No. 90-247, 20 Stat. 919 (1967).

Bilingual Education Act, Pub. L. No. 93-380, 88 Stat. 503 (1974).

Bilingual Education Act, Pub. L. No. 95-561, 92 Stat. 2268 (1978).

Bilingual Education Act, Pub. L. No. 98-511, 98 Stat. 2370 (1984).

Bloom, B. (1984). The search for methods of group instruction as effective as one-to-one tutoring. *Educational Leadership, 41*(8), 4–17.

Boggs, S. T. (1972). The meaning of questions and narratives to Hawaiian children. In Cazden, C., John, V., and Hymes, D. (Eds.), *Functions of language in the classroom.* New York: Teachers College Press.

Boggs, S. T., and Watson-Gegeo, K. (1978). Interweaving routines: Strategies for encompassing a social situation. *Language in Society, 7*(3), 375–392.

Bok, D. (1990). *Universities and the future of America.* Durham, NC: Duke University Press.

Boykin, A. W. (1983). The academic performance of Afro-Americans. In J. T. Spence (Ed.), *Achievement and achievement motives: Psychological and sociological approaches.* San Francisco: W. H. Freeman.

———. (1986). The triple quandary and the schooling of Afro-American children. In U. Neisser (Ed.), *The school achievement of minority children* (pp. 57–92). New York: New Perspectives.

Braker, J. S. (1975). From communication to language—A psychological perspective. *Cognition, 3,* 3–21.

Brophy, J., and Good, T. (1986). Teacher behavior and student achievement. In M. Wittrock (Ed.), *Handbook of research on teaching* (3rd ed.). New York: Macmillan.

Brown v. Board of Education, 327 U.S. 483(1954).

Calderón, M. (1991). Trainer of trainers: Professional development for diversity. In Office of Bilingual Education and Minority Language Affairs (Ed.), *Proceedings of the First National Research Symposium on limited English proficient students* (pp. 119–138). Washington, DC: U.S. Department of Education.

———. (1994). *Cumulative reports: Vol. 1. Bilingual teachers' development within school learning communities: A synthesis of the staff development model. Vol. 2. The impact of the bilingual cooperative integrated reading and composition model on bilingual programs.* El Paso: University of Texas, Department of Educational Leadership.

California Commission on Teacher Credentialing. (1991). *Teacher credentialing in California: A special report.* Sacramento: Author.

California Department of Education (1990). *High school curriculum frameworks.* Sacramento: Author.

California Tomorrow. (1995). *The unfinished journey: Restructuring schools in a diverse society.* San Francisco: Author.

———. (1996). *Looking in, looking out: Redefining child care and early education in a diverse society.* San Francisco: Author.

———. (July 1997). *The schools we need now: How parents, families, and communities can change schools.* San Francisco: Author.

Calkins, L. M. (1986). *The art of teaching writing.* Portsmouth, NH: Heinemann.

Campbell, A., and Frey, G. (1970). *Methods in social science research.* New York: Appleton Books.

Carter, T. P., and Chatfield, M. L. (1986). Effective bilingual schools: Implications for policy and practice. *American Journal of Education, 95*(1), 200–234.

Castaneda v. Pickard, 648 F.2d 989, 1007 5th Cir. 1981; 103 S. Ct. 3321 (1981).

Cazabon, M. T., Nicoladis, E., and Lambert, W. E. (1998). *Becoming bilingual in the Amigos Two-Way Immersion Program* (Research Rep. No. 3). Santa Cruz, CA: Center for Research on Education, Diversity, and Excellence.

Cazden, C. B. (1988). *Classroom discourse: The language of teaching and learning.* Portsmouth, NH: Heinemann.

Center for Applied Linguistics and Center for Research on Education, Diversity, and Excellence (CREDE). (1993). *Improving teaching and learning conditions: Erminda García's first grade classroom.* Washington, DC: Author.

Center for Research on Education, Diversity, and Excellence (CREDE): *http://www.cal.org/crede*

Chamot, A. U., and O'Malley, J. M., (1986). *A cognitive academic language learning approach: An ESL content-based curriculum.* Washington, DC: National Clearinghouse for Bilingual Education.

Chavez, L. (1991). *Out of the barrio: Toward a new politics of Hispanic assimilation.* New York: Basic Books.

Chavez, R. C. (1995). *Multicultural education in the everyday: A renaissance for the recommitted.* Washington, DC: The American Association of Colleges for Teacher Education.

Cherry, L. J. (1981). Teacher-student interaction and teachers' expectations of students' communicative competence. In O. Garnica and M. King (Eds.), *Language, children, and society* (pp. 246–261). New York: Pergamon Press.

Christian, D. (1994). *Two-way bilingual education: Students learning through two languages.* (Educational Practice Rep. No. 12). University of California, Santa Cruz: National Center for Research on Cultural Diversity and Second-Language Learning.

———. (1997). *Vernacular dialects in U.S. schools.* ERIC Digest. Washington, DC: ERIC Clearinghouse on Languages and Linguistics.

———. (1999). *Applied linguistics in 2000 and beyond.* Remarks presented at the annual meeting of the Linguistic Society of America, Los Angeles.

Christian, D., and Livermore, G. (1970). A comparison of Anglo-American and Spanish-American children on the WISC. *Journal of Social Psychology, 81,* 9–14.

Christian, D., and Whitcher, A. (1995). *Directory of two-way bilingual programs in the United States* (Rev. ed.). Santa Cruz: University of California, National Center for Research on Cultural Diversity and Second-Language Learning.

Chu, H., and Levy, J. (1988). Multicultural skills for bilingual teachers. *NABE Journal, 12*(2), 17–36.

Civil Rights Act of 1964, Pub. L. No. 88–352, 70 Stat. 241(1964).

Clark, K. B., and Clark, M. P. (1939). Segregation as a factor in the racial identification of Negro preschool children. *Journal of Experimental Education, 8,* 161–163.

Clark, R. M. (1983). *Family life and school achievement: Why poor black children succeed or fail.* Chicago: University of Chicago Press.

Cloud, N., Genesee, F., and Hamayan, E. (2000). *Dual language instruction: A handbook for enriched education.* Boston: Heinle and Heinle.

Cohen, N. E., and Pompa, D. (1994). *Multicultural perspectives on quality in early care and education: Culturally specific practices and universal outcomes.* Quality 2000, Advancing Early Care and Education. Working paper, Yale University, New Haven, CT.

Colangelo, N., Foxley, C. H., and Dustin, D. (Eds.). (1982). *The human relations experience.* Monterey, CA: Brooks/Cole.

Cole, R. W. (1995). *Educating everybody's children: What research and practice say about improving achievement.* Alexandria, VA: Association for Supervision and Curriculum Development.

———. (1996). *Cultural psychology: A once and future discipline.* Cambridge, MA: Belknap Press of Harvard University Press.

Coleman, J. S. (1963). *The adolescent society: The social life of the teenager and its impact on education.* New York: The Free Press.

College Board (1999). *Report of the task force on minority high achievement.* New York: Author.

College Board and the Western Interstate Commission for Higher Education. (1991). *The road to college: Educational progress by race and ethnicity.* New York: College Board.

Collier, V. P. (1985). University models for ESL and bilingual teacher training. Washington, DC: National Clearinghouse for Bilingual Education.

———. (1995). Acquiring a second language for school. *Directions in Language and Education, 1*(4) [On-line]. Washington, DC: National Clearinghouse for Bilingual Education. Available: *http://www.ncbe.gwu.edu*

Comer, J. P. (1997). *Waiting for a miracle: Why schools can't solve our problems—and how we can.* New York: Dutton.

Committee for Economic Development. (1991). *The unfinished agenda: A new vision for child development and education.* New York: Author.

Coons, J. E., Clune, W., III, and Sugarman, S. D. (1970). *Private wealth and public education.* Cambridge, MA: Harvard University Press.

Cooper, C. R., Baker, H., Polichar, D., and Welsh, M. (1991). *Ethnic perspectives on individuality and correctedness in adolescents' relationships with family and peers.* Paper presented at the meeting of the Society for Research in Adolescence, Alexandria, VA.

Corder, S. P. (1967). The significance of learners' errors. *International Review of Applied Linguistics in Language Teaching, 5,* 161–170.

Council of the Great City Schools: *http://www.cgcs.org*

Crawford, J. (1995). *Bilingual education : History, politics, theory, and practice* (3rd ed.). Los Angeles: Bilingual Educational Services.

Cuellar, J. B. (1980). A model of Chicano culture for bilingual education. In R. Padilla (Ed.), *Ethnoperspectives in bilingual research, Vol. II: Theory in bilingual education.* Ypsilanti, MI: Eastern Michigan University, Department of Foreign Languages and Bilingual Studies.

Cultural diversity and early education: What children bring to school [On-line]. Available: *http://www.nap.edu/reading room/books/earlyed/chapter3.html*

Cummins, J. (1979). Linguistic interdependence and the educational development of bilingual children. *Review of Educational Research, 19,* 222–251.

———. (1981). The role of primary language development in promoting educational success for language minority students. In California State Department of Education, *Schooling and language minority students: A theoretical framework* (pp. 3–50). Los Angeles: Evaluation, Dissemination, and Assessment Center.

———. (1984a). Wanted, a theoretical framework for relating language proficiency to academic achievement among bilingual students. In C. Rivera (Ed.), *Language proficiency and academic achievement.* Clevedon, UK: Multilingual Matters.

———. (1984b). *Bilingualism and special education.* San Diego: College Hill Press.

———. (1986). Empowering minority students: A framework for intervention. *Harvard Educational Review, 56*(1), 18–35.

———. (1989). *Empowering minority students.* Sacramento: California Association for Bilingual Education.

———. (1991). Interdependence of first- and second-language proficiency in bilingual children. In E. Bialystok (Ed.), *Language processing in bilingual children* (pp. 70–89). Cambridge, UK: Cambridge University Press.

Dalton, S., and Sison, J. (1995). *Enacting instructional conversation with Spanish-speaking students in middle school mathematics* (Research Report 12). Santa Cruz: University of California, National Center for Research on Cultural Diversity and Second-Language Learning.

D' Andrade, R. (1995). *The development of cognitive anthropology.* New York : Cambridge University Press.

Darcy, N. T. (1953). A review of the literature of the effects of bilingualism upon the measurement of intelligence. *Journal of Genetic Psychology, 82,* 21–57.

———. (1963). Bilingualism and the measurement of intelligence: Review of a decade of research. *Journal of Genetic Psychology, 103,* 259–282.

Davies, S. N. (1991). The transition toward bilingual education of deaf children in Sweden and Denmark: Perspectives on language. *Sign Language Studies, 7,* 169–195.

Davis, D., Davis, T., and Leppo, M. (1999). *First class teachers speak out.* Washington, DC: Sallie Mae Education Institute.

Davis, D., and Leppo, M. (1999). *A first–class look at teaching.* Washington, DC: Sallie Mae Education Institute.

Davis, R. B., Maher, C. A., and Noddings, N. (Eds.). (1990). *Constructivist views on the teaching and learning of mathematics.* Reston, VA. : National Council of Teachers of Mathematics.

DeAcosta, M. (1996). *Characteristics of successful recruitment and retention programs for Latino students* (Research Report No. 15). Cleveland, OH: Cleveland State University Urban Child Research Center.

Delgado-Gaitan, C. (1991). Involving parents in schools: A process of empowerment. *American Journal of Education, 100*(1), 20–46.

Delgado, R. (Ed.). (1995*). Critical race theory: The cutting edge.* Philadelphia: Temple University Press.

Delpit, L. (1995). *Other people's children: Cultural conflict in the classroom.* New York: New Press.

Delpit, L. D. (1988). The silenced dialogue: Power and pedagogy in educating other people's children. *Harvard Educational Review, 58*(3), 280–298.

Developmental Associates. (1984). *Final report: Descriptive study phase of the national longitudinal evaluation of the effectiveness of services for language minority limited English proficient students.* Arlington, VA: Author.

———. (1993). *Final report: Descriptive study phase of the national longitudinal evaluation of the effectiveness of services for language minority limited English proficient students.* Arlington, VA: Author.

Dewey, J. (1916). *Democracy and education: An introduction to the philosophy of education.* New York: Macmillan.

———. (1921). *Reconstruction and philosophy.* London: University of London Press.

Diaz, R. M. (1985). Bilingual cognitive development: Addressing these gaps in current research. *Child Development, 56,* 1376–1388.

———. (1983). The impact of bilingualism on cognitive development. In E. W. Gordon (Ed.), *Review of research in education* (Vol. 10, pp. 23–54). Washington, DC: American Educational Research Association.

Diaz, R. M., and Klinger, C. (1991). Towards an exploratory model of the interaction between bilingualism and cognitive development. In E. Bialystock (Ed.), *Language processing in bilingual children* (pp. 140–185). New York: Cambridge University Press.

Diaz, S., Moll, L. C., and Mehan, H. (1986). Sociocultural resources in instruction: A context-specific approach. In Bilingual Education Office (Ed.), *Beyond language: Social and cultural factors in schooling language minority students* (pp. 197–230). Los Angeles: California State University, Evaluation, Dissemination, and Assessment Center.

Diversity Database: *http://www.inform.umd.edu:8080/EdRes/Topic/Diversity*

Dolson, D. (1984). *The influence of various home bilingual environments on the academic achievement, language development, and psychosocial adjustment of fifth- and sixth-grade Hispanic students.* Unpublished doctoral dissertation, University of San Francisco.

Donald, M. (1991). *Origins of the modern mind: Three stages in the evolution of culture and cognition.* Cambridge, MA: Harvard University Press.

Drasgow, E. (1993). Bilingual/bicultural deaf education: An overview. *Sign Language Studies, 80,* 243–266.

———. (1998). American Sign Language as a pathway to linguistic competence. *Exceptional Children, 64*(3), 329–342.

Dugger, W. E. (1999). Putting technology education standards into practice. *NASSP Bulletin, 83*(608), 57–63.

Dulay, H., and Burt, M. (1974a). A new perspective on the creative construction process in children. *Language Learning, 24,* 253–278.

———. (1974b). *Natural sequence in child second-language acquisition.* Working paper on bilingualism, The Ontario Institute for Studies in Education, Toronto.

Duquette, G. (1991). Cultural processing and minority language children with needs and special needs. In G. Duquette and L. Malve (Eds.), *Language, culture, and cognition.* Philadelphia: Multilingual Matters.

Duran, R. (1983). *Hispanics' education and background: Predictors of college achievement.* New York: College Entrance Examination Board.

———. (1986). *Improving Hispanics' educational outcomes: Learning and instruction.* Unpublished manuscript, Graduate School of Education, University of California, Santa Barbara.

Dwyer, C. (1991). *Language, culture and writing* (Working paper 13), Berkeley: University of California, Center for the Study of Writing.

Dyson, A. H. (1983). The role of oral language in early writing processes. *Research in the Teaching of English, 17,* 1–30.

———. (1995). *Writing children: Reinventing the development of childhood.* Berkeley: University of California, National Center for the Study of Writing; and Washington, DC: U.S. Department of Education, Office of Educational Research and Improvement, Educational Resources Information Center.

Eckert, P. (1989). *Jocks and burnouts: Social categories and identity in high school.* New York: Teachers College Press.

Edelsky, C., Altwerger, B., and Flores, B. (1991). *Whole language : What's the difference?* Portsmouth, NH: Heinemann.

Eder, D. (1982). Difference in communication styles across ability groups. In L. C. Wilkinson (Ed.), *Communicating in the classroom* (pp. 245–263). New York: Academic Press.

Edmonds, R. (1979a). Effective schools for the urban poor. *Educational Leadership, 37,* 20–24.

———. (1979b). Some schools work and more can. *Social Policy, 9*(5), 28–32.

Education Alliance: *http://www.brown.edu/Research/The_Education_Alliance/*

Edwards, J. (1981). *Ratings of black, white and Acadian children's speech patterns.* Unpublished doctoral dissertation, Mount St. Vincent University, Halifax, Nova Scotia, Canada.

———. (1995). A commentary on discursive and cultural psychology. *Culture and Psychology, 1,* 55–65.

Elam, S. (1972). Acculturation and learning problems of Puerto Rican children. In F. Corradasco and E. Bucchini (Eds.), *The Puerto Rican community and its children on the mainland.* Metuchen, NJ: Scarecrow Press.

Elementary and Secondary Education Act of 1965, Title II, Pub. L. 89-10, Stat. 27 (1965).

Epstein, J. L. (1995). School/family/community partnerships: Caring for the children we share. *Phi Delta Kappan, 76*(9), 701–712.

Equal Educational Opportunities and Transportation Act of 1974, Pub. L. 93-830, Stat. 514 (1974).

ERIC Clearinghouse on Urban and Minority Education: *http://www.tc.columbia.edu/academic/iume/iume.htm*

Erickson, F. (1987). Transformation and school success: The politics and culture of educational achievement. *Anthropology and Education Quarterly, 18*(4), 335–355.

Ervin-Tripp, S. M. (1974). Is second-language learning like the first? *TESOL Quarterly, 8*(2), 111–127.

Escalante, J., and Dirmann, J. (1990). The Jaime Escalante math program. *Journal of Negro Education, 59*(3), 407–423.

Faltis, C. J., and Hudleson, S. J. (1997). *Bilingual education in elementary and secondary school communities: Toward* *understanding and caring*. Boston: Allyn and Bacon.

Fashola, O. S., Slavin, R., Calderón, M., and Durán, R. (1997). *Effective programs for Latino students in elementary and middle schools* (Report No. 11). Baltimore: Center for Research on the Education of Students Placed at Risk.

Fasold, R. W. (1972). *Tense marking in Black English: A linguistic and social analysis* (Urban Language Series, No. 8). Arlington, VA: Center for Applied Linguistics.

Feldman, C., and Shen, M. (1971). Some language-related cognitive advantages of bilingual five-year-olds. *Journal of Genetic Psychology, 118*, 235–244.

Feldt, L. S., and Brennan, R. C. (1989). Reliability. In R. L. Linn (Ed.), *Educational Measurement* (3rd ed., pp. 105–146). New York: American Council on Education and Macmillan.

Fernandez, R., and Shu, G. (1988). School dropouts: New approaches to an enduring problem. *Education and Urban Society, 2*(4), 363–386.

Ferreiro, E. (1988, April). *Emergent literacy*. Paper presented at the annual convention of the American Educational Research Association, New Orleans.

Ferreiro, E., and Teberosky, A. (1982). *Literacy before schooling*. Exeter, NH: Heinemann.

Fiere, P. (1970). *Pedagogy of the oppressed*. New York: Seabury Press.

Figueroa, R., and García, E. (1994). Issues in testing students from culturally and linguistically diverse backgrounds. *Multicultural Education, 2*(1), 10–24.

Figueroa, R., and Hernandez, S. (2000). *Testing Hispanic students in the United States: Technical and policy issues*. Washington, DC: President's Advisory Commission on Educational Excellence for Hispanic Americans.

Fillmore, L. W. (1982). Language minority students and school participation: What kind of English is needed? *Journal of Education, 164*(3), 143–156.

Fine, M. (1993). A parent involvement. *Equity and Choice, 9*(3), 4–8.

Finley, M. K. (1984). Teachers and tracking in a comprehensive high school. *Sociology of Education, 57*(4), 233–243.

Fishman, J. A. (1990). What is reversing language shift (RLS) and how can it succeed? *Journal of Multilingual and Multicultural Development, 11*(1–2), 5–36.

Fix, M., and Passel, J. S. (1994). Immigrants and social services. *Migration World Magazine, 22*(4), 22–25.

Flores, B. M., and García, E. M. (1984). A collaborative learning and teaching experience using journal writing. *NABE: The Journal for the National Association for Bilingual Education, 8*(2), 67–83.

Fordham, S. (1988). Racelessness as a factor in black students' school success: Pragmatic strategy or pyrrhic victory? *Harvard Educational Review, 58*(1), 54–83.

Fradd, S. (1997). School-university partnerships to promote science with students learning English. *TESOL Journal, 7*(1), 35–40.

Frankenburgh, R. (1993). *The sociolinguistics of society*. Oxford, England: Blackwell.

Frase, M. (1989). *Dropout rates in the United States: 1988* (Analysis report). Washington, DC: Superintendent of Documents, U.S. Government Printing Office.

Frederiksen, J. R., and Collins, A. (1989). A systems approach to educational testing. *Educational Researcher, 18*(9), 27–32.

Freedman Warshauer, S. (1994). *Exchanging writing, exchanging cultures: Lessons in school reform from the United States and Great Britain*. Cambridge, MA: Harvard University Press.

Freeman, Y. S., and Freeman, D. E. (1997). *Teaching reading and writing in Spanish in the bilingual classroom*. Portsmouth, NH: Heinemann.

Friedson, E. (1986). *Professional powers*. Chicago: University of Chicago Press.

Galambos, S. J., and Hakuta, K. (1988). Subject-specific and task-specific characteristics of metalinguistic awareness in bilingual children. *Applied Psycholinguistics, 9,* 141–162.

Gallas, K. (1991). Arts as epistemology: Enabling children to know what they know. *Harvard Educational Review, 61,* 40–50.

Gallimore, R., et al. (1986). Self-regulation and interactive teaching: The effects of teaching conditions on teachers' cognitive activity. *Elementary School Journal, 86*(5), 613–631.

Gallimore, R., and Tharp, R. G. (1989). *Challenging cultural minds.* London: Cambridge University Press.

Gándara, P. (1995). *Over the ivy walls: The educational mobility of low-income Chicanos.* Albany: State University of New York Press.

———. (1997). *High School Puente evaluation report No. 3.* Davis: University of California.

———. (Ed.). (2000). *The dimensions of time and the challenge of school reform.* Albany : State University of New York Press.

Gándara, P., and Bial, D. (1999). *Paving the way to higher education: K–12 intervention programs for underrepresented youth.* Unpublished manuscript.

Gándara, P., and Maxwell-Jolly, J. (1999). *Priming the pump: Strategies for increasing the achievement of underrepresented minority undergraduates.* New York: College Board.

García, E. (1983a). *Bilingualism in early childhood.* Albuquerque: University of New Mexico Press.

———. (1983b). *The Mexican-American child: Language, cognition, and social development.* Tempe: Arizona State University, Center for Bilingual Education.

———. (1986). Bilingual development and the education of bilingual children during early childhood. *American Journal of Education, 95* (1), 96–121.

———. (1988). Effective schooling for language minority students. In National Clearinghouse for Bilingual Education (Ed.), *New Focus* (pp. 49–62). Arlington, VA: Author.

———. (1989). Instructional discourse in "effective" Hispanic classrooms. In R. Jacobson and C. Faltis (Eds.), *Language distribution issues in bilingual schooling* (pp. 104–120). Clevedon, UK: Multilingual Matters.

———. (1990a). Language minority litigation policy: The law of the land. In A. Barona and E. García (Eds.), *Children at risk* (pp. 53–64). Washington, DC: National Association of School Psychologists.

———. (1990b). Bilingualism and the academic performance of Mexican-American children: The evolving debate. *ERIC Digest.*

———. (1991a). Attributes of effective language minority teachers: An empirical study. *Journal of Education, 173,* 130–141.

———. (1991b). Bilingualism, second language acquisition in academic contexts. In A. Ambert (Ed.), *Bilingual education and English-as-a-second language: A research annual* (pp. 181–217). New York: Garland.

———. (1991c). *Characteristics of effective teachers for language minority students: A review* (Education Report No. 1). Santa Cruz: University of California, National Center for Research on Cultural Diversity and Second-Language Learning.

———. (1991d). *The education of linguistically and culturally diverse students: Effective instructional practices.* Santa Cruz: University of California, National Center for Research on Cultural Diversity and Second-Language Learning.

———. (1992a). Effective instruction for language minority students: The teacher. *Journal of Education, 173*(2), 130–141.

———. (1992b). Hispanic children: Theoretical, empirical, and related policy issues. *Educational Psychology Review, 4*(1), 69–93.

———. (1993). Language culture and education. In L. Darling-Hammond (Ed.), *Review of research in education* (pp. 51–98). Washington, DC: American Education Research Association.

———. (1994a). Addressing the challenges of diversity. In S. L. Kagan and B. Weissbourd (Eds.), *Putting families first* (pp. 243–275). San Francisco: Jossey-Bass.

———. (1994b). The impact of linguistic and cultural diversity in American schools: A need for new policy. In M. C. Wang and M. C. Reynolds (Eds.), *Making a difference for students at risk* (pp. 156–182). Thousand Oaks, CA: Corwin Press.

———. (1994c). *Understanding the needs of LEP students.* Boston: Houghton Mifflin.

———. (1995). Educating Mexican American students: Past treatments and recent developments in theory, research, policy, and practice. In J. Banks and C. A. Banks (Eds.), *Handbook on research on multicultural education* (pp. 372–384). New York: Macmillan.

———. (1996). Early childhood education reinvention and education policy: Addressing linguistic and cultural diversity. *Early Child Development and Care, 123,* 203–219.

———. (1997). The education of Hispanics in early childhood: Of roots and wings. *Young Children, 52*(3), 5–14.

———. (1999). *Student cultural diversity : Understanding and meeting the challenge* (2nd ed.). Boston: Houghton Mifflin.

———. (2001). Bilingualism and schooling in the United States. *International Journal of the Sociology of Language* [in press].

García, E., Casimir, M., Sun Irminger, A., Wiese, A., and García, E. (1999). Authentic literacy assessment (ALA) development: An instruction-based assessment that is responsive to linguistic and cultural diversity. *Educators for Urban Minorities, 1,* 51–60.

García, E., and Gonzales, G. (1984). Spanish and Spanish-English development in the Hispanic child. In J. V. Martinez and R. H. Mendoza (Eds.), *Chicano psychology* (pp. 98–114). New York: Academic Press.

García, E., and Gonzalez, R. (1995). Issues in systemic reform for culturally and linguistically diverse students. *College Record, 96*(3), 418–431.

García, E., and McLaughlin, B. (1995). *Meeting the challenges of linguistic and cultural diversity in early childhood.* New York: Teachers College Press.

García, E., and Stein G. B., (1996). Multilingualism in U.S. schools: Treating language as a resource for instruction and parent involvement. *Early Childhood Development and Care, 127–128,* 141–155.

García, R. (1979). *Teaching in a pluralistic society.* New York: Harper and Row.

Gardner, H. (1983). *Frames of mind: The theory of multiple intelligences.* New York: Basic Books.

Gardner, R. C., and Lambert, E. (1972). *Attitudes and motivation in second-language learning.* Rowley, MA: Newbury House.

Garth, T., Elson, T., and Morton, M. (1936). The administration of non-language intelligence tests to Mexicans. *Journal of Abnormal and Social Psychology, 31,* 53–58.

Gay, G. (1975). Organizing and designing culturally pluralistic curriculum. *Educational Leadership, 33,* 176–183.

———. (1997). The relationship between multicultural and democratic education. *Social Studies, 88*(1), 5–11.

Geertz, F. (1973). *The interpretation of cultures: Selected essays.* New York: Basic Books.

Genishi, C. (1981). Code switching in Chicano six-year-olds. In R. Duran (Ed.), *Latino language and communicative behavior* (pp. 133–152). Norwood, NJ: Ablex.

Genishi, C., and Dyson, A. H. (1984). *Language assessment in the early years.* Norwood, NJ: Ablex.

Genzuk, M., and Hentschke, G. (1992). *Career pathways for practitioners: Progress report.* Los Angeles: University of California, USC Latino Teacher Project.

George Washington University Center for Equity and Excellence in Education. (1996). *Promoting excellence: Ensuring academic success of limited English proficient students.* Arlington, VA: Evaluation Assistance Center East.

Gibson, M. A. (1987). The school performance of immigrant minorities: A comparative view. *Anthropology and Education Quarterly, 18*(4), 262–275.

———. (1995). Promoting additive acculturation in schools. *Multicultural Education, 3*(1), 10–12, 54.

Gibson, M. A., and Ogbu, J. (Eds.). (1991). *Minority status and schooling: A comparative study of immigrant and involuntary minorities.* New York : Garland.

Giroux, H. A. (1992). *Border crossings: Cultural workers and the politics of education.* New York: Routledge.

Giroux, H. A., and McLaren, P. (1986). Teacher education and the politics of engagement: The case for democratic schooling. *Harvard Review, 56,* 213–238.

Gleason, J. B. (1988). *The development of language.* Columbus, OH: Merrill.

Goals 2000: Educate America Act, Pub. L. No. 103-227, 108 Stat. 125 (1994).

Goldenberg, C. (1992). *Instructional conversations and their classroom application* (Education Practice Report No. 2). Santa Cruz: National Center for Research on Cultural Diversity and Second-Language Learning, University of California.

———. (1993). Instructional conversations: Promoting comprehension through discussion. *Reading Teacher, 46*(4), 316–326.

Goldenberg, C., and Gallimore, R. (1990). *Meeting the language arts challenge for language-minority children: Teaching and learning in a new key* (Progress Report for 1989–90 to Presidential Grants for School Improvement Committee, University of California, Office of the President).

———. (1991a). Local knowledge, research knowledge, and educational change: A core study of early Spanish reading improvement. *Educational Researcher, 20*(8), 2–14.

———. (1991b). *Teaching and learning in a new key: The instructional conversation.* Paper presented at the annual meeting of the American Educational Research Association, Chicago, IL.

Goldenberg, C., and Patthey-Chavez, G. (1991). *Discourse processes in instructional conversations: Interactions between teacher and transition students.* Manuscript submitted for publication.

Goldman, S., and Trueba, H. (Eds.). (1987). *Becoming literate in English as a second language: Advances in research and theory.* Norwood, NJ: Ablex.

Gollnick, D. M., and Chinn, P. C. (1986). *Multicultural education in a pluralistic society.* New York: Maxwell Macmillan, International Press.

———. (1990). *Multicultural education in a pluralistic society* (3rd ed.). Columbus, OH: Merrill.

———. (1994). *Multicultural education in a pluralistic society* (4th ed.). New York: Maxwell Macmillan, International Press.

Gonzalez, G. (1990). *Chicano education in the segregation era: 1915–1945.* Philadelphia: The Balch Institute.

———. (1991). Spanish language acquisition research among Mexican-American children. *Early Childhood Research Quarterly, 6,* 411–426.

———. (1994). *Labor and community: Mexican citrus worker villages in a southern California county, 1900–1950.* Urbana: University of Illinois Press.

———. (1999). *Mexican consuls and labor organizing: Imperial politics in the American Southwest.* Austin: University of Texas Press.

Gonzalez, V. (Ed.). (1999). *Language and cognitive development in second language learning: Educational implications for children and adults.* Boston: Allyn and Bacon.

Gonzalez, V., Brusca-Vega, R., and Yawkey, T. (1996). *Assessment and instruction of culturally and linguistically diverse students with or at-risk of learning problems : From research to practice.* Boston: Allyn and Bacon.

Goodenough, W. H. (1981). *Culture, language, and society* (2nd ed.). Menlo Park, CA: Benjamin/Cummings.

Goodlad, J. (1984). *A place called school.* New York: McGraw-Hill.

Goodman, Y. (1980). The roots of literacy. In M. P. Douglass (Ed.), *Reading: A humanizing experience* (pp. 286–301). Claremont, CA: Claremont Graduate School.

Gordon, E. W. (1999). *Education and justice: A view from the back of the bus.* New York: Teachers College Press.

Grant, C. A. (1977a). The mediator of culture: A teacher role revisited. *Journal of Research and Development in Education, 11*(1), 102–117.

———. (Ed.). (1977b). *Multicultural education: Commitments, issues, and applications.* Washington, DC: Association for Supervision and Curriculum Development.

———. (1999). *Multicultural Research: A reflective engagement with race, class, gender, and sexual orientation.* London Philadelphia: Falmer Press.

Grant, C. A., and Secada, W. G. (1990). Preparing teachers for diversity. In W. R. Houston (Ed.), *Handbook of research on teacher education* (pp. 403–422). New York: Macmillan.

Grant, C. A., and Sleeter, C. E. (1987). An analysis of multicultural education in the United States. *Harvard Educational Review, 57,* 421–444.

———. (1988). Race, class, and gender and abandoned dreams. *Teachers College Record, 90*(1), 19–40.

———. (1996). *After the school bell rings* (2nd ed.). Washington, DC: Falmer Press.

Graves, D. H. (1994). *A fresh look at writing.* Portsmouth, NH: Heinemann; Toronto: Irwin.

Grosjean, F. (1996). Gating. *Language and Cognitive Processes, 11*(6), 597–604.

Guerra, M. H. (1979). Bilingualism and biculturalism: Assets for Chicanos. In A. Trejo (Ed.), *The Chicanos: As we see ourselves* (pp. 129–136). Tucson: University of Arizona Press.

Hakuta, K. (1974). *A preliminary report on the development of grammatical morphemes in a Japanese girl learning English as a second language.* In The Ontario Institute for Studies in Education, *Working Papers in Bilingualism* (Vol. 3, pp. 294–316). Toronto: Author.

———. (1986). *Mirror of language: The debate on bilingualism.* New York: Basic Books.

Hakuta, K., and August, D. (Eds.). (1997). *Improving schooling for language-minority children: A research agenda.* Washington, DC: National Academy of Sciences—National Research Council, Board on Children, Youth, and Families.

Hakuta, K., and D'Andrea, D. (1992). Some properties of bilingual maintenance and loss in Mexican background high-school students. *Applied Linguistics, 13,* 72–99.

Hakuta, K., Diaz, R., and Ferdman, M. (1986). *Bilingualism and cognitive development: Three perspectives and methodological implications.* Los Angeles: CLEAR.

Hakuta, K., and García, E. (1989). Bilingualism and bilingual education. *American Psychologist, 44*(2), 374–379.

Hakuta, K., and Snow, C. (1986, January). *The role of research in policy decisions about bilingual education.* Washington, DC: Testimony before the U.S. House of Representatives, Education and Labor Committee.

Hall, N. (1987). *The emergence of literacy.* Portsmouth, NH: Heinemann.

Halliday, M. A. K. (1973). *Explorations in the functions of language.* London: Edward Arnold.

Halliday, M. A. K., and Martin, R. J. (1993). *Writing science: Literacy and discursive power.* Pittsburgh: University of Pittsburgh Press.

Hamayan, E. V., and Perlman, R. (1990). *Helping language minority students after they exit from bilingual/ESL programs: A handbook for teachers.* Washington, DC: National Clearinghouse for Bilingual Education.

Hamers, J. F., and Blanc, M. (1989). *Bilinguality and bilingualism.* New York: Cambridge University Press.

Harrison, J. (1985). Functions of language attitudes in school settings. *Language in Society, 22,* 1–21.

Hawley, W. D., and Jackson, A. W. (Eds.). (1995). *Toward a common destiny: Improving race and ethnic relations in America.* San Francisco: Jossey-Bass.

Haycock, K., and Navarro, M. S. (1988). *Unfinished business: Fulfilling our children's promise: A Report from the Achievement Council.* Oakland, CA: Achievement Council.

Heath, S. B. (1981). Towards an ethnohistory of writing in American education. In M. Farr-Whitman (Ed.), *Variation in writing: Functional and linguistic cultural differences,* (Vol.1, pp. 225–246). Hillsdale, NJ: Erlbaum.

———. (1982). Questioning at school and at home: A comparative study. In G. D. Spindler (Ed.), *Doing the ethnography of schooling: Educational anthropology in action* (pp. 102–131). New York: Holt, Rinehart and Winston.

———. (1983). *Ways with words: Language, life, and work in communities and classrooms.* Cambridge, UK: Cambridge University Press.

———. (1986). Sociocultural contexts of language development. In California Department of Education, *Beyond language: Social and cultural factors in schooling language minority students* (pp. 143–186). Los Angeles: California State University, Evaluation, Dissemination, and Assessment Center.

———. (1989). Oral and literate traditions among black Americans living in poverty. *American Psychologist, 44*(2), 367–373.

Heath, S. B., and Mangiola, L. (1991). *Children of promise: Literate activity in linguistically and culturally diverse classrooms* (NEA School Restructuring Series). Washington, DC: National Education Association.

Henderson, R. W., and Landesman, E. M. (1992). *Mathematics and middle school students of Mexican descent: The effects of thematically integrated instruction* (Research Report No. 5). Santa Cruz: University of California, National Center for Research on Cultural Diversity and Second-Language Learning.

Henze, R., Regan, K., Vanett, L., and Power, M. (1990). *An exploratory study of the effectiveness of the Lower Kuskokwin School District's bilingual program.* Paper prepared for the Lower Kuskokwin School District, Oakland, CA.

Hernstein, R. J., and Murray, C. (1994). *The bell curve: Intelligence and class structure in American life.* New York: Free Press.

Hetherington, E. M., and Parke, R. D. (Eds.). (1988). *Contemporary reading in child psychology* (3rd ed.). New York: McGraw-Hill.

Hewitt, G. (1995). *A portfolio primer: Teaching, collecting, and assessing student writing.* Portsmouth, NH: Heinemann.

Hinton, L. (1994). *Flutes of fire: Essays on California Indian languages.* Berkeley, CA: Heyday Books.

Hoffman, D. M. (1988). Cross-cultural adaptation and learning: Iranians and Americans at school. In H. Trueba and C. Delgado-Gaitan (Eds.), *School and society: Learning content through culture.* New York: Praeger.

Hoffmeister, R. (1990). ASL and its implications for education. In H. Bornstein (Ed.), *Manual Communication in*

America (pp. 81–107). Washinton, DC: Gallaudet University Press.

Holms, A., and Holms, W. (1994). *The status of Navaho language: Retrospect and prospects.* Presentation at the 15th Annual American Indian Language Development Institute. Tucson, AZ: University of Arizona.

Hopwood v. Texas. 78 F.3d. 932 (5th Cir. Tex. 1996).

Huerta, A. (1977). The development of code switching in a young bilingual. *Working Papers in Sociolinguistics, 21,* 1–27.

Hughes, A. (1989). *Testing for language teachers.* Cambridge, UK, and New York: Cambridge University Press.

Hurtado, A., Figueroa, R., and García, E. (Eds.). (1996). *Strategic interventions in education: Expanding the Latina/Latino pipeline.* Santa Cruz: Regents of the University of California.

Hurtado, A., and Gurin, P. (1987). Ethnic identity and bilingualism attitudes. *Hispanic Journal of Behavioral Sciences, 9*(1), 1–18.

Hutton, W. R. (1942). *Glances at California, 1847–1853: Diaries and letters of William Rich Hutton.* San Marino, CA: The Huntington Library.

Irujo, S. (1988). An introduction to intercultural differences and similarities in nonverbal communication. In J. Wurzel (Ed.), *Toward multiculturalism.* Yarmouth, ME: Intercultural Press.

Jackman, M. R. (1973). Education and prejudice or education and response-set. *American Sociological Review, 38,* 327–339.

Jankowski, K. (1994). Reflections upon Milan with an eye to the future. In B. Snider (Ed.), *Post Milan ASL and English literacy: Issues, trends and research* (pp. 1–36). Washington, DC: Gallaudet University College for Continuing Education.

Jaynes, G. D., and Williams, R. M., Jr. (Eds.). (1989). *A common destiny: Blacks and American society.* Washington, DC: National Academy Press.

Jencks, C., Smith, M., Acland, H., Bane, M., Cohen, D., Gintis, H., Hynes, B., and Micelson, S. (1972). *Inequality: A reassessment of the effects of family and schooling in America.* New York: Basic Books.

Johnson, D. L., Teigen, K., and Davila, R. (1983). Anxiety and social restriction: A study of children in Mexico, Norway, and the United States. *Journal of Cross-Cultural Psychology, 14,* 439–454.

Joyce, B., Murphy, C., Showers, B., and Murphy, J. (1989). School renewal as cultural change. *Educational Leadership, 47*(3), 70–77.

Kagan, S. (1983a). Interpreting Chicano cooperativeness: Methodological and theoretical considerations. In J. L. Martinez and R. H. Mendoza (Eds.), *Chicano psychology* (2nd ed., pp. 289–333). Orlando, FL: Academic Press.

———. (1983b). Social orientation among Mexican-American children: A challenge to traditional classroom structures. In E. García (Ed.), *The Mexican-American child.* Tempe: Arizona State University.

———. (1984). Interpreting Chicano cooperativeness: Methodological and theoretical considerations in Chicano psychology. In E. García (Ed.), *The Mexican-American child.* Tempe: Arizona State University.

———. (1986). Cooperative learning and sociocultural factors in schooling. In *Beyond language: Social and cultural factors in schooling language minority students.* Los Angeles: California State University, Evaluation, Dissemination, and Assessment Center.

———. (Ed.). (1993). *The essential functions of the early care and education system: Rationale and definition.* Working paper, Quality 2000, Advancing Early Care and Education, Yale University, New Haven, CT.

Kagan, S., Knight, G. P., Martinez, S., and Espinosa-Santana, P. (1981). Conflict resolution style among Mexican children: Examining urbanization and ecology effects. *Journal of Cross-Cultural Psychology, 12*, 222–232.

Kaufman, P., and Frase, M. J. (1990). *Dropout rates in the United States: 1989.* Washington, DC: National Center for Education Statistics.

Keefe, S. E. (1979, summer). Urbanization, acculturation, and extended family ties: Mexican-Americans in cities. *American Ethnologist*, 349–362.

Keefe, S. E., and Padilla, A. M. (1987). *Chicano ethnicity.* Albuquerque: University of New Mexico Press.

Keefe, S. E., Padilla, A. M., and Carlos, M. L. (1979). *Mental health issues of significance in Mexican American families.* Hispanic Mental Health Working Papers, University of California, Los Angeles.

———. (1979). The Mexican-American extended family as an emotional support system. *Human Organization, 38*, 144–152.

Kessler, C., and Quinn, M. E. (1987). Language minority children's linguistic and cognitive creativity. *Journal of Multilingual and Multicultural Development, 8*(1), 173–185.

Knight, G. P., Bernal, M. E., and Carlos, G. (in press). Socialization and the development of cooperative, competitive, and individualistic behaviors among Mexican American children. In E. García, L. Moll, and A. Barona (Eds.), *The Mexican American child: Language, cognition, and socialization* (Vol. 2). Tempe: Arizona State University.

Knight, G. P., and Kagan, S. (1977). Acculturation of prosocial and competitive behaviors among second- and third-generation Mexican American children. *Journal of Cross-Cultural Psychology, 8*, 273–284.

Kozol, J. (1991). *Savage inequalities: Children in America's schools.* New York: Crown.

Krashen, S. D. (1981a). Bilingual education and second-language acquisition theory. In California State Department of Education (Ed.), *Schooling and language minority students: A theoretical framework* (pp. 3–50). Los Angeles: California State University, Evaluation, Dissemination and Assessment Center.

———. (1981b). *Second-language acquisition and second-language learning.* New York: Pergamon Press.

———. (1985). *The input hypothesis: Issues and implications.* New York: Longman.

Krashen, S. D., Tse, L, and McQuillan, J. (Eds.). (1998). *Heritage language development.* Culver City, CA: Language Education Associates.

Kraus, M. (1992). The world's languages in crisis. *Language, 68*, 6–10.

Kraus, N. (1997). Storytelling figures: A Pueblo tradition. *Book Links, 7*(3), 32–36.

Kreinberg, N., and Nathan, H. (1991). *Teachers' voices, teachers' wisdom: Seven adventurous teachers think aloud.* Berkeley: University of California, EQUALS, Lawrence Hall of Science.

Kroeber, A. L., and Kluckhohn, D. (1963). *Culture: A critical review of concepts and definitions.* New York: Vintage Books.

Labov, W. (1972a). *Sociolinguistic patterns.* Philadelphia: University of Pennsylvania Press.

———. (1972b). The logic of nonstandard English. In W. Labov (Ed.), *Language in the inner city: Studies in black English vernacular* (pp. 201–240). Philadelphia: University of Pennsylvania Press.

Ladson-Billings, G. (1994). *The dreamkeepers: Successful teachers of African American children.* San Francisco: Jossey-Bass.

Ladson-Billings, G., and Tate, W. (1995). Toward a critical race theory of education. *Teachers College Record, 97*(1), 47–68.

Lambert, W. E. (1990). *Issues in foreign language and second language education.* Washington, DC: U.S. Department of Education, Office of Educational Research and Improvement, Educational Resources Information Center (Report No. FL020039). East Lansing, MI: National Center for Research on Teacher

Learning. (ERIC Document Reproduction Service ED 341 269)

Language Minority Research Institute: *http://lmrinet.gse.ucsb.edu/*

Laosa, L. M. (1978). Maternal teaching strategies in Chicano families of varied educational and socioeconomic levels. *Child Development, 49,* 1129–1135.

———. (1982). School, occupation, culture and family: The impact of parental schooling on the parent-child relationship. *Journal of Educational Psychology, 74*(6), 791– 827.

———. (1984). Ethnic, socioeconomic, and home language influences upon early performance on measures of abilities. *Journal of Educational Psychology, 76*(6), 1178–1198.

———. (1995). *Intelligence testing and social policy* (Research Report 95-32). Princeton, NJ: Educational Testing Service.

Lareau, A., and Shumar, W. (1996). The problem of individualism in family-school policies. *Sociology of Education,* 24–39.

Lau v. Nichols. 414 US 563 (1974).

Lave, J. (1988). *Cognition in practice: Mind, mathematics and culture in everyday life.* Cambridge, UK: Cambridge University Press.

Lee, L. C. (1991, winter). The opening of the American mind: Educating leaders for a multicultural society. *Human Ecology Forum,* 2–5.

Leighton, M. S., Hightower, A. M., and Wrigley, A. M. (1993). *Model strategies in bilingual education: Professional development.* Washington, DC: U.S. Department of Education.

Leighton, M. S., Russo, A. W., and Hightower, A. M. (1993). *Improving education for language minority students: Promising practices in professional development.* Unpublished manuscript, Policy Studies Associates, Washington, DC.

Lempke, J. (1990). *Talking science: Learning, language and values.* Norwood, NJ: Ablex.

Leopold, W. F. (1939). *Speech development of a bilingual child: A linguist's record. Vol. I: Vocabulary growth in the first two years.* Evanston, IL: Northwestern University Press.

Levin, H. M. (1986). *Educational reform for disadvantaged students: An emerging crisis.* Washington, DC: National Education Association.

Levin, I. (1988). *Accelerated schools for at-risk students* (CPRE Research Report Series RR-010). New Brunswick, NJ: Rutgers University, Center for Policy Research in Education.

Lindholm, K. (1999). *Two-way bilingual Education: Past and future.* Presentation at the American Education Research Association, Toronto.

Lindholm, K., and Christiansen, A. (1990). *Directory of two-way bilingual programs.* Washington, DC: Center for Applied Linguisitics.

Lucas, T. (1987). *Black English discourse in urban contexts.* Unpublished doctoral dissertation, Georgetown University, Washington, DC.

———. (1997). *Into, through, and beyond secondary school: Critical transitions for immigrant youths.* New York: Columbia University, The National Center for Restructuring Education, Schools, and Teaching, Teachers College.

Lucas, T., Henze, R., and Donato, R. (1990). Promoting the success of Latino language minority students: An exploratory study of six high schools. *Harvard Educational Review, 60,* 315–334.

Luria, A. R. (1928). The problem of the cultural development of the child. *Journal of Genetic Psychology, 35,* 493–506.

Mahiri, J. (1998). *Shooting for excellence: African American youth and culture in New Century schools.* New York: Teachers College Press.

Mahshie, S. (1995). *Educating deaf children bilingually.* Washington, DC: Gaullaudet University Pre-College Programs.

Mas, C. (1994). Bilingual education for the deaf in Paris. In I. Ahlgren and

K. Hyltenstam (Eds.), *Bilingualism in deaf education, Stockholm, Sweden* (International Studies on Sign Langauge and Communication of the Deaf, Vol. 27). Hamburg: Signum Press.

Matute-Bianchi, M. E. (1990). *A report to the Santa Clara county school district: Hispanics in the schools.* Santa Clara, CA: Santa Clara County School District.

McAdoo, H. P., and McAdoo, J. L. (Eds.). (1985). *Black children: Social, educational, and parental environments.* Beverly Hills, CA: Sage.

McClintock, C. G. (1972). Social motivation: A set of propositions. *Behavioral Science, 17,* 438–454.

———. (1974). Development of social motives in Anglo-American and Mexican-American children. *Journal of Personality and Social Psychology, 29,* 348–354.

McClintock, E., Bayard, M. P., and McClintock, C. G. (1983). The socialization of prosocial orientations in Mexican-American families. In E. García (Ed.), *The Mexican-American child: Language, cognition, and social development* (pp. 143–162). Tempe: Arizona State University.

McDermott, R. P. (1987). The exploration of minority school failure, again. *Anthropology and Education Quarterly, 18*(4), 361–364.

McGahie, W. C. (1991). Professional competence evaluation. *Educational Researcher, 20*(1), 3–9.

McLeod, B. (1996). *School reform and student diversity: Exemplary schooling for language minority students.* Washington, DC: George Washington University, Institute for the Study of Language and Education.

McNab, G. (1979). Cognition and bilingualism: A re-analysis of studies. *Linguistics, 17,* 231–255.

Mead, M. (1937). *Cooperation and competition among primitive people.* New York: McGraw.

———. (1939a). Native languages as fieldwork tools. *American Anthropologist, 41,* 189–205.

———. (1939b). *Culture of the islander.* New York: Academic Press.

Mehan, H. (1979). *Learning lessons: Social organizations in the classrooms.* Cambridge, MA: Harvard University Press.

———. (1987). Language and schooling. In G. Spindler and D. Spindler (Eds.), *Interpretive ethnography of education at home and abroad* (pp. 109–136). Hillsdale, NJ: Erlbaum.

Mehan, H., Villanueva, I., Hubbard, L., and Lintz, A. (1996). *Constructing school success: The consequences of untracking low-achieving students.* New York: Cambridge University Press.

Milk, R. D. (1986). The issue of language separation in bilingual methodology. In E. García and B. Flores (Eds.), *Language and literacy in bilingual education* (pp. 67–86). Tempe: Arizona State University.

Milk, R. D., Mercado, C., and Sapiens, A. (1992). *Re-thinking the education of teachers of language minority children: Developing reflective teachers for changing schools.* Washington, DC: National Clearinghouse for Bilingual Education.

Miller, L. S. (1995). *An American imperative: Accelerating minority educational advancement.* New Haven: Yale University Press.

Minicucci, C., and Olsen, L. (1992). *Programs for secondary limited English proficient students: A California study* (FOCUS No. 5, Occasional Papers in Bilingual Education). Washington, DC: National Clearinghouse for Bilingual Education.

Miramontes, O., Nadeau, A., and Commins, N. (1997). *Linguistic diversity and effective school reform: A process for decision making.* New York: Teachers College Press.

Mirón, L. F. (1996). *The social construction of urban schooling: Situating the crisis.* Cresskill, NJ: Hampton Press.

Moll, L. (1996). Educating Latino students. *Language Arts, 64,* 315–324.

———. (1998). Bilingual classroom studies and community analysis: Some recent trends. *Educational Researcher, 21*(2), 20–24.

Moll, L., and Diaz, S. (1983). *Bilingual communication skills in classroom contexts.* San Diego, CA: University of San Diego, Laboratory of Comparative Human Cognition.

Montone, C. (1995). *Teaching linguistically and culturally diverse learners: Effective programs and practices.* Santa Cruz: University of California, National Center for Research on Cultural Diversity and Second-Language Learning.

Moreno, J. (Ed.). (1999). *The elusive quest for equality: 150 years of Chicano/Chicana Education.* Cambridge: Harvard Educational Review.

Morine-Dershimer, G. (1985). *Talking, listening, and learning in elementary classrooms.* New York: Longman.

Moss, B. (Ed.). (1994). *Literacy across communities.* Cresskill, NJ: Hampton Press.

Multicultural education: Strategies for linguistically diverse schools and classrooms: *http://www.ncbe.gwu.edu/ncbepubs/pigs.pig16.html*

Nanda, S. (1990). *Cultural anthropology.* New York: D. Van Nostrand.

National Association of Bilingual Education. (1992). *Professional standards for the preparation of bilingual/multilingual teachers.* Washington, DC: National Association for Bilingual Education.

National Association for the Education of Young Children. (1997). *Leadership in early age and education.* Washington, DC: Author.

National Board for Professional Teaching Standards. (1996). *Proposed English as a new language standard.* Washington, DC: Author.

National Center for Children in Poverty. (1995). *Five million children: A statistical profile of our poorest young citizens.* New York: Columbia University.

National Center for Education Statistics. (1991). *The condition of education* (Vols.

1–2). Washington, DC: U.S Government Printing Office.

———. (1995). *The condition of education.* Washington, DC: U.S. Government Printing Office.

———. (1996). *The condition of education* (Vols. 1–2). Washington, DC: U.S. Government Printing Office.

———. (1999). *The condition of education 1999.* Washington, DC: U.S. Government Printing Office.

———. (2000). *Educational statistics quaterly* (Vol. 1, No. 2). Washington, DC: U.S. Government Printing Office.

National Center of Effective Secondary Schools. (1991). *Annual report: Effective secondary schools.* Madison, WI: National Center of Effective Schooling.

National Clearinghouse for Bilingual Education (NCBE): *http://www.ncbe.gwu.edu/*

National Commission on Children. (1991). *Beyond rhetoric. A new American agenda for children and families* (Final report of the National Commission on Children). Washington, DC: Author.

National Commission on Excellence in Education. (1983). *A nation at risk: The imperative for education reform.* Washington, DC: U.S. Department of Education.

National Council of Teachers and International Reading Association. (1996). *Standards for the English language arts.* Urbana, IL, and Newark, DE: Authors.

National Research Council. (1993). *Losing generations: Adolescents in high-risk settings.* Washington, DC: National Academy Press.

———. (1998). *From generation to generation: The health and well-being of children in immigrant families.* Washington, DC: National Academy Press.

National Task Force on Minority High Achievement. (1999). *Reaching the top: A report of the National Task Force on Minority High Achievement.* New York: College Board Publications.

National Teachers Association. (1991). *Beyond rhetoric: A new American agenda for children and families.* Washington, DC: Author.

New Jersey State Board of Education Handbook. (1991). *Guidelines for development of program plan and evaluation summary, bilingual/ESL programs and English-language services, fiscal year 1991.* New Jersey State Department of Education.

Nieto, S. (1979). *Curriculum decision-making: The Puerto Rican family and the bilingual child.* Unpublished doctoral dissertation, University of Massachusetts, Amherst.

———. (1992). *Affirming diversity: The sociopolitical context of multicultural education.* New York : Longman.

———. (1996). *Affirming diversity: The sociopolitical context of multicultural education* (2nd ed.). White Plains, NY: Longman.

———. (1999). *The light in their eyes: Creating multicultural learning communities.* New York: Teachers College Press.

Nine Curt, C. J. (1984). *Nonverbal communication.* Cambridge, MA: Evaluation, Dissemination, and Assessment Center.

Noddings, N. (1973). Comments on the wisdom of scientific inquiry on education. *Journal of Research in Science Teaching, 10*(3), 279.

———. (1996). Rethinking the benefits of the college-bound curriculum. *Phi Delta Kappan, 78*(4), 285–289.

Nora, A., Rendon, L. I., and Cuadraz, G. (1999). Access choice and outcomes: A profile of Hispanic students in higher education. In A. Tashakkori and S. H. Ochoa (Eds.), *Education for Hispanics in the United States* (pp. 261–283). New York: AMS Press, Inc.

Oakes, J. (1984). *Keeping track.* New Haven, CT: Yale University Press.

———. (1989). What educational indicators? The case for assessing the school context. *Educational Evaluation and Policy Analysis, 11*(2), 181–199.

———. (1991). *Lost talent: The underparticipation of women, minorities, and disabled persons in science.* Santa Monica, CA: Rand Corp.

———. (1992). Can tracking research inform practice? Technical, normative, and political considerations. *Educational Researcher, 21*(4), 12–21.

Oakes, J., and Lipton, M. (1992). Detracking schools: Early lessons from the field. *Phi Delta Kappan, 73*(6), 448–454.

Ochs, E., Taylor, C., Rudolph, D., and Smith, R. C. (1989). *Narrative activity as a medium for theory-building.* Unpublished manuscript, University of Southern California.

Ogbu, J. (1982a). Cultural discontinuities and schooling. *Anthropology and Education Quarterly, 13*(4), 168–190.

———. (1982b). Socialization: A cultural ecological approach. In K. M. Borman (Ed.), *The social life of children in a changing society* (pp. 253–267). Hillsdale, NJ: Erlbaum.

———. (1983). Minority status and schooling in plural societies. *Comparative Education Review, 27*(22), 168–190.

———. (1986). The consequences of the American caste system. In U. Neisser (Ed.), *The school achievement of minority children: New perspectives.* Hillsdale, NJ: Erlbaum.

———. (1987a). *Minority education and caste: The American system in cross-cultural perspective.* New York: Academic Press.

———. (1987b). Variability in minority school performance: A problem in search of an explanation. *Anthropology and Education Quarterly, 18*(4), 312–334.

———. (1992a). Adaptation to minority status and impact on school success. *Theory into Practice, 31*(4), 287–295.

———. (1992b). Understanding cultural differences and school learning. *Education Libraries, 16*(3), 7–11.

———. (1992c). Understanding cultural diversity and learning. *Educational Researcher, 21*(8), 5–14, 24.

———. (1999). *Collective identity and schooling.* Paper presented at the meeting of the Japan Society of Educational Sociology, Tokyo.

Ogbu, J., and Matute-Bianchi, M. E. (1986). Understanding sociocultural factors: Knowledge, identity and school adjustment. In Bilingual Education Office (Ed.), *Beyond language: Social and cultural factors in schooling language minority students* (pp. 73–142). Los Angeles: California State University, Evaluation, Dissemination, and Assessment Center.

Olsen, L. (1988). *Crossing the schoolhouse border: Immigrant students and the California public schools.* San Francisco: California Tomorrow Policy Research.

———. (1997). *Made in America: Immigrant students in our public schools.* New York: New Press.

O'Malley, M. J. (1981). *Children's and services study: Language minority children with limited English proficiency in the United States.* Rosslyn, VA: National Clearinghouse for Bilingual Education.

———. (1992). *Children's and services study: Language minority children with limited English proficiency in the United States.* Rosslyn, VA: National Clearinghouse for Bilingual Education.

Orfield, G., and Miller, E. (Eds.). (1998). *Chilling admissions: The affirmative action crisis and the search for alternatives.* Cambridge, MA: Harvard Education Publishing Group.

Ovando, C. J., and Collier, V. P. (1985). *Bilingual and ESL classrooms: Teaching in multicultural contexts.* New York: McGraw-Hill.

Ovando, C. J., and McLaren, P. (Eds.). (2000). *The politics of multiculturalism and bilingual education: Students and teachers caught in the crossfire.* Boston: McGraw-Hill.

Padden, C. (1997). *Deaf students as readers and writers: A mixed-mode research approach.* Washington, DC: U.S. Department of Education, Office of Educational Research and Improvement, Educational Resources Information Center.

Padilla, A. M., and Liebman, E. (1975). Language acquisition in the bilingual child. *The Bilingual Review/La Revista Bilingüe, 2,* 34–55.

Paley, V. (1981). *Wally's stories.* Cambridge, MA: Harvard University Press.

———. (1986). *Mollie is three: Growing up in school.* Chicago: University of Chicago Press.

Paul, B. (1965). Anthropological perspectives on medicine and public health. In K. Skipper, Jr., and R. C. Leonard (Eds.), *Social interaction and patient care* (pp. 187–124). Philadelphia: J. B. Lippincott.

Peal, E., and Lambert, W. E. (1962). The relation of bilingualism to intelligence. *Psychological Monographs: General and Applied, 76*(546), 1–23.

Pearl, A. (1991). Democratic education: Myth or reality. In R. Valencia (Ed.), *Chicano school failure and success* (pp. 101–118). New York: Falmer Press.

Pease-Alvarez, L., García, E., and Espinoza, P. (1991). Effective instruction for language minority students: An early childhood case study. *Early Childhood Research Quarterly, 6*(3), 347–363.

Pelto, P., and Pelto, G. H. (1975). Intracultural variation: Some theoretical issues. *American Ethnologist, 2*(1), 1–45.

Phelan, P., Davidson, A. L., and Cao, H. T. (1991). *Students' multiple worlds: Negotiating the boundaries of family, peer, and school cultures.* Palo Alto, CA: Stanford University,Center for Research on the Context of Secondary Teaching.

Philips, S. U. (1972). Participant structures and communication incompetence: Warm Springs children in community and classroom. In C. Cazden, D. Hymes, and W. J. Johns (Eds.), *Function of language in the classroom* (pp. 161–189). New York: Teachers College Press.

———. (1983). *The invisible culture: Communication in classroom and community on the Warm Springs Indian reservation.* New York: Longman.

Piper, T. (1998). *Language and learning: The home and school years* (2nd ed.). Upper Saddle River, NJ: Merrill.

Policy Analysis for California Education. (1998). *Californians speak on education and reform options: Uneven faith in teachers, school boards, and the state as designers of change.* Berkeley: University of California, and Palo Alto: Stanford University.

Porter, C., and Cleland, J. (1995). *The portfolio as a learning strategy.* Portsmouth, NH: Boynton/Cook.

Portes, A. (1996). *The new second generation.* New York: Russell Sage Foundation.

Portes, A., and Rumbaut, R. G. (1996). *Immigrant America: A portrait* (2nd ed.). Berkeley: University of California Press.

Purkey, S. C., and Smith, M. S. (1983). Effective schools: A review. *Elementary School Journal, 83,* 52–78.

———. (1985). School reform: The district policy implications of the effective schools literature. *Elementary School Journal, 85*(3), 353–389.

Ramirez, A. (1985). *Bilingualism through schooling.* Albany: State University of New York Press.

Ramirez, J. D., and Merino, B. J. (1990). Classroom talk in English immersion: Early-exit and late-exit transitional bilingual education programs. In R. Jacobson and C. Faltis (Eds.), *Language distribution issues in bilingual schooling* (pp. 61–103). Clevedon, UK: Multilingual Matters.

Ramirez, J. D., Yuen, S. D., Ramey, D. R., and Pasta, D. J. (1991). *Final report: Longitudinal study of structured English immersion strategy, early-exit, and late-exit transitional bilingual education programs for language minority children.* San Mateo, CA: Aguirre International.

Ramirez, M., and Castaneda, A. (1974). *Cultural democracy, bi-cognitive development and education.* New York: Academic Press.

Ramsey, P. G. (1998). *Teaching and learning in a diverse world: Multicultural education for young children* (2nd ed.). New York: Teachers College Press.

Rendon, L., and Hope, R. (Eds.). (1996). *Educating a new majority: Transforming America's educational system for diversity.* San Francisco: Jossey-Bass.

Reynolds, A., and Elias, P. (1991). *What is good teaching: A review of the literature.* Princeton, NJ: Educational Testing Service.

Riley, R. W. (1995). *Turning the corner: From a nation at risk to a nation with a future* (Second annual address). Washington, DC: U.S. Department of Education.

Rodriguez, C. E. (1989). *Puerto Ricans born in the USA.* Winchester, MA: Unwin Hyman.

Rodriguez, R. (1982). *Hunger of memory.* New York: Bantam.

Rogoff, B. (1990). *Apprenticeship in thinking: Cognitive development in social context.* Oxford, UK: Oxford University Press.

Romo, H. (1999). *Reaching out: Best practices for educating Mexican-origin children and youth.* Charleston, WV: Clearinghouse on Rural Education and Small Schools.

Romo, H., and Falbo, T. (1996). *Latino high school graduation: Defying the odds.* Austin: University of Texas Press.

Rosaldo, R. (1993). Culture and truth: The remaking of social analysis (With a new introduction). Boston: Beacon Press.

Rose, M. (1989). *Lives on the boundary.* New York: The Free Press.

———. (1995). Calexico: Portrait of an educational community. *Teachers and Writers, 26*(5), 1–15.

———. (1996). *Possible lives: The promise of public education in America.* New York: Penguin Books.

Rosenshine, B. (1986). Synthesis of research on explicit teaching. *Educational Leadership, 43*(3), 60–69.

Rueda, R., and Mehan, H. (1987). Metacognition and passing. *Anthropology and Education Quarterly, 17*(3), 145–165.

Rumbaut, R. (1997). *Children of immigrants: The adaptation process of the* *second generation* (Report to the Russell Sage Foundation). New York: Russell Sage Foundation.

Rumbaut, R. G. (1997). *Immigrants in San Diego County*. New York: Russell Sage Foundation.

Rumbaut, R. G., and Cornelius, W. A. (1995). *California's immigrant children*. San Diego: Center for U. S.–Mexican Studies.

San Antonio Independent School District v. Rodriguez, 11 U. S. 1 (1973).

Sarason, S. B. (1990). *The predictable failure of educational reform: Can we change course before it's too late?* San Francisco: Jossey-Bass.

Scarcella, R. (1999). *Academic English: A conceptual framework*. Santa Barbara, CA: University of California Language Minority Institute.

Schneider, S. G. (1976). *Revolution, reaction, or reform: The 1974 Bilingual Education Act*. New York: Las Americas.

Schuman, H., and Harding, J. (1964). Prejudice and the norm of rationality. *Sociometry, 27*, 353–371.

Schuman, H., Steeh, C., and Bobo, L. (1985). *Racial attitudes in America: Trends and interpretations*. Cambridge, UK: Cambridge University Press.

Schumann, J. H. (1976). Affective factors and the problem of age in second-language acquisition. *Language Learning, 25*, 209–239.

Schwartz, T. (1978). Where is the culture? Personality as the distributive locus of culture. In G. Spinder (Ed.), *The making of psychological anthropology*. Berkeley: University of California Press.

Scollon, R., and Scollon, B. K. (1981). *Narrative literacy and face in interethnic communication*. Norwood, NJ: Ablex.

Scribner, S., and Cole, M. (1981). Unpackaging literacy. In Farr-Whiteman, M. (Ed.), *Variation in writing: Functional and linguistic-cultural differences: Vol. 1. Writing: The nature, development, and teaching of written communications* (pp. 71–88). Hillsdale, NJ: Erlbaum.

Secada, W. G. (1996). Urban students acquiring English and learning mathematics in the context of reform. *Urban Education, 30*(4), 422–448.

Seginer, R. (1989). *Adolescent sisters: The relationship between younger and older sisters among Israeli Arabs*. Paper presented at the meeting of the International Society for the Study of Behavioral Development, Jyvaskyla, Finland.

Seliger, H. W. (1977). Does practice make perfect? A study of international patterns and L2 competence. *Language Learning, 27*(2), 263–278.

Sells Dick, G., and McCarty, T. L. (1996). Mother tongue literacy and language renewal: The case of the Navajo (Report No. RC021314). Springfield, VA: ERIC Document Reproduction Service (EDRS). (ERIC Document Reproduction Service No. ED 422 133)

Shimberg, B. (1983). What is competence? How can it be assessed? In M. R. Stern (Ed.), *Power and conflict in continuing professional education* (pp. 17–37). Belmont, CA: Wadsworth.

Skinner, B. F. (1957). *Verbal behavior*. Englewood Cliffs, NJ: Prentice Hall.

Skrabanek, R. L. (1970). Language maintenance among Mexican Americans. *International Journal of Comparative Sociology, 11*, 272–282.

Skutnabb-Kangas, T. (1979). *Language in the process of cultural assimilation and structural incorporation of linguistic minorities*. Rosslyn, VA: National Clearinghouse for Bilingual Education.

Slavin, R. E. (1989). Pet and the pendulum. Fadism in education and how to stop it. *Phi Delta Kappan, 70*(10), 752–758.

Slavin, R., Karweit, N., and Madden, N. (1989). *Effective programs for students at risk*. Needham Heights, MA: Allyn and Bacon.

Sleeter, C. E., and Grant, C. A. (1987). An analysis of multicultural education in the U.S. *Harvard Educational Review, 57*(4).

————. (1999). *Making choices for multicultural education: Five approaches to race, class, and gender* (3rd ed.) Upper Saddle River, NJ: Merrill.

Smith, J. P., and Edmonston, B. (Eds.). (1997). *The new Americans: Economic, demographic, and fiscal effects of immigration.* Washington, DC: National Academy Press.

Smith, T. (1997). Lessons and questions: Excerpts from the 1996 Kurt Hahn Address. *Journal of Experiential Education, 20,*(1), 22–26.

Smith, T. W. (1971). *Understanding reading.* New York: Holt, Rinehart and Winston.

————. (1990). *Ethnic images* (GSS Topical Report No. 19). Chicago: University of Chicago, National Opinion Research Center.

Smith, T. W., and Sheatsley, P. B. (1984). American attitudes towards race relations. *Public Opinion, 7,* 14–15, 50–53.

Snow, C. E. (1990). The development of definitional skill. *Journal of Child Language, 17*(3), 697–710.

————. (1991). The theoretical basis for relationships between language and literacy in development. *Journal of Research in Childhood Education, 6*(1), 5–10.

Snow, C. E., Burns, M. S., and Griffin, P. (1999). *Language and literacy environments in preschools.* Committee on the Prevention of Reading Difficulties in Young Children, Commission. Washington, DC : National Academy Press.

————. (1999). Language and Literacy Enviroments in Preschools. *ERIC Digest* (Report No. EDO-PS-99-1). Washington, DC: Office of Educational Research and Improvement. (ERIC Document Reproduction Service No. ED426818)

Snow, C. E., and Dickinson, D. K. (1987). Interrelationships among prereading and oral language skills in kindergartners from two social classes. *Early Childhood Research Quarterly, 2*(1), 1–25.

Social Context of Education: *http://nces. ed.gov/pubs*

Solorzano, D. G. (1997). Images and words that wound: Critical race theory, racial stereotyping, and teacher education. *Teacher Education Quarterly, 24*(3), 5–19.

Sorenson, A. P. (1967). Multilingualism in the Northwest Amazon. *American Anthropologist, 69,* 67–68.

Soto, L. D. (1997). *Language, culture, and power: Bilingual families and the struggle for quality education.* Albany: State University of New York Press.

Spencer, M. B. (1988). Self-concept development. In D. T. Slaughter (Ed.), *Black children and poverty: A developmental perspective* (pp. 103–116). San Francisco: Jossey-Bass.

Spencer, M. B., and Horowitz, F. D. (1973). Effects of systematic social and token reinforcement on the modification of racial and color concept attitudes in black and in white preschool children. *Developmental Psychology, 9,* 246–254.

Spindler, G. (1955). *Anthropology and education.* Palo Alto: Stanford University Press.

————. (1974). *Education and cultural process: Toward an anthropology of education.* New York: Holt, Rinehart and Winston.

————. (1982). *Doing the ethnography of schooling: Educational anthropology in action.* New York: Holt, Rinehart and Winston.

————. (1987). *Education and cultural process: Anthropological approaches.* Prospect Heights, IL: Waveland Press.

Spindler, G., and Spindler, L. (1989). Instrumental competence, self-efficacy, linguistic minorities, and cultural therapy: A preliminary attempt at integration. *Anthropology and Education Quarterly, 20*(1), 36–50.

Spiro, M. E. (1951). Culture and personality: The natural history of a false dichotomy. *Psychiatry, 14,* 19–46.

Stanton-Salazar, R. (1997). A social capital framework for understanding the socialization of racial minority children and youths. *Harvard Educational Review, 67*(1), 1–40.

Sternberg, R. J., and Wagner, R. K. (Eds.). (1986). *Practical intelligence.* New York: Cambridge University Press.

Stiggins, R. J. (1995). *Sound performance assessments in the guidance context.* Greensboro, NC: ERIC Clearinghouse on Counseling and Student Services.

Stritikus, T., and García, E. (In Press). Education of Limited English Proficiency in California schools and assessment of the influence of Proposition 227 on selected teachers and classrooms. *NABE Journal.*

Suarez-Orozco, M. M. (1985, May). *Opportunity, family dynamics, and school achievement: The sociocultural context of motivation among recent immigrants from Central America.* Paper presented at the University of California Symposium on Linguistics, Minorities, and Education, Tahoe City, CA.

———. (1987). Becoming somebody: Central American immigrants in U.S. inner-city schools. *Anthropology and Education Quarterly, 18,* 287–299.

———. (1996). California dreaming: Proposition 187 and the cultural psychology of racial and ethnic exclusion. *Anthropology and Education Quarterly, 27*(2), 151–167.

Suarez-Orozco, M., and Suarez-Orozco, C. (1995). *Transformations: Immigration, family life, and achievement motivation among Latino adolescents.* Palo Alto, CA: Stanford University Press.

Sue, S., and Okazaki, S. (1990). Asian-American educational achievements: A phenomenon in search of an explanation. *American Psychologist, 45*(8), 913–920.

Sue, S., and Padilla, A. (1986). Ethnic minority issues in the United States: Challenges for the educational system. In California Bilingual Education, *Beyond language: Social and cultural factors in schooling language minority students* (pp. 35–72). Los Angeles: California State

University, Evaluation, Dissemination, and Assessment Center.

Sullivan, P. (1992). *ESL in context.* Newbury Park, CA: Corwin Press.

Suzuki, R. H. (1984). Curriculum transformation for multicultural education. *Education and Urban Society, 16*(133), 294–322.

Swain, M., and Lapkin, R. (1991). The influence of bilingualism on cognitive functioning. *Canadian Modern Language Review, 47,* 635–641.

Tajfel, H. (1978). *The social psychology of minorities.* London: Minority Rights Group.

Tharp, R. G. (1989). Psychocultural variables and *k* constants: Effects on teaching and learning in schools. *American Psychologist, 44,* 349–359.

———. (1991). Cultural diversity and treatment of children. *Journal of Consulting and Clinical Psychology, 59*(6), 799–812.

Tharp, R., and Gallimore, R. (1988). *Rousing minds to life: Teaching, learning, and schooling in social context.* New York: Cambridge University Press.

———. (1989). *Challenging cultural minds.* London: Cambridge University Press.

———. (1991). *The instructional conversation: Teaching and learning in social activity* (Research Report No. 2). Santa Cruz: University of California, National Center for Research on Cultural Diversity and Second-Language Learning.

Thomas, S. V., and Park, B. (1921a). *Culture and personality* (2nd ed.). New York: Random House.

———. (1921b). *Culture of immigrants.* Cambridge, MA: Newcome Press.

Thomas, W. P., and Collier, V. P. (1995a). *A longitudinal analysis of programs serving language minority students.* Washington, DC.: National Clearinghouse on Bilingual Education.

———. (1995b). *Language minority student achievement and program effectiveness* [Research summary of ongoing study, results as of September].

Thornton, S. (1981). *The issue of dialect in academic achievement*. Unpublished doctoral dissertation, University of California, Berkeley.

Tikunoff, W. J. (1983). *Compatibility of the SBIF features with other research on instruction of LEP students* (SBIF-83-4.8/10). San Francisco: Far West Laboratory.

Trueba, H. T. (1987). *Success or failure? Learning and the language minority student*. Scranton, PA: Harper and Row.

———. (1988a). Peer socialization among minority students: A high school dropout prevention program. In H. Trueba and C. Delgado-Gaitan (Eds.), *Schools and society: Learning content through culture* (pp. 178–193). New York: Praeger.

———. (1988b). *Rethinking learning disabilities: Cultural knowledge in literacy acquisition*. Unpublished manuscript, Office for Research on Educational Equity, Graduate School of Education, University of California, Santa Barbara.

———. (1999). *Latinos unidos*. Lanham, MD: Rowman and Littlefield.

Trueba, H. T., Moll, L. C., Diaz, S., and Diaz, R. (1982). *Improving the functional writing of bilingual secondary students*. Washington, DC: National Institute of Education.

Trujillo, F. X. (1989). *The teacher* [Poem prepared for the celebration of the teacher]. Sacramento, CA.

Ueda, R. (1987). *Avenues to adulthood: The origins of the high school and social mobility in an American suburb*. Cambridge, UK: Cambridge University Press.

U.S. Bureau of the Census. (1991). *Census of the Population*. Washington DC: U.S. Government Printing Office.

U.S. Department of Commerce. (1989). *School enrollment: Social and economic characteristics of students: October 1989*. Washington DC: U.S. Government Printing Office.

———. (1994). *School enrollment: Social and economic characteristics of students: October 1994*. Washington DC: U.S. Government Printing Office.

U.S. Department of Education. (1998). *No more excuses: Final report of the U.S. Department of Education Hispanic dropout project*. Washington, DC: Author.

U.S. Department of Education and the White House Initiative on Educational Excellence for Hispanic Americans. (1999). *What works for Latino youth?* Washington, DC: Author.

U.S. General Accounting Office. (1987, March). *Research evidence on bilingual education* (GAO/PEMD-87-12BR). Washington, DC: Author.

———. (1994). *Limited English proficiency: A growing and costly educational challenge facing many school districts* (GAO/HEHS-94-38). Washington, DC: Author.

U.S. Immigration and Naturalization Services. (1995). *Statistical yearbook of immigration and naturalization services*. Washington, DC: U.S. Government Printing Office.

———. (1999). *Statistical yearbook of immigration and naturalization services*. Washington, DC: U.S. Government Printing Office.

United States v. Texas, 647 F.2d 69 (9th Cir. 1981).

Valdés, G. (1996). *Con respeto: Bridging the distances between culturally diverse families and schools. An ethnographic portrait*. New York: Teachers College Press.

———. (1998). The world outside and inside schools: Language and immigrant children. *Educational Researcher, 27*(6), 4–18

Valencia, R. (1991). Chicano school failure and success: Research and policy agendas for the 1990s. New York: Falmer Press.

Valenzuela, A., and Dornbusch, S. M. (1994). Familism and social capital in the academic achievement of Mexican origin and Anglo adolescents. *Social Science Quarterly, 75*(1), 18–36.

Valsiner, J. (1989). How can developmental psychology become "culture inclusive"?

In J. Valsiner (Ed.), *Child development in cultural context* (pp. 1–8). Lewiston, NY: Hogrefe and Huber.

Veltman, C. (1988). *The future of the Spanish language in the United States.* New York: Hispanic Policy Project.

Villegas, A. M. (1991). *Culturally responsive pedagogy for the1990's and beyond.* Princeton, NJ: Educational Testing Service.

Villegas, A. M., Clewell, B. C., Anderson, B. T., Goertz, M. E., Joy, M. F., Bruschi, B. A., and Irvine, J. J. (1995). *Teaching for diversity: Models for expanding the supply of minority teachers.* Princeton, NJ: Educational Testing Service.

Vizenor, G. (1998). *Fugitive poses: Native American Indian scenes of absence and presence.* Lincoln: Univeristy of Nebraska Press.

Vogt, L., Jordan, C., and Tharp, R. (1987). Explaining school failure, producing school success: Two cases. *Anthropology and Education Quarterly, 18*(4), 276–286.

Vygotsky, L. S. (1929). The problem of the cultural development of the child. *Journal of Genetic Psychology, 36*, 414–434.

———. (1956). *The genesis of higher psychological functions.* Moscow: Academy of Pedagogical Sciences.

———. (1981). The genesis of higher mental functions. In J. V. Wertsch (Ed.), *The Concept of activity in Soviet psychology.* Armonk, NY: Plenum.

Waggoner, D. (1984). The need for bilingual education: Estimates from the 1980 census. *NABE Journal, 8*, 1–14.

———. (1991). Numbers and needs: Ethnic and linguistic minorities in the United States. *Numbers and Needs, 1–2.*

Walberg, H. (1986a). Synthesis of research on teaching. In M. Wittrock (Ed.), *Handbook of research on teaching* (3rd ed., pp. 15–32). New York: Macmillan.

———. (1986b). What works in a nation still at risk. *Educational Leadership, 44*(1), 7–11.

Waldinger, R., and Bozorgmehr, M. (Eds.). *Ethnic Los Angeles.* New York: Russell Sage Foundation.

Walker, C. L. (1987). Hispanic achievements: Old views and new perspectives. In H. Trueba (Ed.), *Success or failure? Learning and the language minority student* (pp.15–32). Cambridge, MA: Newbury House.

Wallace, A. F. C. (1970). *Culture and personality* (2nd ed.). New York: Random House.

Walsh, D. (1990, October 12). Minority students in Santa Clara County continue to deteriorate academically. *San Francisco Examiner,* pp. B1–4.

Waters, M. C. (1999). *Black identities: West Indian and American realities.* Cambridge, MA: Harvard University Press.

Weinberg, M. (1990). *Racism in the United States : A comprehensive classified bibliography.* New York: Greenwood Press.

Weis, L. (Ed.). (1988). *Class, race, and gender in American education.* Albany: State University of New York Press.

Wertsch, J. V. (1985). *Vygotsky and the social formation of the mind.* Cambridge, MA: Harvard University Press.

West, C. (1999). The new culture of politics of difference. In C. Lemert (Ed.), *Social theory: The multicultural and classics readings* (pp. 521–531). Boulder, CO: Westview Press.

White House Initiative on Educational Excellence for Hispanic Americans: *www.ed.gov/offices/oiia/hispanic*

Whiting, B. B., and Edwards, C. P. (1988). *Children of different worlds: The formation of social behavior.* Cambridge, MA: Harvard University Press.

Wiese, A., and García, E. (1998). The Bilingual Education Act: Language minority students and equal educational opportunity. *Bilingual Research Journal, 22*(1), 1–18.

Wiesner, T. S., Gallimore, R., and Jordan, C. (1988). Unpackaging cultural effects on classroom learning. Native Hawaiian peer assistance and child-generated activity. *Anthropology and Education Quarterly, 19*(4), 327–353.

Wigdor, A. K., and Garner, W. R. (Eds.). (1982). *Ability testing: Uses, consequences, and controversies. Part I: Report of the committee.* Washington, DC: National Academy of Sciences–National Research Council, Assembly of Behavioral and Social Sciences.

Wiggins, R. A. (1994). Large group lessons/small group follow-up: Flexible grouping in a basal reading program. *Reading Teacher, 47*(6), 450–460.

Wilbur, R. B. (1979). *American sign languages and sign systems.* Baltimore: University Park Press.

Wiley, M. S. (1996). Environmental education in the school culture: A systemic approach. *Clearing, 94,* 25–27.

Williamson, M. (1993). An introduction to holistic scoring: The social, historical and theoretical context for writing assessment. In M. Williamson and B. Hout (Eds.), *Validating holistic scoring for writing assessment: Theoretical and empirical foundations* (1–14). Cresskill, NJ: Hampton Press, Inc.

Williamson, J. N. (1993). *Don't take away the light.* New York: Kensington.

Wilson, W. J. (1987). *The truly disadvantaged: The inner city, the underclass, and public policy.* Chicago: University of Chicago Press.

———. (1999). *The bridge over the racial divide: Rising inequality and coalition politics.* New York: Russell Sage Foundation.

Wolfram, W. (1993a). Ethical considerations in language awareness programs. *Issues in Applied Linguistics, 4*(2), 225–255.

———. (1993b). A proactive role for speech-language pathologists in sociolinguistic education. *Language, Speech, and Hearing Services in Schools, 24*(3), 181–185.

Wong-Fillmore, L. (1976). *The second time around: Cognitive and social strategies in second-language acquisition.* Unpublished doctoral dissertation, Stanford University, Palo Alto, CA.

———. (1991). When learning a second language means losing a first. *Early Childhood Research Quarterly, 6*(2), 323–347.

Wong-Fillmore, L., Ammon, P., McLaughlin, B., and Ammon, M. S. (1985). *Final report for learning English through bilingual instruction* (NIE Final Report No. 400-360-0030). Rosslyn, VA: National Clearinghouse for Bilingual Education.

Wong-Fillmore, L., and Snow, C. (1999). *What educators—especially teachers—need to know about language: The bare minimum.* Santa Barbara, CA: Language Minority Research Institute.

Wong-Fillmore, L., and Valadez, C. (1985). Teaching bilingual learners. In M. S. Wittrock (Ed.), *Handbook on research on teaching* (3rd. ed., pp. 481–519). Washington, DC: American Educational Research Association.

Wood, D. (1992). Culture, language, and child development. *Language and Education, 6*(2–4), 123–140.

Zentella, A. C. (1981). *Ta bien* you could answer me *en cualquier idioma:* Puerto Rican code switching in bilingual classrooms. In R. Duran (Ed.), *Latino language and communicative behavior* (pp. 109–132). Norwood, NJ: Ablex.

Zhou, M. (1997). Growing up American: The challenge confronting immigrant children and children of immigrants. *Annual Review of Sociology, 23*, 61–95.

Index